Remnants of Conquest

Remnants of Conquest

The Island Caribs and their Visitors, 1877–1998

PETER HULME

OXFORD
UNIVERSITY PRESS

OXFORD
UNIVERSITY PRESS

Great Clarendon Street, Oxford OX2 6DP

Oxford University Press is a department of the University of Oxford.
It furthers the University's objective of excellence in research, scholarship,
and education by publishing worldwide in

Oxford New York

Athens Auckland Bangkok Bogotá Buenos Aires Calcutta
Cape Town Chennai Dar es Salaam Delhi Florence Hong Kong Istanbul
Karachi Kuala Lumpur Madrid Melbourne Mexico City Mumbai
Nairobi Paris São Paulo Shanghai Singapore Taipei Tokyo Toronto Warsaw

and associated companies in Berlin Ibadan

Oxford is a registered trade mark of Oxford University Press
in the UK and certain other countries

Published in the United States
by Oxford University Press Inc., New York

© Peter Hulme 2000

The moral rights of the author have been asserted
Database right Oxford University Press (maker)

First published 2000

British Library Cataloguing in Publication Data
Data available

Library of Congress Cataloging in Publication Data
Data available

ISBN-0-19-811215-7

1 3 5 7 9 10 8 6 4 2

Typeset by Best-set Typesetter Ltd., Hong Kong
Printed in Great Britain
on acid-free paper by
T.J. International Ltd,
Padstow, Cornwall

for Susan

(ED 249)

Contents

List of Illustrations and Maps

Abbreviations

APS	Aborigines Protection Society
AS&APS	Anti-Slavery and Aborigines Protection Society
BAE	Bureau of American Ethnology
BEB	'Black Exercise Book' (Jean Rhys Collection, McFarlin Library, University of Tulsa)
BP	Hesketh Bell papers (Royal Commonwealth Society collection, Cambridge University Library)
CO	Colonial Office papers (Public Record Office, Kew, London)
DPP	David Plante Papers (Special Collections, McFarlin Library, University of Tulsa)
IR	'The Imperial Road' (unpublished story by Jean Rhys)
JC	Papers of Joseph Chamberlain (The Chamberlain Papers, Special Collections, University of Birmingham)
JRC	Jean Rhys Collection (Special Collections, McFarlin Library, University of Tulsa)
LH	Papers in the possession of Lennox Honychurch, Dominica
NAA	National Anthropological Archives (Smithsonian Institution, Washington)
NC	Papers of Neville Chamberlain (The Chamberlain Papers, Special Collections, University of Birmingham)
PRO	Public Record Office, Kew, London
SIA	Smithsonian Institution Archives, Washington
TP	'Temps Perdi' (Rhys 1987: 256–74)
WM	*Wild Majesty* (ed. Hulme and Whitehead 1992)
WSS	*Wide Sargasso Sea* (Rhys 1997)

Note on References

References will be via the name/date system; full titles are listed at the end of the book. During runs of references, second and subsequent name/dates may be omitted as long as clarity is not impaired. Primary sources will usually require a footnote, but will employ the abbreviations.

1. Visiting the Caribs

It is saddening to reflect that no great ancient races inhabited these lovely Isles, that no great man ever lived, and laboured, and worked, and fought, and died, and left a name for posterity to honour and to cherish as a 'household word'; that no time-honoured tower or world-famed temple, or pilgrim-haunted shrine ever stood on yonder cape—in short, that the past is all a blank. (Grenville John Chester, *Transatlantic Sketches in the West Indies, South America, Canada and United States* (1869: 17–18))

While doing the research for this book I constructed for myself a moment of beginning, a touchstone of what the project was *about*, as that wonderfully vague and useful preposition has it. In a pocket guide book to the West Indies, first written in 1907 and frequently republished, there is a one-sentence paragraph appended to the chapter about Dominica: 'By those desirous of visiting the Caribs the coastal steamer should be taken to Marigot, whence their settlement can be reached on foot or horse-back, the distance being eleven miles' (Aspinall 1914: 239). I will touch the stone of this sentence at various points in the chapters to come, trying to untangle the special magic of its combination of desire and geographical precision. Its most important phrase, though, and the one around which cluster the kinds of questions I want this book to pose, is 'visiting the Caribs'.

THE VISITORS AND THEIR WRITINGS

The Caribs—it should briefly be explained, in advance of the lengthier explanations that follow—were by 1907 the relatively small groups descended from the indigenous population of the Caribbean and resident on Dominica and St Vincent, two of the islands of the Lesser Antilles in British possession (see fig. 1). In one sense they were 'merely' another of the native peoples of

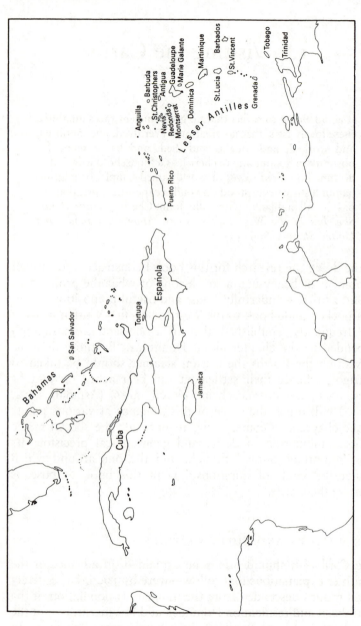

FIG. 1. Map of the Caribbean.

the world sheltering as best they could in some corner of a European empire where they had been left to rot after their usefulness had been exhausted or their fight for survival overcome. But the Caribs had always been recognized as special, in part because their widespread reputation as cannibals had earlier made them into the archetype of unregenerate savagery, in part because, as sole survivors of the native peoples who inhabited the Caribbean at the time of Columbus's arrival, they still stood as symbols of the first encounter of Europe with America, an encounter much discussed in the 1890s, as it was in the 1990s.

Nobody knows for sure what the inhabitants of the islands of Waitukubuli (now Dominica) and Iouloumain (now St Vincent) called themselves at the end of the fifteenth century, although in the seventeenth French missionaries recorded *karifuna* and *kalligonam* for the men and women respectively on Dominica. The Spanish term *caribe*, French *caraïbe*, and English *carib* (along with many variants), were used by the colonizing powers, asserting a connection, first in behaviour, later in ethnic and cultural affiliations, with some of the populations of the South American mainland, affiliations that are still much disputed. Anthropologists and linguists have attempted to make distinctions between different 'Carib' groups—between Black and Yellow Caribs on St Vincent, between the 'True' Caribs of the mainland and the Island Caribs with whom they may have relatively little in common except their name and deeply embedded assumptions about them generated by colonial ideologies. In Belize—to where they were deported in 1797—the Black Caribs refer to themselves as Garifuna, a name now widely accepted by others. In Dominica and St Vincent Carib is still the usual name, although Karifuna is used on occasions of formal or cultural significance. In the interests of simplification 'Carib' will be used here to designate the surviving indigenous population of the islands.

The verb 'visit' has ten principal meanings according to the *Oxford English Dictionary* (I summarize): 1. to comfort (usually referring to a visit by God); 2. to examine or subject to scrutiny; 3. to harm; 4. to afflict (usually referring to sickness); 5. to punish; 6. to call upon as an act of friendliness; 7. to attend (as a doctor); 8. to go to look at or examine; 9. to go to worship;

10. to go to for the purpose of sightseeing. In what sense in 1907 could the Caribs *be visited*? If you take the following entry in the *OED*, which serves to elucidate the verb, the Caribs were 'visitable' in two senses: 'Liable to visitation by some competent authority' and 'capable of being visited'. What is common to both these senses is that the party being visited has no choice in the matter. The Caribs were not 'visitable' in the third *OED* sense—'having some social position in a neighbourhood', and therefore 'capable of being visited on more or less equal terms by those of some standing in society'; they were very definitely 'liable' or 'capable' of being visited, passive recipients of the 'visits' of those who deemed them 'visitable', in either a supervisory or a touristic capacity. 'To see' was in these cases—to paraphrase Roland Barthes—an intransitive verb, a self-contained activity that was limited to the visual dimension and rarely involved significant or extended communication. The Caribs were there to be looked at, the term suggests. Appropriately enough, the period covered by this book is the era of the camera, the emblematic technology of the visit, and the visual recording of the Caribs has been an important feature of modern accounts.

This sense of 'visiting' is a relatively new phenomenon at the turn of the century and one that characterizes this recent period of writing about the Caribs, over the last 100 years or so. It is to be distinguished from all the other possible kinds of contact—basically going to kill, to trade with, to convert, or to study. 'To visit' is the verb that belongs to sightseeing and tourism, but it also incorporates—at this period and at this place—independent travel and intellectual curiosity, without which we would have little first-hand evidence of any kind to draw on.

The chapters that follow try to unpack the texts of those who have proved 'desirous of visiting the Caribs' over the last century and a quarter. The visitors range from an ornithologist who stumbled across the Caribs while looking for birds to a novelist fulfilling a childhood ambition; from a colonial official expecting to meet Red Indians in warpaint to a British naval officer who bombarded the Reserve with starshells; from an anthropologist who had a family with a Carib woman to contemporary travellers looking for signs of cultural difference.

The main geographical focus is extremely narrow—a piece of land approximately 3,700 acres in area, ocupied by about 3,000 people (out of a total Dominican population of around 76,000), whose boundaries were established in 1903 as demarcating 'The Carib Reserve' on the island of Dominica and formalized in the laws of the independent Commonwealth of Dominica after 1978. '*Quartier*' or 'quarter' are earlier designations still found well into the twentieth century; 'Carib Territory' is the term preferred by the Caribs themselves. Some references will be made for comparative purposes to the Carib community in St Vincent, which may indeed have been at least as significant as the Dominican Carib community before its virtual destruction in the volcanic eruption of 1902, but which has been little visited in recent years.[1]

The concentration on the modern period is quite deliberate. Too often the Caribs have been consigned to the past as a picturesque ornament to the story of the Caribbean, an ornament whose 'remnant' is sometimes allowed to have survived precariously into the writer's present tense: almost all the writers under consideration use the word 'remnant' to refer to the Caribs, judging their supposed loss of population after 1492 as a cultural deterioration through which they are supposedly doomed to extinction, usually soon after the moment of writing.

The present work is a literary study in the sense that it offers an analysis, informed by literary approaches, of a relatively self-contained body of texts, even if many of those texts are not conventionally 'literary' in form. A fundamental starting point—familiar from what has recently been codified as a relatively coherent body of postcolonial studies—is that what offers itself as a representation of a culture, or a series of events, or an individual body, or a national history, is deeply marked by its own positionality, its own historicity, its own ideology, and must therefore be read with due care. This does not make such material meaningless—I would hardly have spent so many years reading it if I thought so; but it does put its *authority* into question, in particular the authority that has traditionally accrued

---

[1] According to Frederick Ober, who visited both islands in 1877, Carib traditions were better preserved in St Vincent than in Dominica (1880: 99). The St Vincent Caribs were extensively studied by the anthropologist Charles Gullick (esp. 1985). For recent work on the Trinidadian Carib community in Arima, see Forte 2000.

to the metropolitan eyewitness, sometimes formalized into the anthropological participant-observer.

This is a textually-based study, then, but it makes no claims for the self-sufficiency of texts or of any internal reading that may be offered of them. These texts are embodied in a history of Western observation of indigenous peoples, and that history intersects—if at times somewhat tangentially—with the history of the Caribs themselves, a history inseparable from that of the decline of one empire, the rise of another, and the travails of Dominican independence.

THE CARIB STEREOTYPE

My focus, as I have said, is on the modern period, with 'modernity' occasionally given some weight as a concept since the Caribs, like other indigenous peoples, are often classified with respect to their negative or at least tardy relationship to the modern world. But visitors' interest in the Caribs is almost always predicated upon an understanding of their past, on what they once were but have ceased to be; so, although subsequent chapters will proceed more or less chronologically from 1877 to 1998, they will sometimes refer back to earlier periods of Carib history or of the history of Carib–European relationships. What the Caribs now 'are', for visitors, is frequently a function of them not being what they once were. Since their present 'being' is predicated upon their past, even if negatively, it is important to understand the governing sense of what that history has been.

Like other indigenous peoples—'the Apache', 'the Maori', 'the Hottentot'—'the Carib', in the singular, has been for almost exactly five hundred years one of the staple stereotypes of Western colonial discourse, a stereotype that has operated across the lines of official, fictional, and scholarly writing. The fundamentals of that stereotype are that the Caribs were a fiercesome warrior tribe, probably cannibalistic, which swept northwards through the Caribbean islands shortly before the arrival of the Europeans, killing the Taino (Arawak) men and taking the women as their wives. Unlike the settled and cultured Taino, who retained possession of the larger islands of Hispaniola, Cuba, and Puerto Rico, the Caribs supposedly had few cultural pretensions and little political sophistication. However, their martial attributes allowed them to resist the European invasion with some success, small numbers surviving on several of the Lesser Antilles until the seventeenth century, and on St Vincent and Dominica until the present day.

The historical 'evidence' for the antagonism of the two 'tribes' goes back to Columbus's very first account of Native Caribbean life written on the evening of his arrival in the Bahamas on 12 October 1492: 'I saw some who had marks of wounds on their bodies and I made signs to them asking what they were; and they showed me how people from other islands nearby came there and tried to take them, and how they defended themselves; and I believe that they come here from tierra firme to take them captive' (Columbus 1989: 67); and the Taino/Carib contrast has been a staple of all descriptions of the Native Caribbean from Columbus to, say, the recent summation of his own anthropological and archaeological career given by the Yale anthropologist Irving Rouse, doyen of this normative view of indigenous Caribbean culture (1992). Standard historical accounts follow the same path. The leading early twentieth-century historian of the British Empire summed the Caribs up with typical pith: 'They were a restless and migratory race, often moving from island to island, and when evicted by Europeans prone to return with their friends in unexpected force. This mobility, coupled with their secret and treacherous mentality, rendered them a formidable obstacle to the early settlers, and the ultimate solution to the problem was provided only by a war of extermination' (Williamson 1926: 4). 'Carib means cannibal', a more recent and much reprinted history of the area tells us, 'and cannibalism . . . was one of the characteristics of these canoe-borne marauders who were pushing north along the line of the Lesser Antilles and enslaving or destroying the earlier inhabitants in their way' (Parry and Sherlock 1956: 1–3).

The longevity and persistence of this stereotype will be a feature of many of the pages that follow. That visitors should find the stereotype not to correspond with what they see with their own eyes on Dominica will often provide for them an occasion to reflect on how times have changed and how the mighty are fallen, rather than an opportunity to reject the inadequacies of the stereotype itself. However, as the next two chapters will demonstrate, the late nineteenth century did mark a shift in Western attitudes towards indigenous peoples, with some resulting inflections in responses towards the surviving Caribs. Slowly, too, over the second half of the twentieth century, the prevailing scholarly paradigm has collapsed under the weight of its own contradictions, even if no new orthodoxy has yet replaced it.

One persistent aspect of the Carib stereotype is that of visibility. At the end of the fifteenth century, the Italian humanist Peter Martyr, who lived in Spain, analysed in great detail reports on the inhabitants of the New World. Finally, after some captured Caribs were shipped to Spain as slaves, he got an opportunity to see some for himself in the city of Medina del Campo: 'There was no one who saw them who did not shiver with horror, so infernal and repugnant was the aspect nature and their own cruel character had given them. I affirm this after what I have myself seen, and so likewise do all those who went with me in Medina to examine them'.[2] No modern visitor would use such terms, but many would share Peter Martyr's assumption that nature and character are immediately visible to the eyes of an examiner, whatever the circumstances.

The nearest twentieth-century equivalent to Peter Martyr's examination of the Caribs probably took place in 1935 when the Italian poet, Lionello Fiumi, travelling in the French West Indian islands, came across a group of Caribs from Dominica on display in an Exposition in Fort-de-France, Martinique.[3] The encounter prompted a brief poetic meditation, perhaps even a prose poem, published in his *Images des Antilles* under the inevitable title 'Les derniers Caraïbes'—the last Caribs:

To the poet of the Antilles, Daniel Thaly, friend of the last Caribs.

At an exposition in Fort-de-France, I see—inoffensive objects in the pavilion, resigned to the sideshow—those who, one day—heads arrogant with parrot feathers, bodies glowing with roucou—had leapt boldly from their narrow canoes, arrowtips drenched in the deadly

---

[2] D'Anghera (1912: i. 75–6), translation amended. All translations are mine, unless otherwise noted. Original language texts are in the Appendix.

[3] Lionello Fiumi (1894–1973), Italian poet, critic, and travel writer; who often wrote in French: see Clerici 1962.

juice of the mancenillier, the raiders of the sea that bears their name: the Caribs.

The sparse and poverty-stricken descendants who were there—reaching us just as if they had been survivors on a raft from some sad shipwreck—were not from Martinique, they had been unearthed from the neighbouring island of Dominica. A man in a straw hat had brought them here, a clean-shaven, brick-red face, gentle eyes behind glasses, and it was good to find out that this shepherd was a poet—the poet of the Antilles—as if poetry alone still knew how to offer, in a world set on destroying itself, a trace of love to a dying seed.

Straight hair wrapped in oilcloth—an unusual contrast with the frizzy froth of negro heads all around—, prominent cheekbones in olive faces—the mystery of racial affinities: have I not seen similar traits among the Lapps?—, the last Caribs stood there, without smile or pride, taciturn.

Exposed to all the impertinent looks, calm in the face of all the clicking Kodaks, those who had been so shy and hidden themselves in the forest as soon as they had spied on the sea those trees they had never seen before—the masts carrying Columbus's flags.

Looking at them, one thought of the cobra seen in the zoo, behind the glass which renders useless any impulse to poison.

The glass for these survivors is time: the two or three centuries of European guns which have been enough to bring the race to an end, and to sweeten the cruelty of it all.

And for the descendants of those cannibals who, in order to boost their courage, would harden their body in a hairshirt of carnivorous ants, there does not even remain the stoicism of that American bird called the *quetzal* which, put into a cage, kills itself. (Fiumi 1938: 80–1)

Although the image of the cobra retains some trace of the terror that Peter Martyr felt, Fiumi's dominant note is pathos, which his writing wants to conjure in the reader for the fall of the Caribs from bravery to taciturnity, from cannibalism to the absence even of the pride that would lead to suicide. Instead, for the modern reader, he conjures only the pathos of the event itself. We see not just the Caribs in their 'cage', but also the tourists with their cameras and the poet with his notebook and his aesthetic sensibility.[4]

In 1935 France was celebrating the three hundredth anniversary of its first settlement of Martinique. Since all Martinique's

---

[4] For the general background to these ethnographic showcases, see Corbey 1993.

Caribs had been unfortunately killed or exiled during the colonial period, Dominica was called on to provide replacements, brought by their 'friend' the poet Daniel Thaly, whom Fiumi revealingly refers to as 'berger' (shepherd).[5] One of the French magazines celebrating this tricentenary was picked up in Dominica the next year by Jean Rhys, its picture of a Carib reminding her of one she used to look at on the wall of her family house in Roseau, forty years previously.

EARLIER VISITORS

From the earliest moments of contact the Caribs have always had a special place in the European imagination. They were, according to Columbus's understanding of what the first people he met in the Caribbean told him, the hostile and man-eating inhabitants of the islands he did not quite get to visit on that epochal journey. When he landed on Marie-Galante at the beginning of his second voyage, in late 1493, he was in no doubt that he was in Carib country; and the name stuck to refer to the native inhabitants of the islands north and south of that landfall, from St Croix in the north to Grenada in the south. Columbus himself never gave a name to the first people he met, nor referred to what they called themselves, if anything. Subsequently, Arawak came to be used (extended from the mainland of northern South America), with Taino a later, but now widely used name for the chiefdoms that had developed on Hispaniola (now the Dominican Republic and Haiti), Cuba, and Puerto Rico.

Spanish interest and attention were focused on those larger islands, with their more sophisticated political classes, before moving to the mainland. However, the political and trading balances of the whole region were irrevocably altered by the Spanish presence, especially when the other islands began being raided for slaves to work in the Hispaniolan goldfields. The islands supposedly inhabited by Caribs, who were supposedly cannibals, were for a while the only ones that could legally be raided, although such a law did not obviously assist the survival

---

[5] Dr Daniel Thaly (1879–1950) was himself one of Dominica's best-known writers (see Paravisini-Gebert 1999).

of the undesignated populations. However, the effectiveness of the resistance from the denizens of the Lesser Antilles only served to confirm their reputation for hostility, although it also brought with it a certain grudging respect, which was carried over into the reports from other European visitors. The favoured sailing ship route from Europe to America caught the north-easterly trade winds off the Canary Islands and made landfall on either Guadeloupe or Dominica. The north-east coast of Dominica offered no landing points, but the sheltered bay on the north-west coast, now known as Prince Rupert Bay, provided a useful first landing place, where bartering with the Caribs took place at least until the mid-seventeenth century (see Honychurch 1997a).

Four kinds and periods of writing about the Carib communities before 1877 can be established. In the second half of the sixteenth and early years of the seventeenth century English and French sailors left short accounts of those short visits for 'wood and water' or for trade, although the crew of the wrecked *Olive Branch* had more extensive contact during an enforced stay on St Lucia in 1606–7. After the beginnings of French and English settlement on the islands, from the 1620s, a series of French missionaries and officials spent lengthy periods on the islands, sometimes living with Carib groups for many years, and in several cases compiling accounts of language and lifeways which provide an extraordinarily rich body of material about indigenous life in the Lesser Antilles after nearly two centuries of cultural contact. Raymond Breton, Charles de Rochefort, Jean Baptiste du Tertre, and Jean Baptiste Labat are the most important names.[6]

As far as modern visitors have been concerned, the most significant of these earlier writers was the engaging French Jesuit, Père Labat. Labat's popularity has resulted partly from him being the most recent of the quartet and partly from a short selection of his writings being available since 1931 in English

---

[6] See WM chs. 9, 10, 11, and 13. Their principal works are as follows: Raymond Breton, *Dictionnaire caraïbe–françois*, 2 vols. (1665–6); Jean Baptiste Du Tertre, *Histoire générale des Antilles habités par les François*, 4 vols. (1667–71); Charles de Rochefort, *Histoire naturelle et morale des Îles Antilles de l'Amérique* (1665); and Jean Baptiste Labat, *Nouveau Voyage aux isles de l'Amérique*, 6 vols. (1722).

translation.[7] Labat's colourful career in Martinique and his keen interest in all aspects of the islands he inhabited for eleven years make him a lively guide to the early eighteenth-century Caribbean. However, he arrived in the region after three centuries of European colonization had wrought dramatic changes to Carib culture and lifeways and, in any case, had himself only rather brief contacts with surviving Carib communities. None of this prevented him from becoming established as the authority on what the Caribs 'were really like'. Frederick Ober, who will appear in Chapter 2 as the modern 'rediscoverer' of the Caribs, begins his very first piece of writing about them by saying how different they are from the Caribs as described by Père Labat.

A further series of eighteenth-century writings, mostly English, concerns the intermittent conflict between the planters on St Vincent and the strong groups of surviving Amerindians, popularly divided between the Yellow Caribs and the Black Caribs, the latter group supposedly having mixed with escaped or shipwrecked Africans. The length and difficulty of this conflict occasioned much writing. After their final military defeat in 1796, a large number of Caribs were deported to Central America, but small groups stayed and have been visited and studied, though less often than the Caribs in Dominica. The fourth and final kind of writing consists of the very fragmentary material produced in the period between the Revolutionary wars in the Caribbean at the end of the eighteenth century and the 'rediscovery' of the Caribs in the 1870s. Most of this was written by missionaries or planters: there was very little interest from the rest of the outside world.[8] By this time the Carib communities in Dominica and St Vincent were quite small and isolated on the parts of their islands most remote from the larger European settlements. With respect to the Native Caribbean, the past did indeed seem 'all a blank', as Grenville Chester suggested in 1869.

These last two periods of writing—mostly English—come after the landmark settlement in the Caribbean, the 1763 Treaty of Paris, after which British sugar planters were supposed to

---

[7] Labat 1931. Rochefort was translated in full into English as early as 1666 (Davies), but the translation is not easily available.

[8] All this writing about the Caribs is represented in *WM*, especially chs. 5, 6, 9, 10, 11, 13, and 14–20.

complete the plantation of the Lesser Antilles, control of which had until then been contested with France. Benedict Anderson notes this particular decade—following the invention of an accurate chronometer—as marking the beginning of a new phase of colonial development which saw the squaring off of empty seas and unexplored regions in measured boxes, and Dominica was accordingly 'boxed' and enthusiastically bought by lot all over England, with unfortunate disregard for the fact that the island consists almost entirely of steep and forested mountain sides: an early and devastating defeat for the geometrical grid (Anderson 1991: 173). As the very first description of Dominica as an English island graphically put it:

One would be tempted to believe that Nature had given birth to it, when labouring in convulsions; or that, by subterranean fires, it had been heaved from the bed of ocean. The angels and devils in Milton, when engaged in horrid strife, tore up such rocks and craggy mountains, and Dominique stands erected an accumulated monument of this direful contest (*Some Observations* 1764: 6–7)

The 'boxed' plan reserved two small sections of land on the remote north windward coast for the Caribs (Byres 1777). This was a symbolic allocation—a handful of acres in the most remote part of the most remote island of the Caribbean—and in the 1760s the Caribs were undoubtedly more widely spread throughout Dominica, as Byres's map actually indicates. However, the settlement acted as an expression of official intent, an intent which may have coincided with Carib desires to keep as far away from British settlements as possible: the 1903 Reserve of 3,700 acres incorporates that original allocation (see fig. 2).[9]

Unlike the Vincentian Caribs, the Caribs on Dominica seem to have played little part in either the Revolutionary wars at the end of the eighteenth century or the intermittent struggles with maroons, although maroon contact with Caribs may simply be under-represented in the colonial archives.[10] The anonymous

---

[9] The absence of a river valley on that part of the island meant that no large plantation had developed there (Honychurch 1997b: 118).

[10] See Marshall 1976. In one of the documents addressed to the Colonial Secretary of the time, Earl Bathurst, by the local supporters of Governor Ainslie, who received much metropolitan criticism of his harsh treatment of the maroons, 'a poor harmless Carib' is listed as being murdered by maroons (*A Collection of Plain Authentic Documents* 1815: 14).

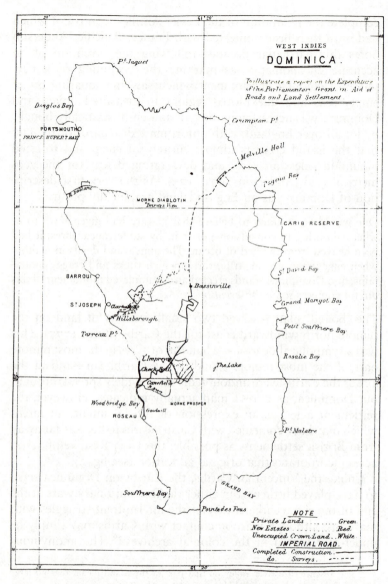

FIG. 2. Map of Dominica, drawn to accompany Hesketh Bell's, *Dominica. Roads and Land Settlement. Report on the Expenditure of the Parliamentary Grant in Aid* (Colonial Reports—Miscellaneous, no. 23, London: HMSO, 1903).

pamphleteer of 1764 refers to them as 'the poor native Caribbees, who are a quiet well-disposed people, and should be taken kind care of' (*Some Observations* 1764: 7). Thomas Atwood, who wrote the first history of Dominica in 1791, certainly suggested that the few remaining Caribs on the island— not more than twenty or thirty families—had already been left to their own devices:

The Indians, natives of Dominica, are descended from the ancient inhabitants, who were found there when this island was first discovered by Europeans, and are the people properly called 'Caribbes'. Of these there are not more than twenty or thirty families, who have their dwellings on the east part of the island, at a great distance from Roseau, where they are seldom seen.

They are of a clear copper colour, have long, sleek, black hair on their heads; their persons are short, stout, and well made; but they disfigure their faces by pressing flat their noses, which is done in their infancy. They are a quiet, inoffensive people, speak a language of their own, and French, but none of them speak English.

They live chiefly by fishing in the rivers and the sea, or by fowling in the woods, at both of which they are very expert with their bows and arrows. They will kill the smallest bird with an arrow, or transfix a fish at a great depth in the sea; and are very serviceable to the planters near their settlement, whom they chiefly supply with fish and game. They are also very ingenious, making curious wrought panniers, or baskets of silk grass, or the bark of trees.

It is much to be regretted, that since this island has been in the possession of the English, so little pains have been taken to cultivate an union with these people, as they might be capable of essential service to its internal security, especially against the accumulation of runaway negros in the time of peace; and in war they might be induced to join in its defence, should it be invaded. Yet they are permitted to roam wherever their fancies lead them, as much unnoticed as if no such people were in existence. They are men as well as we, are born with the same degree of sensibility; and by proper encouragement, might be of material benefit to a country which was originally their own. (Atwood 1791: 221–3)

There are already a number of notes here that will be played again in the 200 years that follow Atwood's remarks, not least the emphasis on defining physical features, especially skin colour and hair, the skill at basketwork, the possibility of mutual English–Carib interests against blacks, and the Caribs' peculiar social invisibility: 'as much unnoticed as if no such people were in existence'. There is no indication that Atwood visited the Carib territories.

Atwood's description was echoed thirty-seven years later by an anonymous (temporary) resident in a sketch of the island and its history which was, like so many written at this time, a defence of the stern measures employed against maroons and a warning to the metropolis not to abolish the institution of slavery:

A few families of Caribs, or free Indians, however, inhabit the mountains, and occasionally visit Roseau, to sell their bows and arrows, and other curiosities. They are very quiet and inoffensive, live entirely by themselves, and have never, at any time, given any disturbance to the planters, as those in St Vincent's and Jamaica have. These people are short in stature, yellow in complexion, with long hair and dark eyes. They have flat foreheads, and small hands and feet; shew no curiosity, or anger; seem little sensible of either joy or sorrow; are peacable and harmless, silent and indolent, and mix neither with negroes nor people of colour. (*Sketches and Recollections* 1828: 148)

Atwood's advice was ignored. The infrequent travellers who left any written accounts of Dominica did little more than mention the Caribs, simply passing on the new version of the stereotype. This is Daniel McKinnen in 1804: 'There are some few wandering red Charaibs in this island; but I did not accidentally meet with any of them' (50); this Henry Nelson Coleridge in 1832: 'There are a few families of the aboriginal Caribs living on the windward side of the island, but they have scarcely any intercourse with the rest of the population, and all I learned about them was, that although they usually lived to a great age, they were gradually decreasing from a continued system of intermarrying within a very narrow circle' (153–4); and this Mrs Henry Lynch in 1856: 'Some descendants of the Caribs are yet found in the Windward Islands, and though they have lost their ferocity, and with it their spirit of independence, though slothful and careless in their habits, they remain to this day a peculiar and distinct people' (1856: 13).

When Grenville Chester visited the island in the late 1860s, he—like many others—failed to convert his interest in the Caribs into a journey to their part of the island: 'It was a matter of regret that the shortness of my stay prevented a visit to the Charaib or Carib Indians, who still inhabit a portion of Dominica.' But, as he notes, even residents claiming an interest in the Caribs had not actually managed a visit: 'Neither the rector, nor an intelligent and scientific Scotch physician who has buried himself alive in Dominica, nor any of the merchants with whom I conversed, had ever visited them, nor were they able to give any information on the subject' (1869: 16–17).[11] Chester does note, however, that a Roman Catholic priest living among the Caribs had recently left the island, taking with him all knowledge of the habits 'of these interesting people'. This may be a reference to Father du Lettré, usually regarded as the converter of the Caribs to Catholicism in the 1850s and 1860s, perhaps the most decisive moment of cultural change for the Caribs, but one for which there is practically no documentation (see *WM* 233–40).

THE CARIBS IN SCIENTIFIC WRITING

The third edition of Johann Friedrich Blumenbach's *De Generis Humani Varietate Nativa* was published in 1795, at the very moment of the outbreak of the war in St Vincent which would lead to the final military defeat of the Caribs. For Blumenbach there were five principal varieties of the human species: the middle, or Caucasian, variety; two extremes, Mongolian and Ethiopic; and two intermediate varieties, the Malay and the American. Five skulls took pride of place in the engravings illustrating this treatise, one for each variety; and the American was represented by the skull of a Carib chief from St Vincent, 'a gift of Sir Joseph Banks, Bart.'.[12] Banks himself had received the skull from Alexander Anderson, head of the Botanical Garden in St Vincent, who had explained in a 1789 letter to Banks just

---

[11] The 'Scotch physician' was Dr John Imray (1812–80), a distinguished botanist and medical researcher. While Imray and his successor, Dr Henry Alfred Alford Nicholls (1851–1926), were based near Roseau, one doctor, Joseph Numa Rat, worked on the east coast and wrote a valuable study of the Carib language (Rat 1897). Cf. Clyde (1980: 52–3, 73–5, 91–2).

[12] Blumenbach (1865: 156). The skull, marked 'Caribaei', is reproduced in an endplate.

how hard it was to get an indigenous skull since the Caribs' burial places 'are not easily found & an attempt to disturb them is look'd upon as the greatest of crimes'.[13] The Caribs were still seen as special, able to represent 'America', although Anderson notes that most of the Vincentian Caribs are now mixed with Africans.[14] During the popularity of phrenology in the first half of the nineteenth century, casts of Carib skulls were of particular interest as representing 'as cruel a people as any known'— and by now distinguished from the American Indian, 'whose character is known to be far superior'.[15]

Then, during the middle of the nineteenth century, when there was a general hiatus in interest in the Caribs as a surviving population, they were remembered and discussed in one of the institutional forums within which the discipline of anthropology found its eventual shape, the London Ethnological Society, when the question of American Indian origins was addressed—with particular reference to the Caribs—in a startling lecture delivered by James Kennedy on 15 March 1854.[16]

Kennedy's approach to the general question of American Indian origins is relatively eclectic inasmuch as he suggests that the American continent was peopled from different places and at different times, a view which—though now unorthodox—is still given some credence by those sceptical of the theory of initial continental population across a Bering Straits ice bridge. The Caribs enter Kennedy's argument during his discussion of pre-Columbian African contacts with America. Early theorists had posited all kinds of possible Old World origins for American Indians, including African ones: traditions ultimately finding their authority in Aristotle, who had spoken of Carthaginian merchants discovering and settling land beyond the Pillars of Hercules (Huddleston 1967: 17). In 1580 Suarez de Peralta posited an Ethiopian origin for some Indians, but neither he nor Hugo Grotius, who linked Ethiopia with the

---

[13] The letter is in Blumenbach's papers (MS Blumenbach 3:30ᵛ, University of Göttingen Library) as quoted by Turnbull (1999: 217).

[14] For a suggestion that this evidence should be treated sceptically, see Hulme 1999*b*.

[15] De Ville (1828: 11); and cf. Cooter 1984.

[16] Kennedy had been a judge in Havana and had also, he says, met the Revd Mr Henderson of Belize, who had translated the Gospel of St Matthew into Carib in 1847.

Yucatán because of the practice of circumcision, seems to have made an issue of skin colour (37). However, Kennedy's argument is premissed upon the differential *colour* of the Caribs. He notes to begin with that from Peter Martyr and from Ferdinand Columbus's biography of his father, 'we learn that the discoverers fell in with several tribes of a darker colour than the general body of Indians, and some of them actually black'. Most notorious was 'a widely-diffused tribe of dark colour and peculiar ferocity, [found] throughout the islands, designated Caribs or Cannibals'. They were, Kennedy notes, too intractable to submit to any intercourse with the Spaniards. Darkness of skin colour, ferocity, intractability—the associations are clearly inescapable for Kennedy: '[T]hough the name Carib might thus have been given them extraneously, yet, as they seem to have taken it as their own, it might possibly have been also their proper name, as in Africa are found people bearing one of a similar sound, Karabàs and Carabalis' (1855: 31-2). Kennedy considers the views of Charles de Rochefort and William Robertson on Carib origins before giving his backing to Bryan Edwards's theory of the African descent of the Caribs, an opinion Kennedy had, he says, come to independently 'from what had come under the observation of this people':

Their general appearance and features, notwithstanding their straight shining hair, gave me the idea more of the African than the American Indian; and the fact of their having come over from Africa was not, even according to Rochefort's account, inconsistent with their traditions, as these merely stated that they had come by sea from a far country, without distinctly shewing whether it was from the east or the west. (36)

Kennedy recalls the features of Carib customs that suggested an African origin to Edwards—contemptuous behaviour to females, cotton buskin worn by women, disfiguration of the face—to which he adds their use of the tom-tom, mentioned by Rochefort. Then Kennedy lists twenty-nine Carib words taken from Breton and Rochefort, and gives similar-sounding words from West African languages, though the demonstration of similarity is somewhat weakened by the fact that he has to draw from nine different African languages in order to make his point.[17]

---

[17] On Rochefort, see n. 6 above. William Robertson was the Scottish author of the influential *History of America* [1777]; Bryan Edwards, his contemporary, the

As to the voyage which brought them from Africa, Kennedy recalls Spanish accounts of Carib navigational skill and physical endurance. And, '[f]rom their appetite for human flesh, learned not improbably in Africa, they would have been able to obtain sufficient sustenance for the long voyage across' (41). Why human flesh should be superior to animal flesh in this regard is not explained, unless it is assumed that once their food supplies had run out they would have been able to eat each other until the journey was over, always assuming that at least one man and one woman survived to perpetuate the species.

British speculation about Carib origins is not unrelated to colonial wars in the Caribbean, culminating—for the Caribs—in the massive deportation of Caribs from St Vincent to Central America in 1797. Bryan Edwards, for example, had started his history of the British West Indies in the 1780s, a moment of relative stability in the region, only to have to cope in the latter stages of the book's composition and in its new editions with events on Saint-Domingue and the war with France, where the Caribs of St Vincent played—according to British accounts—a significant role. The major issue—dealt with most explicitly by William Young, who edited posthumous editions of Edwards's *History*—involved the question of the 'Black Caribs', as they were called, a new ethnic group with whom the British had considerable problems in the period from 1763 to 1797.[18] Kennedy's suggestion of an African origin for the Caribs themselves—and not just for the 'black' component of the Black Caribs—completes an 'Africanization' of the Caribs which in part refines and in part displaces their 'Orientalization' by Edwards. The Carib Wars darkened the Caribs; the early nineteenth-century exploration of Africa, in British eyes, soldered the chain of signifiers which associated darkness of skin colour with intractability and ferocity (especially cannibalism).[19]

---

author of a much reprinted history of the British colonies in the West Indies (1819). Edwards considered the Caribs different enough from all other indigenous American populations to be conceived of as 'a distinct race', and floated the idea of an oriental ancestry (previously suggested in 1652 by the Dutchman Georg Horn in his *De Originibus Americanis* (Edwards 1819: i. 145–6).

[18] See *WM* chs. 14–19; Hulme (1986: 225–63); and Hulme 1999.

[19] In the Pacific, by what seemed at first pure coincidence, Europeans found two major peoples, one, the Polynesians, light-skinned and peaceful, just like the Arawaks, the other, the Melanesians, dark-skinned and cannibalistic, just like the

During the nineteenth century a number of expatriate anti-
quarians, visiting scientists, and colonial officials took some
kind of interest in native Caribbean history. Two large collections of antiquities (George Latimer's from Puerto Rico and M.
L. Guesde's from Guadeloupe) were donated to the Smithsonian Institution in 1863 and 1885 respectively (see Mason 1877
and 1885). Two other large collections, compiled by E. L.
Atkinson of Trinidad and Sir Thomas Graham Briggs, one of
the largest West Indian landowners, went to the Horniman
Museum in south London (see Im Thurn 1884, Quick 1902,
and Branch 1907); and important artefacts were found in
Jamaica (Anon. 1896; Handler 1978). However, this interest in
Caribbean antiquities developed entirely without reference to
surviving indigenous populations. J. Ballet, 'chef du service de
l'enregistrement' on Guadeloupe, produced a memoir on the
Caribs for the first International Congress of Americanists in
Paris in 1875. He recognized that the people who inhabited the
Lesser Antilles at the time of Columbus 'have almost entirely
disappeared', but the focus of the memoir is entirely on 'the
causes that led to their extermination', despite the existence of
Carib families on Guadeloupe at this time (Ballet 1875: 394–5).

US MOVES/CREOLE PERSPECTIVES

James Kennedy's detailed, if phantasmagoric, consideration of
Carib origins was an exception for its period. For the most part,
if the Caribs appeared at all in mid-nineteenth-century writing,
they did so in repetitions of the early Spanish accounts of Native
Caribbean history, retailed in the course of the various ideological repositionings of the period with respect to the Spanish-
speaking islands of the Caribbean. These repositionings can be
divided into two broad streams. The expansionist interests of
the US republic had, from its earliest days, had at least half an
eye on the Caribbean, even if its army and colonists were more

Caribs. Eventually someone—the US scholar Harold Gladwin in 1949—suggested
the irresistible conclusion 'that the Caribs may represent the Melanesians in South
America in much the same way that the Arawaks may have been derived from some
of the Polynesians' (1949: 250–1). Not surprisingly, the Melanesia/Polynesia division has come in for something like the same kind of reassessment in recent years
as the Arawak/Carib division: see, for example and for further references, Thomas
1989.

actively involved in Texas, Florida, and the remaining Indian territories to the west of the States. John Quincy Adams was only one of many politicians to voice the opinion that Cuba belonged 'naturally' within the ambit of the USA and there were various, usually half-baked, attempts to annex parts of the Dominican Republic, which was in mid-century moving out of and back into the Spanish Empire at irregular intervals. This political and economic interest had some small anthropological counterpart: the antiquarianism that marked the new country's intellectual life, with its rash of historical societies, found an echo among US expatriots in the Caribbean. In particular, the century saw a growing interest in the figure of Christopher Columbus, culminating in the Chicago Exposition of 1892 (which I will say more about in the next chapter). Initially, Columbus had offered the independent United States a figurehead usefully detached from its British antecedents. In 1828 Washington Irving had used newly discovered Columbus materials (especially the journal of the first voyage, in Bartolomé de Las Casas's summary) to produce an important biography; and US expansion south and west was leading to a growing interest in the country's Hispanic roots. The association with Columbus linked the USA to the beginnings of Western (and therefore Christian) influence in the New World, a connection sanctioned when John Vanderlyn's painting, *Landing of Columbus at the Island of Guanahani, West Indies* was added in 1847 (along with the disembarkation of the pilgrims, the baptism of Pocahontas, and the discovery of the Mississippi by De Soto) to Trumbull's four panoramas of Independence as murals on national history in the US Capitol in Washington, DC, soon to be followed by Randolph Rogers's bronze doors to the Rotunda illustrating the life of Columbus in nine tableaux.[20]

US interests and ambitions in the Caribbean clarified over the course of the century, leading in 1898 to the invasion of Cuba and the annexation of Puerto Rico, the geriatric presence of the Spanish Empire finally displaced.[21] That outcome had long been

[20] See Fryd (1992: 42–61 and 125–54).
[21] On general US interest in Caribbean (and on imperial developments): Knight 1928; Tanshill 1938; Calcott 1942; Merk 1963; LaFeber 1963; Langley 1976; Horsman 1981; Drinnon 1980. US interest in Caribbean anthropology and archeology was relatively slight before 1898, with the exception of Ober's works (and

on the cards; and it implied two kinds of possible relationship to the historical Caribs, however rarely these were actually spelled out. It was always likely that Spain, rather than Britain or France, would prove the eventual US antagonist in the Caribbean. Early in the century there might have been US support for a war against Britain in the Caribbean to take over its slave plantations but, once slavery had been ended, there was little economic motivation for such a move and the growing influence of the ideology of Anglo-Saxonism tended to stress common interests based on common racial background. In any case, the USA was likely to be interested in the same islands as Spain, which had had first choice, and for the same reasons—the larger islands had greater economic potential, underdeveloped by their Spanish owners; they had significant natural resources, both mineral and agricultural; and they offered great strategic positions from which to control the Caribbean sea-lanes.[22] And, in addition, in Cuba there was a strong movement towards independence from Spain, which allowed the USA to appear as a liberator, with Cuba as a younger version of itself, seeking freedom from imperial control.

The indigenous implications of all this may not seem too obvious. However, as the USA positioned itself with respect to Spain, the old Black Legend of Spanish cruelty to the indigenous population was a useful stick to wave, a tactic which led to the present populations, especially in Cuba, being identified, at least ideologically, as new indigenes still under attack from an old and vicious enemy. The islands themselves could therefore be

leaving aside books whose primary focus was on Columbus), though in an incident it is difficult not to see as symbolic, what the Smithsonian Institution recognized as 'the first evidence as to the antiquity of man in the West Indies' (the words of Spencer Baird, Secretary to the Smithsonian) was a bone scraper cut from a shell and discovered in a quantity of cave earth brought to Philadelphia in 1868 by a firm of phosphate manufacturers who had obtained it from a cave in Anguilla (Cope 1883).

[22] The strategic position was succinctly stated by Captain Mahan in May 1897: 'In the Caribbean Archipelago—the very domain of sea power, if ever region could be called so—are the natural home and centre of those influences by which such a maritime highway as a canal must be controlled, even as the control of the Suez Canal rests in the Mediterranean . . . In the cluster of island fortresses of the Caribbean is one of the greatest of the nerve centres of the whole body of European civilization; and it is to be regretted that so serious a portion of them now is in hands which not only never have given, but to all appearances never can give, the development which is required by the general interest' (1918: 261).

seen as not *essentially* Spanish (and also, helpfully, as not in any way African). The old stories could be told again, in which the islands' native inhabitants were under threat from the Caribs, but 'saved' by outside intervention from Spain—only for Spain to destroy them instead. The implication was that the modern Cubans (seen as Native Caribbeans), groaning under alien hegemony (this time Spanish), would again be rescued by an outside force (this time the USA), which would—this time—*not* betray them; or so the story went.[23]

What I am suggesting was, of course, a largely unconscious set of identifications. But take, for example, De Bonneville Randolph Keim's *San Domingo. Pen Pictures and Leaves of Travel, Romance and History, from the Portfolio of a Correspondent in the American Tropics* (1870). Keim was sent to the Dominican Republic by his editor to drum up support for President Ulysses Grant's unsuccessful attempt to annex the country. His book has materials on the contemporary political situation (including an interview with President Baez); extensive comments on the progress of negotiations; accounts of his travel through the country; and a brief history of the republic. However, surprisingly, about a quarter of the book is given over to a retelling of the narratives of first contact between Spaniards and native people, including the story of the founding of Santo Domingo through the tragic love of Zameaca (Catalina) for the fugitive Miguel Diaz, and—inevitably—the story of the Spanish Governor, Nicolás de Ovando's, entrapment and murder of Anacaona, the Taino queen, retold largely through the perspective of Washington Irving, although Keim claims to have had the story from a lady in Santo Domingo.[24]

---

[23] In all of this, the indigenous inhabitants stood metonymically for the mineral resources of the island, I have suggested (Hulme 1997*a*, 1997*b*).

[24] On the political background to Keim's visit, see Tanshill (1938: 370). The execution of Anacaona is usually seen as one of the most cold-blooded killings in what was in any case a blood-soaked period. The original Anacaona has many manifestations in colonial historiography and legend. The important point to emphasize here is that Anacaona was presented by Washington Irving (through his reading of Las Casas) as the archetypal *victim* of Spanish brutality, an image Keim reflects (as Frederick Ober does later in his novels), though the historical reality may well have been considerably more complicated, with Anacaona a more active and potentially powerful native leader. On the indigenous background to Anacaona, see Sued Badillo 1985.

Irving plays an important role here in disseminating ideas about Columbus and about the Caribs: his biography of Columbus had 175 editions and translations between 1828 and 1900 (Irving 1981: p. lxxxvi). By the end of the century new scholarly work on Columbus was appearing, but the popularity of Irving as a writer ensured his influence at least until the Great War. Although Irving's qualities as a historical scholar have often been called into question, he was properly sceptical about the orthodox picture of the Caribs which was, he says, 'coloured by the fears of the Indians, and the prejudices of the Spaniards'. Irving's conclusion is that 'the warlike and unyielding character of these people, so different from that of the pusillanimous nations around them, and the wide scope of their enterprizes and wanderings, like those of the nomade tribes of the old world, entitle them to distinguished attention' (1981: 192).

Building on this perspective, but with a different spin, the Caribs could also become 'beneficiaries' of a US revisionism which wanted a full restoration of the Black Legend, as in this post-1898 extravaganza:

Already, on his third expedition, Columbus suggested that the natives of the West Indies, the gentle Caribs, should be sold as slaves, in order to raise money for the Government, and in 1494 five hundred were brought to Spain and sold. Slave auctions of Caribbee Indians became an institution in Seville, but the money raised did not by any means make up for the chests of gold and precious stones that Columbus had led his friends at home to expect . . . The instructions to Columbus had been very explicit as to the importance of converting the natives to Christianity, and while the Church had some scruples regarding slavery when applied to those of its own faith, the Pope looked upon it as a fair punishment for those who remained heretic. Of course it would have been most inconvenient had all the natives turned Christian for then there would have been an end to slavery. So the natives were hunted down by bloodhounds; they were addressed in Spanish, and they answered in Caribbee. The white slave-raider swore that the Carib had refused to become a Christian, while the poor Carib knew nothing of what was expected of him. In any event, the white man's word was taken, the Carib was branded, sold as a slave, and thus was laid the foundation of Spain's colonial fortune. From the very outset Columbus inaugurated the policy that every Indian owed more or less of his labor to the white man, without remuneration, and that policy was not reversed until Admiral Dewey trained his twelve-inch guns upon Manila in the summer of 1898. (Bigelow 1901: 6–7)

So, in the USA during the second and third quarters of the nineteenth century, there was substantial interest in retelling the history of the Native Caribbean, often in fictionalized form, even if very little interest in, or even recognition of, the tenuous survival of indigenous communities. This perspective had also been apparent in the creole societies of the Spanish Caribbean in their struggles to form national identities at this period, with indigenous figures, particularly those who had fought against the Spanish, providing inspiration for such significant works of fiction as Manuel de Galván's *Enriquillo* (Dominican Republic, 1882) and Eugenio María Hostos's *La peregrinación de Bayoán* (Puerto Rico, 1863). There was little role here for the Caribs, however, except—again—as playing the allegorical part of Spaniards in the more mournful work of the Cuban poets known as the *ciboneyistas* (from the presumed name of the island's first inhabitants). As José Fornaris wrote, in the 1888 edition of his *Cantos del Siboney* (1855), drawing out the political implications of *ciboneyista* writing:

Only symbolically would the poet have been able to express the love for his country and to protest against the unjust and insulting manner of ruling over it. The word *patria* rang like a call to insurrection in our rulers' ears. I know very well that that was the idea that the poetry expressed. Within the poetry, as a symbol, the Siboney Indians represented the oppressed Cubans, and the Carib Indians represented the unjust oppressors.

That the colonial regime recognized the political charge to this imaginative indigeneity is demonstrated in the story of how the Spanish military commander in Cuba, General José de la Concha, summoned Fornaris, saying: 'I have called you here to warn you that if you want to continue writing about the Siboneyes, you should go to the United States. On this island we are Spaniards, not Indians; do you understand?, all Spaniards'.[25] The Cuban military leader, Antonio Maceo, would later invoke Indian suffering at the hands of brutal Spaniards,

---

[25] Both quotations from Vitier (1970: 158–60). Cf. Arrom 1980; and Roberts 1997.

and during the Cuban War of Independence comparisons were often made between Maceo and Guama (the best-known Cuban Indian resistance leader in the sixteenth century) and between Máximo Gómez and the Taino, Hatuey (both of whom came from the neighbouring island of Hispaniola to assist their comrades in the struggle on Cuba). But the most striking indication of the political valency of indigeneity had come early in the piece: the adoption of the island's aboriginal name, Haïti, by Dessalines and the first black government of the newly independent Saint-Domingue (see Geggus 1997).

Another element to the creation of national consciousness in the islands of the Spanish Caribbean was historical and antiquarian enquiry of the kind that would emphasize local, insular developments, rather than seeing the islands as part of an imperial history. Andrés Poey gave a paper on 'Cuban Antiquities' to the American Ethnological Society as early as 1851; the first exhibition of 'relics of our Indians' was held in Puerto Rico in 1854; a Cuban Anthropological Society was started in 1877; and a considerable body of writing on the subject was produced in the latter part of the nineteenth century, especially in Cuba—even though most modern accounts of the scholarship of the Native Caribbean only begin with the US investigators who followed hard on the heels of their army in 1898.[26]

MODERN TRAVELLERS

One April morning in New York, in the mid-1880s, a young North American called William Agnew Paton was suddenly asked by a family friend if he fancied a trip to the West Indies, where the friend, a doctor, was going for a rest and change of air. Paton agreed; and they left that afternoon. When he got back Paton wrote one of the first modern travel-books about the Caribbean, called *Down the Islands: A Voyage to the*

[26] Poey 1851; Alegría 1978; Rivero de la Calle 1966. For appreciations of nineteenth-century Caribbean scholarship in the area, see Ortiz 1922; Sued Badillo 1978; and Davis 1996. Much of this work obviously concentrated on Taino material remains, language, and culture, drawing largely on the work of the early Spanish chroniclers and historians but gradually involving knowledge of local sites and study of surviving linguistic forms, both in toponyms and in the spoken vernacular. However, Juan Ignacio de Armas published a fine assessment of the Carib myth (1884).

Caribbees (1888). Like many subsequent travellers, Paton found himself most fascinated by the island of Dominica:

Of all the Caribbees, Dominica most awakened my curiosity and excited my imagination. It seemed so inaccessible, so mysterious, a great wilderness in the midst of the sea, unexplored and unexplorable. What wonder that the Caribs longest remained in possession of it; the mention of its name suggests an inquiry into the history of that interesting race. Just as at Barbados it seems natural to inquire into the statistics of sugar-planting, in St Lucia to rehearse the stories of the wars between England and France, so in Dominica one is tempted to discourse of the legends of the Carib people, to learn of their struggle for liberty, their mad fight for existence. The legends of this ill-fated people seems to haunt the mountain-heights and valleys where they longest made a stand in defence of their old homes, as echoes calling back from hill and glen.

In the least-explored mountain-retreats and gloomiest valleys of Dominica there still exists a miserable remnant of this once powerful and numerous nation, a few wretched survivors preserving some traditions, and until within a few years a vestige of the ancient language of a great and warlike people—the undisputed, unconquerable masters of all the Caribbean islands in years gone by. For years and years after the coming of Columbus the 'Caribs' and the 'Canibals', the 'Robbers' and the 'Man-eaters', successfully resisted all attempted invasions, and were only after ages deprived of their inheritance, as the ancient Britons were in the end dispossessed by the Danes and Norsemen. Inch by inch, foot by foot, in continual struggle the natives defended their island settlements. It is the old story of the North American Indians over again, of savage races in all parts of the world when in conflict with Europeans—a competition of arrows and clubs against gunpowder and rum; savage cunning against civilized diplomacy. This process of civilizing the Caribs went ruthlessly on—Carib against Spaniard, Frenchman, Dutchman, Englishman, Carib against the whole world, until there remains of the ancient possessors of these islands but a handful on Dominica and a wretched band of half-breeds (half Carib, half runaway-slave) on the island of St Vincent; nor will it be many years until the last Carib shall be gathered to his forefathers, leaving nothing but a tradition—the imperfectly remembered story of a once mighty people. (96–7)

Paton's words constitute a classic example of the elegies that have constantly been written for the Caribs from the eighteenth century onwards. The magnificent scenery of Dominica is evoked and the story of 'a once mighty people' recalled—their

ancient dominance of the Caribbean, their fiercesome reputation as cannibals and fighters, their brave struggle to defend
their liberty. Now, however, all that remains is 'a miserable
remnant', a 'handful' of this ill-fated people, whose eventual and
inevitable demise is broached in that elegantly turned phrase:
'nor will it be many years until the last Carib shall be gathered
to his forefathers'. The civilizational process is not exactly called
into question. Progress is no doubt inevitable, 'savage cunning'
no doubt doomed; but a sentimental pity still attaches to the
'interesting race'. The tone of the writing is so elegiac, so romantic, so involved, that it is initially surprising to learn, if ultimately appropriate, that Paton never set foot on Dominica, let
alone visited the Caribs: his boat merely anchored in the roadstead off Roseau while it took on passengers and mail.[27]

Paton's elegy speaks of the Caribs in tones rather different from
those attached to the dominant story told in the West about the
Native Caribbean, in which kindly and peaceful Arawaks suffered at the hands of rapacious Caribs, depredations only halted
by the arrival of Columbus; but, however interesting the story
of their ancestors, the 'wretched survivors' are of little concern
to Paton. Nevertheless, by the time Paton visited Dominica,
the surviving Caribs had re-entered Western writing in a travel-
book by the US ornithologist, Frederick Ober: writing in 1938
Douglas Taylor, the foremost authority this century on the
Dominican Caribs, pointed out that Ober 'appears to have been
the first person since the middle of the eighteenth century to take
the slightest interest in this last isolated island tribe' (1938:
110).[28] Ober's writings—beginning with *Camps in the Caribbees*
in 1879—do constitute almost a second 'discovery' of the
Caribs, and make his work the essential starting point for this
book. Ober will therefore be the dominant figure in Chapter 2,
emerging as a prolific writer with broad Caribbean interests, to
be situated with respect to the development of US anthropology
and to the genre of travel writing. The key dates here are
1876–8, the nearly two years that Ober spent in the Lesser

[27] Brief biographical information about 'visitors' to the Caribs can be found at
the end of the book in 'Notes on Visitors'.
[28] For some minor exceptions to Taylor's statement, see *WM* 231–7; and cf.
Chester (1869: 16–17).

Antilles, and the early 1890s, when he returned in an official capacity. Chapter 2 groups Ober with other US and British visitors from the period—doctors such as Frederick Treves and William Birge, naturalists like A. Hyatt Verrill and Symington Grieve, and the French Catholic priest, René Suaudeau; described as Ober's 'followers' because of the frequency with which they use him as an authority or reference point. In all this work the keynotes sounded in Paton's elegy are repeated and extended, and others added, most notably the almost everpresent concern about racial intermixing; but these visitors, like Ober, do at least mostly see and report from the Reserve itself, rather than from Roseau, or from a ship off the Dominican coast.

As Ober dominates Chapter 2, so Hesketh Bell, the British Administrator of Dominica at the beginning of the twentieth century, dominates Chapter 3, since his action in formalizing the Carib Reserve on Dominica in 1903 set the territorial boundaries with which the Dominican Caribs still live. Hesketh Bell started writing about the Caribs in the early 1890s; he was still writing about them fifty years later. However, in counterpoint, other voices begin to be heard at the turn of the century, voices belonging to the emergent coloured bourgeoisie on Dominica, who have their own ideas about the Caribs, with whom they share the island, even if—at least in these early days—they were not themselves frequent visitors to their neighbours.

The principal writer in Chapter 4 is Douglas Taylor, the Yorkshire-born linguist who lived with a Carib woman, settled in Dominica, and became an authority on the lifeways and language of the people. He played an important part in the political developments of the 1930s and his anthropological work has had a lasting influence on Carib studies. Taylor first visited the Reserve shortly before the incident which became known as the 'Carib War', in which two Caribs were shot dead by policemen in a dispute over smuggled liquor. The subsequent trial—of Caribs, not of the policemen—and a later Commission of Enquiry, after the local jury had come to the wrong verdict, produced a valuable set of papers which this chapter analyses.

In Chapter 5 Ella Gwendoline Rees Williams, a white Dominican who left the island in 1907, returns as Jean Rhys the novelist for a brief visit in the summer of 1936, another resonant year. Her writing about the Caribs is as laconic as Taylor's is voluminous, but for both that Carib War provides a singular point of reference, a caustic reminder that the Caribs belong in the present as well as in the past. Rhys's deep familial involvement in Dominica, across racial lines, provides a further opportunity to see the modern Carib community within the full insular context of Dominica.

Writing about the Caribs shows no sign of decline. The heterogeneity of Chapter 6 perhaps demonstrates a new degree of specialization with its professional anthropologists and its professional travel writers, as well as the usual motley array of passers-by: Patrick Leigh Fermor and Jean Raspail are given most attention; Fermor, like Ober before him, becomes a frequent enough reference point to be given 'followers'. The year 1998 is taken as the book's terminus, 505 years after Columbus first sighted Dominica, with the Caribs, now not so evidently close to extinction, interacting with their multiple visitors in an attempt to find a way of doing more than simply surviving into the twenty-first century.

The subtitle of this book, 'The Island Caribs and their Visitors', suggests, not inappropriately, a dual focus, both on the Caribs themselves, a community whose history has never adequately been told, and on the visitors, mainly from Europe and the United States, who have spent time passing through the small Carib Territory on the windward coast of Dominica. Properly speaking, however, neither group finds anything like a full history here. Rather my focus is on the space of the encounter between them, a space which is physical, psychic, and ideological, a space which finds its shape in the narratives constructed by the visitors, narratives of travel, of encounter, of observation, and of fantasy. So, the implicit geography of the book must include not just the Carib Reserve itself, but also the places from which visitors have travelled to it; and those places are themselves associated with institutions, ideas, and theories about indigeneity, which have been practised, tested, and sometimes challenged on Carib grounds. For example, for many of the years covered in this study, the most important lines of control have run to the Carib Reserve from the Colonial Office in London, via the Administrator's House in Roseau, the island capital. In practice, the Administrator, as local colonial official, had a good deal of influence over policy, although he himself was also inevitably influenced by local opinion in Roseau. Since Dominican independence the politics of the Carib Reserve have in one way become more local, with Roseau replacing London as the central political authority, but in another way become more international, as the Caribs themselves have developed links with international organizations, especially the United Nations.

Those kinds of links will be briefly examined in Chapter 6. Earlier in the book attention will be paid to the contexts of late nineteenth- and early twentieth-century travellers, principally the development of anthropology in both the USA and Britain, and the changing attitudes towards American Indians generally during this period; since it is clear that—at least before the Second World War—many travellers arrived in Dominica with expectations developed from reading accounts of the Indian Wars of the 1870s or the novels of Fenimore Cooper. By the end of the nineteenth century the overarching perspective in which American Indians were seen—Caribs as much as Lakotas or Apaches—was that of the Vanishing Indian: a perspective that controlled anthropological as much as popular or literary accounts. The trope of the 'remnant', so almost universally present in accounts of the Caribs that I have little option but to use it as a title, comes marked by its use in Cooper and, memorably, in Longfellow, with Hiawatha's mournful words:

> I beheld our nations scattered,
> All forgetful of my counsels.
> Weakened, warring with each other;
> Saw the remnants of our people
> Sweeping westward, wild and woeful,
> Like the cloud-rack of a tempest,
> Like the withered leaves of Autumn![29]

---

[29] Longfellow (1855: XXI. 157); for the broader context, Carr (1996a: 120–47). Cooper had referred to the 'remnant of the original possessors of these regions' (*Notions of the Americans: Picked up by a Travelling Bachelor*, 2 vols. (London, 1828), ii. 367; quoted by Stafford (1994: 239)).

Shortly after the publication of Longfellow's poem, Charles Darwin—writing in 1871 about the inevitable extinction of races—noted that 'Some small and broken tribes, remnants of former races, still survive in isolated and generally mountainous districts' (1913: 281), setting a scientific stamp on the language with which the Caribs would be described in the years to come.

LETTERS FROM TWO CARIB CHIEFS

By the end of the nineteenth century, the Island Caribs and their history had become much more visible to interested outsiders than at any time over the previous hundred years, largely thanks to Frederick Ober's 'rediscovery' of the Dominican Caribs in 1877. This lively US interest in a surviving Carib community tended to offset, at least to some small degree, identification with the indigenous Taino cultures of the islands it was taking over from Spain (Cuba and Puerto Rico)—although US archaeology and anthropology would largely inherit from Spain a Taino-centred view of Native Caribbean history. At the same time, and as part of the same larger historical process, Britain made an effort to avoid the fate of the Spanish Empire by injecting new thinking and finance into its impoverished Caribbean colonies, an initiative which also served—quite incidentally—to draw the Dominican Carib community into a new relationship with the British state, a development outlined in Chapter 2. However, I will end this introductory chapter by registering the moment when the historical record first shows any indication of a Carib response to this gradual intensification of outside interest.

What Frederick Ober initiated was a concern for the surviving Caribs expressed from beyond the island of Dominica, a concern which led ultimately to the island itself, at least through its colonial officials, having to take the Caribs more seriously than before. This raised for the first time in many years the question of representation: who would represent the interests of the Carib community to these outsiders? As a result (one can speculate), the institution of 'chief' came again to have an importance not seen since the mid-eighteenth century, as the

Caribs began a tentative re-engagement with the colonial authorities.[30] During Sir Robert Hamilton's 1893 Royal Commission to Dominica, two letters were delivered to him from the Caribs, one letter from the 'official' chief, Auguste François, and one from his 'rival', Bruni Michelle, who clearly had to do without the assistance of the official interpreter. Auguste François, writing 'as CHIEF of the Caribs', lays a few facts before Hamilton 'as cause of discontent': the need for a school in the quarter, the need for a hospital, and the fact that he receives no remuneration for conducting 'the affairs of the settlement'. The letter is presented according to all the conventions of late nineteenth-century letter-writing, and presented in the name of 'Augustus Francis'. A note below the letter states that it has been read over to the above Augustus Francis 'and sworn by him to represent the wants of the Caribs'.[31]

'Represent' assumes here some of its richness as a signifier. Auguste swears that the letter 'represents' accurately what he has wanted to say, that it is in other words an accurate rendition of the words he has spoken in creole, the French-based patois spoken in Dominica. Those words he has spoken, and which are translated by the interpreter, are themselves representative of 'the wants of the Caribs' because Auguste is himself the representative of the Caribs and can therefore speak of those wants. This claim is complicated, to say the least, by the existence of the second letter to Hamilton by another person claiming some authority to speak for the Caribs about their wants:

PETITION from BRUNI MICHELLE, Rival Chief of the Caribs. To HER MAJESTY.
In the Name of God.
MY LORD,
   We humble beg of your kindness to accept our petition of your poor people, Indians or Caraibe, of Salibia, to unbrace the favarable opportunity to addressing to you to emplore the marcy of our Beloved Mother and Queen Victoria, for her poor and unfortunate childrens. We dont have nothings to supported us, no church, no school,

---

[30] In 1864 a priest apparently arranged for the Caribs to elect a 'king', who chose to call himself Canute I, supposedly because of the saint day of his election although it is tempting to read the name allegorically (*WM* 236–7).

[31] Hamilton (1894: 91) [repri. in *WM* 237].

no shope, no store. We are very far in the forest; no money, no dress, etc., etc. They call us wild savages. No my beloved Queen, it is not savages, but poverty. We humble kneel down in your feet to beg of your assistance. Accept from your humble childrens of Salibia, in the care of

MR. BRUNI MICHELLE

11 December 1893 Make at Salibia.[32]

When faced with the multiple significations imposed upon the Caribs by outsiders, from Columbus to the present day, the temptation is to endow with special significance the examples of direct Carib speech or writing, the few places where Carib priorities seem to lodge themselves within the dominant discourse. These moments are indeed worth careful attention, but exactly how they are to be read is by no means unproblematically clear. In the case of Auguste François's letter to Hamilton an initial question is posed by the act of translation or interpretation, which immediately sets a screen between the reported words and any supposed 'original'. Auguste François's letter is then turned, presumably by the interpreter or one of Hamilton's officials, into the 'correct' format, just as he himself is turned into Augustus Francis.

Because it so comprehensively breaks with the 'proper' conventions of the chiefly word, Bruni Michelle's letter to Hamilton certainly strikes the modern eye as the more unmediated of these Carib letters. Contextualization is very difficult here. Although there is some suggestion of Auguste's unpopularity amongst the Caribs, this letter is almost the only evidence that there was a rival chief in the 1890s, and seems to be the only extant example of Bruni Michelle's writing.[33] For all that, his stark plea, written almost exactly a hundred years before the end of the United Nations Year of Indigenous Peoples, stands

[32] Hamilton (1894: 117) [repri. in *WM* 237–8].

[33] While giving evidence before the Commission of Enquiry which followed the 'Carib War' in 1930, Edward Green, retired Government Officer and Acting Magistrate for the Eastern District from 1890 to 1893 and again from 1905 to 1924, recalled the situation on the Carib Reserve in the 1890s: 'The Carib Chief was a man called Ogiste who claimed to be Chief but the Carib whom I had dealing with was named Bruney. He was regarded as the Chief. Both of them were Chiefs. It was rather a difficult thing. I found Ogiste not very steady. I preferred Bruney. Neither of them had been appointed by the Government' (CO 152/42511 (Evidence of Edward Richard Green, 18 May 1931)).

in ironic counterpoint to Western discourses. Its string of negatives—'no church, no school, no shope, no store . . . no money, no dress' almost parodies Gonzalo's utopian fantasy in *The Tempest*, and that engagement with the ethnographic view ('They call us wild savages') and rejection of it ('it is not savages, but poverty') serves as a poignant reminder that Carib priorities are not necessarily the same as their visitors'.

2. Northern Hunter and Dusky Carib: Frederick Albion Ober and his Followers (1877–1907)

> Over hidden precipices
>   Falls the unseen torrent's thunder;
> Windy shrieks and sibilations
>   Fill the pathless gorge with wonder;
> And the dusky Carib hears
> Cowering with mysterious fears.
>
>   (Lucy Larcom, 'The Cry of the
>   Sunset Bird' (1884: 250–1))

Not many ornithologists are the subjects of poems, but when Frederick Ober got back in 1879 from his long trip to the Caribbean, Lucy Larcom, a well-known New England poet and neighbour of the Ober family in northern Massachusetts, wrote a poem about him called 'The Cry of the Sunset Bird', originally published in her 1880 volume, *Wild Roses of Cape Ann*. The appended note to the name 'sunset bird' explains that 'the cry of this bird, just before nightfall, which sounds like the words *'Soleil coucher!'* is supposed by the Caribs to be the voice of a spirit; and they believe that whoever tries to follow it will be led into some dreadful calamity' (Larcom 1884: 250).[1] While the 'dusky Carib' cowers fearfully, a man of destiny strides forward:

> 'Hark!' The Northern hunter listens:
>   Down the jungles of the highland
> Steals a melody unearthly,
>   Wavering over sea and island;

---

[1] On Lucy Larcom (1826–93) and her family connections with Frederick Ober, see Dow 1921, Bacon 1902, and Marchalonis 1989. Her poem is based on Ober (1880: 40–3): the bird was named *Myiarchus Oberi*.

> Can that tender music start
> From the crater's hollow heart?
>
> .   .   .   .
>
> 'Stay thee, stranger!' called the Carib;
>   'Vain to track a wandering spirit,
> Bodiless as breeze of sunset.
>   'T is no living creature! hear it!
> "Day is waning!" without woe
> None upon his track may go.'

Needless to say, the fearless northern hunter ignores the words of superstition and sets off after the bird. The Caribs are now fearful for the safety of their intrepid visitor:

> 'Will he come again?' They shudder,
>   Into lengthening shadows peering;
> Through the sudden veil of nightfall
>   Joyfully his footfall hearing;
> There the dark-eyed hunter stands,
> Sheltering something in his hands!
>
> 'Look! a gray bird is your spirit!
>   On his breast the sunset lingers,
> Golden as the hour he sings in:
>   Touch him! stroke him with light fingers!
> Still a spirit, though with wings
> Shaped like other birds, he sings.'

Ober is the scientist adventurous enough to investigate nature for himself in spite of the Caribs' superstitious warnings, and he is able to demonstrate to them the baselessness of their way of interacting with the natural world. For all Ober's sympathy and concern for the Caribs, he remains a pioneer from the future, from the modern world, who knows more than the Caribs do. That their world is both fascinating and doomed is suggested by the slightly ponderous Longfellovian metre, still popular for writing about Indians twenty-five years after the phenomenal success of *Hiawatha*.

OBER BEFORE THE CARIBBEAN

Frederick Albion Ober was born in 1849 in Beverly, Massachusetts, where he trained as a shoemaker, the traditional winter occupation of the fishermen of the village, though his boyhood passion was ornithology. In his youth he made a series of trips to Florida, about which he wrote a number of articles in the early 1870s. For the next twenty-five years, he was an almost constant traveller, principally in the Caribbean, but also in Mexico, Spain, North Africa, and northern South America. For a while he had great difficulty financing his expeditions: a lengthy correspondence survives concerning the Smithsonian Institution's intermittent willingness to back his early Caribbean and Mexican trips. At first Ober clearly saw himself as a collector: he sent back a lot of material from the Caribbean to the Smithsonian, mostly birds, two species of which carry his name, and the Smithsonian published his field-trip report. However, after the commercial success of his first travel-book about his Caribbean expeditions, *Camps in the Caribbees: The Adventures of a Naturalist in the Lesser Antilles*, first published in 1879, it clearly occurred to Ober that he could make a better living as a writer since the Smithsonian was not going to give him the job that he wanted. Ober's descriptive accounts of the Caribs of Dominica and St Vincent and his keen interest in their lifeways and history received only one mark of recognition from the new science of ethnology, when he was invited to work as special commissioner for the World's Columbian Exposition, a task that involved liaison with local groups sending material to Chicago, and the collecting of objects of interest, especially those with some relevance to Columbus. Works that resulted from this commission were Ober's second Caribbean travel account, *In the Wake of Columbus: Adventures of a Special Commissioner Sent by the World's Columbian Exposition to the West Indies* (1893) and his most scholarly piece of writing, 'Aborigines of the West Indies' (1894), which sums up the results of his extensive reading and combines them with personal experience to produce a sixty-page summary of the native cultures of the Caribbean and their fate during the course of the Spanish Empire. Natural history and anthropology remained interests, but he also broadened his horizons and, after some struggles, made a career for himself as travel writer, journalist, public lecturer, and novelist. Eventually, after thirty years as traveller and writer Ober settled down as a real-estate dealer in Hackensack, New Jersey, where he died in 1913.[2]

[2] For a study of one of Ober's novels and a fuller account of Ober's life, see Hulme 1997a. On his family history, see Loring and Toomey 1941, and 'Genealogical Record of the Descendants of Andrew Kimball Ober' (Beverly Historical Society, n.d.).

FIG. 3. Frederick Ober's business card, *c*.1910 (National Museum of Natural History, Smithsonian Institution).

By neither wealth nor social class did Ober's family belong to the patrician elements that dominated nineteenth-century New England culture, although Larcom and Ober were both Huguenot families—La Combe and Aubert—who had been in New England from the seventeenth century. But the area around

Beverly did have a depth of local settler history scarcely equalled elsewhere in the USA, and a strong liberal and humanitarian tradition, Abolitionist and pacifist in its politics, moral and reforming in its outlook. J. G. Whittier was its exemplary writer, and Lucy Larcom was his friend and pupil: so the Ober–Larcom connection suggests some possible routes for Ober's eventual literary ambitions.[3] In 1812 the publisher Isaiah Thomas had founded the American Antiquarian Society in Massachusetts, and Ober's father, Andrew Kimball Ober, was a local collector and enthusiast, who had corresponded with the Smithsonian in his own right over Indian remains, and who made maps showing the landings of the Norsemen and the country explored by them.[4] Ober's father's store (at Mackeral Cove, just outside Beverly) was, according to Ober's sister, Sara, 'a kind of reading room or forum, where uneducated though intelligent men gained much information' through the family's subscription to the best New York and Boston newspapers (Sara Endicott Ober, n.d.: 5).

In Ober's youth, this part of New England was changing fast, with the industrial system beginning to establish itself, pre-eminently in Lowell, leading to the coastal area around Beverly becoming popular with summer visitors, a move resented by many local families. Through a dialectic with which we are now all too familiar, the threats to the natural world that accompanied these developments spawned a series of students and enthusiasts, working inevitably in the shadow of Thoreau, who had died in 1862.[5] Ober's early work belongs to this tradition of natural history writing, which flourished in New England in the middle decades of the nineteenth

---

[3] This area is recalled in Van Wyck Brooks's *New England: Indian Summer, 1865–1915* (1940: 45–65). See also *Historic Beverly* (1937) and Sara Endicott Ober's reminiscences (n.d.); and for a slightly earlier period, Lucy Larcom's autobiography (1961 [1889]). Whittier twice wrote to Ober in praise of *Camps in the Caribbees*, claiming it as the equal of anything in Audubon or Wallace (Ober to Baird, 23 Jan. 1880: SIA, Office of the Secretary, 1879–1882 (Spencer F. Baird), Incoming Correspondence, Box 27, p. 8006).

[4] See e.g. the letter from A. K. Ober to Baird of 26 July 1871 (SIA, Assistant Secretary 1850–77: Incoming Correspondence 1871–4, vol. VIII, nos. 1–8). Cf. Falnes 1937, for background.

[5] Henry David Thoreau (1817–62), author of *Walden, or Life in The Woods* (1854), and also of the small-scale but influential travel account, *A Week on the Concord and Merrimack Rivers* (1849).

century.[6] The institutional centre for that interest became Louis Agassiz's new Museum of Natural History at Harvard, and it seems that it was the young Ober's collection of New England bird-skins which first gave him a connection to Harvard, interesting Alexander Agassiz, Louis's son: Harvard's purchase of the collection provided some finance for Ober's earliest expeditions. Buoyed by the success of this sale, Ober—now 20 years old—wrote in September 1869 from Beverly to Joseph Henry, the Secretary of the Smithsonian Institution, asking for employment stuffing birds: 'Craving pardon for my boldness; if worthy of an answer, could I have one soon? As I wish otherwise, not meeting your views, to resume my studies.'[7] Resuming his studies, Ober's interest in natural history took him to Florida on several occasions in the late 1860s and early 1870s, after which the Smithsonian, in the persons of Joseph Henry and Spencer Baird, presumably impressed by Ober's assiduity, was prepared to finance, at least partially, the ornithological visit to the Lesser Antilles that Ober planned for late 1876.[8]

As Larcom's poem suggests, on his return from that visit Ober was still seen as primarily an ornithologist and, indeed, his first writing about the Caribbean was 'Ornithological Exploration of the Caribbee Islands', which appeared in the *Annual Report of the Smithsonian Institution (1878)* (Ober 1879). This five-page article is a summary of the twenty months that Ober spent in the Caribbean islands, emphasizing his ornithological work but also demonstrating the descriptive skills that would be soon more extensively deployed. He begins the conclusion to that article by noting 'that in ornithology alone my collections contained *eighteen species and varieties new to science*, a result that cannot fail to be considered gratifying'; only to add the complaint that would grow to an obsession: 'Fortunate as I have been, I cannot but regret that the appropriations for finishing my search and completing a work but little more than half accomplished were not forthcoming' (450).

[6] Hicks (1924) is still the standard study.

[7] SIA, Secretary 1863–79: Incoming Correspondence 1868–9, vol. 86, box 223, no. 48 (Ober, F.A.).

[8] See Baird's draft letter of recommendation (SIA, Secretary, Outgoing Correspondence, vol. 74, p. 312 (Nov. 1876)).

Ober's mentor as an ornithologist was the naturalist George Lawrence, who prepared catalogues from Ober's notes and specimens (reproduced as an appendix to *Camps in the Caribbees)*, and with whom Ober had an extensive correspondence.[9] For five years after his return, Ober kept referring in letters to both Baird and Lawrence to his determination to complete his *Birds of the Lesser Antilles*, but the Smithsonian was unresponsive ('I have asked Prof. Baird about it so many times that I am tired' (Letter to Lawrence, 31 Dec. 1879)), while publishers provided money for guide books and newspapers money for articles 'of a popular character' (13 June 1881), many written for the *Boston Herald*. At the end of 1882, after completing his mammoth book on Mexico, *Travels in Mexico, and Life among the Mexicans* (1884), Ober again wrote to Lawrence: 'notwithstanding my diversion into more popular paths than ornithological pursuits afford, I still cherish a longing to return' (19 Dec. 1882). His marriage in 1885 seems to have finally put paid to his ornithological pretensions: 'My lectures are paying me quite well, but taking all my time. I am *out* with ornithology, I fear. I had a living to get, and could not get it out of birds . . . I have a darling little wife; but we are as poor as rats, and I don't suppose we ought to have married. However, life is a little pleasanter than it once was, and we will live happy so long as possible' (6 Feb. 1886). His wife died within two years. Writing about himself in the third person in 1891, Ober summarized: 'Although at first travelling for the sake of adventure and rare birds, latterly Mr. Ober has drifted away from the study of natural history, and has shaped his journeys with a view to the exposition of the early history of America' (1891: p. x).

THE NATURAL HISTORY OF FLORIDA INDIANS

In a sense, then, the living that Ober could not get out of birds he eventually got out of the Native Caribbean, its history and its present inhabitants. There had already been suggestions of

---

[9] In the George Newbold Lawrence (1806–95) Collection (American Museum of Natural History, New York): Box Five, Correspondence (Frederick A. Ober, 1874–94). Subsequently referred to in the text by date of letter.

Ober's ethnographic interests embedded within his ornithological adventures. His earliest publications of any substance were the first two parts of his report from the Florida expedition sponsored by *Forest and Stream*, which he undertook in 1872–3: under the general heading 'Wild Life in Florida', both are entitled 'Camping among the Seminoles'.[10] The three Seminole Wars had been significant features of US nation-building. In the first, the USA conquered Spanish Florida, and then began to explore its new possession, an exploration which led inexorably to the second war (1835–42), relentlessly pursued by Andrew Jackson and resulting in massive loss of life on both sides. A high proportion of the Seminoles who survived (about 80 per cent) were deported to Indian Territory (now Oklahoma)—providing one of several links to the Caribs, a similar proportion of whom were deported from St Vincent to Central America after their defeat by the British in 1796. The third Seminole War (1855–8), really little more than a prolonged series of skirmishes, led to a few deaths and some 240 deportations. By 1860 there were fewer than 200 Seminoles in Florida, all of whom had survived by withdrawing into the remote swamplands. The draining of the Florida wetlands from the 1880s eroded Seminole economic independence, and consequently their social cohesiveness. Reservations were established in the 1920s and 1930s.

William Sturtevant, the distinguished ethnohistorian, notes a significant break in the documentation concerning the Seminoles for nearly twenty years after the end of the third war (1858). He counts this as 'an extremely important period of cultural and social adjustment to radically new ecological and demographic conditions' and notes how, in the new sources of the 1870s and 1880s, the Seminole appear 'as though discovered afresh' (1971: 111). This is precisely the note that Ober strikes (although his reports from 1873 feature in almost no ethnohistorical writing about the Seminole).[11]

---

[10] Eight articles on Florida appeared in *Forest and Stream* between November 1873 and May 1874, followed by three further sketches and two pieces in *Appleton's Journal*. The three articles that refer to the Seminoles are referenced as Ober 1873a, 1873b, and 1875.

[11] Ober is mentioned in Kersey (1975: 9) as writing the first report on the Seminoles since the 1850s.

The opening paragraph of Ober's first *Forest and Stream* piece recapitulates:

By the treaty of 1842, the few Seminoles remaining in Florida after the war were confined to the southern portion of the peninsula. There they still remain, between two and three hundred in number, leading a peaceful life, cultivating their fields and hunting. They are governed by two chiefs; those around the southern shore of Lake Okeechobee by 'Tustenuggee,' and those east of that great lake by 'Tiger Tailee.' Their intercourse with white men is limited to occasional trading visits to Indian River and the Keys. Though they have existed as a nation for one hundred years, very little is known regarding their language, customs, and social life. (1873*a*: 193)

The reworked version, for the more literary *Appleton's Journal*, begins with the contrast between the new tourists who do not see beyond their pleasures and the historical remnant holding themselves in a rather dignified seclusion:

The waters of the St. John's, the mighty river which the Seminole once held as his own, is the winter resort of hundreds who little suspect, as they pass the forest-covered fields and mounds that the Indian once owned and cultivated, that the descendants of the aboriginal inhabitants yet live in the State. Far down in the swampy Everglades a ruined and degraded people eke out a bare existence upon a tithe of the lands which their ancestors once claimed by right of conquest. (1875: 142)

The tone is detached and factual, the attitude to the Seminoles respectful: their life is peaceful and agricultural, under settled government. Yet, although living within the boundaries of the United States, they remain little known. They are, note, in Ober's eyes, a nation, a judgement echoed in recent ethnohistorical work, which sees the Seminole of the Everglades as developing a unique subculture in the relative isolation in which they lived for about a century from the 1840s (not from the 1780s, as Ober suggests). Against this slightly sober background, the narrator characterizes himself and his visit in a much lighter tone: 'It was with the avowed object of studying the Indian in his native wilds that I left Indian River one beautiful spring morning in '72. I had provided myself with an ox-cart, oxen, of course, and a guide—though just what he was a guide of, and to where, I have not satisfactorily determined to this day—and the usual amount of hunters' traps' (1873*a*: 193).

Very little that might pass as 'studying' in any scientific or anthropological sense occurs during Ober's travels, and the section headings at the beginning of the piece indicate its range of concerns: 'The Everglades—Lake Okeechobee—Tiger Tail—Black Cypress Swamp—Alligators—Dog Meat Ragouts—Indian Belles—Queer Experiences' (193). And yet, as with the later writings about the Caribs, there is an engaging frankness of approach, underlain by an open romanticism, which comes out most clearly in the description of the first Seminoles they encounter:

'Tiger', the oldest, was about seventy years old, and had fought in the Seminole war. He was rather above medium height, broad-shouldered, massive arms, and legs like mahogany pillars, worn smooth and polished by many a brush with thicket and briar. His nose and lips indicated a trace of negro blood. His iron gray hair straggled over a greasy bandana bound about his temples. His broad shoulders were artistically draped in two ragged shirts of 'hickory,' or striped homespun, the inner one about a foot longer than the outer, and reaching nearly to his knees. A breech cloth and moccasins completed his attire. 'Charley Osceola' was a young man of twenty, claiming to be a descendant of the famous chief Osceola. Over six feet high, with broad shoulders and finely-shaped limbs, erect and straight, he was my *beau ideal* of an Indian brave. His eyes were small, black, and keen, his voice was musical, and he spoke in a firm, gentle manner that won my heart at once. His hair was thick, coarse, and black, with the changeable purple of the raven's wing. It was shaved close at the sides, leaving a ridge on the crown, spreading toward the neck, and hanging in braids over the shoulders. (193)

Individual descriptions are always telling, and inevitably function metonymically as a way of passing comment on the larger community. In these two figures that chance brings Ober's way, he discerns in the first case the representative Seminole—the red-black figure tempered in the wars of the 1830s and 1840s, his limbs polished, his hair steely, but his remnant status suggested by his ragged clothes; and the openly idealized Indian brave, touched with the reputation of Osceola, and crowned by the encomium to his hair, ultimate symbol of Indianness.[12] In the *Appleton's Journal* essay Ober notes that 'No tribe—or remnant

---

[12] In the *Appleton's Journal* version, Ober describes the hair as having 'the changeable, metallic lustre of a raven's wing', and a ridge on the crown 'which ran from the forehead back like the crest of a helmet' (1875: 142).

of a nation, rather—has preserved its blood so free from con-
tamination as this' (1875: 142), making Charley Osceola the
typical figure rather than Tiger (though the 'tribe' was itself of
recent vintage). The original Osceola had been a renowned figure
since his exploits in the second Seminole War in the 1830s, and
was the subject of one of George Catlin's most famous paintings.
Nothing is known of Osceola's children, so Charley may have
been a grandson. But the Seminoles, far from being the remnant
of a pure nation, as Ober suggests, were a complex amalgam,
forged out of the wars in the south-east of northern America
between various combinations of groups such as the Cowetas,
Kasihtas, and Coosas, and later the Yuchis, Alabamas, and
Choctaws, and various complements of black maroons. The
Spanish, French, British, and later US forces had also left their
mark. Creek and, later, Seminole, were terms used by whites, in
part as a way of cutting through the onomastic jungle, which
slowed comprehension and control as effectively as the briars of
Ober's Big Cypress swamp slowed the traveller's progress.
'Seminole', like 'maroon', is a version (via the Muskogee *simanó
li*) of the Spanish *cimarrón*, or runaway, probably a word of
indigenous Caribbean origin (see Arrom 1986). Osceola had a
white father and possibly African ancestry, and one of his wives
was black; so Charley, if a descendant, is unlikely to have been
the pure Indian that Ober clearly wanted him to be.[13]

The peculiar ferocity—even by frontier standards—of the
second Seminole War can probably be explained by one of its
principal objectives: the recovery of runaway black slaves who,
again as in St Vincent, clearly worked in close alliance with
Indian groups, sometimes in mixed communities, sometimes
in separate.[14] Indian-hating may be a constant of American history, but the red-black alliances in Florida and the Caribbean
seem to have provoked a language of special virulence. For one

---

[13] On the onomastic complexity, and history of the area, see Wright 1986. It is
no accident that the first classic study of ethnogenesis is dedicated to this area:
Sturtevant 1971. On the figure of Osceola, see Wickman 1991. Ober later wrote a
novel about Osceola (1908).

[14] 'Seminole resistance . . . led General Jesup and his successors to violate flags of
truce, capture Indians invited to negotiate, hold them as hostages, threaten them
with execution if they did not bring in their followers, employ bloodhounds against
the tribe, and kill cattle that American troops did not need in order to deprive the
Indians of food' (Rogin 1991: 239–40; cf. Mahon 1967).

writer: 'The Seminole Indians are not a *"legitimate"* tribe of *native* Americans. They are an association of desperados, who have been banished from other tribes, and who have drawn into their confederacy, many runaway negroes, whose African sullenness, has been aroused to indiscriminate vengeance, by the frantic fury of the American natives'.[15]

There is no evidence that Ober sought out such groups as the Seminoles and Black Caribs because of some special interest in mixed groups. If anything, it was probably because, paradoxically, his Indian interests came second to his ornithological that he did not, like his contemporaries, head for the areas such as the north-west coast or the South-west, where relatively 'untouched' Indian cultures could be contacted and where other pioneers in natural history and ethnology were heading in the wake of Powell's exploration of the Colorado River in 1869: Frank Hamilton Cushing, James and Matilda Stevenson, Washington Matthews, and Jesse W. Fewkes (who would later work in the Caribbean). As Curtis Hinsley suggests, by 1880 the South-west presented the most alluring ethnographic prospect: 'An invigorating climate; sedentary populations of artisans in weaving, pottery, and silver; mysterious, bird-like cliff-dwellers of the remote past; possible links between the high civilizations of Central America and the North American aborigines: these were some of the appealing aspects that fed a popular romance with the South-west that blossomed into commercial exploitation with the new century.'[16] As anthropology, still in its very early stages of development, sought out examples of the culturally pristine Indian culture as it supposedly had existed before European contact, it was left to the travel writers and ornithologists to speak about the mixed communities of the Greater Caribbean, that contact zone in which nothing had been 'pristine' for a very long time.

CHANGING DIRECTION

That Ober's imagination next turned towards the Caribbean islands can probably be explained by two factors. For a start,

---

[15] 'Report of the House Committee on Indian Affairs' (21 Feb. 1823), American State Papers, Indian Affairs (Washington, DC: US Congress, 1834), ii. 411–12; quoted in Rogin (1991: 197).

[16] Hinsley (1981: 192); and cf. Stegner 1954; and Goetzmann 1966.

coastal New England positioned Ober in potentially significant ways. The fishing and sailing community of Beverly (adjacent to Salem and Marblehead) led naturally to overseas connections. As Lucy Larcom's most recent biographer explains: 'Beverly's economy was for many years a balance of land and sea, farming and sailing, with shops and small businesses in support, and a small cottage industry of shoemaking. Like Salem, but always more sedate than its bustling neighbor, the Larcoms' home village was cosmopolitan. Most of the men and many of the women had made long voyages and were familiar with foreign places and ways.'[17]

Frederick Ober's sister's memoir of their father's store (written in the third person) confirms this picture:

The Bermudas, Bahamas and other West Indias were but back-door neighbors, and the Azores only just around the corner, on the broad Atlantic which lapped the shores of Mackeral Cove. She had thrilled over narrow escapes from English privateers, Malay pirates, cannibals and savages, had grieved over sufferings from scurvey, Yellow Jack (yellow fever), starvation and thirst, for she had 'salt water in her veins', as the old sea dogs said. And well she might, for her mother's father and four brothers and their father before them had been sea captains and owners of their ships. All the brothers had died at sea or in foreign lands before they were middle-aged. (Sara Endicott Ober, n.d.: 4)

That is the language of her brother Frederick's novels, which may well have been inspired by family stories as well as by his reading of early American history and of novelists such as G. A. Henty. The less attractive reality behind Sara's language of adventure is that Beverly was a slave port in the middle of the nineteenth century, although of course the town's inhabitants would only have seen the Caribbean goods that filled the ships on the last leg of the triangle, from Havana to Beverly, not the slaves that had been transported from Africa to Cuba. By 1870 there was a huge trade between Cuba and the northeastern seaboard of the USA, including a thriving banana trade which would serve as a route to Cuba for Ober's adolescent New England hero in his novel, *Under the Cuban Flag* (1897). Other travellers and writers from New England would develop Caribbean interests in this period, for a variety of political,

---

[17] Marchalonis (1989: 12–13); cf. Larcom (1961: 93–6).

journalistic, and economic reasons: Richard Henry Dana, Alexander Agassiz, Henry Adams, Clarence King, and—rather later—Stephen Crane; but Ober was the only one to sustain a long-term interest in the whole area and its history.

So, from the Beverly shore, the Caribbean probably seemed much closer, geographically and even culturally, than the deserts of the South-west. In addition, Ober's travels in Florida had already brought him to the very edge of the Caribbean, indeed to the area that in one influential account, that of Charles de Rochefort's, was the origin of indigenous Caribbean culture.[18] So the extension of his natural history interests from Florida to the Caribbean, although pioneering, was logical; and, given his lively interest in the Florida Seminoles when he came into contact with them, it was hardly surprising that, early in his trip to the Caribbean, Ober should have requested an extension of his remit to include the indigenous population of Dominica, about whose existence he had just been made aware. Joseph Henry wrote to him from the Smithsonian in June 1877: 'We have carefully considered your proposal to continue the work, in the way of collecting and spending a considerable period of time among the remnants of the Carib tribes of Dominica, in securing photographs and objects illustrating the habits and customs of this people and facts relating to their general history and characteristics', and offered $500 towards the expenses, in return for first refusal of 'specimens of ethnology and material history without exception, as well as a series of the photographs, as also the notes and observations you may make'.[19]

Ober's extension of focus, which eventually became a shift, from the ornithological to the ethnographic, had been foreshadowed in Florida and was, in any case, not an unusual or major move in terms of contemporary norms: anthropology was regarded (as Joseph Henry's words, quoted several pages below, suggest) as quite precisely 'the natural history of man'; and the

---

[18] Rochefort's (1665) graphic account of the indigenous migrations from Florida to the Caribbean was long influential. Scholarly consensus has more recently favoured the theory of population movement from the South American mainland, but cultural contact of some kind between Florida and Cuba remains likely. (Currier (1902) was still retailing Rochefort's ideas at the beginning of the twentieth century).

[19] Joseph Henry to Frederick Albion Ober, 12 June 1877 (SIA, Secretary: Outgoing Correspondence, vol. 56, p. 148).

various forms of natural history had not yet been separated into academic specialisms. Spencer Baird himself had begun as an ornithologist before broadening his interests as Secretary to the Smithsonian Institution. Henry R. Schoolcraft began his career as a geologist and mineralogist, before becoming an Indian agent and ethnologist, as did John Wesley Powell, founder of the Bureau of American Ethnology; while Lewis Henry Morgan combined ethnological and natural historical interests throughout his life, and Edward Palmer, one of the Smithsonian's chief ethnological collectors, was primarily a botanist. George Bird Grinnell, conservationist and ethnographer, had taken part as a naturalist in exploratory army expeditions to the West in 1874 and 1875, and had—like Ober—published in *Forest and Stream*, a journal he would edit from 1880 to 1911. Grinnell founded the first local Audubon Society in 1886, but then turned to the study of Indian cultures, especially the Cheyenne, writing one of the classic elegies for the disappearance of Plains Indian culture, *Where the Buffalo Ran*, in 1920. In another sense, though, Ober's shift of focus was remarkably timely since it coincided almost exactly with what is now recognized as the founding moments of the establishment in the USA of the modern discipline of anthropology.[20]

For obvious reasons US anthropology had at its centre the study of the American Indian, but scientific attention had hardly been constant. Indeed, after a brief flourishing of what might be thought of as ethnographic activity around the time of independence, actively encouraged by Thomas Jefferson in particular, expansion of territory had taken precedence over any kind of intellectual interest in the cultures that stood in the way of that expansion until the 1870s, when the last wave of Indian

---

[20] Terminology is complex and unstable at this period—and US, British, and French terms still differ. For my purposes, I use 'anthropology' here to imply the academic discipline; ethnography for the study of living communities. A rough analogy might be drawn between Ober and Alfred Haddon, who wrote that 'In 1888 I went to Torres Strait to study the coral reefs and marine zoology of the district; whilst prosecuting these studies I naturally came much into contact with the natives, and soon was greatly interested in them' (1901: p. vii). Haddon's *Head-Hunters*, of which this is the opening sentence, is the equivalent of Ober's *Camping in the Caribbees*, but Ober did not go on to produce the vast scientific work to which Haddon contributed in his role as leader of the Cambridge Torres Strait expedition (see Herle and Rouse, eds. 1998).

wars coincided with the first wave of ethnographic field trips. Indeed, between 1848, the date of Squier and Davis's *Ancient Monuments of the Mississippi Valley*, and 1894, when Cyrus Thomas's huge report finally proved to everyone's satisfaction that those monuments had been built by the ancestors of the native people still living in that valley, US Indian wars were fought against 'savages' who were often regarded as having wiped out their more 'civilized', mound-building predecessors, rather as the Caribs were supposed to have done to the 'settled' Taino of the islands. Andrew Jackson, as usual, did not beat about the bush: 'In the monuments and fortresses of an un-known people, spread over the extensive regions of the west, we behold the memorials of a once powerful race, which was exterminated, or has disappeared, to make room for the exist-ing savage tribes. Nor is there anything in this, which, upon a comprehensive view of the general interests of the human race, is to be regretted'.[21] This division between present savage and previous city-dweller was sharpened after the US invasion of Mexico in 1846 when the wonderful monuments of the Maya and Mexica were contrasted with the poverty and supposed sav-agery of that country's peasantry.[22] Archaeology might therefore be worthwhile, but for much of the first two-thirds of the nine-teenth century little serious attention was paid to the actually existing peoples of North America. By the mid-nineteenth century, the national mood had reached its most myopic, with George Bancroft as spokesman in his immensely popular *History of the United States From the Discovery of the American Continent*:

And yet it is but little more than two centuries, since the oldest of our states received its first permanent colony. Before that time the whole territory was an unproductive waste. Throughout its wide extent the arts had not erected a monument. Its only inhabitants were a few scattered tribes of feeble barbarians, destitute of commerce and of political connection. The axe and the ploughshare were unknown. The soil, which had been gathering fertility from the repose of

---

[21] 'Message from the President of the United States to the Two Houses of Con-gress . . . December 7, 1830', US 21st Cong. 2nd House Doc. No. 2 (1830): 19–22 (quoted in Bieder 1986: 112 n. 17).

[22] On these questions, see Kennedy 1996. For the literary impact of the slowly growing knowledge about the Incas and the Aztecs, see Wertheimer 1999.

centuries, was lavishing its strength in magnificent but useless vegetation. In the view of civilization the immense domain was a solitude. (Bancroft 1840: 4)

Such a view, similar in tone and content to Grenville Chester's, which provided the epigraph to Chapter 1, was unlikely to lead to much interest in the survivors of those 'feeble barbarians'.

The Smithsonian Institution itself, founded in 1846, supported anthropological work, but only as one small part of its much larger remit; although there were voices—such as that of Henry Rowe Schoolcraft—urging Indian study as essential to the development of a national science (Hinsley 1981: 20). However, the second half of the 1870s—just the period that Ober spent travelling in the Caribbean and writing his book about those travels—is exactly the moment when more general shifts in attitudes and interests can be located. An American Ethnological Society had existed in the 1840s, but barely survived the death of Albert Gallatin: Ezequiel Squier had briefly but unsuccessfully tried to revitalize it as the Anthropological Institute of New York in 1871. However, in 1879 the Bureau of American Ethnology[23] was founded by John Wesley Powell, and in the same year a meeting was held to found a Society of American Archaeology. 'Archaeology' soon became 'Anthropology' and Powell was elected first President: 'The object of this Society shall be to encourage the study of the Natural History of Man, especially with reference to America, and shall include Archaeology, Somatology, Ethnology, and Philology' (quoted in Laguna 1960: 94). *American Anthropologist* eventually appeared as the society's journal in 1888.[24]

A sharp insight into the fraught relationship between the scientific interests of public institutions and the living practices of indigenous communities is glimpsed in the correspondence surrounding the Smithsonian's ultimately ill-fated attempt to organize an Indian dimension to the Centennial Exposition at Philadelphia in 1876, shortly before Ober left for the Caribbean. Spencer Baird, the man in charge, initially accepted the

---

[23] Strictly speaking, the Bureau of Ethnology: it gained the adjective in 1894.
[24] See the essays in Murra, ed. 1976. On general developments in US archaeology and anthropology in this period, see Hallowell 1960; Willey and Sabloff 1980; Hinsley 1981; Mitchell 1981; Stocking 1982; Patterson 1986; Carr 1996a.

suggestion of Indian Commissioner J. Q. Smith that the so-called partly civilized tribes be excluded on the grounds that 'their mixture with whites and negroes and their adoption of their manners and customs renders them less interesting as objects of ethnological display'. What was wanted—in theory— was the 'authenticity' of the non-civilized. However, Baird realized that the behaviour of the *actual* Indians invited might reflect badly on him and the Smithsonian, and so a thirteen-point checklist was drawn up, insisting, for example, that the individuals selected had to be more white than Indian, have influence in their tribe, speak English, have a pleasant disposition, be 'the cleanest and finest looking', and have a clean child, a dog, and a pony.[25] Perhaps fortunately, Congress refused to supply any money and so plans for Indian participation had to be abandoned. However, the Smithsonian still gave over one-third of its space allocation to Indian exhibits, emphasizing 'those tribes of Indians which have come least under the influence of civilized men'.[26] The possibility of embarrassing behaviour was minimized by the use of mannequins, although one of them, widely taken to be a depiction of the Sioux leader, Red Cloud, was described by one visitor as being 'ready to pounce on some unsuspecting victim'.[27] Probably few visitors got too close to the mannequin after news reached Philadelphia in July 1876 of the outcome of the Battle of the Little Big Horn in which Custer had met his match at the hands of Crazy Horse.

Undaunted, the Smithsonian's director, Joseph Henry, affirmed in the following year's report that anthropology should consist of both archaeology and ethnology—taking account of present Indian inhabitants:

[A]nthropology, or what may be considered the natural history of man is at present the most popular branch of science. It absorbs a large share of public attention and many original investigators are assiduously devoted to it. Its object is to reconstruct, as it were, the past history of man, to determine his specific peculiarities and general

[25] Letter to Baird, 9 Mar. 1876; and anonymous memo, probably by Baird (quoted in Trennert 1974: 125 nn. 31 and 34).

[26] *Smithsonian Annual Report, 1876*, p. 34 (quoted in Trennert 1974: 127 n. 43).

[27] Quoted in Trennert 1974: 128 n. 50. There was a small Indian presence at the Philadelphia Exposition, under the supervision of renowned Indian fighter, George Anderson (Rydell 1987: 27).

tendencies ... American anthropology early occupied the attention of the Smithsonian Institution ... to collect all the facts which could be gathered in regard to the archaeology of North America, and also of its ethnology, or in other words, an account of its present Indian inhabitants, was considered a prominent object in the plan of operations of the establishment.[28]

The anthropological impulse was towards conserving Indian lifeways and languages by recording them before they disappeared: what would eventually become known as 'salvage ethnography'. In the same year, 1877, this turn from the grand ethnological syntheses of the early nineteenth century to the more empirical and methodical collection of data associated with modern anthropology was marked by Lewis Henry Morgan, himself a great synthesizer, but now striking an empiricist and conservationist note in the Preface to his *Ancient Society*:

While fossil remains buried in the earth will keep for the future student, the remains of Indian art, languages and institutions will not. They are perishing daily, and have been perishing for upwards of three centuries. The ethnic life of the Indian tribes is declining under the influence of American civilization, their arts and languages are disappearing, and their institutions are dissolving. After a few more years, facts that may now be gathered with ease will become impossible of discovery. These circumstances appeal strongly to Americans to enter this great field and gather its abundant harvest.[29]

This was the impulse behind Powell's determination to turn the Bureau of American Ethnology away from its authorized study of historical sites towards ethnological study among living tribes (Mitchell 1981: 179). The investigative direction here was, as noted, usually south-west, following Powell's own celebrated

---

[28] *Annual Report of the Smithsonian Institution, 1877* (Washington: Government Printing, 1878, p. 36); quoted in Hallowell (1960: 26).

[29] Lewis Henry Morgan, *Ancient Society; or Researches in the Lines of Human Progress from Savagery through Barbarism to Civilization*, ed. Eleanor Burke Leacock (Cleveland, Oh., 1963), preface, quoted in Dippie 1982: 229. Powell used exactly the same argument in pushing for the establishment of the BAE (see Gruber 1970: 1295). The metaphor of the harvest moved to the Caribbean in 1904 when, encouraging Jesse Fewkes to pursue a thorough ethnological research of the area, Otis Mason remarked revealingly that the Caribbean would open 'a new and rich field as a relief from the overthrashed straw of our own native tribes' (NAA, Mason to Fewkes, 1 July 1904: quoted in Hinsley 1981: 116).

exploration of the Colorado. Powell had some success here, focusing the BAE's work on the compilation of language dictionaries and the study of cultural behaviour. However, he was to an extent hamstrung by the BAE's subsidiary position to the National Museum's Department of Anthropology (which, despite its name, was mainly dedicated to the collection of Indian artefacts) and therefore to its director, Spencer Baird. Indeed, Baird exercised his influence in securing authorization for the establishment in 1879—the same year as the BAE—by one of his long-time military collectors, Captain Richard H. Pratt, of the Carlisle School, well known for its determination to turn Indians into good citizens of the nation state (Rivinus and Youssef 1992: 189). The theme of the Vanishing Indian was constantly used by Powell and Baird in trying to get funds for the Bureau of Ethnology and the Anthropology Division of the US National Museum—while Baird's support for the Carlisle School was further helping the vanishing process.

Against this background, Ober's 'discovery' that there were Indians still in the Caribbean was a step of a quite different kind—at least in the long run—because these Indians were not living in the territory claimed by the US state, which was, throughout the middle years of the century, engaged in a huge surveying operation of the continental resources it claimed, even if it did not fully control. Admittedly, this distinction was not always apparent. The great intellectual synthesizers of the first part of the century would put Caribbean materials into their large Americanist picture, evidence both of a perspective wider than the boundaries of the USA and of an incipient identification of the USA with the continent itself, an identification increasingly encouraged by US politicians and cemented in the appropriation of Columbus as the nation's founding father.[30]

---

[30] Interest of this kind was still very much in the *ancient* Caribbean, as part of a general history of, in Cornelius Rafinesque's 1836 title, *The American Nations; or, Outlines of their General History, Ancient and Modern*, in which one chapter is devoted to 'The Poetical Annals and Traditions of the Haytians or Tainos of the Antilles' (162–259) (based on the 1494 report of Columbus's ethnographer, Father Ramón Pané (1978)), or in Daniel Brinton's pioneering linguistic work which established connections between the mainland Arawak and what he called the Island Arawak (Rafinesque's 'Taino') (Brinton 1871). Mid-nineteenth-century ethnology saw 'the American race' as 'essentially separate and peculiar' (Samuel Morton,

The natives of the Caribbean could then hold a special position as the first Americans encountered by Columbus and be favoured with some attention, especially in the aftermath of the quatercentenary in 1892.[31] The Smithsonian Institution was building American collections, and so Ober's Caribbean purchases and contacts were regarded as relevant. In 1877, for example, Joseph Henry wrote to a collector in Antigua with whom Ober had put him in contact. He was still thinking largely in terms of natural history, but also wanted Carib antiquities 'for determining the primitive character of the group ... The extension of our West Indian series is a matter of great interest to us'.[32] In part as a result of Ober's efforts, the BAE saw Caribbean/Florida connections which it wanted to pursue after 1898: in its report for 1900, Powell reported that he and W. H. Holmes had:

repaired to Cuba and Jamaica for the purpose of tracing lines of cultural migration between the great continents of the Western Hemisphere. The researches of the last two decades have shown clearly that the customs of the aborigines in what is now south-eastern United States were affected by extraneous motives and devices; the phenomena have suggested importation of objects and ideas belonging to what is commonly styled 'Caribbean art' from South America by way of the Antilles; and it was thought desirable to seize the opportunity offered by recent political changes for special studies in the Antillean islands. (Powell 1901: 59)

By the end of the century, with Ober's help, the Caribbean had been drawn into the circle of US cultural interests.

On the northern continent the American Indian was still persistently present and intermittently dangerous. While Ober was in Florida the US Army was defeating—with great difficulty—the Modocs under Captain Jack on the California/Oregon

Distinctive Characteristics of the Aboriginal Race of America [1844], 35–6; quoted in Nott and Gliddon 1857: 629); building on the classification established by Blumenbach which, it will be remembered, had a Carib skull as its representative.

[31] See Holmes 1894; Fewkes 1891, 1903, 1904, 1907 (and for a useful survey Watters 1976). Most of the early *Contributions from the Museum of the American Indian Heye Foundation* related to the Caribbean (New York: Museum of the American Indian 1913–15).

[32] Letter from Joseph Henry to Revd. B. Romig, St Johns, Antigua, 18 Dec. 1877 (SIA, Secretary: Outgoing Correspondence, vol. 59, p. 240). For similar letters to Caribbean collectors (all 1878), see vol. 64, p. 310; vol. 75, pp. 30, 36, and 39.

border; a few months before Ober visited the Caribbean for the first time, Custer and his men were killed at the Battle of the Little Big Horn; while Ober was in the Caribbean, the Nez Percé began their memorable trek from Idaho towards Canada, only to be defeated by Colonel Nelson Miles's command in late September 1877, at the very moment Ober was making contact with the Dominican Caribs; his second visit to them took place just after the decisive massacre of the Lakota at Wounded Knee in 1890. American Indians were already sentimentalized in certain forms of fiction, and they were already being packaged and domesticated for exhibition in shows like that put together by William Cody (Sell and Weibright 1955); but at least until 1890 they were an active military force in some parts of the USA. Perhaps by contrast to these military and political complications, the Island Caribs offered a simple originality, as among the first Indians encountered by Columbus; and they seemed also to offer survival in something like their primitive form—with little sense then, as there is still often little sense now, of a complex colonial history involving their interaction with a number of imperial powers. But above all they offered distance: the physical distance of Dominica from the USA and the inaccessibility of the Caribs even within the island itself: I used Paton as an example in the previous chapter because the purity of his idea of the Caribs is unsullied by anything so mundane as contact with them.

By this yardstick, Ober's work was to be first in the field, not least because of the *ethnographic* attention it paid to the surviving indigenous population. His first published words on the subject, in the Smithsonian *Annual Report*, are therefore of special interest:

I found the Caribs of to-day different from the *Charaibs* of one hundred and fifty years ago, as described by Père Labat. They speak a French *patois* and are good Catholics, and through the influence of the French priests, who make them monthly visits, they have been compelled to intermarry with negroes to such an extent that the individuality of the Carib is gone. There are not more than twenty families of uncontaminated blood in the island. These, with a few in St. Vincent, comprise *the whole* of the remainder of the many thousands found in these islands by Columbus. A few old men and women only can speak the ancient Carib tongue; from these I obtained a good vocabulary, which, by comparing with another I secured in St Vincent, I found to be correct. The Caribs are more peaceful citizens than the negro, more cleanly and intelligent, but not a whit more industrious or virtuous. They subsist by fishing and cultivating provision grounds in the mountains, but very few of them follow the chase. I remained with them six weeks, secured many valuable photographs, and many notes respecting them of value to the ethnologist and philologist. (1879: 447)

Perhaps the most striking comment here is Ober's suggestion that the Caribs have been 'compelled to intermarry with negroes' by the influence of the French priests who visit them. It is not clear what form such compulsion could have taken, but the motive would presumably have been to prevent coupling between close blood relatives, difficult to avoid in a small population. So the influence of the priests is seen, as so often by anthropologists, to have been responsible for the loss of indigenous individuality. Carib spiritual beliefs have been replaced by Catholicism, Carib language by French patois, and the supposed purity of the Carib race by an adulterated mixture, leaving only twenty or so families of 'uncontaminated blood'. Ober has arrived just in time to secure valuable information and photographs; with the implicit suggestion that time is running out for the Caribs.

CAMPING IN CARIB COUNTRY

By the time the Smithsonian report appeared, Ober had already written his 1879 travel book, *Camps in the Caribbees*, in which this brief picture would be amplified and put into narrative form. The immediate success of *Camps in the Caribbees* suggests that Ober judged the market well. His only obvious model was the work of his friend Nathaniel Bishop, author of *A Thousand Miles' Walk Across South America* (1869), who, in 1875, had just returned from an extraordinary trip of 2,500 miles by water from Quebec to the Gulf of Mexico, an account of which he would publish during Ober's first Caribbean sojourn as *Voyage of the Paper Canoe* (1878)—and to whom *Camps in the Caribbees* is dedicated. In November 1878 Ober wrote to George Lawrence that: 'Lee and Shepard [his publishers] very much desire me to write out my travels at once and promise to give me as good a dress as Bishop's 'Paper Canoe'—which is a great deal to offer these times' (23 Nov. 1878).

In the Preface to *Camps in the Caribbees* Ober writes of exploring the islands of the Lesser Antilles under the auspices of the Smithsonian Institution 'with the especial view of bringing to light their ornithological treasures' (1880: p. v). Yet the book itself offers to its readers descriptions and stories, rather than scientific discoveries: it belongs to a genre of travel writing which remains familiar, and indeed is probably as popular at the beginning of the twenty-first century as it has ever been. Its American roots lie in such travel narratives as William Bartram's *Travels* (published 1793) and Francis Parkman's *The Oregon Trail* (published 1846), but more immediately in the spate of personal travel-books by members of various United States Geological Surveys, most notably John Wesley Powell's *Exploration of the Colorado River of the West and Its Tributaries* (published 1875) and Clarence King's *Mountaineering in the Sierra Nevada* (published 1872). King's work, both personal and scientific—and probably fictionalized—sets Ober's tone: King had reworked his travel notebooks as 'an experiment . . . to see if the mere description of scenery could be made into popular reading' (Wilkins 1958: 139). Not accidentally, 1872 is also the date of Mark Twain's *Roughing It*, in part a satire on romantic expectations of the American wilderness in the West—suggesting that travel writers might have to start looking further afield for material.

Firm lines are impossible to draw here, but Ober's work and interests can probably be situated as part of the 'outdoor movement' that became so popular in so many different forms in the USA during the last quarter of the nineteenth century. The outdoor movement was not a *movement* in any political sense, though it did breed clubs such as the Appalachian Mountain Club (1876), the Boone and Crockett Club (founded by Roosevelt and Grinnell in 1888) and the Sierra Club (1892), which brought together a whole spectrum of outdoor interests, some more compatible than others: climbing, conservation, hunting, cycling, natural history, antiquities, camping. Initially these were activities for fairly rich or sponsored men, rarely women, early forms of what we now think of as alternative or ecological tourism. That connection would associate Ober with

Clarence King rather than with John Wesley Powell, and with
Nathaniel Bishop rather than with John Muir, because both
King and Bishop were interested in writing rather than in the
national institutions and public policy that concerned Powell
and Muir.[33] Clarence King was famously presented, in Brooks's
study, *New England: Indian Summer 1865–1915* (1940), as the
type of the 'restless man' of the generation of 1870, a brilliant
talent for which his culture, to its discredit, could find no place.
That is Ober's generation and geographical background, but he
belonged to a different class, which needed to make a living out
of its writing and therefore looked to the new magazines like
Harper's and *Atlantic Monthly*, founded in the 1850s, which
accepted serious travel pieces, and to the publishers who were
ready to exploit the new interest in a great outdoors which was
slightly less intimidating when it was a little further away from
New York or Boston than it had been in 1800; when the natives
were either safely dead or definitely friendly; and when somebody else was doing the travelling and taking the risks.[34] As
Powell, for one, was very aware, anthropology had quickly
become inseparable from questions of national policy and
administration: Indians were increasingly the concern of the
Department of Interior rather than the War Department, and
the Bureau of American Ethnology, ultimately dependent on the
government for funding, needed to stress its ability 'to produce
results that would be of practical value in the administration of
Indian affairs'.[35] By contrast, the Caribbean, at least until 1898,
offered adventure without responsibility and without immediate political implication.

---

[33] Powell's journal was only published at the insistence of his political pay-
masters (1875). The popular account, *The Exploration of the Colorado River
and Its Canyons* was not written and published until 1895.

[34] The elegiac was certainly one of the notes struck at this time, although the sad
loss of Indian cultures was often regarded as a by-product of the even sadder loss
of the American wilderness: 'The stern and solemn poetry that breathed from her
endless wilderness is gone,' wrote Francis Parkman in 1844, 'and the dullest,
plainest prose has fixed its home in America' (quoted in Nash 1973: 110). As
Roderick Nash points out, it was these sentiments that were behind the first expressions of the idea of *preserving* what remained of that wilderness, sentiments
expressed in George Catlin's paintings of Indians just as they were in the movement
to establish a national park at Yellowstone.

[35] Powell's 1877 report (quoted in Hinsley 1981: 150).

The words of Ober's title say much about how his book is positioned. Camping had become popular as a vacation pastime in the 1860s and 1870s, preferably in the 'wilderness'; and the Caribbean, although not entirely off the beaten track, was distant enough from most readers' experience for Ober to get away with the word 'adventure' in his subtitle.[36] By 1879 the term 'Caribbees' already had a sense of the exotic, invoking an older, more poetic world of buccaneers and buried treasure.[37] The adventures, though, are 'of a Naturalist', the scientific note adding a respectable and serious side to the expedition, when Ober desires to exploit it.

The modest claims Ober makes for himself in his Preface depend upon the impact of the Caribbean forest, 'where everything reposes in nearly the same primitive simplicity and freshness as when discovered by Columbus, nearly four centuries ago'. 'My only claim', he writes, 'is that these sketches are original, and fresh from new fields—new, yet old in American history,—and that they are accurate, so far as my power of description extends. They have not, like the engravings, had the benefit of touches from more skilfull hands, and they may be crude and unfinished, and lack the delicate shadings and half-tones a more cunning artist could have given them; but they are, at least, true to nature' (pp. vi–vii).

'New, yet old': this paradox says much in small compass about the developing relationship between the USA and the Caribbean. The islands are 'new' in the sense that they have not been extensively explored or written about by US travellers and writers; yet they are 'old'—and therefore worthy of an historian's attention—because of their connection back to Columbus:

[36] An article in *Scribner's Monthly* in August 1874, entitled 'The Tent Under the Beach', recommended camping. Next year the magazine noted that 'camping out' was growing in favour. A guide to popular resorts in 1874 made 'camping out' the subject of a whole chapter (Huth 1972: 111; cf. Gould 1877). William H. H. Murray's *Adventures in the Wilderness; or, Camplife in the Adirondacks* (1869) is probably the immediate progenitor of Ober's titles, first essayed in 'Camping among the Seminoles'.

[37] Ober connects himself to the minor strain of nineteenth-century writing in English about the Native Caribbean, mostly based on Washington Irving, by quoting as his epigraph Tom Moore's lines from 'A Dream of Antiquity': 'Tomorrow I sail for those cinnamon groves, | Where nightly the ghost of the Carribee roves' (Moore 1929: 107). Moore was not the first or last whose interest in the 'Caribbees' is not matched by his ability to spell the word.

the Caribbean has 'settlements antedating Jamestown and Plymouth' (p. v). With Columbus moving into position through the
course of the nineteenth century as a significant US forefather,
the Caribbean can be gradually drawn into US national history.

Ober was a keen photographer and the engravings in the book
are based on his photographs. But photography also provides
him with the image of his writing, a telling image since, as I suggested in the opening chapter, photography is the technology of
the visit: 'As with the illustrations, so with the sketches in type.
I have but photographed the scenes I visited and the people
I saw and lived among' (p. vii). There are no ethnographic
pretensions here, but the phrase 'have but photographed' still
serves to claim a form of objectivity—supported by the scientific analogy to photographic technique; and suggests, equally
significantly, that the objects of the descriptions are worthy of
being so described.

Ober's presentation of himself as a writer is superficially self-
deprecatory but in fact very much in keeping with the development of adventure and romance as masculine genres which
would increasingly challenge the supposed effeminacy of the US
domestic novel as the century drew to a close. As a writer not
precious nor gilded nor skilful, but simple and honest and accurate, a producer of sketches which are 'true to nature', Ober
presents himself as pre-eminently masculine, 'strenuous' in the
sense that would soon become associated with Theodore
Roosevelt (1901). This may well be relevant both to Ober's self-
image as the active and solitary ornithologist, and to his literary self-presentation as an adventurer beyond the US frontiers,
part of that 'new vitality' of the time, which John Higham suggests 'may be understood as an infusion of lower-class and
upper-class aggressiveness into the middle-class world' (1970:
87). Ober quotes Trollope, impressed by Dominica's beauty,
writing in 1859 that 'it fills one with an ardent desire to be off
and rambling among these mountains', a desire Trollope immediately and no doubt gratefully qualifies by 'as if one could
ramble through such wild bush country, or ramble at all with
the thermometer at eighty-five degrees'.[38] Trollope may be the

---

[38] Trollope (1968: 160) (quoted, without reference, and with minor errors, in
Ober 1880: 5–6).

better writer, Ober implies, but his desire was not ardent enough. If you want to know the pleasures of the isle, then Ober is your man, as he suggests by quoting Caliban's offer to be Stephano's tour-guide—'I prithee, let me bring thee where crabs grow' (1880: 35).[39]

Writing after the event, Ober can invest his travels with the rhetoric of mock-heroism, leaving it for the reader to decide just how seriously the author ever took the 'reports that came from Carib country' that the Caribs lived 'secluded from the world', wandered 'naked . . . at will in the forest', and occupied a 'stronghold' which he would need to 'penetrate' (78–9). As author, Ober knows what is to come in his descriptions, knows how inappropriate the language of heroism would be in these circumstances, and so offers a slightly ironic picture of himself and his preparations. None the less, he is the ever-curious Yankee who wants to see things for himself—in implicit contrast to the incurious British who sip tea and play tennis in Roseau, the island's capital. He notes, rightly, that many writers have stopped off in Roseau, interviewed the natives 'and then have hastened off to England or the States, and written books about them'. None has 'penetrated beyond the line of civilization' (p. v). This new kind of writing will focus more on the protagonist and his adventures, the travel *itself* rather than the political agenda that tended to interest British travellers; and it will seek the untrodden paths. Nationality is important here: as a fairly rare white visitor Ober could not (and clearly did not want to) avoid the colonial paths through Roseau and the large estates—he was a particular friend of William Stedman, an important landowner, and knew the island President. But, unlike his British counterparts, he was also keen to leave 'the beaten path of travel', and could claim to have visited areas 'that few, if any, *tourists* ever reached before' (p. v) (my emphasis). This, then, is travel writing which distinguishes itself from the beaten track of tourism, but is aware that it is itself beating new tracks which others will soon follow, that it is not exploration and discovery in any grand sense: Ober's life is not in danger, despite the rather dramatic tones of Larcom's poem.[40]

---

[39] Quoting *The Tempest*, II.ii.161.

[40] In other words Ober is playing with that dialectic between travel and tourism which James Buzard (1993), among others, sees as fundamental to travel writing.

Ober's first camp in Dominica was at Laudat, just above Roseau, in a hut owned by Jean Baptiste, grandson of the Jean Baptiste Laudat who had founded the village in the eighteenth century. There is Carib blood here, Ober notes, in these five Laudat families; and after a month's stay, hearing intermittent reports about the Caribs, he decides that he will cross the island to visit them.

Ober's introduction to the chapter of *Camps in the Caribbees* called 'Among the Caribs' offers an idyllic picture, rather gentler than the tones of his Smithsonian report:

In two of the smaller islands of the Caribbean Sea lives a vestige of a once powerful people. A people with a history; an unwritten and forgotten history, running back unnumbered ages, farther than we can trace it; but beginning to be known to civilized man when the existence of America was first becoming evident to his awakened senses.

Peaceful and gentle, singularly mild and affectionate, they dwell happily in their rude houses of thatch, drawing their sustenance from mother earth with occasional forays upon the sea . . .

In a land that is theirs by right; beneath a sky ever genial, though not always smiling; able to satisfy hunger by a little toil in the garden, or exertion upon the sea, or in the river, it is not strange that they should be content with the bounties of the present, nor care to question the precarious prospects of the future. (73)

'A land that is theirs by right' sets the tone: words that a British writer would find difficult to compose about the Caribs on an island in the British Empire and that a US writer would find difficult to utter in a US context. Ober goes on to give an account, drawn largely from Washington Irving and Père Labat, 'of the discovery and condition of the first cannibals ever beheld by white men' (77) (neglecting to point out that Irving dismissed the charge of cannibalism), in order, as he says, 'to begin at the beginning, to bring before you the Carib as he was when found, nearly four centuries ago, and to show, by contrast with his present life, how he has been almost civilized out of existence' (78). Nothing is more important to national self-understanding than the notion of 'beginning': for Ober, *the* beginning for the Caribs is synonymous with 'beginning to be known' and not with the 'unnumbered ages' which might have been assumed to place any such beginning into distant millennia. The consequence, as so often in accounts of Carib history, is to collapse the 'true' Carib, 'as he was', into the Caribs as they responded to the European invasion of the Caribbean islands. This is rather like taking the dog's word that cats are essentially tree-dwelling creatures. So Ober's sense of Carib history is a repetition of the imperial story: 'We can trace them from South America northward, killing and devouring as they went. In the time of Columbus the people of Porto Rico were beginning to feel alarm from their incursions; and the Spaniard may be consoled by the thought that if he had not murdered his millions, the Caribs would have eventually depopulated these peaceful isles' (110).

In keeping with tradition, Ober's first meeting is with the Chief, but the offhand manner emphasizes Carib decline: 'As I rode along, every house seemed deserted; no face appeared, and I met no one save the ancient king, old George, who was named for King George III, tottering towards the plantations, to spend some money he had earned' (79–80). Ober notes that there are two sovereigns, because the Carib chief holds a gold English coin in his hand, the 'real' sovereign showing by implicit contrast the inauthenticity of the Carib replica.

Ober goes on to give a generally sympathetic picture of the social life of the Dominican Caribs, emphasizing the good relationships between the sexes, the outstanding hospitality ('a virtue he possesses in perfection' (95)), and the beauty of Carib baskets: 'Basket-making is the only art they have preserved from the teaching of their ancestors; but in this they indeed excel' (88).[41] He seems to have treated his neighbours without condescension, to have genuinely enjoyed their company, and to have been willing to learn from them, particularly the lore of the forest; and he names many of the individuals he had contact with, especially his servant Meyong, and his friend Coryet. This approach can properly be contrasted with what Edward Tylor, founding father of the discipline of anthropology, wrote about the Caribs at this time:

---

[41] The woven basket is noted by Lee Clark Mitchell as the single most important artifact in educating white collectors to Native American culture (1981: 180), so the presence and importance of Carib basketry placed the West Indies as part of the larger American Indian picture.

The people whom it is easiest to represent by single portraits are uncivilized tribes, in whose food and way of life there is little to cause difference between one man and another, and who have lived together and intermarried for many generations. Thus Fig. 18 [here fig. 4], taken from a photograph of a party of Caribs, is remarkable for the close likeness running through all. In such a nation the race type is

FIG. 4. A group of Caribs, from Edward B. Tylor, *Anthropology: An Introduction to the Study of Man and Civilization* (London: Macmillan and Co., 1892, fig. 18).

peculiarly easy to make out. It is by no means always thus easy to represent a whole population. To see how difficult it may be, one has only to look at an English crowd, with its endless diversity. (1892: 79)

Ober's picture of life among the Caribs could also be seen as opposite to 'an English crowd', but in a very different way. The crowd was, in the late nineteenth century, the very sign of modern life—impersonality, bustle, business. Against this, life in the tropics, especially at noon, is sweetly indolent: 'Everything is hushed in universal calm, and even the insects and birds feel the influence of the solar rays and are silent, drowsy, and indulging in mid-day siestas. *Dolce far niente* is the life these people lead; the sweet-do-nothing more than is absolutely necessary' (1880: 96).

Associated with this is a kind of dignification of Carib life. They may have been cannibals, but that habit, allied to their military prowess, led to important literary associations—with *The Tempest*, on which Ober quotes Daniel Brinton's *Myths of the New World*; and with *Robinson Crusoe*, since Friday was a Carib, as Ober would later 'demonstrate' at length.[42] In addition, they have their fireside stories and superstitions: they have lost their cannibal appetite but acquired a hearth around which stories of olden days can be told: one of Ober's chapters is called 'Indian Home Life'. In addition, and of special importance to Ober, though not irrelevant to many of those who follow him, the Carib villages—in the remotest part of the remotest island—are close to the wildernesses which interest natural historians. In fact, Ober's 'ethnographic' chapter, 'Among the Caribs' is followed by 'The Haunts of the Parrot' and 'A Day in the Deep Woods', for both of which he needs his Carib guide.

However, the main—and related—emphases of Ober's account are on physical descriptions and on historical change. The Caribs' 'form and color . . . make them different from people of other nationalities'; but

[t]hrough the changes of climate and residence, and the greater changes wrought by intermarriage with other tribes and with the negroes, the

---

[42] Brinton referred to Caliban as 'undoubtedly the word Carib' and pointed to the Patagonian origin of Setebos (1876: 240n.). Ober's book on Tobago expounds the Friday–Carib association (1898).

true Carib type is likely soon to be lost. It is, however, lighter in complexion than that of the North American Indian,—so light, that, from their peculiar cast of golden-brown, they have acquired the name of *Yellow* Indians ... One beautiful feature about them is their hair, which is abundant, long, and purple-black; it is finer than that of our Indians, though not so fine as that of the Caucasian type. (1880: 92)

Only about twenty families are seen as 'uncontaminated with negro blood' (95) (and only six will be in St Vincent). The loss of the true 'Carib type' is accompanied by, and associated with, the loss of the Carib language. Ober's stay saw the passing of the community's oldest inhabitant, 'whose death I lamented, as I was awaiting her recovery to secure from her a vocabulary of Carib words', though his lamentation over her death is alleviated by the idea of exhuming her skeleton and taking it back for the Smithsonian Museum's collection (98).

The dominant note is that of loss:

How changed are the Caribs of the present day! They have intermarried with the negroes to such an extent that their individuality is nearly lost. Their free mode of life, their long journeys by sea, their language even, are all things of the past. This remnant of a race, living so quietly in these islands, hemmed in between forest and ocean, peacefully cultivating their gardens and weaving baskets, quietly breathing away existence, are slowly but surely passing on into the great gulf of forgetfulness. Already they have forgotten the deeds of their fathers, the dread prowess of their ancestors. The bow, the hatchet, the war-club, mighty weapons in willing hands, are lost. In all their settlements one cannot find a bow. Here, then, are people who have lost language, prestige, tradition, ambition; and it is a matter of comparatively little time ere they will have ceased to exist, and the forests and rivers, the cool fern-shaded baths and tropic streams, no longer know their presence. (110–11)

THE WHITE CITY

In 1879 Ober was a young travel writer putting together his first book, whose moderate success led him into a career as a writer, journalist, and popular historian. Ten years later a combination of his early links with Harvard and the Smithsonian and his quite extensive knowledge of the Caribbean islands led to his invitation to act as Special Commissioner for the Caribbean in the preparations for the Chicago Columbian Exposition, the quatercentenary celebrations of Columbus's first voyage. Ober took his role very seriously indeed, travelling through Spain and the Caribbean in 1890 and 1891, collecting large amounts of material for Chicago, and writing his own account of his travels, published in 1893 as *In the Wake of Columbus: Adventures of the Special Commissioner Sent by the World's Columbian Exposition to the West Indies*. Whereas in the 1870s Ober travelled independently and alone, in the 1890s he travelled at government expense and in an official capacity, often meeting with politicians and other men of influence. Inevitably, therefore, the writing persona in the later book is less humorous, less personal, less self-deprecating, than the adventurous ornithologist of *Camps in the Caribbees*. In addition, Ober's main task was to collect material relating to Columbus, so his attention was directed more to the Spanish-speaking islands.

The Chicago Columbian Exposition was, according to Ober, 'the grandest work of its kind the world has ever seen; the crowning event of a century filled with wonders and miracles of man's invention' (1893: preface). This was certainly its self-image. Recent commentators note that World's Fairs offer a privileged site for social interpretation, a compacted statement, operating on many levels, of how a particular social formation articulates its idea of itself. Robert Rydell has analysed these fairs in terms of the 'symbolic images' they constructed, reading the turn-of-the-century fairs in the USA in psychocultural terms: 'To alleviate the intense and widespread anxiety that pervaded the United States, the directors of the expositions offered millions of fairgoers an opportunity to reaffirm their collective identity in an updated synthesis of progress and white supremacy that suffused the blueprints of future perfection offered by the fairs' (1987: 4). Columbus's first voyage was the named reason for the Exposition—although it was nearly the quatercentenary of his second by the time it opened—and so Columbus needed integrating into the Exposition's ideology, even if his actual achievements were as little relevant as they were to Chicago's late twentieth-century equivalent, in Seville in 1992 (see Harvey 1996).

By the 1890s Spain's influence in the Americas was limited to Cuba and Puerto Rico, and the commercial—and indeed military—involvement of the USA in the area was gathering ominous force. The significance and belonging of Columbus were deeply contested, and Chicago was a crucial moment in his 'Americanization,' a process in which Columbus became, in Ober's words, 'the hero of America's initial appearance upon the stage of history' (1893: 4), the major symbol of what Thomas J. Schlereth has called '*Columbianism*, a late nineteenth-century form of patriotic Americanism that involved cultural and political hegemony and various ethnic and religious identities', especially for Italian, Hispanic, and Catholic communities in the USA, who vied to commemorate and celebrate Columbus. Such enthusiasm eventually took on the form of a civic religion: 'Columbianism, as an aspect of this civic faith of creed, code, and cult, added to its sacred texts (Irving's biography), feast days (October 12), credo (Pledge of Allegiance), hymns ("Hail Columbia"), and icons (Columbian statuary). In this context, the Columbian Exposition served as a summer-long civic liturgy, replete with invocations, dedications, odes, homilies, and benedictions.'[43] To this list could be added the 'relics' that Ober was asked to collect in his role as commissioner: 'Your attention is particularly called to that portion of the Classification which relates to a collection of the relics of Columbus. The field to which you are assigned must contain many things of great value and interest, and you will devote your energies to securing articles for this collection'.[44]

For Ober, as for the Exposition generally, Columbus was a dividing line: modernity had its origins in Columbus but had developed new elements over the centuries as the mantle of progress passed from Europe to America, as the Exposition was supposed to demonstrate—westward the course of empire. For

---

[43] Schlereth (1992: 938 and 963); cf. Bushman (1992: 176–9).
[44] Quoted in Ober (1893: 128). William Eleroy Curtis, assistant to the Director-General of the Exposition and Chief of the Latin-American Department, used the phrase *The Relics of Columbus* as the title of his book to illustrate the material exhibited at Chicago in the reproduction of the convent of La Rábida, much of it collected by Ober: see Hulme 1997c.

this purpose, the Exposition needed to juxtapose the past and present peoples of America, including those who were living on the continent when it was discovered by Columbus. In this way, according to Frederick Ward Putnam, Chief of the Department of Ethnology and Archaeology for the Exposition, the stages of the development of man on the American continent could be 'spread out as an open book from which all could read', with such a collection forming the basis of a permanent ethnological museum 'which would grow in importance and value as time goes on and the present American tribes are absorbed by the peoples of the several republics'.[45] In this rich metaphoric brew, the demands of salvage anthropology are associated with an idea of the museum as an open book, a kind of great map of mankind as envisioned by Edmund Burke, in which past and present co-exist, with—in the usual paradox—'present American tribes' actually representing the 'past' peoples who are on the point of disappearing.

In the event, it was the popular and informal world of the Midway Plaisance which represented this 'past', developing in ways with which Putnam—who had notional control over it—was not happy. The Midway had 3,000 people from forty-eight nations or dependent colonies in its myriad stalls and camps, performing and hustling. Buffalo Bill's Wild West Show and Congress of Rough Riders ran for 618 performances in six months, and reputedly netted a million dollars (Fogelson 1991: 75). Curtis Hinsley sees all this in Benjaminesque terms: 'The eyes of the Midway are those of the *flâneur*, the stroller through the street arcade of human differences, whose experience is not the holistic, integrated idea of the anthropologist but the segmented, seriatim fleetingness of the modern tourist "just passing through"' (1990: 356). In his 1894 address to the Philosophical Society of Washington, 'America's Relation to the Advance of Science', George Brown Goode, assistant secretary to the Smithsonian and that institution's representative at Chicago, concluded by quoting from Whitman's *Leaves of Grass*, defining the demonstration of scientific progress at the

---

[45] Quoted in Dexter (1966: 316). Putnam was Curator of the Peabody Museum of Archaeology and Ethnology and Peabody Professor of American Archaeology and Ethnology at Harvard. The 'permanent ethnological museum' came to pass at the Field Museum in Chicago.

Chicago Exposition as an attempt precisely 'to formulate the Modern'.[46] As a result of all this, the spatial arrangement of the Exposition manifested the idea of civilizational progress. At the centre was the White City, the gleaming celebration of technology, science, and commerce. Outside the central core were ethnic displays and performances of popular arts, and at the periphery were the exotic primitives, the freaks, and the immensely popular side-shows. A contemporary critic saw it this way too. Nearest to the White City were the Teutonic and Celtic races as represented by the two German and two Irish villages. The centre of the Midway contained the Mohammedan world, West Asia, and East Asia. Then 'we descend to the savage races, the African of Dahomey and the North American Indian, each of which has its place' at the opposite end of the Plaisance. There seemed only one way to understand this 'living museum of humanity': 'Undoubtedly, the best way of looking at these races is to behold them in the ascending scale, in the progressive movement; thus we can march forward with them starting with the lowest specimens of humanity, and reaching continually upward to the highest stage. In that way we move in harmony with the thought of evolution, and not with that of the lapse or fall.'[47] In this way Chicago offered its spectators an ambulant gloss on history itself—the opportunity to walk in a couple of hours from primitivism through barbarism to civilization, with a final glimpse of what a technological future might hold.

The kinds of problems Baird had confronted in planning Indian groups at Philadelphia could now largely be circumvented. Living tableaux were established, but of a 'safe' variety, pretty much guaranteed not to embarrass organizers or tourists. Flanking the living tableaux were the popular shows on the Midway Plaisance and—sponsored by the Smithsonian— the plaster-of-Paris life groups developed by William Henry Holmes, which allowed the imaginative reconstruction of pre-Columbian lifeways: 'snapshots of primitive life long vanished' (Hinsley 1981: 108).

[46] George Brown Goode, 'America's Relation to the Advance of Science', *Science*, NS 1 (4 Jan. 1895), 8–9 (quoted in Rydell 1987: 45–6).
[47] Denton J. Snider, *World's Fair Studies* (Chicago, 1895), 255–7 (quoted in Rydell 1987: 65).

Ober still harboured some determination to see a Carib presence in Chicago:

My [1891] visit to the Caribs of Dominica was for the purpose of ascertaining how many of them, of pure blood, could be prevailed upon to go to the Exposition; it being the intention of the managers to gather there all the representative Indians of North and South America.

The Caribs, as the last living representatives of the Indians found in these islands by Columbus, possess a peculiar interest for the ethnologist, and it was my desire to secure from them not only an exhibit, but the best types of the people themselves. There are very few of pure Indian blood remaining, as in the course of generations, they have become mixed to a great extent with the blacks. (1893: 464–5)

Here the Exposition is seen—in keeping with Putnam's vision—as a Linnaean tableau for the display of 'all the representative Indians' of the Americas, and Ober's task is to encourage 'the best types' of the Caribs to attend which, in this instance, means the families 'of pure Indian blood'. As so often, the sense of decline—which calls forth the elegiac tones—is combined with a sense of continuity, which guarantees the authenticity of the 'representations': they need to live in the *same* primitive style as their ancestors, as if undisturbed by the turbulent history of the colonial period. Although largely unrealized in Chicago, Putnam's real interests lay firmly within the anthropological paradigm of establishing pre-contact authenticity: '[The native tribes] have about vanished into history, and now is the last opportunity for the world to see them and to realize what their condition, their life, their customs, their arts were four centuries ago.'[48] The Exposition's instructions to Ober and his colleagues were quite specific on this score: 'Particular attention should be paid to the fact that the most important things to be collected are those of genuine native manufacture, and especially those objects connected with the olden times. Objects traded to the natives by whites are of no importance and are not desired; the plan being to secure such a complete collection from each tribe as will illustrate the condition and mode of life of the tribe *before contact with*

[48] A draft speech, quoted from Putnam's papers (in Harvard) by Hinsley (1990: 347).

Europeans' (Johnson 1897–8: ii. 319, my italics). Needless to say, this was a particular challenge when the date of contact was 1492 or soon afterwards, which may explain why Ober chose to expend most of his energies on collecting items associated with Columbus.[49]

However, undeniably 'genuine'—and moreover representative of the disappeared races of the Caribbean—were skulls and skeletons. Blumenbach's physical anthropology had found one culmination in Samuel George Morton's skull collections, which had turned American Indians into specimens as Morton sanctioned the activities of those who, in the name of science, travelled to the West to collect Indian crania for phrenological purposes and for museums.[50] Ober's failure to find a skull of this sort on Watlings Island (San Salvador), the site of Columbus's first landfall in the Caribbean, is presented in a rather self-consciously jocular tone, suggestive of a certain unease about the whole process:

We groped for hours, on that and succeeding days, in the dark and dismal caves, finding many disjected fragments of skeletons and moldering bones, but no skeleton in its entirety—as its owner left it when he shuffled off this mortal coil. If Columbus only could have known—if the Indians themselves could—what a value would now attach to an aboriginal skeleton in this quadri-centennial of their discovery, perhaps some of them might have kindly bequeathed their bones to the investigators of posterity . . .

Subsequently, in Cat Island, I found other bones, and, as these were added to those obtained here, and the whole given in charge of Prof. Putnam, of the Department of Ethnology, something of interest may eventuate. Yes, I must confess to grievous disappointment, and I really feel quite incensed at Columbus and the aborigines that they should have been so inconsiderately forgetful as to leave no vestige of their remains. (1893: 77–8)[51]

---

[49] As far as I am aware there is no information as to whether Ober succeeded in taking the Caribs to Chicago. Relevant work on the Exposition and on the exhibition of indigenous peoples in the period includes Fogelson 1991; Hinsley 1990; Rydell 1987; Bogdan 1988.

[50] Hinsley (1981: 25–6); and cf. Bieder 1986.

[51] Bones Ober earlier found in the Bahamas were examined by Prof. W. K. Brooks of Johns Hopkins University (*Popular Science Monthly*, Nov. 1889) (according to Ober 1893: 75–6). Ober's ethnological materials were acknowledged in Chicago (Johnson 1897–8: iii. 423).

IN ST VINCENT

After leaving Dominica in the autumn of 1877, Ober continued
his bird-hunting in St Lucia and St Vincent, eventually descending from the latter's volcanic peak to the north-east coast:

> Carib country is that portion of the island of St. Vincent lying between
> the central ridge of mountains and the Atlantic coast. It is the most
> fertile and level, spreading from the foot of the hills in gentle slopes
> and undulating plains. Formerly in possession of the Caribs, it early
> attracted the English by its fertility, and, by processes well known to
> the white man when he desires his red brother's land, it soon changed
> hands. Though one may lament this usurpation of the Indian's terri-
> tory, and deprecate such deeds on general principles, one is soon rec-
> onciled to the change after he has been domiciled among the people
> in present possession. (1880: 208)

Rarely can a conscience have been so easily assuaged—in this
case by the hospitality of the mostly Scottish planters. In
Dominica, Carib territory was far away from the main estates
where Ober visited, and there was no obvious planter or creole
'position' with respect to the Caribs. In St Vincent the situation
was very different. There were two main Carib villages, one of
which, Morne Ronde, inhabited by Black Caribs, was on the
north-west coast. Sandy Bay, whilst also—like the Carib Reserve
on Dominica—on the north-east coast of an island whose
capital is in the south-west, was less difficult of access than its
Dominican counterpart and, as Ober notes, close to fertile
plains where European settlement had developed. In addition,
the Caribs of St Vincent had been defeated in a bloody military
conflict almost within living memory. So the plantocracy of St
Vincent had a much clearer and more articulated set of views
about the Caribs than their Dominican counterparts. Ober was
also quite ill for much of his time on St Vincent and therefore
reliant on the warm hospitality of his new friends, whose views
he seems often to reflect.[52]

Unsurprisingly these views tend to concern the labouring
population of the island, black and East Indian, rather than the
Caribs, who would not have been employed by the planters on

---

[52] George Lawrence's Appendix to *Camps in the Caribbees* notes two attacks of
fever, the second of which prostrated Ober for well over a month (in Ober 1880:
358). During this time he stayed with a planter, James Milne.

a regular basis. So, the emancipated negro is said to prefer 'hunger and inferior food . . . to plenty and work', with the breadfruit, imported from the Pacific to provide cheap food for slaves now ironically blamed for having run wild in the forest where it provides this 'inferior food' in return for the labour of picking it off the tree. 'To aid the planters in their difficulty,' Ober writes, 'natives of the East Indies were imported as laborers.' But due to the machinations of the anti-slavery party, it has proved difficult to extract the necessary labour from these new imports. Indeed, Ober suggests, with a touch of hyperbole: 'The Coolie is protected by government to such an extent that the planter is really the slave of the "laborer"' (232–3). To be honest, Ober may not have needed much encouragement in his negrophobia, to use the late nineteenth-century term, which emerges throughout his work. It probably differs little from that of many of his contemporaries, and would therefore not be worthy of note were it not for the contrast it affords to his attitude towards the Caribs. One incident will suffice. In Grenada, Ober goes hunting for monkeys with a young black boy as guide. Presented with the opportunity to shoot them, he hesitates: 'what if there was some remote relation in that throng? or—what was more probable—some descendant of an ancestor in common with the little negro crouching by my side?' The boy encourages him: 'He at least had no misgivings on the score of relationship, even though the resemblance between the two— the monkey in the tree, and the African, the monkey on the ground—was strong enough to excite a smile' (276–8).

Captain George, a Black Carib, was Ober's near neighbour and informant in St Vincent, especially about the eighteenth-century wars in which the Caribs had been dispossessed. More of his words are quoted in the book than any other Carib's. On Dominica, the Caribs at that time spoke the same French-based patois as the majority Afro-Dominican population. Ober, who regarded the language with disdain as a bastardized French, quotes it in translation, with some Gallic markers, such as the overuse of sibilance ('pleeze'), but in moderation. On St Vincent, the Caribs—again like the majority population—speak a form of English which Ober can transcribe according to fairly established models of southern US black speech. Some literary licence was no doubt employed—after all, Ober had no tape-recorder—

but the extensive paragraphs of direct speech do allow an individual character to emerge.

Captain George regales Ober 'with numerous stories of the achievements of the Caribs during the war with the English in the last century', which Ober seems inclined to accept at face value, giving credit to the Caribs' military skill and to their persistence in the face of overwhelming numbers. The war was only won for the British in 1796 with the arrival of General Abercrombie and 4,000 troops. The French troops on St Vincent, who had fought alongside the Caribs, were released on parole and allowed to leave; the Caribs, abandoned, refused unconditional surrender and fought on until starved into submission. Nearly five thousand were removed to the small island of Balliceaux and kept there for several months: 'Captain George declared that the English government aimed to destroy as many of them as possible, and caused lime to be mixed in their bread; but of course this was false, and probably arose from the fact that the water, being impregnated with lime, caused much sickness and death' (217). Here—in the second, 'corrective' part of the sentence—it is possible to see how Captain George's Carib version of the facts has been 'revised' by the planters in whose houses Ober was staying.[53]

In February 1797 most of these Caribs were deported to Roatan, an island off the Honduras coast, where after many vicissitudes they established the Black Carib (Garifuna) community which now thrives up and down that Atlantic littoral, the one surviving community still speaking the indigenous language of the Caribbean islands. Noting that the few remaining Black Caribs seem to have been better treated than their 'Yellow' counterparts, Ober speculates that the Black Caribs did not take part in the war, due to their 'innate cowardice . . . born of their negro blood' (217), a view diametrically opposed to that of the British, which was that the Black Caribs were more aggressive than the Yellow Caribs precisely because of the *presence* of that 'negro blood'.[54]

---

[53] Cf. 'It is noteworthy that Central American Carib traditions about the aftermath of the Carib War includes mention of lime being mixed with the flour given to the Caribs during their deportation' (Gullick 1985: 88).

[54] The 'black' and 'yellow' designations have still not been fully understood: see Gullick 1976 and 1985; Gonzalez 1988; Hulme 1999*b*.

Our images of cultures are shaped by the comparisons and analogies we use to place and describe them. As Spartans of the Caribbean, the Caribs were militaristic, aggressive, and uncultured (relative to the 'Athenian' Arawaks): worthy of a guarded respect. Ober, looking through the eyes of New World experience rather than Old World learning, saw in these Vincentian Caribs the story of the Florida Seminoles, the first Indians with whom he had had contact:

How similar has been the fate of the Caribs to that of the Seminoles of the Southern States! At the beginning of the present century, the latter were peaceful and happy, cultivating their gardens with an intelligence that shows them to have been superior people. They, too, were driven to war, stripped of their property, and hunted by white troops. Their resistance lasted for seven years, but in the end, nearly all were captured and transported far from their homes. Of them a remnant lingers in the hunting-grounds of their fathers, engaged, like the present Carib, in agricultural pursuits. With them, too, the negro found a home, married with them, and to them communicated the curse of his race. (Ober 1880: 218)

Like the Seminoles, the Caribs may have survived several centuries of European aggression, but they have no chance against a few drops of negro blood.

Ober gets to visit the island of Balliceaux, by 1877 a game reserve, and Battowia, an even smaller island where a native *duho* or stool had been found fifteen years earlier. He refers to Otis Mason's account of Puerto Rican antiquities, including stools similar to this one, quoting Mason's words from the Spanish historian Herrera about how in Cuba the welcoming chiefs caused Columbus's party 'to sit down on seats made of a solid piece of wood in the shape of a beast with very short legs and the tail held up, the head before, with eyes and ears of gold'.[55] Ober speculates that this object had been taken by the Caribs from their enemies in Haiti or perhaps belonged to an Arawak captive living among the Caribs, making the assumption that the 'ferocious' Caribs were too uncivilized to make the kinds of ritual objects which conventionally mark a culture as having climbed at least a couple of rungs on the ladder of

[55] Ober (1880: 224), quoting Mason 1877.

progress. However, Ober himself finds a wooden *zemi* in the form of a tortoise (222), suggesting that Battowia might have been a place of refuge for sacred objects.

On his return in 1891 Ober provides one of the last descriptions of the Carib community at Morne Ronde before it was decimated by the 1898 hurricane and destroyed by the 1902 volcanic eruption: 'They have a fine reservation, extending from the sea far up into the mountains, and containing over four hundred acres. In all they number about two hundred; old François went out and took the census, while I waited in the hut . . . There was but one of them who could speak, or pretended to speak, the Carib tongue, and as no one else knew the sense of his lingo, it had to pass at that' (1893: 479). Morne Ronde also contains 'the great hut where the basket-makers worked' (478): 'The baskets made by these Black Caribs are in such demand that they are kept busy filling orders, and seem much more industrious than their Indian brothers of Dominica' (480). It may be that the best of the nineteenth-century photographs of Carib basket-makers is of this 'great hut' at Morne Ronde.[56]

A short visit to Sandy Bay introduces a more sombre note than usual, not just because Ober can mark the changes since his previous visit—a pretty child grown into a coarse woman, Captain George now a widower, but remarried. A recent hurricane had destroyed gardens and huts, and the friends who came to see Ober told him 'the same sad stories that all the world is familiar with—of sickness and death, and struggles with poverty' (482).

There is just one other snapshot of Sandy Bay written relatively soon after Ober's visits. Among the more unusual vessels cruising the Lesser Antilles in the summer of 1888 was the sailing canoe *Liberdade*, constructed by Joshua Slocum after the wreck of his boat *Aquidneck* earlier that year on the Brazilian

---

[56] Reproduced in *WM* 251. There is some confusion over this photograph. The caption in *WM* is drawn from its description in Fewkes (1907). However, an earlier version describes it as 'Six Vincentian Caribs at Jamaica International Exhibition in 1891 weaving baskets in a model village' (S. P. Musson and T. Laurence Roxburgh, comp., *Handbook of Jamaica for 1891–92* (Kingston 1891), 578; quoted in Taylor (1993: 65–6)).

coast.[57] On his return home, one of Slocum's sons, Victor, told his friend Frederic Fenger about this enforced but spectacular cruise, and Fenger hatched the idea of repeating it himself, a plan he finally put into practice during the course of 1911, shipping his small sailing canoe, the *Yakaboo*, from New York to Grenada, where he met a Carib boy who had fled from St Vincent after the volcanic eruption in 1902. 'If I would sail from island to island after the manner of the Carib, why not seek out the native and learn the truth from him?' (Fenger 1958: 30). Fenger sails into a group of Black Carib canoes off the coast of St Vincent (near Layou) and is persuaded to visit their village ('I felt like an explorer on the coast of Africa being entertained by the people of a friendly tribe' [117]). A couple of days later he is taken by Batiste (son of the man who had been Ober's guide) to visit the 'Yellow' Caribs at Sandy Bay on the windward coast, to which, Fenger explains, they had now almost all (who had survived the volcano) returned after several years living among the Black Caribs along the leeward coast. There he spends what he calls his 'Days with a Vanishing Race'. That first evening Fenger sat at the door of his tent having some sea eggs removed from his foot by an old Carib woman:

It would have been one of the best photographs of my whole cruise could I have caught those faces around that burning flambeau. Now for the first time I could really observe them in unconscious pose. Notwithstanding a considerable amount of admixture they must have undergone with the blacks, there was still a satisfying amount of Indian blood left in these people. I said Indian purposely for I do not care to use the expression Carib in this sentence. I believe these people to be more of the peaceful Arawauk than the fierce Carib, although time and environment and subjugation may have had this softening effect upon them. (137–8)

He retells the usual story of Carib raids on Arawak settlements, the killing of the men, the taking of the women as wives, but draws what for the time was an unusual conclusion: 'Through their offspring by their Carib masters the Arawauk women introduced their language and their softening influence into the tribes so that little by little the nature of the Carib was perceptibly changed. Thus the Arawauk became ultimately the race

[57] Slocum (1962: 39–124); cf. Teller (1971: 53).

conquerors' (138). This is certainly one explanation for Carib 'change', but by no means the usual one.

IN OBER'S FOOTSTEPS

Partly, no doubt, as a result of the success of *Camps in the Caribbees*, the following decades saw a sharp increase in the number of Caribbean travel-books, with several writers making the still difficult trek across Dominica to visit the Caribs. The travellers that followed this path were usually aware of Ober's work, often referring to it or quoting from it. The later 1880s were a particularly busy time. James Anthony Froude, anatomist of the British Empire, was in Dominica in 1887, the same year as William Paton, and wrote that the Caribs 'still lingered in the forests' (1909: 113), though, like Paton, he himself did not get as far as the north-east coast to visit them.[58] The New England doctor, W. S. Birge, actually visited the Caribs that same year, although his written account had to wait for publication until 1900. A. H. Verrill made the first of several visits in 1888, though his account of that visit is part of a much later retrospective survey of his long career as ornithologist and writer. Despite this surge of interest, a contemporary guide for settlers—perhaps a different constituency from tourists—was adamant that '[t]here are no natives proper to the Lesser Antilles . . . the few now bearing the name of such can hardly be called true descendants of the former aborigines' (Bulkeley 1889: 177). Frederick Treves, a well-known Edwardian doctor, provides a final pre-war visitor.

Alpheus Hyatt Verrill calls his *Thirty Years in the Jungle* (1929) 'neither a book of travel, a novel, a narrative of adventure, nor a treatise on jungle life; but, in a way . . . a combination of all' (p. v)—which may act as a warning to read it with some care. He has, he writes, tried to demonstrate 'the customs, beliefs, habits and admirable traits of the wild, unspoiled aborigines, for the purpose of studying whom most of my expeditions have been undertaken' (p. xii). A generation younger than Ober,

---

[58] Paton was discussed in Chapter 1; Froude reappears in more detail in Chapter 3.

Verrill's writing output is very similar in kind to Ober's: travel writing in the Americas, which is a mixture of natural history, popular ethnography, and adventure; and novels aimed mainly at an adolescent market. Verrill makes no mention in this book that Ober had been in Dominica a decade before he had, although many of the incidents Verrill describes are remarkably similar to those in *Camps in the Caribbees*, from the visit to the Boiling Lake, to the shooting of the parrots, and the unavailing search for the Diablotin, the famous giant petrel not seen on the island since the eighteenth century.[59]

During this first visit to Dominica, in 1888, Verrill describes spending much time in Laudat, where most people, he says, had Carib features, although the family he stays with also have a Carib servant called Beché with whom Verrill goes hunting for parrots.[60] Beché's native village is La Soir (La Soie, now more commonly Wesley, just north of the present borders of the Reserve). When Verrill visited the Reserve, the inhabitants were 'shy, friendly, smiling and hospitable, and it was hard to believe that it was these peaceful, timid aborigines who, for nearly two hundred years . . . brought terror to the hearts of all enemies, white, black or yellow' (27–8). The tribe numbered about two hundred, he recalls, with less than a score speaking Carib. Beché had been purchased as a child and was virtually a slave— 'although a very well-treated one' (28).

The chief, an elderly fine chap, became fascinated with a pair of scissors I was using, and as I had bestowed several small gifts on Beché's parents and other members of the tribe, I presented the scissors to the chief. The old fellow grunted, grinned, and hurrying off returned presently leading a very pretty Carib girl, perhaps fifteen years of age. Through the medium of Leon as interpreter, he informed me she was his daughter and that she was mine in exchange for the scissors.

In vain I protested and declined to accept the girl, who appeared to take the deal as a matter of course. To the chief my protests meant merely that I was not satisfied with the bargain, and he became quite excited, declaring she was the prettiest girl in the village, and he

[59] Verrill does mention Ober as his prime inspiration for going to Dominica in his unpublished autobiography, 'Never a Dull Moment' (MS: 212).

[60] The Laudat dynasty had apparently passed to another generation since Ober was there eleven years previously: André Laudat is now the patriarch, with Leon, his son, and Rolles, his son-in-law, acting as Verrill's guides and interpreters.

appeared quite peeved and even insulted at my attitude. It would never do to incur the displeasure of the chief, and something had to be done which would satisfy all the parties concerned. So I accepted my involuntary purchase, appeased the ruffled chief by giving him a file and a knife for full measure, and, explaining that I could not be encumbered by the girl on my long trip to Morne Diablotin, I gave her into her father's keeping until I should return to claim her. Evidently Carib custom provides that goods left unclaimed beyond a certain time can be disposed of, for when I next visited La Soir, nearly twenty years later, I found my feminine chattel married to a strapping Carib in whom I failed to recognize my old friend Beché, and the mother of several yellow-skinned aborigines. (28–9)[61]

The trope of the diverted or repressed sexual encounter between Western traveller and Carib girl is a staple element of travel writing about the Caribs, especially in the earlier part of the period covered here—although at least in Verrill's case the girl is not much younger than he was at the time. Ober's *Camps in the Caribbees* has the picture of Marie, a 16-year-old girl from Laudat, part Carib, part African, and part French, who is able to deliciously embarrass Ober with her propensity for removing articles of clothing and then diving for crayfish:

These she handed to the little girl on the rock near me, and then climbed out and stood erect, with heaving bosom and parted lips, and nonchalantly gathered up her dripping skirts and wrung from them the water. Outlined against that wonderful background of tropical leaves, with its depths of shade and gleams of light, with the water dashing against the rock upon which she stood, and parting in sheets of foam, what a charming naiad she appeared! Naiad she may have been, but she could hardly have been called a Dry-ad, as the water had caused her garment to cling closely to her shapely figure, and was pouring from it. (1880: 37–8)

Marie is described as breathless and excited from her exertions, her finger red and swollen from the bite of a crayfish. All adjectives apply equally well to the writer.

This theme emerges in something like its purest and most naïve form in W. S. Birge's *In Old Roseau*, published in 1900. The first half of this book sees Birge, a doctor from Province-

---

[61] Verrill was also in Dominica in June 1902 collecting birds for a Chicago museum. He named a new species of humming-bird *Tharulania Belli* after Hesketh Bell, the subject of Chapter 3 (see Bell 1946: 66).

town on holiday in the West Indies, lazing around 'old Roseau' doing very little. One day he stands on the bridge overlooking the Roseau River, at a loose end. He tires of watching the 'Dominican damsels washing clothes in the river, every one conspicuous by her bright-colored petticoat, very short, coming some three inches above the knees, showing in most of them an exquisite contour of dusky limbs below' (Birge 1900: 66), and turns inland to look at the mountains: ' "Those are the Dominican Mountains," I said to myself, "and what lies beyond? Is it not the Mahoe country, inhabited by the remnant of that once powerful tribe, the Carib Indians, so memorable in the early Columbian history?" ' (67).

He recalls reading Washington Irving and quotes him at length on the subject of the Caribs:

Columbus found the Caribs a powerful and warlike people, entirely different from the peaceful mild-mannered natives that he first encountered. They were trained to war from their infancy; their distant roamings by sea made them observant and intelligent. They went, on predatory enterprises, in canoes made from the hollowed trunks of trees, to the distance of one hundred and fifty leagues. Their arms were bows and arrows, pointed with the bones of fishes, or shells of tortoise, and poisoned with the juice of a certain herb. They made descents upon the various islands, ravaged the villages, carried off the youngest and handsomest of the women, and made prisoners of the men, to be killed and eaten. When the men went forth on these expeditions, the women remained to defend their shores from invasion. The natives of the other islands only knew how to divide time by day and night by the sun and moon; whereas, these had acquired some knowledge of the stars, by which to calculate the times and seasons. (Birge 1900: 68–9; compressing several paragraphs from Irving (1981: 187–9)).

The resulting visit enables him to entitle Part II of his book 'Reminiscences of a Sojourn Among the Remnants of a Once Powerful People' (63), a sojourn which begins when Birge travels to the Mahoe country (around Mahaut River) with Jean Baptiste Pierre, the son of a French father and Carib mother, who proves a perfect 'informant', fully accepted as Carib and yet with a sense of himself as an outsider. He also has two sisters, Louise and Marcella, aged 15 and 17: ' "Bon jour, monsieur," exclaimed the elder of the two, as she came forward and

extended her hand, "we with plaisure welcome ze gentleman."
A flush stole over the olive cheeks, and the rich red lips parted
in a smile, showing a set of pearly teeth that would have created
envy in the heart of a society belle' (77).

A variety of incidents ensues, including one in which Birge—
like Ober before him—is embarrassed by the number of clothes
that the two sisters are prepared to shed in order to cross a
swollen stream, and another in which Marcella enters his room
at night and kisses him softly on the forehead. The day before
he leaves, Marcella comes to ask questions about his life in
America. He describes himself as 'an old bachelor' (97). She
wishes she could go to his country, and he asks her what she
would do there:

'Why'—there was a slight hesitation in her voice, and a deeper tinge
of color overspread her cheeks—'I would live with you, monsieur.'
   'That could hardly be, my child; I have no home of my own, besides
it would not be considered the proper thing in my country.' (97)

They spar in this fashion for a while, the dialogue interspersed
with his comments about 'her magnificent hair' falling about
'her dainty neck and shoulders' and 'those great dark eyes' (98).
Birge claims to be taken aback by her line of questioning: 'I had
looked upon her as hardly more than a child' (99).

'Oh! monsieur,' she continued; 'you leave Mahoe to-morrow—do pity
poor Marcella. Take me with you. I do not ask to be your wife, zat
would be impossible. You no marry poor Carib girl. I will be your
slave. Anything you wish, monsieur; only take me with you. You do
not love me, but you can like me one little bit. I love you, monsieur,
so much.'
   Her bosom heaved with emotion, and throwing her arms around my
neck, she pressed her warm cheek against my own, her raven tresses
hanging in reckless profusion around us both. I will not attempt to
describe what transpired during the next few moments. How I tried in
vain to reason with her, telling how different from her own were the
ways and customs of the American people. How the climate was bleak
and cold. How she would soon wither and pine like a tropical flower
transplanted from the warmth and sunshine of its own heather. It was
of no avail and, finally, when I disengaged her arms from about my
neck, she flung her quivering form upon the ground and wept as if her
heart would break. I thought it best to let her feelings have sway, and
walked away and left her. (99–100)

In Old Roseau, written thirteen years later, has a touching dedication: 'To My Wife, who has been a constant companion and help through years of a busy professional life, this little book is dedicated with a feeling of respect and honest affection'. The opposite page is decorated with a picture of the 17-year-old Carib beauty, Marcella (fig. 5).

Frederick Treves's travel books, written over the first twenty years of the new century, offer a kind of 'report on Empire', a fairly leisurely survey written in a distinctly less anguished tone than that of Froude some thirty years earlier. They were the product of Treves's retirement, after a distinguished career as a surgeon. In *The Cradle of the Deep* (1908) he recounts his West Indian voyage, including a visit to Dominica, although it appears that Treves—like Paton and Froude—did not actually visit the Carib Territory. Dr Henry Nicholls, the physician and planter, who had taken an interest in the Caribs, acted as an

FIG. 5. Marcella, a Carib beauty (frontispiece to William S. Birge, *In Old Roseau: Reminiscences of Life as I found it in the island of Dominica and among the Carib Indians*, New York: The Blanchard Press 1900).

intermediary, offering the figure of the young girl Victorine as an emblem of 'Caribness' for Treves to contemplate and around whom to weave his historical meditations. Although Victorine belongs to the strain of adolescent Carib girls that has fascinated male travellers, in the photograph that forms Treves's frontispiece (*WM* 278) she is wearing more clothes than most.

Treves recapitulates the familiar history, though with a slant even more distinctly sympathetic to the Caribs than his immediate predecessors. For example, the Arawaks are described as 'savages of a low type, indolent, gentle and unprogressive', whereas the Caribs were 'fierce, warlike and intelligent.' 'They could claim to be a race of fine people', he writes, and in support quotes Francis Drake as calling them 'very personable and handsome strong men'. He goes on to conjure a powerful picture of October 1492 from the viewpoint of a 'naked savage of San Salvador' ('Now, on this October morning, there came from out of the unknown three fearsome things that moved upon the sea'), before describing the one actual Carib he meets:

During my stay on Dominica I was able, through the kindness of Dr. Nicholls, to make the acquaintance of a pure-blooded Carib from the Reservation. She was a girl of ten, whose name was Victorine. She was a picturesque little maid, with pretty manners and singularly sweet voice. Her complexion was yellow-brown, her hair long, lank and black. She had the lacquer-black eyes of a Japanese doll, almond shaped and a little oblique, a fine mouth and lips, slightly prominent cheeks. The type of her face was distinctly Mongolian, without the least suggestion of the negro in its outlines . . . Victorine could claim at least an interesting ancestry. Her people roamed the island for centuries before Columbus came. They saw the sailing hither of the first great ship the Marie Galante. They watched the landing of Drake and Hawkins when they came for 'refreshing', just as now they may gaze at blue jackets coming ashore from the modern ironclad. Victorine may not be 'the daughter of a hundred earls,' but among her forefathers might have been that 'King of the Cannibal Islands' who is for ever famous in the English nursery song.

She might still have been attracted by a scarlet cap, a string of beads, or a hawk's bell. None of these being at hand, she was offered her choice of certain commonplace articles. With a remarkable precision and with more than mere instinct she selected a purse and two half-crowns, those being the largest of the coins laid out before her. It was impossible not to feel that the most fitting present for this little wild thing, with her brown skin and piercing eyes and her wilder ancestry, would still have been a hawk's bell. (Treves 1908: 173–4).

Victorine may be picturesque and wild, but the real interest lies in the even wilder ancestry that she can claim—or, to be more precise, that Treves can claim for her. Again, though, as with Ober, the interest is dependent upon the purity of the blood, which serves to underwrite the connection back to Columbus and to the primitivism which Treves is determined to find. Victorine's instinct may be determinedly 'modern' as she unerringly selects the two half-crowns: Treves has to resort to the notion of grammatical impossibility in order to present the hawk's bell which he feels would have been most fitting.

In the cases of Verrill and Birge, the sexual encounters narrowly avoided were with teenage girls. Treves's Victorine is slightly younger, as is the semi-naked girl who appears in Symington Grieve's photograph of a couple of years earlier, having her hair washed in a stream (*WM* 272). The connotations are again complex. These are 'wild' Indians, but their ferocity belongs to the past, so they are, it seems, best represented by the children, especially young girls, who suggest the 'freshness' of that supposedly primitive world, enhanced by the metonymic transfer of wildness to the setting. In this respect Grieve's photograph belongs to a long tradition not seriously challenged in the Native Caribbean context until H. M. and E. L. Ayers's photographs in the early 1940s, discussed below in Chapter 4.

The psychodynamics of Caribbean colonial encounters have not been paid much attention. In the Spanish sources, for example, there are already signs of a deeply repressed identification between the Spanish and the Caribs; indeed the strongest form of this argument would be that what exists as 'the Caribs' in the early Spanish sources is a disavowed and projected self-image: marauders from across the seas who kill the native men and 'marry' the native women. That identification is much more open in many of these late nineteenth-century Anglo-American sources: the peaceful and gentle Arawaks have become pusillanimous and backward, the ferocious Caribs have became manly and sporting and even imperialistic—just like the British have been and the citizens of the USA are in the process of becoming.

The politics of *erotic* encounter have a different inflection. What can be called the 'Pocahontas syndrome' takes many forms, but it always involves a native woman who is more responsive to the European colonist than her male counterparts, often saving his life as Pocahontas does for John Smith, or Yarico for Inkle in the Caribbean version. In one sense the theme of the welcoming Carib girl reproduces the original Arawak/Carib division—which was itself already inflected discursively as a female/male division: not just because Carib men 'married' Arawak women, but because Carib women were seen as 'masculine' and Arawak men as 'feminine'. In the narratives here under consideration the previously Arawak features (gentle, peaceful, welcoming) become attached—at least in the colonial imagination—to Carib women; just as in St Vincent in the eighteenth century Arawak features had become attached to the so-called Yellow or pure Caribs while the supposedly impure Black Caribs retained the original martial Carib features.

As such an account suggests, in all of these cases the supposedly ethnographic description is in fact a function of the ideological and/or psychological needs of those offering the descriptions. However, although this particular body of turn-of-the-century Caribbean material is relatively small, a national distinction could also be discerned here, with two very different images of empire on offer. The US travellers are, in however mediated a fashion, imagining—even if, or especially if, they deny it—a sexual relationship with an adolescent Carib girl, a relationship that figures on the larger ideological map as the desire for a degree of involvement which cannot, for whatever reason, yet be achieved. That desire is no doubt in one register the great American search for innocence, but it is also, I would argue, an unconscious aspect of the negotiation of a more direct political relationship between an expansionist USA and the Caribbean islands. Treves and Grieve, on the other hand, the British travellers, encounter pre-pubescent girls. There is certainly an element of the ethnopaedophiliac here, but perhaps the dominant feature is the infantilization of the Caribs. As Britain's power in the region declines, the representative figure amongst the aboriginal population becomes a child in need of protection:

indeed, as the next chapter will discuss, the Aborigines Protection Society was an important influence on the development of British anthropology. It was commonplace for so-called savage or primitive peoples to be seen as childlike, or even for the colonized culture to be regarded as undergoing a process of development which, under careful tutelage, might result in adulthood. The novelty of Benjamin Kidd's argument, enormously influential at the time, was his articulation of the administrative principle 'that in dealing with the *natural* inhabitants of the tropics we are dealing with peoples who represent the same stage in the history of the development of the race that the child does in the history of the development of the individual' (1898: 51–2). In which case the Caribs could expect to remain 'in trust', as minors, for the rest of their existence.

In this process, as we have seen with Ober and several of his followers, the supposed ferocity and martial qualities of the Caribs are confirmed but reassessed. The obvious reason for the reassessment is that that 'ferocity' is not any longer a danger to any of the colonial or would-be colonial powers in the area. Equally important, though, in this largely English-speaking rewriting of the history of the Native Caribbean, is that Carib aggression had been aimed entirely at European colonial powers and principally at Spain; and Spain features in English and, of course, especially in US writing of this period, as a decadent colonial power holding back the possible development of islands like Cuba and Puerto Rico. So what tends to happen now is that the conventional dualism—peace-loving Arawaks destroyed by ferocious Caribs—is maintained but discursively reinflected. So Frederick Treves, for example, calls the Arawaks 'gentle', a traditional adjective to describe them, but embeds the term within a sentence which runs 'savages of a low type, indolent, gentle and unprogressive', whereas the Caribs are 'fierce, warlike' . . . and 'intelligent'. Birge's resumé of Washington Irving strikes a similar note: 'powerful and warlike', but also 'observant and intelligent'.[62] For the turn-of-the-century Caribs, this reassessment was a double-edged sword: it gave them a

---

[62] All these phrases are taken from the longer quotations over the previous three pages.

more highly regarded history—intelligent soldiers rather than mindless cannibals; but that only meant that their present degradation marked an even greater fall.

THE ARRIVAL OF THE TOURISTS

In one sense all the visitors considered thus far who actually reached the Carib territory were tourists: none of them was a professional ethnographer, none of them 'went native', none of them was a resident of Dominica. However, they are entitled to be considered travellers inasmuch as they spent some time with the Caribs and took at least a passing interest in their history and culture. The first visitor who seems identifiably a tourist in the modern sense was Stephen Bonsal, the US journalist and later diplomat, who visited Dominica in the early years of the century, probably around the time of the publication in 1907 of Algernon Aspinall's travel guide, from which I extracted the phrase 'desirous of visiting the Caribs' at the beginning of Chapter 1.[63] The guiding idea behind Bonsal's travels through the Caribbean is given by his quotation from the historian Brooks Adams: 'Should the future resemble the past and the conditions of competition remain unchanged, the Caribbean archipelago must either be absorbed by the economic system of the United States or lapse into barbarism.'[64]

Bonsal's introduction to the Caribs comes via 'a weather-worn, worm-eaten copy of Père Labat's celebrated book' (1912: 232), which he finds in a monastery high above the port of Charlotte Amalie, on St Thomas, one of the Virgin Islands, north of Dominica. The Belgian Fathers of the monastery place the book at his disposal, and together they spend many long afternoons talking 'of the passing of the Carib Kings' (233). Bonsal recounts several stories from Labat, including the much-

---

[63] Although the book was published in 1912, Bonsal's description of the Carib chief as 'a dried-up little man, who had evidently attained a very great age' (1912: 240) seems to suit Auguste François, who died in 1908, better than his successor, Jules Corriette, who would have been 54 in 1912. Hesketh Bell, the subject of the next chapter, had written a short guide for tourists ('Ten Days in Dominica') while he was the island's Administrator, so short visits were clearly becoming more common as steamship services developed in the early years of the new century (Bell 1904*b*).

[64] Bonsal (1912: 20); quoting Adams's *The New Empire*, published in 1902.

repeated episode during the Caribs' unavailing defence of
Grenada against the French when the surviving natives, pressed
back onto a high promontory, threw themselves to their death
rather than surrender, leading to that cliff getting the name it
still bears, of Le Morne de Sauteurs (233); a story which has
always cast an awkward light on surviving Carib communities,
as if they somehow had not possessed the courage or principles
of their suicidal brethren.

Full of Labat's stories, Bonsal arrives on Dominica determined
to visit the Caribs: to make what he refers to as a 'pilgrimage'
(237). He has a local informant, an English planter who insists
that 'You must go to see the Caribs by night, because just at
sunrise there is a touch of wild light in their eyes, which fades
as the days wear on, and the King is magnificent.' This sounds
impressive, fully within the discourse of wild majesty, but the
sentiment is immediately poisoned by the worm of modernity:

'Only, don't stay with him too long', the planter continues: 'I did. The
look of disdain which curled his lips when I first saw him had vanished, and his haughty carriage seemed about to relax. A sudden panic
seized me, and I fled from the Carib court circle somewhat uncere-
moniously, for I feared, and almost expected, he would come up to me
and whisper in my ear, as did a certain king in the Blue Mountains
of Jamaica: "Buckra! Won't you give me a pair of your old shoes?"'
Naturally, after this we went by night, and were determined not
to stay too long. (Bonsal 1912: 238)

So Bonsal and his companions travel by night from Roseau, a difficult journey across swollen torrents made with a hesitant guide.

After six hours' travelling through the night, the first light of dawn
revealed to us the little shacks of thatch in which these refugees from
civilisation house. These huts were aligned, somewhat irregularly, it is
true, and embowered in shrubbery, along the bank of a mountain
stream, which, a few yards farther on, suddenly ended its musical
course through the rock barriers, and, with a wild cry of freedom,
sprang into the ocean that lay so still fifty feet below.[65]

All is quiet in the village and the tourists remain hidden in
the shrubbery, like twitchers, waiting for the Caribs to bestir
themselves.

---

[65] Six hours by night from Roseau to Salybia in 1907 seems unlikely.

[A]t last our patience was rewarded. One by one, and without a word to each other, several young men came out of the silent huts, slipped down the mountain-side, and plunged into the ocean. For a few moments, like porpoises, and quite as silent in their play, they plunged and gambolled about, and then, with great overarm strokes, came swimming back to the shore. Other forms were stirring now in and about the straw-huts, and when the bathers seated themselves upon the rocks which dotted the strand, their women came down to them with strange guttural cries, and gave them their morning smokes of loosely-rolled tobacco-leaves. Then, slowly and lovingly, they streaked and smeared the still dripping bodies of the returned swimmers with a yellow ochre chalk or paint. A moment later the young men were gone, darting out through the breakers in their canoes, with the wonderful watermanship which is their still unimpaired inheritance from the fifteenth-century Caribs, who astonished Columbus and the early navigators with their aquatic exploits. (239)

The picture is dramatic, even moving; but distinctly unsettling. The departing fishermen sing a mournful song, which the visitors' black guide ('who did not seek to conceal the disdain in which he held the shiftless Caribs') translates as follows: 'In olden times we were men and ate our enemies. | Now we are women and only eat Cassava cakes.'

When we came out of hiding, we were personally conducted about the village by the King, who, we understood, had achieved this proud position, not by birth, but by reason of seniority. He was a dried-up little man, who had evidently attained a very great age, and he showed more signs of the negroid admixture than any of his subjects. We were not invited to enter any of the thatched huts, but, as far as we could see from the outside, they differed in no wise from the usual habitations of the negro islanders.

The only reported conversation with the Caribs themselves involves barter with 'the King' for limes and baskets: 'The monarch relaxed, and there were symptoms of approaching talk about old shoes and other worn-out baubles of our artificial civilization. So, as the sun began to climb towards its zenith, and flood the dark mountain paths with its light and warmth, we left the Carib reservation' (240–1).

Bonsal's summary of this brief visit is as 'an interesting experience, and one which I am not likely to forget', and he takes care, in words which recall Aspinall's, to 'recommend the little journey as being worth the trouble to those who come this way'. There was 'the feeling, or illusion, if you will', that they had seen the aboriginal West Indians 'much as Columbus presented them to the astonished gaze of the Catholic Kings'; and the certainty—from cranial formation and skin colour—that the Caribs are a 'new ethnological type', quite different from their various cousins in Central America or Guiana (241–2).

This conclusion is reached, even through what Bonsal admits is 'the untrained eye of the unscientific observer' (242), on the basis of a visit which lasted, on a generous estimate, about four hours, less than a third of the time it took to get to the Reserve and back to Roseau. The briefness of the visit looks forward to the 'classic' visitors in the middle of the century, like Jean Rhys and Patrick Leigh Fermor, and then on to the vehicular visitors considered in Chapter 6, many of whom stay for less than four hours. Bonsal, however, stands as a landmark in the long history of condescension. His primary response to the Caribs is aestheticizing—'wonderfully proportioned bodies . . . golden bronze hue . . . resplendent colour of their skins' (240–2), epithets attached to people he watched swimming from the cover of the local shrubbery, an activity rather closer to voyeurism than to ethnography. The only conversation he held was to barter with the Chief, an 'entering-wedge of commercialism' (241), which is deplored at the same time as it is encouraged. And, untrained eye or not, some ethnological conclusions are portentously conveyed. Definitely worth four hours of anyone's time—except perhaps the Caribs'.

The one touristic trope Bonsal does not offer is the photographic pose although, from Ober onwards, photographs had been taken of the Caribs, despite the difficulty of carrying the unwieldy equipment. Shortly after Bonsal's flying visit, a very fine, but pseudonymous, amateur photographer, writing under the name 'Vaquero', visited Dominica, his 'principal inducement', he wrote, being 'to see the Caribs who live in their reservation called Salybia' (1914: 169).[66] Of the twelve pages of his book dedicated to 'seeing the Caribs', ten describe the difficulties of getting to and from Salybia from Roseau, and

[66] He took the photograph reproduced in *WM*: fig. 25 (p. 271).

one-and-a-half the difficulties in getting a group of Caribs together for a photograph. The problem was not their unwillingness to be photographed: just the opposite—they were delighted, but wasted so much time going home to change into their best clothes that the light almost disappeared. 'Vaquero' repeats the now familiar phrases—'last strongholds of the unfortunate Caribs', 'now peacefully become extinct as a race', 'this interesting and fast disappearing race', 'inundated by such a quantity of negro blood' (169, 170, 174, 174), but his other comments, mostly glossing this final phase, are based entirely on observation of physical characteristics.

3   The Administrator's Fiat: Henry Hesketh Bell and the Establishment of the Carib Reserve (1900–1921)

> These Caribs appear to have had almost every quality which would ennoble a race; indominitable courage, patriotism, and a high sense of military honour. Unlike the effeminate *Arawaks* and Yellow Caribs, which peopled Jamaica, the larger islands and part of the mainland, the Caribs of St. Vincent, Grenada, St. Lucia & Dominica preferred death to slavery, and perished almost to a man in defence of their liberty. (Hesketh Bell, unpublished letter)[1]

The imperialistic tone of Stephen Bonsal's 1912 travel book, which closed the previous chapter, had of course been made possible by the USA's comprehensive military defeat of Spain in 1898, prompting the most far-reaching shift in the geopolitics of the Caribbean since the triumph of the Haitian revolution. For Britain, 1898 made abundantly clear what had already been on the cards for some time: that it should either take steps to shore up its weaker colonies in the West Indies or risk losing them to a resurgent USA, or even possibly to France. In the British debates that followed, Dominica played a special part. Financially it was in a weak position, with a small revenue and large annual expenses. Culturally, it was an island that often seemed to visitors more French than English, and its local connections tended naturally to be with the neighbouring French islands of Martinique and Guadeloupe. And yet every visitor remarked on its special qualities and enormous potential. So, when the pro-imperialist Joseph Chamberlain took over the Colonial Office in 1895, Dominica was set to become a test case

---

[1] Draft of a letter to *The Times*, probably never sent (BP5: A1). For an explanation of the references to Bell's papers, see the note on Manuscript Collections at the beginning of the References section.

for the 'new imperialism', with Henry Hesketh Bell as Chamberlain's instrument. The effects of all this on the situation of the Caribs would turn out to be surprisingly far-reaching, and Bell himself, as well as wielding considerable influence as the island's Administrator, was also a voluminous writer about the Caribs, penning newspaper reports, an official Colonial Office report, and drafts of various chapters towards a book he never completed, along with a later autobiographical memoir. However, this period also sees the beginnings of the long process of contact between the Caribs and the majority Dominican population, especially its political class, responsible for slowly forging the nationalist ethos that would inherit the island after independence. The local political situation will therefore require some extensive exposition.

DOMINICA AT THE END OF THE NINETEENTH CENTURY

Dominica is an exception to most generalizations about the West Indies, but one can risk saying that, like the other British islands in the area, its economy suffered badly during the second half of the nineteenth century and its problems were generally of little interest to the metropolis unless some act of violence impinged on the national consciousness—as it had done in 1844 over the brutal execution of Jean Pierre Motard during the so-called 'guerre nègre', an incident which involved several members of the maternal family of the novelist Jean Rhys, and around family memories of which she was much later to write the novel *Wide Sargasso Sea*.[2]

Two distinguished imperial travellers produced damning words about Dominica and its governance during this period. After a brief visit in mid-century, Anthony Trollope had written about Roseau's 'desolation, apathy, and ruin', the people 'chattering, idle and listless', the streets 'covered with thick, rank grass', and, worst of all, 'no sign either of money made or of money making' (1968: 161). Then, thirty years later, in his influential travelogue, *The English in the West Indies, or The Bow of Ulysses* [1887], James Anthony Froude struck exactly the

---

[2] See Hulme (1994*a*), and cf., for another aspect of Lockhart involvement in Dominican political affairs, Thomas (1999: 168–71).

same note, but after a more extended stay on the island. On its political affairs he reflected the views of his host, John Spencer Churchill, the local President, who was clearly frustrated at his lack of power and influence: 'the duty of an administrator of Dominica, it appears', noted Froude, 'is to sit still and do nothing, and to watch the flickering in the socket of the last remains of English influence and authority' (1909: 130).[3] Froude had come to Dominica with a lively sense of its historical importance as an island that Britain had fought hard, on several occasions, to take out of French hands. But only 100 of the population of 30,000 were English, and the only influential Europeans were the Catholic priests. What Froude saw on the streets of Roseau was enough to convince him that, although Dominica had once been regarded as 'the choicest jewel in the necklace of the Antilles', it was now deeply neglected: 'For the last half-century we have left it to desolation, as a child leaves a plaything that it is tired of' (135). As the language suggests, Froude laid the blame for this state of affairs firmly at the imperial gate. Dominica would surrender herself tomorrow to France or to the United States: 'Why should she care any more for England, which has so little care for her? Beauties conscious of their charms do not like to be so thrown aside' (142). Froude combines the language of chivalry: Dominica as the prize England had won in manly contest with her French rival, with the language of enterprise: Dominica as the virgin garden of the world which, if not 'cultivated' by the youth of England, will turn elsewhere.

Froude met one exemplary figure on Dominica, the medical officer and planter, Dr H. A. A. Nicholls, 'an English gentleman who has gone the right way to work there' (145). Froude went to visit Nicholls's small estate, cultivated on scientific principles, and was deeply impressed by the quality of the limes and coffee, but also by the number of botanical experiments under way, and by the 'innocent affection' with which the black labourers clung to Nicholls. Needless to say, 'being the only man in the island

---

[3] Writing in one of the local newspapers, William Davies identified Froude's other guide ('Mr F——') as Acton Don Lockhart, Jean Rhys's uncle (*Dominica Dial*, 19 Mar. 1888). Sue Thomas (1999: 18) suggests that 'lost heart', Froude's naming of the malady of the English whites on the island, could even be a pun on Lockhart, especially as the phrase occurs in a paragraph describing his tours with Mr F——.

of really superior attainments, he had tried in vain to win one of the seats in the elective part of the legislature' (146). Nicholls and Froude discuss why it should be that Englishmen flock to Ceylon and Borneo to become planters when, 'comparatively at their own doors', there is this immeasurably more fertile island. The explanation, Froude supposes, 'is the misgiving that the West Indies are consigned by the tendencies of English policy to the black population, and that a local government created by representatives of the negro vote would make a residence there for an energetic and self-respecting European less tolerable than in any other part of the globe' (146).

Froude's conclusion is a rousing call for renewed imperial action:

If the Antilles are ever to thrive, each of them ... should have some trained and skilful man at its head, unembarrassed by local elected assemblies. The whites have become so weak that they would welcome the abolition of such assemblies. The blacks do not care for politics and would be pleased to see them swept away to-morrow if they were governed wisely and fairly. Of course, in that case it would be necessary to appoint governors who would command confidence and respect. But let governors be sent who would be governors indeed, like those who administer the Indian presidencies, and the white residents would gather heart again, and English and American capitalists would bring their money and their enterprise, and the blacks would grow upwards instead of downwards. Let us persist in the other line, let us use the West Indian governments as asylums for average worthy persons who have to be provided for, and force on them black parliamentary institutions as a remedy for such persons' inefficiency, and these beautiful countries will become like Hayti, with Obeah triumphant, and children offered to the devil and salted and eaten, till the conscience of mankind wakens again and the Americans sweep them all away. (144)

The response to Froude was vehement, although it is not clear that many of the counter-voices were heard in London. J. J. Thomas's *Froudacity* is the best-known riposte from inside the West Indies; C. S. Salmon's was also noteworthy, coming from a respected colonial official with experience of the West Indies.[4]

---

[4] Thomas 1969 [1889] and Salmon 1888. See also Davis 1888, writing from British Guiana.

Within Dominica itself, one of the local newspapers, which had serialized Froude's chapters on Dominica, then poured particular scorn on his picture of Dr Nicholls, accusing Nicholls of appropriating to himself the botanical experiments that had in fact been initiated by his predecessor, Dr John Imray, who had 'bequeathed to his unworthy and ungrateful assistant the fruits of his own talent and industry'; and suggesting in no uncertain terms that Nicholls had lied shamelessly about the actual financial returns possible: 'As for the "£1,000 a-year from 30 acres of land," hardly anyone who can read and write has not had his little joke on the subject.'[5] Another interesting critic, writing from within the West Indies, was Hesketh Bell, future Administrator of Dominica but at this time a minor colonial official in Grenada. Bell criticized Froude's dismissive view of Grenada to which, Bell sharply notes, Froude devotes a whole chapter despite having only come ashore for dinner and left the same evening. Interestingly, in the light of his later experience in Dominica, Bell criticizes Froude for judging the prosperity of a colony by the number of English-born inhabitants: 'We are inclined to think, however, that a colony derives more benefit from a settled population of well-educated and energetic creoles', making it clear that the term 'creole' can apply equally well to 'those born in the West Indies, of English parents' as it can to a 'coloured' population (Bell 1893: 195–6). Bell's attitudes towards the 'energetic creoles' would change dramatically after he went to Dominica, as the rest of this chapter will demonstrate.

Since 1831 free non-whites had had full political and social rights on Dominica. Given the much smaller number of white planters, merchants, and attorneys than on other British West Indian islands, this quickly led to the rise of what became known as the 'mulatto ascendancy' or, later, the *gros bourg*, a group of closely related families who had a significant say in the direction of island politics and who made life very difficult for a series of colonial administrators.[6] This rather large, active, and

---

[5] [William Davies], *Dominica Dial*, 24 Mar. 1888.
[6] This grouping consisted of a Roseau-based group of lawyers and merchants, a mixture of free coloured families, sometimes descendants of settlers from Martinique, and the outside children of white planters. The social base of the

influential, but by no means unified group, certainly served to complicate Dominican racial politics during the nineteenth century, often siding ultimately with the forces of colonial law and order despite being regarded by the representatives of those forces as fundamentally unreliable (Trouillot 1988: 102).

As the tide of metropolitan opinion moved back towards direct control of the West Indian islands' affairs from London (Crown Colony government), Dominica was the most vociferously opposed to this measure. In 1865 the size of the Legislative Assembly on the island had been drastically reduced, taking power from the elected representatives, and in 1871 Dominica had became part of a new Leeward Islands federation with its seat of government on Antigua—a further sleight, in Dominican eyes. The main opposition to the move towards Crown Colony government came from two men within the 'mulatto ascendancy' who inherited the mantle (and the printing press) of the radical politician and journalist Charles Gordon Falconer, namely William Davies and Alexander Lockhart.[7] The *Dominican* was edited by Lockhart from 1872 to 1880 and by Augustus Righton (known as Papa Dom), from 1880 to 1907. Davies founded and edited the *Dominica Dial* from 1882 to 1891, supporting the Party of Progress which had been founded to push for progressive legislation (compulsory education, founding of grammar school and public library) and to defend representative democracy on the island against what was correctly seen as the authoritarian intentions of the Colonial Office.[8]

Froude's analysis of British neglect, and of the failure of the federal system, was music to the ears of this group, but it was horrified by his disdain for democracy and by the casual racism

group would gradually encompass some white Dominicans who identified themselves with the island rather than with the British 'home', and a rising black middle class. The best studies of this period in Dominica are Boromé 1969, on which much of the next few paragraphs is based, and Trouillot (1988: 1–140; 1989, and 1992). For general background on Dominican history over the last 150 years, see in particular Honychurch 1995; also Baker 1994; Clyde 1980; Green 1999; André and Christian 1992; and Paravisini-Gebert 1999.

[7] Charles Gordon Falconer (1819–72: see Boromé 1959–60); William Davies (1840–1916); Alexander Ramsey Capoulade Lockhart (d. 1924). Davies and Lockhart were both coloured descendants of white settlers.

[8] Even the foundation of reading clubs and, eventually, a public library were issues both politicized and racialized on Dominica (see Boromé 1970). On the development of the press in the Caribbean, Lent (1977: 22–56).

which assumed that, as long as they are firmly led, 'the blacks there, as everywhere, are happy with their yams, and cocoa nuts and land crabs' (Froude 1909: 128). Most of all, perhaps, it was distraught at his failure to even recognize its members as a distinct group, racially, commercially, and politically. As elected local members of the Assembly, they were left to recognize themselves in the 'black parliamentary institutions' which would lead inevitably to satanism and cannibalism—not the most flattering of portraits for those who tended to see themselves as progressive liberals and democrats.[9]

Froude's attitudes towards blacks were indicative of mainstream British opinion in the second half of the nineteenth century. The humanitarian accents of earlier decades now tended to be drowned out by the aggressive response to any forms of native resistance to imperialist projects. In the West Indies, in particular, growing dissatisfaction (among whites) with the effects of Emancipation intensified the kind of sentiments so forceably uttered by Thomas Carlyle in his essay on 'The Nigger Question', first given in 1849, which provided scenarios and imagery for the decades which followed, and in particular for the public debate following the uprising at Morant Bay in Jamaica, the execution of several of its supposed leaders, and the indictment (and acquittal) of the Governor, Edward Eyre.[10]

During this period the British Colonial Office's policy had been to cover economic shortfall in the smaller West Indian

---

[9] See [William Davies], *Dominica Dial*, 17 Mar. 1888. Unlike Froude, Trollope had well understood that in order to understand the West Indies one needed to discuss the position of 'coloured men' (see Gikandi 1996: 96). In these years positive assessments of miscegenation were uncommon, so it is not surprising that the *Dominican* (28 Jan. 1897) reproduced a long and thoughtful article from the *Spectator* reflecting on the remarkable achievements of half-breeds and mulattos, despite the popular racial prejudices about cross-breeding. The article was prompted by the death of Antonio Maceo in Cuba. The dominant view at the time, expressed in Eugene Talbot's *Degeneracy: Its Causes, Signs and Results* [1898], was that mulattoes tended to 'morbid proclivities' and 'retrogressive tendencies' (Stepan 1985: 112–13).

[10] On Morant Bay, see Heuman 1994; for the public debate, Hall 1989. Most of this developing discourse of racism had had predictably little to say about the indigenous population of the Caribbean, although in 'The Nigger Question' Carlyle did contrast the resilience of the black African with 'all manner of Caribs and others [who] pine into annihilation in presence of the pale faces' (1915: 311). Froude was Carlyle's literary executor and constant reference point.

islands by raising more local taxes, an approach that was opposed by most local politicians, who would stand to lose by any reorganization of the islands' extremely uneven tax patterns. In Dominica the serious problems which dominated the decade following 1888 were started by the fiasco of an attempted road construction programme, a scheme which would eventually—but almost a century later—have a decisive impact on the life of the Caribs. In 1887 a Road Board had been established and an English engineer, Edward Robins, contracted to oversee the building of nineteen bridges over rivers between Roseau and Layou, and a carriage road the length of the island. The bridges Robins started building soon collapsed, and a street he constructed in Roseau flooded badly because of poor drainage. He unwisely tangled with the Road Board, on which William Davies sat, and ended by being held up to public ridicule and needing police protection. A damning report from the commander of the Royal Engineers in the West Indies confirmed the Road Board's charges of incompetence and extravagance. Local feelings were hardly assuaged when the disastrous 1891 flood swept away most of the Roseau–Layou road and the one bridge at Canefield which Robins had succeeded in building. The underlying problem was that Dominica's finances permitted no loans to support development or even to repair its infrastructure, yet its cultivation was coming to a standstill and labourers were leaving the island for work in Venezuela and French Guiana.[11]

After Emancipation, British policy in the West Indies had been to try to maintain the availability of a workforce on the plantations by making it exceedingly difficult for emancipated slaves and their descendants to buy their own land: Crown Land prices were pitched deliberately beyond reach, abandoned estates were used as collateral elsewhere, land taxes were introduced. On Dominica, matters came to a head when a resident of La Plaine,

---

[11] The contrast with Martinique is instructive. Visiting in 1887, Lafcadio Hearn wrote a paean of praise to 'the excellent national roads,—limestone highways, solid, broad, faultlessly graded,—that wind from town to town, from hamlet to hamlet, over mountains, over ravines; ascending by zigzags to heights of twenty-five hundred feet; traversing the primeval forests of the interior; now skirting the dizziest precipices, now descending into the lowest valleys' (1923: 106). There were 303 miles of these roads: nearly 300 miles more than there were on Dominica at the same time.

a poor community on the windward coast with very difficult communications with Roseau, was about to have his house sold for non-payment of the tax due on it under the 1888 Land and House Act. After a bailiff and a policeman were driven off by protesters, the Governor of the colony, William Frederick Haynes Smith, ordered the resident ejected—with a little help from nine policemen and twenty-five sailors Smith had in the meantime rustled up from HMS *Mohawk*. The crowd threw stones, the police opened fire, eight policemen and sailors were slightly injured, four protestors were shot dead. Davies's newspaper, the *Dial*, had recently folded. However, faced with this new crisis he and his allies founded the *Dominica Guardian*, under the management of Joseph Hilton Steber, a professional journalist. The new paper proposed 'to *guard* and protect our people and country from the tyranny of those who believe it to be their duty to add oppression to our misfortunes'.[12]

The Secretary for the Colonies, Lord Ripon, faced with the Governor's advice that the only solution for Dominica was Crown Colony government, decided to initiate an inquiry into conditions on the island, which he entrusted to Sir Robert G. Hamilton, who had just retired as Governor of Tasmania. It was Hamilton's report that produced the two intriguing letters from rival Carib chiefs discussed in Chapter 1. As far as the contemporary political wrangling was concerned, Hamilton tended to side with the local elected members of the Legislature against the Governor, demonstrating an independence of approach which did not enamour him to the Colonial Office.[13] One official noted—privately—that Hamilton had fallen victim to 'clever but slimy local politicians who represent one of the least desiderable results of the advance of civilization in our West Indian Colonies' (quoted Boromé 1969: 42). In practice, Ripon authorized many of Hamilton's ideas, baulking however at the

---

[12] 3 June 1893 (quoted in Boromé 1969: 40). The community in La Plaine was far from fully integrated into the island. It was described in the Colonial Office 'Notes on West Indian Riots, 1881–1903' as: 'situated on the Windward coast of the island, to a large extent isolated from the capital, Roseau, and the more prosperous parts of the Colony, and the home of an unruly population continually engaged in a smuggling traffic with Martinique' (CO 884/9/no.147: 3). On the general Caribbean problem of access of land, see Holt 1992.

[13] Hamilton had been Gladstone's permanent under-secretary to Ireland and a strong supporter of home rule.

suggestion that substantial credit was due the island for £312,000 received by the British Treasury for the sale of Dominica's Crown Lands between 1763 and 1778. However, at this point, in 1895, matters took a decisive turn with the appointment of Joseph Chamberlain as Secretary for the Colonies.

By the 1890s the whole idea of imperial life had been rejustified, not just by Froude, but also by writers such as John Seeley and Charles Dilke.[14] These three were the grand ideologists of the Empire, whose writings had already shaped Chamberlain's attitudes; so, when asked by Lord Salisbury to join the new coalition government in June 1895, Chamberlain opted for the post of Colonial Secretary and was determined to make an immediate mark. Although nearly 60, he was vigorous, confident, and opinionated, and ready for action after nine years out of office. Froude (who had just died) had provided probably the strongest influence on Chamberlain's views: they had known each other since the early 1880s and shared many opinions, especially as to the need for a firm white metropolitan hand in the colonies. Other influences on Chamberlain included C. S. Salmon, a career diplomat with much experience of the Caribbean who, as noted above, had written a detailed response to Froude, but who was also keen to attract 'young Englishmen' to start cultivating the islands' neglected estates (Salmon 1888: 41), a call Chamberlain would soon echo; and one of the undersecretaries at the Colonial Office, C. P. Lucas, who had written the standard modern guide, *A Historical Geography of the British Colonies* (1890), and whose two sentences on the Caribs may have been the source of Chamberlain's evident interest.[15] A

---

[14] Dilke had preceded Froude with his tour of the Empire (1868); Seeley wrote one of the century's most popular history books about the expansion of the Empire (1914 [1883]). For recent studies of these two writers, see Nicholls 1995; and Wormell 1980; and, for a more general perspective, Madden 1959.

[15] 'In Dominica there is still found a remnant of the aboriginal population of the West Indies, for the thick woods on the north-eastern side of the island give shelter to some 300 Caribs, a shy and retiring people, whose chief intercourse with the other inhabitants is for the purpose of selling their baskets, hammocks, or bows and arrows. They are in no way a striking race, but better featured than the negro' (Lucas 1890: ii. 165). Will stresses the influential role of Lucas as a conduit for many of these current discussions of imperial issues, although Chamberlain would have known some of them directly (1970: 229–45).

more unexpected influence soon emerged. Of humble background—in fact a civil servant in the Department of Inland Revenue when his book was published—Benjamin Kidd distilled many late nineteenth-century ideas into his extremely popular *Social Evolution*, which appeared in 1894, with nine reprints within twelve months, just at the right moment to have an impact on Chamberlain in his new job. *Social Evolution* was a paean to the solid Anglo-Saxon qualities of 'humanity, strength, an uprightness of character, and devotion to the immediate calls of duty without thought of brilliant ends and ideal results' (1896: 350). These qualities had served the Empire well and were absolutely necessary for the development of the tropical zones of the world, inhabited as these were by 'peoples of low social efficiency': 'The love of action, the insatiable desire for strenuous energetic labour is everywhere characteristic of the peoples who have come to occupy the foremost places in the world' (1896: 57–8).[16] Kidd offered updated versions both of Lockean improvement and of Carlylean racial ideology: European races owed it to mankind to unlock the vast resources of the tropics which had been left untapped by the indolent 'natives' living there. As a general argument about the Caribbean this was a two-edged sword from the British point of view: after all, just who had had political control of many of the islands for the last two centuries? In the particular case of Dominica, however, such an argument could be useful since the non-whites and even the section of the white creoles who had made life difficult for a string of colonial administrators could therefore be blamed, at least in part, for not 'developing' the island's resources. For Kidd, the tropics were an alien environment for Europeans, but too economically important to be left to the natives.[17] Fortunately, he did offer a sense of duty:

[16] *Social Evolution* was reviewed by Theodore Roosevelt (*North American Review*, 161 (1895))—and was the source of his popular phrase about the 'strenous life' (1901). Kidd developed his argument in *The Control of the Tropics* (1898).

[17] Robert Knox's foundational text, *The Races of Men* (1850), had suggested that barriers to acclimatization would make European colonization of the tropics impossible (Stocking 1987: 64–5). The US physician J. Aitken Meiggs, contributing to Nott and Gliddon's *Indigenous Races of the Earth* (1857), refined this view by suggesting that the white race could only live in the tropics as a master race, with physical labour left to the natives (Stepan 1985: 103).

The tropics in such circumstances can only be governed as a trust for civilization, and with a full sense of the responsibility which such a trust involves. The first principle of success in undertaking such a duty seems to the writer to be a clear recognition of the cardinal fact that in the tropics the white man lives and works only as a diver lives and works under water. Alike in a moral, in an ethical, and in a political sense, the atmosphere he breathes must be that of another region, that which produced him, and to which he belongs. Neither physically, morally, nor politically, can he be acclimatized in the tropics. The people among whom he lives and works are often separated from him by thousands of years of development; he cannot, therefore, be allowed to administer government from any local and lower standard he may develop. If he has any right to be there at all, it is in the name of civilization; if our civilization has any right there at all, it is because it represents higher ideals of humanity, a higher type of social order. (Kidd 1898: 53–4)[18]

In August 1895, soon after taking office, Chamberlain stated his ideological position with respect to the colonies in a major speech to the House of Commons. He deplored the fact that Britain had in many cases neglected its duty. If the people of 'this country' are not willing to invest some of their superfluous wealth in the colonies, then it would, Chamberlain stated categorically, have been better never to have gone there in the first place. Although South Africa was soon to take all his attention, his first concern was for the West Indian islands, typical examples of what he called—in a much-quoted phrase—the 'undeveloped estates', that were in need of imperial assistance.[19] Chamberlain's private view, although it did not appear so openly in his public speeches, was that it was necessary to keep up the number of white colonists 'with a view to preventing the islands from sinking to the level to which other negro communities have sunk'.[20]

---

[18] *The Control of the Tropics* was written in response to the war of 1898 in the Caribbean. Chamberlain praised the book in an article in *Scribner's Magazine* (1898) and worked with Kidd after 1902 (Crook 1984: 115–25).

[19] 'I regard many of our Colonies as being in the condition of undeveloped estates, and estates that can never be developed without Imperial assistance' (*The Parliamentary Debates*, 4th ser. 36, 641–2 (22 Aug. 1895)). On Chamberlain and the West Indies, see Will (1970: 229–73); and Kubicek (1969: 68–9).

[20] Minute from Joseph Chamberlain to Hicks Beach, 26 Nov. 1895 (JC 14/3/10). For an explanation of the references to Chamberlain's papers, see the note on Manuscript Collections at the beginning of the List of References. The Birmingham

Then, in 1897, in a speech to the Colonial Institute, Chamberlain distinguished between what he called three stages of 'our imperial history'. The first stage lasted until the American War of Independence. The second stage was marked by a sense that all the colonies would eventually break away: the spirit of 'little England' dominated. But now the third stage was under way, the 'new imperialism', or what Chamberlain called 'the true conception of our Empire'. However, that 'truth' is immediately glossed by the distinction, already a cornerstone of colonial policy, between the 'self-governing colonies', no longer thought of as dependencies, and the 'tropical colonies', which are still dependent.[21] In the former, Chamberlain says, the sense of possession has given way to a sense of kinship; in the latter a sense of possession has given way to a sense of obligation. The former are thought of as 'part of ourselves . . . united to us', the latter, by implication, not. In the latter, Chamberlain says, white inhabitants will always be outnumbered by 'the native population', in the former, he does *not* say, whites predominate (Chamberlain 1914: ii. 2–3). The distinction is fundamentally racial.

On coming into office Chamberlain appointed a four-man West India Royal Commission to investigate the local results of the severe economic depression in the West Indies. This was therefore the first region-wide commission since 1842. The three-month investigation produced an extensive report in 1897, which is sometimes regarded as the 'Magna Charta of the West Indian peasant' for its recommendation that the labouring population be settled on small plots of land as peasant proprietors.[22] The report tried to find ways of renewing the sugar industry on most of the islands, while recognizing that on Dominica, where sugar had always been less important, the industry would never be re-established and that the future lay in crop diversification. The report's main recommendation left open the question of land disposition:

culture which formed Chamberlain had a long history of knowledge about and investment in the West Indies.

[21] This is a distinction usually traced back to Lord Grey's commentary, *The Colonial Policy of Lord John Russell's Administration* (1853): see Stocking (1987: 240).

[22] C. Y. Shepherd, 'Peasant agriculture in the Leeward and Windward islands', *Tropical Agriculture*, 24 (1947): 63 (quoted by Richardson (1992: 171)). On the fraught discourse of peasantry in Dominica, see Trouillot 1989.

Some of this land ought to be disposed of under proper regulations to peasant cultivators, and some of it may prove attractive to investors of capital or persons who are in a position to occupy and cultivate estates of their own. The Government of the Colony will have to be guided by circumstances in the disposal of it; it is not possible, under present conditions, to say what opportunities will arise, which may lead to its being occupied and cultivated. (Great Britain 1897: 51)

The reference to 'peasant cultivators' was no doubt a significant breakthrough in terms of official discourse; but the language of 'investors' and 'capital' and 'estates' was still prominent, would still be preferred by Chamberlain, and would still be seen as more appropriate for Dominica.

For Chamberlain, Dominica became the test case of this new imperial policy. Based on Hamilton's recommendations, the Colonial Office had suggested a £15,000 grant to pay off the island's debt, and a £100,000 loan for the construction of new roads, wharves, and a light railway. Hicks Beach, the Chancellor of the Exchequer, agreed the grant but turned down the loan—on the grounds, privately expressed, that Dominica was a worthless possession which might well be swapped with the French 'for something in Africa'.[23] However, he agreed to a relief package for the West Indies when Chamberlain made it clear that the alternative would be retaliatory tariff duties aimed at the European countries who had export bounties on their beet sugar.[24] Chamberlain pushed Dominica's case hard: 'The case of Dominica is altogether an exceptional one. It is, I believe, one of the very richest islands in the possession of the Crown in the West Indies in the natural productiveness of the soil; at the same time it is an island in which practically nothing has been done, and to this day the very best Crown land in the island, amounting to about 100,000 acres, is absolutely unproductive because there are no means of communication.'[25]

In line with Froude's trenchantly expressed views, Chamberlain saw the need for a new planting class, which would have to be persuaded to go to Dominica by the opportunities that the

---

[23] Letter from Hicks Beach to Chamberlain, 19 Dec. 1895 (JC 14/3/15).

[24] After yet another report (Naftel's in 1898), a large grant of £250,000 was given to shore up the ailing West Indian sugar industry while the economy could be diversified through the development of such crops as citrus, coffee, and bananas.

[25] *The Parliamentary Debates*, 4th ser., 37, 1409 (28 Feb. 1896).

Colonial Office could provide. Dr Nicholls was his exemplar, drawn from Froude; and the insular model, it seems, was Ceylon, the leading British colony when it came to tropical agriculture. C. O. Naftel, a leading member of the 1897 Royal Commission, had spent twenty-two years in Ceylon and P. A. Templer, the current Administrator on Dominica, was a former Ceylon resident himself (Boromé 1969: 45). One of the first large purchases of Crown Lands in Dominica—the 1,200 acres known as 'Middleham'—was made by Mr Gordon Fowler, a retired coffee planter from Ceylon, in 1898.[26]

After heated debates in the House of Commons, grants for Dominica were approved early in 1896. However, the catch was that the second sum—for road-building—was dependent upon Dominica accepting Crown Colony status. The Legislative Assembly in Dominica furiously rejected this move, condemning Britain for trying to introduce 'the Oriental style of government' (quoted by Boromé 1969: 47). The voting was on race lines. The seven coloured elected members voted against (including William Davies and Alexander Lockhart), as did the one coloured nominated member. The proposal was supported by the six white nominated members (including Jean Rhys's uncle, Acton Don Lockhart, and Sholto Pemberton, previously a defender of representative government and ally of Davies). Davies, now editor of the *Dominica Guardian*, wrote about a race war. The Administrator, Templer, dissolved the Assembly and after a viciously fought election found himself, when the new Assembly convened in July, with an 8–6 majority in favour of Chamberlain's proposal. The *Guardian* singled out for insult the coloured nominee, James Cox Fillan, who voted in favour. 'He sat in his seat,' it reported, 'like a brown diamond in a Caucasian setting, [and] simply nodded his head like a Chinese doll, together with the other Government dummies, in approval of the measure' (quoted in Boromé 1969: 49). The warship *Intrepid* spent most of this time in the roadstead at Roseau.

[26] Hesketh Bell would later say that he had been looking for 'the same class of young men, from Home, who have been such a success in Ceylon, Burma and Malaya' (1946: 28). Bell thought that his plantation, Sylvania, ought to become the 'Nuwara Eliya of Dominica' (1903a: 7), referring to the famously fertile valley of Ceylon.

After Crown Colony government was established, Alexander Lockhart resolutely refused official positions and acted as President of the Representative Government Association until his death in 1924. William Davies retired altogether from public life to tend his estates at Melville Hall and later Concord, next to the Carib Reserve—in which capacity he will re-enter the story at a much later stage, before being dramatically killed in the hurricane of 1916 which swept his house into a valley, smashing it to pieces. Both men, however, continued to act as irritants to successive Administrators through their regular columns and letters in local newspapers.

The incumbent Administrator, Templer, set the basic pattern for the road scheme that Chamberlain thought would reverse Dominica's fortunes. However, Templer's illness and early retirement in April 1899 set the stage for the appearance in Dominica of Henry Hesketh Bell, the first colonial official to take any significant interest in the island's indigenous inhabitants.

THE IMPERIAL ADMINISTRATOR

Henry Hesketh Bell is widely regarded as having played a key role in the modern history of Dominica. During his six years as Administrator, from 1899 to 1905, he was responsible for many attempts at innovation, which laid the basis for the island's future development. He won over a good number of potential critics on Dominica by his boundless energy and tireless diplomacy. He pioneered hurricane insurance, organized a new building for the public library, experimented with new crops, encouraged new settlers from England, established the steamer service from Roseau to Portsmouth, developed his own plantation (Sylvania), and assisted the growth of the banana industry. However, he is generally best remembered for the Imperial Road, a truck road from Roseau to Bassin Will (still referred to as Bells), in the centre of the island, which would later be continued to the windward coast; and for the establishment, or at least formal recognition, of the so-called Carib Reserve. Bell certainly promoted the bill that Froude had drafted and Chamberlain enacted: restitution of a British planter class, preferably newly minted from the metropolis, assisted by modern experimentation in agriculture and by the establishment of a decent

FIG. 6. Hesketh Bell in 1899, the year he took his appointment as Administrator of Dominica (photograph in the Royal Commonwealth Society Collection, Cambridge University Library (Y3011F/16), reproduced with permission of the Syndics of Cambridge University Library).

set of communications.[27] Bell got full support from Chamberlain and was allowed to correspond directly with him on all Dominican matters, rather than—as had previously been the case—via the Governor of the Leeward Islands, based in Antigua (BP2: 19 July 1901).

[27] Bell said that his powers made him 'practically a Dictator' (BP2: 13 Dec. 1899). His friend Neville Chamberlain had first brought Bell to his father's attention after Bell had asked him 'to use his influence on my behalf with his father' (BP2: 1 Aug.

Bell's assessment—reached so quickly that one might assume he had arrived with it in place—was that the 'natives of Dominica', by which he meant the Dominican-born white and mulatto planters, 'lack[ed] the means for rapidly increasing the productiveness of their lands' (1899: 3), a phrase he later glossed, less ambiguously, by noting that 'The conditions of life are so easy in the West Indies and the climate so conducive to *dolce far niente*, that energy on the part of those who lack the spur of want, is comparatively rare' (22). This 1899 letter to his Governor, in Antigua, is full of the need for 'capital, energy, and roads' (11) to enable the 'opening-up of new lands' (6) which are currently in a condition of 'luxuriant waste' (7).

Bell was a fine publicist and attracted a number of new ventures on Crown Lands, thirty on his own estimation, with a total investment of about £40,000 (BP2: 12 Oct. 1904). In September 1900, while on leave in London, Bell wrote a long letter to *The Times* under the title 'Planting in Dominica', extolling the virtues of the island and seeking young white men: 'Thanks to Mr. Chamberlain's lively interest in our great "undeveloped estates," the Imperial Parliament was, last year, induced to vote a grant-in-aid to Dominica and, by its means, the magnificent highlands and valleys of the interior are now being made accessible. Over 100,000 acres of virgin soil are thus being rendered available for cultivation and the natural conditions for successful enterprise are present everywhere' (Bell 1900).

He received many replies, three planters returning with him to Dominica later that year: Penrice, Kent, and Bryant.[28] In the first of his recruitment pamphlets, published in 1903, Bell laid down his qualifications for would-be settlers:

Any man fond of an open-air life and interested in agriculture would probably make a successful planter in Dominica. He should also be healthy, active, and temperate. Good temper is required in dealing with the laboureres, likewise patience. A man very keen on social pleasures

1899). Bell and Chamberlain had met in the Bahamas, where Bell was Receiver General and Chamberlain in charge of his father's sisal plantation.

[28] BP2: 25 Sept. 1900 and 13 Nov. 1900. A further letter was published under the same title on 5 Jan. 1903. A thousand copies of his recruitment booklet (1903*b*) were distributed to hotels and waiting rooms in England (Bell 1946: 832). Between 1891 and 1911 the number of Europeans residing on the island increased from 44 to 399, a leap for which Bell was largely responsible (Trouillot 1988: 121).

and 'functions' will rarely make a good planter. He should stick to his estate so long as it requires attention . . . An intending settler, if young, should endeavour to get a friend to accompany him to Dominica . . . They will be glad of each other's society when the day's work is done, and can compare notes of progress to their mutual advantage. (1903*b*: 13–14)

THE IMPERIAL ROAD

Within weeks of his arrival in Dominica, Bell wrote a thirty-six-page letter to the Governor of the Leeward Islands Federation (but meant for Chamberlain's eyes, one might assume), outlining his plan for spending the funds granted to Dominica. Rejecting both the conservative plan of the Colonial Engineer to improve existing roads and bridges and the original plan of his predecessor, Templer, to drive a road right across the island from Roseau to Melville Hall, Bell proposed that the Imperial Road should go as far as Bassin Will, in the dead centre of the island, and that an existing but overgrown French road, from Bassin Will down to Layou should be surveyed and opened. A steamer service from Portsmouth to Roseau, calling at the coastal villages between, would create a triangular set of communications (Bell 1899).

By 1904 Bell could report some success. The Imperial Road ran to the centre of the island; the first five or six miles of its course was 'practicable for wheeled traffic', the remainder 'a first class bridle-road'. Ascending through a fertile valley to a 'governing-point' at 1,800 feet, it rendered accessible thousands of acres of land suitable for a wide variety of crops before descending gradually 'into the great punch-bowl which comprises the interior of Dominica' (Bell 1904*a*).

Bell was certainly enthusiastic in trying to entice and encourage a new class of planters, vigorous young men, usually unmarried, in whom he imbued the kind of team-spirit appropriate to the renewed imperatives associated with Chamberlain's imperial policy. Unfortunately, they all failed to master the difficult conditions, the virulence of the crop pests, the occasional devastation of hurricanes (especially that of 1916), and intermittent support from 'Home'.

Jean Rhys's story about Mr Ramage, 'Pioneers, Oh, Pioneers', published in 1969 but drawing on her childhood memories, etches a lasting image of these hopeful but inexperienced planters. As the narrator recalls, Ramage had arrived on the island two years earlier, 'a handsome man in tropical kit, white suit, red cummerbund, solar topee' (Rhys 1987: 276). He was, he said, looking for peace: 'I was told that there were several places going along this new Imperial Road you've got here' (277). He buys an estate called Spanish Castle but quickly drops out of polite society, first by marrying a coloured woman of dubious respectability, then by confronting a neighbour and his wife while wearing nothing but sandals and a leather belt. His estate is untended, his wife disappears, local people stone his house, and the newspaper, the *Dominica Herald and Leewards Island Gazette*, publishes a vitriolic article: 'The so-called "Imperial Road" was meant to attract young English-men with capital who would buy and develop properties in the interior. This costly experiment has not been a success, and one of the last of these gentlemen planters has seen himself as the king of the cannibal islands ever since he landed . . .' The article ends by asking whether black people 'must . . . also bear beastly murder and nothing be done about it?' (282). When concerned citizens visit Spanish Castle they find that Ramage has shot himself. His wife, it later emerges, was away visiting relatives on a neighbouring island. Rosalie, the 9-year old protagonist, daughter of the doctor who had befriended Ramage, is distraught and begins to write the dead man a love letter, which her mother later discovers and throws away.[29]

The real Ramage was, it seems, like Frederick Ober and A. H. Verrill, a serious naturalist who had collected specimens of Dominica's birds for a joint Committee of the Royal Society and British Association for the investigation of the Fauna and Flora of the Lesser Antilles, but who had been apparently driven to distraction by Dominica.[30] In Stephen Hawys's later account: 'His instincts were apparently concentrated upon digging a hole, week after week, without employing assistance by anybody. Month after month he remained at his labour which excited

---

[29] The story was first published—coincidentally (one assumes)—in *The Times* newspaper, where Bell had made one of his early appeals for 'pioneers', as 'My Dear Darling Mr Ramage', *The Times*, no. 57598 (28 June 1969), p. 19. At one time Rhys had been working the story up into a novel (see Angier 1990: 471 n.).

[30] George A. Ramage had collected the birds in 1887 and 1888 (Sclater 1889).

curiosity. He told enquirers that he was digging a private road to China, which meant that he would be obliged to dig right through the earth until he came out at the other side' (Hawys 1968: 165).[31] His attempt to dig a hole to reach China stands as a parody of Chamberlain and Bell's modernizing efforts: much digging to no ultimate purpose. Just as Bell was putting his programme into action he was confronted with the case of someone who had shown how difficult it was to become a planter from scratch at the beginning of the twentieth century: 'The Administrator submitted an application from Mrs Ramage, asking that her husband (a lunatic, native of the United Kingdom) be sent home, by the Government, at her expense. His Honour informed the Council that he had submitted the matter for the consideration of the Governor.'[32] And Bell's Imperial Road was to find a further literary nemesis, as we shall see in Chapter 5.

In a larger perspective, Bell's failure—and Chamberlain's—lay in his attempt to re-establish an estate system deeply anachronistic to the dominant West Indian movement towards peasant proprietorship. Bell's own much-admired energy and commitment to the well-being of Dominica served ultimately only to veil the fundamentally racist assumptions behind his strategy: that only white men could save Dominica. However, of particular interest here is that the road system associated with Bell's efforts did eventually begin to make overland visits to the Carib *quartier* a little more feasible for relatively casual visitors, although it would be the mid-1960s before the Reserve was brought within a three-hour drive from Roseau. Bell himself needed no road, nor were his visits casual. He made two official visits to the Reserve, on horseback, within his first two years on the island, and a third in March 1903 to announce to the Caribs that Chamberlain had accepted that the area of Dominica where they lived should become a recognized Carib Reserve. An official report of the first visit had been sent by Bell to Chamberlain in July 1902 and published later that year by the Colonial Office. Drawing on this report but also on notes, letters, and newspaper reports from the time, and on his

---

[31] Ramage's story had been passed on by word of mouth: Hawys arrived on Dominica several decades after Ramage's departure.

[32] CO 74/37 (25 Nov. 1901).

meticulously kept diary, Bell wrote another account in an article for the *National Review* (1938), expanded in his autobiographical *Glimpses of a Governor's Life* (1946).

BELL'S VISIT AND REPORT

Like many colonial officials, Bell was something of a writer and an amateur anthropologist, whose penchant for graphic descriptions is apparent even within the pages of his official reports to the Colonial Office. After leaving Dominica he took extensive notes with a view to writing a book on the Caribs, but never did. However, his writing about the Caribs actually begins some time before his appointment to Dominica. His early book, *Obeah: Witchcraft in the Caribbean*, written on Grenada and first published in 1889, contains an extraordinary scene in which the discovery of a Carib zemi (a small sacred carved stone) prompts a romantic reverie full of beautiful native maidens and scenes of ghastly human sacrifice, all introduced by a more sober historical resumé:

The island of Grenada was first colonized by the French in the middle of the seventeenth century, and old French historians gravely aver that the island was duly and legally purchased from the Caribs. We find, however, that the price paid was two or three bottles of rum and a few knives, so we can easily understand that the unfortunate natives hardly considered themselves sufficiently compensated for their loss of independence and consequent misery, and we can scarcely blame them for repelling the invaders by all the means in their power. Might, as usual, overcame Right, and the unfortunate Indians were hunted into the woods like animals, and mercilessly destroyed wherever met with. They defended their soil, however, with the utmost bravery, and, unlike the Indians of the larger islands, preferred death to slavery. The last of the Grenada Caribs perished by throwing themselves off a precipitous cliff into the ocean, and the rock was thenceforward known as 'le Morne des Sauteurs'. (1893: 85)

Something of the complexity of Bell's attitudes towards the Caribs is apparent, even from this single early paragraph. Grenada had initially been colonized by the French so 'Might overcame Right' is any easy shot. However, the English record towards the Caribs was no better—indeed in most cases rather worse—than the French, so the forthright indigenist sympathies might be seen as unusual in somebody who was an official in the British colonial service. Bell's background could provide some clue here since, despite his appearance and many of his views, he was not a product of the English public-school system, but born in south-west France and educated in Paris and Brussels. Even though, throughout his voluminous writings, he never said much about his family background, his full name— Henry Hesketh *Joudou* Bell—suggests an English father and a French mother.[33] In the original ending to Jean Rhys's *Voyage in the Dark*, she has Uncle Bo (a figure who may be modelled on Alexander Lockhart) mention with a hint of approval that last year 'the Governor' gave a prize for the best costume in Masquerade: 'Damned half-French monkey somebody said of course he would go and do a thing like that' (Brown 1985: 50). Bell, certainly a fluent French speaker, was the colonial official Rhys knew best and, despite his evident commitment to the ideology of the British Empire, he probably demonstrated more independence than most of his ilk, a trait that evidently retarded his once-glittering career.[34]

In Grenada Bell had come across the signs of stories of a Carib past, which had intrigued him. The Caribs' military attributes held appeal, their various fights to the death added romantic lustre, and he clearly viewed them through the lens of late nineteenth-century fascination with the final battles of the Plains Indians—which he may, like many of his contemporaries, have seen re-enacted in Buffalo Bill's spectacular shows:

In spite of their cannibalistic habits, these Yellow Caribs appear to have been a fine and rather noble race of savages. They fought like sportsmen, and numbers of instances of heroic fortitude, on their part, are recorded by the early writers on the West Indies. They fought openly and to the death, with spears and tomahawks, bows and arrows, and appear rarely to have descended to the use of poisoned weapons. When in full war-paint they must have presented a fearsome appearance, for they painted their bodies a bright red with the juice of the roucou (annatto), and their flashing eyes were encircled by broad rings of

[33] His parents were living in Paris in 1900 (BP2: 7 Aug. 1900), where his mother died in June 1903. Bell visited her grave a year later (BP2: 6 June 1904).

[34] Cf., on Bell's difficulties with the Colonial Office while in Nigeria, Barber (1968: 54–66).

gleaming white pigment. Their long black hair was decorated by coro-
nets of brilliant feathers, while necklaces of human teeth hung from
their necks. French and Spanish missionaries, who wrote about them,
describe these Caribs as of tall stature and handsome shape, and lay
stress upon their pride and self-possession. Many of the characteristics
of these people so closely resemble those of the North American
Indians that one is inclined to conclude that the Yellow Caribs of the
Leeward and Windward Islands must originally have been an offshoot
from the brave and handsome race that peopled the broad prairies of
North America.

One can imagine the terror which these dauntless savages created in
the minds of the early settlers in the islands farther north. Without a
sign of warning, the long black canoes, crowded with painted
warriors, would, in the darkness of the night, suddenly round a head-
land and swarm into the little harbour of a peaceful settlement. Before
the white men could fly to their arms or concert a plan for defence,
the scarlet-hued savages, yelling like fiends, would be in their midst.
In an instant the little town, with its brown thatched dwellings, would
be in a blaze. Overpowered by numbers, the unfortunate traders
and artisans, fighting as best they could in the blare of their burning
homes, would fall under the stone hatchets and tomahawks of the
Caribs, leaving the shrieking women and children at the mercy of their
captors, doomed to a horrible fate in a distant land . . . (Bell 1946:
16–17)[35]

I quote this passage at length because it gives such a powerful
impression of the extraordinary psychological investment made
in the Caribs by some of these turn-of-the-century writers; and
because it demonstrates so clearly that, for Bell at least, the
Caribs are an ideal type of the American Indian—that 'brave
and handsome race'. Almost inevitably the people themselves
were—initially at least—a let-down.

Bell arrived in Dominica in September 1899, with a prior interest in the Caribs and possibly already with instructions, or at
least suggestions, from Chamberlain to take steps to 'protect'

[35] Quoted here from his later memoirs, this passage appeared in only slightly different form in Bell's 1902 report. The report was noticed by publications such as
the *Geographical Journal* (run by the Royal Geographical Society) and *The Lancet*,
as well as by the *Daily Chronicle* and the *Bradford Observer* ('For the modest sum
of twopence the intellectual schoolboy may obtain from His Majesty's Stationary
Office . . . as toothsome a piece of reading as Kingston or Mayne Reid ever supplied
him with at twelve times the price' (BP1 1899–1904)).

the Caribs.[36] He took his first extensive riding tour, with Leslie Jarvis, his private secretary, in December; and visited the 'Carib Reservation' as he was already calling it, on 7 February 1900. This visit was reported in the two local newspapers in articles written by Bell in the third person:

Notice of his arrival having been sent on ahead, the Administrator was able to see a very considerable number of Caribs during his ride through their reserve. This last remnant of a disappearing race proved most interesting, and several good photos of types were obtained. Having frequently heard of the timid and retiring nature of the Caribs, Mr Bell was agreeably surprised to find that he had no difficulty in talking freely to them. He saw a number of men, women and children, who appeared to be of perfectly pure race, and he was much impressed by their extraordinary resemblance to Chinese and Japanese. The children, with their olive complexions, oblique black eyes and straight blue-black hair might have been taken anywhere for thorough-bred little 'Japs'. Judging by the great number of little children scrambling around the cottages, the Carib race may be expected to survive for many a year yet. At St. Marie, or Salybia, the party lunched in the neat little cottage used by the Parish Priest who ministers to the spiritual wants of the Caribs, and here the Administrator was met by some seventy Caribs of all ages, headed by their chief, Mr Ogiste. An earnest request was made for a school at Salybia and Mr Bell had much pleasure reassuring the petitioners that he would do his best to provide them with one.[37]

On this initial tour of the island Bell was not likely to be passing quick judgements, or at least not reporting them in the local newspapers, so the tone is fairly bland, although clearly upbeat about the identity of the group—plenty of people of 'pure race'—with the number of children giving evidence of

[36] Official interest in the Caribs seems to have been more or less non-existent before Bell, the one exception being the difficult four-day trek made by the Chief Justice of the Leeward Islands, John Gorrie, in 1885. In a private letter to a friend in England (Frederick Chesson, who was, perhaps not accidentally, Secretary to the Aborigines Protection Society), Gorrie wrote that 'they seem satisfied as the only two requests the Chief sent to the Governor through me was to have a school and a plan of the lands of the reservation'. In his physical descriptions, he says that 'they are more like the natives of the Gilbert and Marshall group than any other native race I have seen' and that 'they are more Malay than Chinese looking' (quoted in Brereton 1997: 224). However, see Bell (1902: 3) for Chamberlain's prior interest in the Caribs, possibly stemming from Froude or Lucas (see above n. 14).

[37] *Dominican* (1 Mar. 1900); the other report is in the *Dominica Guardian* (21 Feb. 1900). A second visit was made in April 1901 (BP2: 27 Apr. 1901).

their apparent capacity to survive and prosper, at least biologically. The fundamental tone is of course paternal: requests are made to the Administrator, who has pleasure in considering them.

The tone of *Glimpses*, published nearly fifty years later, is rather different:

At the entrance to the Reserve we were met by the old Chief of the Caribs, surrounded by about 150 of his people grouped around a small 'triumphal arch' made of coco-nut branches and decorated with flowers and fruit. I must say that their appearance was a considerable disappointment. After all I had read about the Caribs of the old days, their fine physique, their heroism in battle and their engaging cannibalistic habits, I had conjured up visions of splendid men of the Red Indian type, and half expected to see them covered with feathers and red paint.

The reality was far from my imagination. These last remnants of the magnificent savages that were once the terror of the Caribbean seas wore a distressingly dull and prosaic appearance. Auguste, the Chief, was clad in an old and dilapidated black morning-coat that shone green in the sunlight, with a pair of white cotton trousers, while, on his head, was precariously perched—as it was manifestly much too small for him—one of those flat-topped, hard felt hats beloved of churchwardens. His old wife, who was blind, stood beside him, was dressed in a clean, print gown, and on top of her white head-kerchief wore a man's black, soft felt hat, crushed flat. All the rest of the Caribs were similarly dressed in ordinary European clothing, and there was nothing but their faces to show any difference between them and the ordinary Creole inhabitants of the island . . .

I was pained to see that, out of the three or four hundred individuals, who are now the sole representatives of the dauntless race which occupied all these islands in the time of Columbus, not more than 120 are now of pure blood. I said what I could to make them realize that they are now the last remnant of a fine race and that they should try to keep their breed pure, but I fear that the claims of ethnology will not have much effect on them. (Bell 1946: 16–17, 19–21)

This is the third account of the same moment of encounter. The newspaper version is upbeat, as in slightly more sober fashion is the official report. This much later version may perhaps be based on Bell's still embargoed diaries and therefore actually composed 'to the moment', shortly after the encounter; but it may equally reflect later disappointment at the Caribs' failure to correspond over subsequent years to Bell's expectations of them. Within a couple of years, the local priest was reporting a conversation with Bell in which Bell is supposed to have said: 'Father, it was I myself, two years ago, who got a pension of 200 francs for that old sorcerer direct from the king of England. And I'm really sorry I did so.'[38]

The first photograph taken of a Carib chief seems calculated to confirm this impression of a 'dull and prosaic appearance' with little indication of majesty or indeed of the 'American Indianness' that Bell had expected (*WM* 239). The official report also emphasizes the changes to Carib culture:

A century of peaceful avocations has completely metamorphosed the Carib. Instead of a bloodthirsty, man-eating savage, he is now as law-abiding and mild a subject as any the King has. He no longer paints crimson circles of *roucou* round his eyes and stripes of black and white over his body, but—and I state it with sorrow—on high days and holidays, he wears a tall hat and a black coat. His *Zemis* have been scattered among collections of curios, and instead of yelling round a sacrificial stone, the Carib of to-day goes to confession to the parish priest, and tells his beads with edifying fervour. The picturesque abode depicted by Peter Martyr, where faggots of human bones represented most of the furniture, and a bleeding head hung on a post like a picture, has been replaced by the less romantic, if more comfortable, shingled cabin. (Bell 1902: 10)

The lively, indeed colourful, language that distinguishes Bell's report was in certain instances too indiscreet for the liking of the Colonial Office, which cut several paragraphs before publication, including this pen-portrait of the chief, Auguste François (or Francis, as Bell anglicizes it to):

Auguste must be rather over 60 years of age, and is somewhat of a character. He is about the colour of a Portuguese, rather short but lithe and active, and, when quite sober, has a sharp, intelligent expression. He makes a point of coming to Roseau, two or three times a year, on purpose to shake hands effusively with the Administrator and to make pointed references to the remarkable dryness of the atmosphere. The Chief, however, takes a very serious view of himself and of his position. He pointedly refers to the Carib Reserve as the Carib 'State,' and

---

[38] Suaudeau (1927: 51–3), trans. in *WM* 238–40.

exacts considerable deference from his people. His mien is, nevertheless, not imposing. His gala costume appears to consist of very dilapidated tennis shoes, nankeen trousers, and a greasy old black coat. He glories in a tall hat that may fairly claim to be described as 'shocking bad' and, altogether, he looks like a petty Portuguese trader or a dilapidated gipsy tramp.[39]

The Colonial Office presumably cut this paragraph because it considered it disrespectful to a leader it was 'recognizing', in however small a way. Nevertheless, against the grain of Bell's intentions, the paragraph may reveal a good deal about the Carib sense of the importance of the office of chief, even before that imperial 'recognition'. The punctual visits to the Administrator, the pointed references to the Carib 'State', the exaction of deference: these all suggest a very firm sense of what the office entails. In *appearance* and *demeanour*, Auguste does not correspond to Bell's sense of what a leader of men should look like, and this is a note that will be constantly struck throughout the twentieth century, often applied most forcefully, as we shall see in Chapters 4 and 6, to the Carib chiefs who have evidently been the most effective representatives of their people and attracted the greatest support.[40]

Bell's fundamental gesture was within the best traditions of colonial paternalism: 'No definite allocation of this land had ever been arranged, and it seemed to me highly desirable that the small remnant of the people, who once owned the whole island, should be permanently guaranteed the possession of their last homes' (1946: 19). As always, 'last' lands in the sentence with a thump: history is effectively over for these people—they will not move from these houses. That Bell travels to inform them of 'my decision' (19) just underlines their assumed lack of status.[41] As recent Carib activists have pointed out, the gazetted notice which established the Reserve refers to the land which 'the government

[39] CO 152/275 (Leeward Islands 1902): 32.

[40] Bell's own notes also contain further material about Auguste's conflicts with other Caribs, especially a 'half-breed named Valmond' ('Notes on Ogiste (Auguste) Carib Chief' (BP5: A1).

[41] Bell's main concerns were about territory and race, neither of which was raised by either of the rival Carib chiefs in their letters to the Hamilton Commission (see Chapter 1), though Gorrie had noted Carib interest in 'the plan of the reservation', which will be a constant theme in conversations with visitors.

of Dominica *desires* to reserve for the Caribs for their use': there is no reference to Carib landrights, no guidelines or procedures for entering into possession, no mention of title or treaty, no attempt to accommodate Carib participation in the proceedings. This was the doctrine of benign guardianship.[42]

However, Parliament quickly accepted Bell's report, on Chamberlain's recommendation, so Bell's next official visit, on 13 March 1903, was undertaken to advise the Caribs of the adoption by the Colonial Office of his proposals. The Carib Chief presented an address to Bell, which was read by Mr Angol, the schoolteacher at Salybia, in which he gave profuse thanks to Bell and to the Colonial Secretary, especially for the long-promised elementary school, which had now been in place for several months. About the land-grant he announced, in the address's most memorable sentence: 'We, as a relic of a bye-gone time, are placed by a kind providence in the safe keeping of the British Empire, and we commemorate this day's event as giving us a recognised foothold in this great Empire.'[43] Bell spoke to the Caribs in English and his remarks were translated into patois. He stressed his sense that they had not been treated in the past with either justice or consideration and reviewed his finding that no definite boundaries had been assigned to their settlement, which was why he had lately caused their lands to be surveyed. (At this point the plan of the survey was shown to them). The Secretary of State for the Colonies was taking a lively interest in their welfare, Bell stressed, and had approved of the extension of their Reserve to a total area of around 3,700 acres. This land would be granted to them and their offspring, 'a privilege which they will enjoy so long as they remain in existence and loyal to the British Crown'. Bell was also glad to tell them that the government would duly recognize Francis Auguste as their head and chief of the tribe, and that a small grant of £6 a year would be paid to him during his life.

The Government Notice announcing the formalization of the Carib Reserve was published in the local newspapers on 9 July 1903:

---

[42] *Official Gazette* (26, 4 July 1903) is quoted from Frederick (1983: 10 (italics added)).
[43] *Dominica Guardian* (18 Apr. 1903). A slightly tidied-up version of the letter was copied to London (CO 152/282 (1903)).

Whereas it is considered expedient to delimit the Carib Reserve and to set out the boundaries of their settlement or territory in the Parish of St. David in this Presidency. NOTICE is hereby given that, with the approbation of the Secretary of State for the Colonies, the Government of Dominica desire to reserve to the Caribs for their use ALL that certain portion of land situate in the Parish of St. David and bounded:—

> *Northerly* by the Big River, by Lot 63, and the Ballata Ravive;
> *Easterly* by the Sea;
> *Southerly* by the Raymond River and Crown Lane; and
> *Westerly* by the Pegoua River, by Concord Estate and by parts of
>   Lots 61 and 63.

ALL as the same are set out or delineated on a Plan or Diagram of the said lands drawn by Arthur Percival Skeat, Licensed Surveyor, and filed in the Registrar's Office in this Presidency where the same may be inspected at any time during office hours . . .

> Dated this 30th day of June, 1903.
>   H. HESKETH BELL,
>   *Administrator*.[44]

The boundaries of the Reserve, formally established by this decree, have become such a topic of dissension in recent years that it will be as well to clarify the situation as far as possible (see fig. 7). At the time of European contact the major Carib settlements on Dominica seem to have been on the western, leeward, coast, as would make sense. As British and French settlement developed, so Carib communities moved generally northwards and eastwards. The Byres map, drawn up after the Treaty of Paris had put Dominica into British hands, laid aside a small lot of 134 acres for the Caribs on the north-east coast, but their actual *carbets* or villages were at this point still farther flung, especially down the east coast.[45] By the middle of the nineteenth century, an informal reserve had been consolidated around the villages of Bataca, Salybia, and Gaulette Rivière, but Bell says that he could find 'no trace of any formal arrangement by which the Caribs were allowed to consider as their own the area now held by them'.[46] However, in 1865 the British Gov-

---

[44] *Dominican* (9 July 1903).

[45] Bell says the area was 232 acres: this is corrected in Honychurch (1997*b*: 136) who has examined the original documentation.

[46] Bell 1902: 14. An 1860 missionary census reported 172 Caribs living in thirty-five houses in Bataca, Crayfish River, Pointe, Salybia, Gaulette River, and Mahaut River; pretty much the area covered by the current Carib Territory (Owen 1974: 47).

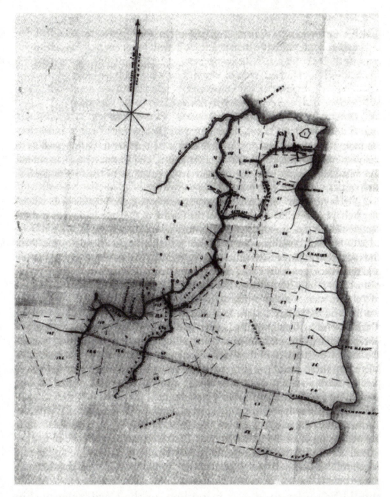

FIG. 7. *Plan of the Proposed Boundaries of the Carib Reserve,* 1901 (Public Record Office, Kew: MFQ/890 188343). This plan was drawn up by the surveyor of Dominica, Arthur P. Skeat, and accompanied Hesketh Bell's 1902 report.

ernment had granted fourteen acres of land in Salybia to Bishop Poirier to be used for the religious salvation of the Caribs, with the land title vested in the Catholic Bishop—a grant that would eventually lead to a dispute over the land when the Caribs wanted a school built there in 1959. In 1879 Frederick Ober used the term 'reserve' without further comment, perhaps extrapolating from the situation in the USA. Visiting in 1885, Sir John Gorrie, Chief Justice of the Leeward Islands, said that the Caribs had 'about 1,000 acres of a Reserve' (quoted in Brereton 1997: 224). According to Bell, the district around Salybia had come to be considered a Carib Reserve 'by a tacit agreement with the Government' (1946: 19) although, as Honychurch points out, most of the land Bell declared to be the Carib Reserve had been sold to British landowners after 1763, so arguably it was not the government's to grant or dispose of. Bell's plan included 3,700 acres, which he considered a slight extension on what was tacitly held, and which he claims was accepted as 'very satisfactory' by the Chief and principal men of the tribe (1902: 15). This land was, though, held in trust by the government, with the Caribs having no title of ownership, so—despite Bell's rather airy language—the Caribs were granted land use privileges but not ownership rights.

In drawing up his recommendations to Chamberlain, Bell appears to have gained his sense of the Reserve's 'proper' boundaries from a statement he took in April 1901 from Mrs Mary Antoinette Burton, whom he describes as the Caribs' 'ex-Maitresse d'Instruction' (BP5: A1). However, the plan drawn up by A. P. Skeat, 'licensed Surveyor', supposedly the basis for the Reserve's boundaries, seems to consist of a tracing of Byres's inaccurate 1776 map, compounded by several misplacings and misnamings, all of which has ensured that the 'original' boundaries of the Reserve remain a subject of dispute.

Lennox Honychurch has recently suggested that the 'original plan of the Reserve' which Caribs often mention to visitors should be understood as a metaphor for the Carib relationship to land and sea before the establishment of the Reserve in 1903. The earlier pattern of landholding, the system of family lands common elsewhere in the Caribbean and much practised on the windward coast of Dominica in the areas not claimed by the large plantations, was a flexible system which allowed access to family plots, individual gardens, and both forest and sea beyond, with no sense of boundary at all until the lands occupied by non-Caribs to the west and south were reached. Rather than confirming Carib practice, Bell was creating a new form of

communal landholding, assuring continued use of Carib domestic land but restricting access to 'the bush': the two systems have
subsequently coexisted with some tension, the 'new' form being
the legally recognized. Outside the Reserve, on the rest of the
island, the old family land system has been replaced by individual legal title, a development prohibited by the terms of the
Reserve. Needless to say, no 'plan' could be drawn of the Caribs'
'original' land use, which depends upon a conception of territory utterly at odds with the one imposed upon Dominica after
1763.[47]

In his 1946 memoir Bell makes it clear that the decision to
'properly' delimit and recognize the Reserve had been taken
within weeks of his appointment, since 'it was with the object
of *informing the Caribs of my decision* that I was making my
journey to their district' (19, my emphasis), this being his very
first visit to the Reserve, in February 1900. Bell's speed in
moving to act on the Carib question may have its roots in his
long-term interest in the Caribs, which dates to the time he spent
in Grenada, but it was probably precipitated by the evident
dispute over the western boundary of the Reserve, which
involved William Davies, proprietor of the Concord Estate.[48] As
could have been predicted, Davies, along with Alexander Lockhart, proved to be Bell's greatest critics: indeed the two of them
were probably responsible for almost all the published remarks
critical of Bell during his tenure of office. Although both
appeared earlier as prominent members of the 'mulatto ascendancy', and both were newspaper proprietors and editors, their
views were by no means identical. Lockhart's father had himself
been a prominent mixed-race politican and so Alexander was a
committed creole nationalist, with his roots firmly in Dominican land and politics. William Davies was second-generation
Dominican, the son of a Welsh father who had emigrated earlier
in the century. After being educated at Winchester, Davies inherited the large plantations of Bath and Emsall from his father and

[47] See Honychurch (1997*b*: 138–43). His point is strengthened by Gorrie's remark
(see above, n. 40), which suggests that Carib concern for 'the plan' actually pre-
dates the map which accompanied Bell's 1902 report.
[48] At his first meeting with Bell, Chief Auguste complained about 'the encroach-
ments of the Dominican peasants' (Bell 1946: 20).

always saw himself as a planter. He had modernizing views which were very much in line with those professed by Chamberlain and Bell—indeed he anticipated many of Bell's schemes; but his favourite idea, to build a small railway, was knocked on the head by Chamberlain in favour of Templer and Bell's road-building ideas, a move which probably ensured that Davies would oppose Bell at every turn.[49]

In his 1902 report Bell refers to Caribs 'working plots of land in a valley that appeared to be outside the northern boundary of their reserve'. This matter came to light, writes Bell, through an application brought by William Davies for a block of Crown Lands which, on inspection by the Government Officer, Mr Robinson, turned out to be under Carib cultivation, with the Caribs believing that these lands formed part of their 'original Reserve'. When he finally saw Bell's report, Davies wrote an article-length letter to the *Dominica Guardian* in order to refute what he saw as Bell's implication that he was attempting to get hold of Carib land by deception (17 Dec. 1904). The story is long and complicated but boils down to Davies having bought an old claim, which had been drawn from Crown Lands in the Pegoua Valley in 1882 in partial substitution for a 'ghost' estate, but on which the government had never issued the promised grant. This land had been squatted by the Caribs *subsequently* to 1882, according to Davies, and he dismisses the idea that the lands were part of an 'original' reserve by noting that they contained the ruins of stone erections: 'These ruins indicate that men of some position, property and civilization occupied them and not the dwellers in those wooden "circular pavilions" which seem to have been the highest architectural effort of the nomadic Carib.' However, Davies's animus is directed at Bell rather than at the Caribs. He claims that Bell had in his possession, and had read, all the relevant documentation but that he chose to ignore it. Bell and Robinson—called by Davies Bell's 'Man Friday'— are accused of being 'Arcadians of a pronounced type'. And, finally, Davies claims that these lands were being worked not only by Caribs but also by some black men from Weirs village, 'and the patient labour of these men has been handed over by Mr. Bell to the Caribs without compensation'.

---

[49] See Trouillot (1988: 193), referring to CO 152/213.

Previously, the main local comment on Bell's report had come in one of Righton's carefully worded editorials in the *Dominica Guardian* in which he welcomed Bell's decision to establish the Carib Reserve, seeing it as a move 'to enable [the Caribs] to embark in the cultivation of cacao, limes and other profitable tropical products, which they have evinced a keen desire latterly to do' (30 July 1902). This may have been the case, but such an intent was not expressed by Bell, nor did he report such a desire as evinced by the Caribs. The point of Righton's welcome for the proposal becomes clearer as his editorial unfolds. The grant of Crown Lands enabling the Caribs to increase the range of their cultigens is 'a step in the right direction' after many years in which nobody on the island took an interest in them 'with the object of bettering their isolated condition'. Carib isolation—the result at least in part of Carib choice—is identified as a condition in need of treatment, with the presumed result of drawing them within the national framework. That the Caribs are, to all intents and purposes, peasant producers just like most other Dominicans is the ultimate thrust of the editorial. Some of the Crown Lands to be awarded to them have, apparently, already been cultivated by them as squatters. 'Perhaps,' Righton concludes, 'this may tend later on to Mr Bell moving in the interest of the many descendants of African settlers all over the island who would be only too ready to take up and cultivate the lands of the Crown.' Righton would have been aware that this fundamental demand of post-Emancipation peasant farmers was exactly what Bell was trying to avoid through his commitment to the establishment of a new class of white English planters. The editorial might best be read, therefore, as a rather subtle accusation that Bell is discriminating in favour of the Caribs and against the Afro-Dominican majority, an accusation that would be made much more stridently by Bell's opponents once he had left the island, as we shall see shortly.

ABORIGINES AND ANTHROPOLOGY

Bell's concern for the Caribs was undoubtedly genuine, although his formalization of the supposed boundaries to the Reserve has proved a double-edged sword, providing some protection both from incursions from outside and—perhaps more importantly—

from sales of land by individual Caribs, but at the same time proving a lasting source of resentment because of inadequate surveying and because of its 'fixing' of the essentially unfixable.

When it comes to understanding the broader circumstances of Bell's actions, there are three relevant contextual circles. The first, and most general, is the development of anthropology as a discipline in Britain, a development which ran on different, if largely parallel, lines to its development in the USA, which was briefly sketched in the previous chapter. The second context—chronologically prior to the first—is the metropolitan interest in aboriginal peoples in general, and in the 'protection' of at least some of them from the more extreme forms of colonial exploitation. And the third, and most particular context, a sub-set of the second, is the way in which a set of evolutionary and racial theories which came to dominate British intellectual life at a time of maximum imperial expansion led inexorably to an interest in the 'lower races', whose rapid 'extinction' was observed with a mixture of horror and fascination, never more so than in the case of the 'last' Tasmanians, William Lanney and Truganini.

In terms of institutions and personnel—as well as, to some extent, intellectual interests—British anthropology developed out of the Aborigines Protection Society, a movement which had its roots in the 1830s, the decade in which humanitarianism had made its greatest impact on colonial policies, partly through the benign influence of the Quaker and Evangelical philanthropists who met in Exeter Hall. The protection of aboriginal peoples was the next great humanitarian issue after the success of the campaign to abolish slavery.

A parliamentary select committee had met from 1833 to 1837 and, although its recommendations were ignored, it led directly into the establishment of the Aborigines Protection Society. In his evidence before the select committee, Thomas Hodgkin, first leading light of the APS, recommended that the best way to eliminate the threat of extermination hanging over various aboriginal groups was to 'have their rights as citizens secured to them and be taught to appreciate these rights, so as to be able to derive advantage from them' (Kass and Kass 1988: 269), a political programme not unlike that adopted by many indigenous groups in the 1990s. However, Henry Fox Bourne's later account of the committee's objectives demonstrates that its aims were hardly radical: 'to consider what measures ought to be adopted with regard to the native inhabitants of countries where British settlements are made, and to the neighbouring tribes, in order to secure to them the due observance of justice and the protection of their rights, to promote the spread of civilization among them, and to lead them to the peaceful and voluntary reception of the Christian religion' (Fox Bourne 1899: 3). The aborigines were to be protected from full-scale exploitation and massacre, but they were to be led peacably towards civilization and Christianity, under the guidance of their superiors: a programme for assimilation.

In 1839 Hodgkin persuaded the leading British ethnologist of the day, James Cowles Prichard, to publicize the work of the APS, which Prichard did, in a forceful address to the British Association for the Advancement of Science in Birmingham. In particular, Prichard lamented the lack of attention to 'ethnography, or the natural history of the human races, while opportunities for pursuing the investigation . . . are every day failing and disappearing for ever'.[50] The British Association then appointed an eight-person committee (including Hodgkin and Prichard—and Charles Darwin, who was apparently not an active member) to draw up and circulate 'a Series of Questions and Suggestions for the use of travellers and others with a view to procure Information respecting the different races of Men, and more especially of those which are in an uncivilised state' (quoted in Kass and Kass 1988: 391). This was a direct descendant of the guidance for travellers issued by the Royal Society in the seventeenth century, but the new version also drew on a recent French model, the 'Instruction Générale Adressée aux Voyageurs' published by the Société Ethnologique de Paris, though the British version put greater weight on anatomical questions. Hodgkin and Prichard's questions were in turn the prototype for the version issued between 1870 and 1920 under

[50] Quoted from Kass and Kass (1988: 390). The full address was reprinted as part of the *Third Annual Report* of the Aborigines Protection Society in 1840. On Prichard, see Stocking 1973. On the development of anthropology in Britain, see Stocking 1987; Kuklick 1993; Rich 1986; Kuper 1988.

the joint auspices of the British Association for the Advancement of Science and the Anthropological Institute, entitled *Notes and Queries on Anthropology, for the Use of Travellers and Residents in Uncivilized Lands*. The APS and those interested in what was still referred to as 'the natural history of the human race' had a common interest in gathering information, and travellers and colonial officials were seen as excellent sources, if properly guided.

The institutional and intellectual development of anthropology in Britain was a fraught process, marked by much bitterness and considerable disagreement over terminology: an Anthropological Society and an Ethnological Society coexisted for several years, with supposedly similar objectives and overlapping membership, yet with deep personal and intellectual differences, often turning on matters of race.[51] By around 1875, however, some kind of consensus between various factions had been reached, the founding of the Anthropological Institute marking the beginning of what George Stocking sees as a period of, in the Kuhnian term, 'normal science'—establishing British anthropology on a solid empirical, theoretical, and institutional footing; even though the collection and analysis of data would for many years largely be in separate pairs of hands, it would not be possible to train as an anthropologist in anything like the modern sense until the beginning of the twentieth century, and the first recognized body of fieldwork did not appear until after the return of the Cambridge Torres Strait expedition of 1898.[52]

Neither the development of anthropology as a scientific discipline nor the humanitarian activities of the APS necessarily indicated a more promising long-term outlook for the future of indigenous cultures. Indeed, underlying both developments was very much the same belief as that held by those who were happy to exploit indigenous peoples in any way they could: that those peoples designated as 'primitive' were in the process of disappearing rapidly off the face of the earth. The Social Darwinist might assume that the disappearance was evidence that these peoples were not well adapted for survival, the APS might want

---

[51] See Stocking 1971; and Rainger 1978-9.
[52] Stocking (1987: 258). On the Torres Strait expedition, see Herle and Rouse, eds. 1998.

to ease their passage into oblivion, and the anthropologist might want to study them before they went; but nobody doubted that they were vanishing. Putting the APS case in the 1850s, R. Montgomery Martin found no 'line of policy likely to prove eventually successful in preserving these wild races, whose extinction—from some inscrutable law of their Creator and ours—seems inevitable; but,' he continued, 'if it be so, is it not the more incumbent on those who are, however regretfully, in some measure the instruments of their fate, to do all in their power to ameliorate it, to evince towards them all possible for-bearance, and to make every attempt to dwell peacably with them in the land from which they are passing rapidly away' (Martin 1852–7: iii. 13). His 'inscrutable law' is a fine example of what Patrick Brantlinger (1995) calls 'rationalizing genocide'. If, in say 1890, this impending disappearance supposedly applied to the still tens of thousands of North American Indians across the continent, then how much more rapidly must it to the few hundred Caribs in Dominica? As was by now usually the case, the most powerful explanations of the process were the scientific ones. The fittest demonstrated their fitness for survival by their energetic expansion. The unfit demonstrated their inability to survive by standing immobile in the face of progress—and dying. Science did not feel entirely comfortable with this: too much potential knowledge was being lost. For Darwin, however, extinction of races was not significantly dif-ferent from extinction of species: 'Extinction follows chiefly from the competition of tribe with tribe, and race with race' (1913: 282)—a different kind of 'inscrutable law', but still one that rationalized genocide. As the impending disappearance of indigenous groups or sub-groups grew supposedly closer, there emerged out of various mists the figure of the 'last man'. The trope of the 'last man' sat comfortably alongside the series of imperial firsts—to discover the source of a great river or climb a previously unknown mountain, with the pathos of extermi-nation merely the reverse of the heroism of exploration. The classical text for the 'last man' in this sense was James Fenimore Cooper's *The Last of the Mohicans*, published in 1826.[53]

[53] On 'last man' stories of various kinds, Stafford 1994; on 'last' indigenes, Goldie (1989: 148–69); on 'vanishing' American Indians, Dippie 1982; and Romero 1981; on 'doomed' Australian Aborigines, McGregor 1997.

The Caribs were not widely known about and therefore not paid attention until the end of the Victorian period: discussion was directed at American and Canadian Indians, Australian Aborigines, Maori and Pacific islanders, but above all at the Tasmanians. The Tasmanians certainly provided the indigenous *cause célèbre* of the second half of the nineteenth century, and therefore a kind of template for reading other indigenous situations.

Although relatively few in number, the Tasmanians had put up spirited resistance to European settlement in the early part of the nineteenth century before being overwhelmed by the usual combination of weaponry, disease, and disruption of lifeways. The well-intentioned George Augustus Robinson had attempted to protect the remaining Tasmanians by moving them in 1833 to a reserved community on Flinders Island, just north of the Tasmanian mainland, an establishment which he turned into what has been called the prototype of the multi-purposed institution for dealing with dispossessed Aborigines: a combination of 'asylum, hospital, training centre, school, agricultural institution, rationing centre, pensioners' home, prison'. After fourteen desperate years, the remaining forty-seven of this group, mostly ill, were moved to Oyster Bay, on the main Tasmanian island.[54]

After 1865, when the *Illustrated London News* ran a feature article on the remaining Tasmanians, the outside world began to take an interest. Charles Dilke's influential study of the Empire at mid-century, *Greater Britain: A Record of Travel in English-Speaking Countries during 1866 and 1867* reported that: 'Fifty years ago, our colonists found in Tasmania a powerful and numerous though degraded native race. At this moment, three old women and a lad dwell on Gun-Carriage Rock, in Bass's Straits, are all who remain of the aboriginal pop-

---

[54] C. D. Rowley, *The Destruction of Aboriginal Society* (Canberra, 1970), 52; quoted by Ryan (1981: 181). Ryan's is the fullest study; see also Ellis 1976; Pybus 1991; Reynolds 1995. As Patrick Brantlinger puts it: 'From 1804 to 1830, the Tasmanian aborigines were harassed and killed with a haphazard but predictable ruthlessness that makes their extinction both unmysterious and unspecial in the history of genocides' (1995: 49). Truganini's equivalent in the USA was the figure of the Californian Ishi (see Heizer and Kroeber, eds. 1979).

ulation of the island' (Dilke 1868: ii. 95). In Nott and Gliddon's encyclopaedic *Indigenous Races of the Earth* (1857), the Tasmanians had come plumb last in the human race: 'we have reached the lowest' (637). As such, they were ripe for being thought of as the 'missing link' between humans and apes. Scientists keen to collect skeletal material hovered over the few survivors like vultures. After February 1862 William Lanney was assumed to be the last Tasmanian male. He was introduced to the Duke of Edinburgh in 1868 as the 'King of the Tasmanians' (Ryan 1981: 214)—though by that stage a 'king' with only two subjects. After Lanney's death in March 1869, the Colonial Secretary and Premier of Tasmania ordered the hospital to take special care of the body on the understanding that after a decent interval the skeleton would be placed in the collections of the Royal Society of Tasmania. However, a Hobart doctor, W. L. Crowther, wanted to send the skeleton to his friend Sir William Flower in London. When Crowther's request was rejected he broke into the dead-house, slit open the back of Lanney's neck, extracted his skull, beheaded a white corpse, and thrust the white man's skull inside Lanney's skin in a rough attempt to conceal the mutilation. The Resident medical officer, G. Stokell, appalled at the theft and determined to prevent Crowther getting the whole skeleton, ordered the hands and feet cut off and left in the custody of the Royal Society. A large and impressive funeral preceded the burial of a coffin containing a white man's skull embedded in an Aborigine's skin and a body minus hands and feet. That night Stokell, seemingly with the collaboration of the police who were supposed to be guarding the grave, dug up the coffin, heaved the body out, placed it in a wheelbarrow and took it to a secluded part of the old hospital. When Crowther's men appeared a couple of hours later, all they found was the skull of the white man, which they tossed to one side. By the time Crowther located the place to which Stokell had removed the body, all that remained was a mass of fat and blood—the skeleton had been removed. When the grave was officially reopened at the request of several prominent citizens who were alarmed at rumours of untoward happenings, it was found to be completely empty (Ellis 1976: 117–21). Crowther lost his job, but Stokell received official protection for his actions, despite some public unease.

After the 'last' Tasmanian, Truganini, died in May 1876, the Tasmanian Royal Society made a formal request for her remains: 'At times like the present when the study of races occupies so much learned attention, types of this kind are of high value and it may safely be affirmed that in future years no specimen in our National Museum would possess greater interest for the learned and scientific traveller from other lands' (quoted in Ellis 1976: 131). The request was refused. An elaborate funeral was planned, but the authorities secretly buried Truganini at night in the yard of a prison. Two years later, in 1878, permission for exhumation was given on the understanding that the skeleton would not be exposed to public view. Several years later, however, it was placed in a glass case at the entrance of the Aboriginal exhibition room in the Tasmanian Museum and Art Gallery, where it remained until 1947. After much legal wrangling, her skeleton was finally cremated in 1976 and her ashes scattered at sea.

The myth of the Tasmanians' disappearance has been effectively disputed by Lyndall Ryan (1981). An 'islander' community in the eastern Bass Strait, descended from Aboriginal Tasmanian women and European sealers, flourished—relatively speaking—and provided the foundation for an existing Aboriginal Tasmanian community, albeit one which has had great difficulty gaining acceptance, so entrenched is the myth of Lanney and Truganini as the 'last' of their race. The Aboriginal Tasmanians' struggles for recognition in recent years have parallels with those of American groups such as the Lumbees, Seminoles, Powhatan, or indeed with the Caribbean Taino, transculturated groups who are often regarded with suspicion on all sides.[55]

However, the small community of disappearing Tasmanians at Oyster Bay told the Victorian world a story it was keen to hear and interpret: it provided Darwin with his central example of the extinction of a race, it was the group referred to by Montgomery Martin on behalf of the APS, and its story, though tragic, offered a sense of completion which was not wholly unsatisfactory to scientific study: as Edward Tylor put it in his preface to Henry Ling Roth's *The Aborigines of Tasmania*: 'In the present work, the recorded knowledge as to the extinct

---

[55] See, respectively, Sider 1993; Sturtevant 1971; Rountree 1990; Guitar 1998.

native race of Tasmania has been brought together with, I think, an approach to absolute completeness.'[56] One of the reasons why the Tasmanians made such an impact on Victorian scientists and general readers was undoubtedly that they were the first indigenous group to be serially photographed, their changing image—as the group got smaller and the survivors older—doubtless offering a dramatic representation of the decline of the weaker races.

Truganani died in the same year as Frederick Ober set out on his Caribbean travels. There may also be a closer link. When Sir Robert Hamilton went to Dominica in 1893, writing his report which included the two letters from the rival Carib chiefs, he had just completed a long spell as Governor of Tasmania, where memories of Truganani and her awful story would still have been fresh, and where—during Hamilton's tenure—learned discussions were still taking place about whether surviving aborigines were full-blooded or not.[57]

BELL THE WRITER

In small compass, Hesketh Bell's contact with and responses to the Carib community can be seen as paradigmatic of imperial attitudes around the turn of the century towards those groups of indigenous peoples no longer perceived as a threat to British interests. Having had his romanticized image of them dashed by the reality of peasant poverty, Bell did his best to isolate the community from what he saw as the ravages of the present—represented by Afro-Dominicans aggressive for land and women. With the boundaries then stabilized, at least momentarily, he set about his duty as an imperial recorder, beginning a book about the Caribs, and contacting the Anthropological Institute in London with information. Bell was precisely the kind of person the Anthropological Institute and the British Association for the Advancement of Science would have had in

---

[56] Darwin 1913; on Martin, see above, p. 135; Tylor (written in 1890), in Roth 1899: p. v.

[57] In September 1889 James Barnard read a paper before the Royal Society of Tasmania called 'Notes on the Last Living Aboriginal of Tasmania': see Roth (1899, Appendix G, p. lxxxiv). (Roth had previously written about the 'Aborigines of Hispaniola' (1887)).

mind when they drew up their guidelines—reliable, curious, scientifically minded, with ethnological interests. According to Bell's letter:

The pure-bred Caribs of Dominica, representing, as they do, almost the only surviving remanant of the natives who peopled these islands at the time of their discovery by Columbus, are very interesting from an ethnological point of view, and it appears advisable that some correct record of their peculiarities should be obtained before they finally disappear. They are now rapidly inter-breeding with Negroes; and it is to be feared that in a generation or two hence, a pure-bred specimen will be hard to find.[58]

In 1904, the 'peculiarities' of the Caribs meant physical peculiarities, and the Institute lent Bell the instruments with which to take anthropometric measurements and gave him detailed guidance as to how to go about the task.[59] *Notes and Queries on Anthropology* had quickly been geared to the kinds of physiological observations necessary to the exercise of anthropometry: 'Consisting of a series of standardising measurements and observations of the human form, anthropometry gave considerable emphasis to the measurement of head length and breadth, the description of facial features, and the calibration of non-measurable traits such as the colour of the skin, hair and eyes, these phenomena being regarded as the primary guide to the classification of race' (Green 1984: 34). But by 1904, the principle that physiognomic characteristics were accurate indicators of intellect and morality had acquired new potency through its association with the eugenics movement. Annie Coombes has noted that museum displays of material culture from the colonies now commonly included photographs, casts of the face, or even skeletons and skulls. These were supposed to demonstrate more nearly the relationship between the inherited and cultural features of any race since 'The man himself as

---

[58] Letter from Hesketh Bell to Anthropological Institute (16 Sept. 1904) (draft in BP5: A1).

[59] Letter from J. Gray (Anthropological Institute) to Hesketh Bell (10 Oct. 1904) (BP5: A1). Gray listed the thirteen key dimensions, helpfully illustrated (see fig. 8), and enclosed a copy of Home & Rowland's price list of anthropometrical instruments. He concluded: 'Measurements of the Caribs, especially as they are fast disappearing, would be extremely valuable to ethnologists & I hope you may be successful in measuring as many as possible.'

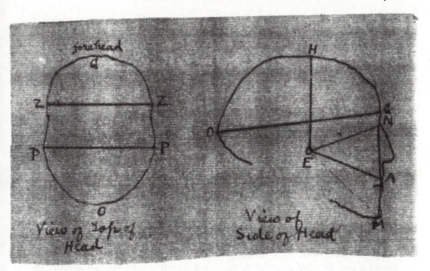

FIG. 8. How to measure heads: a sketch contained in a letter from to Hesketh Bell from J. Gray of the Anthropological Institute, London, 10 Oct. 1904 (in the Hesketh Bell papers (BP5: A1) in the Royal Commonwealth Society Collection, Cambridge University Library, reproduced with permission of the Syndics of Cambridge University).

he appears in his everyday life, is the best illustration of his own place in history, for his physical aspect, the expression of his face, the care of his person, his clothes, his occupations . . . tell the story with much clearness'.[60] In fact, in 1903, just a few months before Bell's letter, the Physical Deterioration Committee had recommended the setting up of an Imperial Bureau of Anthropology, whose anthropometry section was to be responsible for the collating of data on the physical measurements of those races coming under the jurisdiction of the British Empire; so Bell's approach would have been particularly welcome. Unfortunately, in the event, the Caribs seem to have been rather unwilling to submit themselves to this new indignity and the measurements that survive are mostly of Bell and his secretary,

---

[60] W. H. Holmes, 'Classification and Arrangements of the Exhibits in an Anthropological Museum', *Journal of the Anthropological Institute*, 33 (1902): 353–72; quoted by Coombes (1988: 62–3). Cf. Maxwell 1999.

taken no doubt as a standard against which to measure Carib 'peculiarities'.[61]

According to Bell, he 'Started writing a book on Caribs' on 26 September 1903, soon after the formalization of the Reserve's boundaries:

Plan of book

After describing discovery of islands by Columbus and giving partic-ulars of the earliest visits to Dca & other islands, by Europeans, give a full description of the Caribs, their manners & customs etc, before they became affected by contact with foreigners. Inspire the reader with a sympathy for the savages, by a picture of their noble character, courage, independence of spirit, and the justice of the cause . . .

After having gained the readers sympathy in the cause of the Caribs then proceed with their history in chronological order, breaking any impression of 'dryness' by interesting incidents, character studies & legends.

Finally wind up their history with a fairly detailed account of the Caribs of D$^{ca.}$ as they are today. (BP5: A1)

This would, in other words, have been a classic Carib elegy: nobility, independence, and justice are combined with a focus on the pristine state 'before contact', with present issues almost exclusively limited to, and certainly circumscribed by interest in what can count as 'survivals' of that earlier state. The victim of such an approach would, as always, be a real history of inter-cultural contact.

Bell never completed the book, although it often featured among his planned works. At some point, however, possibly after his retirement in 1924, he did sketch out the beginning of an opening chapter:

Depict the scene in a D/ca Carib village at daybreak. As dawn opens, you can make out the array of conical shape huts, (vide Rochefort). A few fowls & guinea birds.—? Any dogs.—No pigs.—The big *carbet* in the middle of the village.—The brown roucout trees with crimson nut.—? Any coconut palms.—Gradually, signs of life in the village.— The women push aside the reed mats hanging in front of the doors and come out of the huts; they start glowing up the embers that had

---

[61] The instruments were returned to London in 1905 with an apologetic letter (11 May 1905: draft in BP5: A1). By this time Bell was about to leave for Africa.

been carefully kept alive since the night before. They put red earthenware pots full of vegetables on the fire. Presently the men appear & saunter down the narrow track leading down to the stream where they will take their morning bath. [...] It would give more point to the description to take one typical homestead in the village & describe it minutely. Let the woman & the man be something in the way of character sketches. For instance, describe the man closely as he appears at the door of his hut, stretching himself lazily, yawning as if only half awake. Describe him as a type of the Carib with all his physical characteristics. The day before had been a festival, of which luckless Arrowak had supplied the principal dish. In spite of his night's sleep after the debauch, his body still shows signs of the finery with which he had been bedecked the day before. His skin from head to foot is still covered with the scarlet roucou paint; rings of jet black encircle his piercing eyes, though considerably smudged, the fantastic designs & streaks in white & yellow that adorned his chest & limbs can still be distinguished. Describe his necklace, armlets & anklets.—A friend comes out of another hut and after the usual Carib salutation, the pair proceed down the narrow track to the mountain stream where they are in the habit of taking their daily bath.

Before getting into the water the Caribs think that they will just push on a few yards further to the mouth of the stream, to see that their canoes are just where they left them the night before. The leader parting the curtain of sea grape branches that masks the beach stood suddenly rooted to the spot and struck dumb with surprise, lays hold of his comrade's arm & silently points to the horizon.

The sun has not yet risen above the straight blue line that separates the ocean from the sky, but the budding effulgence of the morn throws its rosy tints upon the swelling sails of the 3 big carracks & 11 caravels that are smoothly advancing out of the Immensity under the guiding helm of Columbus. Nearer & nearer over the blue water, the ships advance towards the forest clad island until, on the wings of the morn'g breeze is wafted to the ears of the awe struck Caribs the sound of the Salve Regina that is being sung by the grateful Spaniards. [...]

The Caribs of D/ca were not on this occasion, however, fated to make the nearer acquaintance of the white men who were destined to be their implacable foes, & to take from them the last acres of their beautiful islands. On the preceding night, Saturday the 2nd of Nov. Columbus judging by the colour of the sea & appearance of the sky that he was approaching the land he sought, had given orders to shorten sail & to keep a careful watch on board every ship. Nor had he been mistaken in his judgment, for in the early dawn of Sunday

morn'g the forest clad mountains & valleys of D/ca, the most beautiful of all the Caribbees appeared to his delighted eyes rising out of the
ocean. Driven by the favouring trade wind, the stately Marigalante
glided gently towards the promised isle. The deep ultramarine of
the waves was divided from the green of the shore by a long line of
foaming breakers thundering upon a strip of snowy white land. Boldly
& grandly the island rose out from the depths. Hill upon hill & mount
upon mountain, all clad in the most luxuriant verdure rose higher &
higher one behind the other until they culminated in lofty peaks half
hidden by the tropical morn'g. Not a sign of cultivation could be seen
anywhere among the hills nor on the sides of the valleys, and this virgin
land appeared as fresh & pure as if it had only just left the hand of
the Creator. (BP5: A1)

What is remarkable about this piece of writing is its combination of two tropes. On the one hand it offers the 'typical day',
the description of an ordinary day in the life of the village as
described by an imaginary and invisible visitor, a classic element
of ethnographic writing later made famous by Margaret Mead's
chapter, 'A Day in Samoa' in her *Coming of Age in Samoa*,
written in 1928.[62] At the same time, however, Bell introduces
the moment of contact—the arrival of Columbus's ships, which
would for ever change the course of Carib history. The timeless
and the historical are daringly combined. Of course, this was
not the moment of *first* contact with the Native Caribbean,
which had come in the Bahamas on Columbus's first voyage.
This moment came early in the second voyage when, as Bell goes
on to note, having been brought to Dominica by the trade
winds, Columbus found no obvious anchorage and so sailed on
to the north, leaving the Dominican Caribs with that tantaliz-
ing glimpse of large ships and white sails, tokens of a world to
come.

THE LOCAL VIEW

Shortly after Bell left Dominica, the *Leeward Islands Free Press*,
the third and newest of the Dominican newspapers at the

---

[62] 'The life of the day begins at dawn, or if the moon has shown until daylight,
the shouts of the young men may be heard before dawn from the hillside. Uneasy
in the night, populous with ghosts, they shout lustily to one another as they hasten
to their work' (Mead 1981: 19).

beginning of the century, devoted its editorial to the Carib question:

Without exception the 'Carib Quarter' of this island presents the most depressing sight it is possible to find therein. The few dwellings which are passed at long intervals along the public track in no way assist the visitor to a hopeful view of the industrial activities of the section or the formation of a high estimate of the standard of the civilization attained. The District may be shortly described as a half-cleared pasture of the roughest kind, dotted here and there with houses of the lower peasant-proprietor class, which are surrounded with patches of growing cassava. There is an entire absence of any signs of industry in the usual acceptation of the word. Only on festive occasions, Easter and Christmas above all, do the Caribs busy themselves overtly with the production of articles for barter, such as the peculiar baskets which they make and the canoe-shells which they hollow for dug-outs. Their raw materials are supplied by nature without any assistance from the care and skill of man. Apart from those two articles for barter and an occasional output of lumber, there is not any other visible sign of settled occupation by which the tribe may be supposed to live. In the interior of the Carib Reserve a few patches of cacao may be met with, and these supply the experience which operates to prevent the further agricultural development of the quarter. Even the high price of limes which often ruled during the last thirty years has not been sufficiently magnetic to produce any cultivation of the lime tree. Nevertheless, apathy towards agricultural and mechanical enterprise of all kinds is more apparent than real, although it is usually attributed to the influence of the inherited nomad-hunter proclivites of the Carib race. In which connection it is only necessary to state that many Caribs go outside the boundaries of their Reserve to plant permanent crops on secluded spots of Crown Land in order to escape that co-partnership in products which is inevitable under the land settlement of their tribal estate. For a similar stagnation in the progressive development of smaller areas, which had been effected by the vicious system of 'tenancy in common', Governor Haynes Smith devised the remedy of a Partition Act which has been productive of great good to the island. Until some such reform is introduced into the regulations under which the Caribs are allowed to occupy so many thousand acres of land, no change for the better can be expected in their quarter. Without the incentive of personal private ownership of the soil agricultural development will be barred at its present stage, to the detriment of the island as a community and loss to the Carib as an individual. So small an island as ours cannot afford to hand over so proportionately large an area of its land to be locked up in perpetuity as a tribal ranche. The same area under subdivided authorship would suffice to maintain the present Carib population in independence. Instead of this desirable consummation the Carib is forced to hawk his labour about throughout the Windward district in search of wages.

The subject is not one that stops at Carib interests. The tax-payers of the island keep up institutions which are enjoyed by the Carib as well as by the other races settled here. Except the indirect contributions of the import tax in the clothing he wears and the excise duties on the spirits he consumes the Carib does not aid the local revenue in any way. Yet Medical aid, the Courts of Law, and the benefits of the Education Acts are his as a citizen of the State. It is time, therefore, to reconsider the terms of the settlement of this Carib Reservation. What may have suited the last century may not answer under latter-day developments. If the majority of the Carib population should still desire to club their holdings into a common for stock raising no bar can be raised to their perpetuation of the present status. On the other hand, those who may be more industrious and energetic and may also wish to have delimited their share of the tribal patrimony should be accommodated in order that they may prove what they can do when unshackled by the conditions of an archaic system of land tenure.[63]

There are a number of dimensions to this editorial, several of which foreshadow future—indeed still current—debates about the Carib Reserve. The most particular context in which to understand the remarks relates, as one might expect, to the local politics of the time. The owner of the *Leeward Islands Free Press*, a relatively new addition to the roster of weekly newspapers published in Roseau, was Alexander Lockhart, who appeared earlier as a member of the second generation of the 'mulatto ascendancy', the mixed-race politicians and landowners who constituted a powerful local force in Dominica in the second half of the nineteenth century. It was at least in part in tribute to their influence that the Colonial Office forced Crown Colony status on Dominica in 1896, giving all effective power to the island Administrator, under the Governor of the Leeward Islands. No longer 'ascendant', the mixed-race group—who rarely presented a united front—responded in different ways, but several remained close to the local pulse, expressing tren-

---

[63] Unsigned editorial [A.R.C. Lockhart], *Leeward Islands Free Press* (6 Oct. 1906).

chant views in columns, letters, and editorials in the Roseau newspapers. The editors of the two established papers, Steber (the *Dominica Guardian*) and Righton (the *Dominican*), both belonged to this group, but hated each other with a virulence probably unequalled in the annals of newspaper history, despite—or because of—the fact that their political positions were often difficult to distinguish. Lockhart frequently wrote for the *Dominican* but, as the most radical of the three, he clearly felt under constraint and eventually started his own newspaper.[64] The other two papers had always been at least respectful to, and usually supportive of, Hesketh Bell. Lockhart was scornful of the Administrator, who had by now left Dominica and was on his way to Uganda, an attitude that had been quickly manifest in a number of editorials. Behind the scorn was perhaps some sense of social exclusion: Lockhart accused Bell of being 'negrophobic' and of cloistering himself in the whites-only Dominica Club in Roseau. But there also seemed a more personal animus, which emerges in Lockhart's musings on how unlikely it is that Bell, 'who is a rather feminine sort of man, vain, impressionable and finical', is likely to be out of place in Uganda, 'inhabited by warlike races, administered on semi-military methods'. This may pass as a suggestion of homosexuality or it may just be a slight on the unmarried Bell's masculinity, penned by a man who, on my rather rapid glance at the Dominican registry of births for the early part of the century, owned up to seven children by seven different women between 1906 and 1915.[65] So, one element of Lockhart's attitude

---

[64] Three newspapers printing more or less the same news, but with different editorials, was a bizarre development, even by the standards of Dominican journalism. Righton died soon afterwards and Lockhart bought his printing works, incorporating the *Dominican* into his own paper, but the *Leeward Islands Free Press* only lasted until the middle of 1907.

[65] *Leeward Islands Free Press* (6 Jan. 1906); Morne Rouge *Register of Baptisms* (Dominica 1883–1952). Lockhart's twin charges against Bell are combined in his typically barbed obituary for Philip F. Cox, a white settler who went bankrupt and apparently committed suicide in 1906. Lockhart notes Cox's satisfaction with the political change announced by Crown Colony government, preparing the way 'for the social policy of racial sundrance and differentiation, soon commenced by Mr Templer and continued with feminine refinements by Mr Hesketh Bell' (*Leeward Islands Free Press* (17 Nov. 1906)). Lockhart's language (and possibly behaviour) may also have been influenced by the connections sometimes made between mixed-race populations and effeminacy (see Sollors 1997: 131).

towards the Caribs may be explained by the fact that Bell appeared to pay more attention to their welfare than he did to the social group to which Lockhart himself belonged.[66] Lockhart's use of the term 'rather feminine' to describe Bell ironically foreshadows Bell's use of the term 'effeminate' to describe the *Arawaks*—as opposed to the masculine Caribs. This suggests something of the complexity of discursive identifications with respect to the Caribs: Bell implicitly asserts his own sense of manhood by association with the Caribs as they used to be when they were truly themselves, while for Lockhart, Bell's personal demeanour merits the adjective 'effeminate', implicitly associating Bell with the Arawaks of the past—or Caribs of the present—while leaving Lockhart himself to inherit the 'masculine' mantle from the Caribs of the past (and indeed from the 'warlike' Africans about to give Bell a hard time).[67]

But, whatever explanatory power these circumstances may have, the language of the editorial speaks of a commitment to a set of values by which the Caribs are found wanting, not necessarily through any fault of their own. Lockhart's perspective is particularly interesting because he sees in one sense as an outsider—assuming, in the absence of any definite evidence, that the editorial is based on a recent visit. Given the difficulty of travel across the island at this time, it is very possible that this was Lockhart's one and only experience of the Reserve. And yet a Dominican 'outsider' is, on this evidence, likely to look differently and therefore see very different things from a visitor or tourist from outside the Caribbean. For a start, noticing the absences, there is no interest at all in the picturesque, the historical, or the biological. In appearance the Reserve is simply a 'depressing sight'. That the Caribs might have a history of some interest, even if it is one from which the present represents an unfortunate descent, is completely unacknowledged (apart from

[66] Bell had originally prided himself on his good relationship with the local press, achieved through careful cultivation of the newspaper editors (Bell 1946: 72–3), but Lockhart's accusations clearly got under his skin: 'The coloured element in Dominica have started an "ndependent newspaper" called the "Leeward Islands Free Press". Its chief object is to attack me' (BP2: 19 Aug. 1904; also 2 Sept. 1904, 16 Sept. 1904, 1 Nov. 1904 (' "Leeward Islands Free Press" increasingly abusive, accuses one of being a negrophobist').

[67] See Bell's letter quoted as epigraph to this chapter; and on the gendered dimension of the Carib/Arawak discourse, see above, p. 90.

the passing mention of 'inherited nomad-hunter proclivities').
And there is no mention at all, positive or negative, of the racial
composition of the inhabitants, even that argument by 'proclivities' being rejected. The description's positive terms, by
which the Reserve is found wanting, are 'industrial', 'civilization', 'development', and 'enterprise'—the language of that very
modernity from which most 'outside' visitors, after 1877, would
see the Caribs as offering an escape, an alternative, an enclosure of difference.

To some extent this lack of development is laid at the doors
of the Caribs themselves. They have not, it is suggested, made
much of an effort: their specialist commodities (baskets, canoes)
are only made on festive occasions and even the high price of
limes has not induced them to plant lime trees. However, the
main explanation lies in the land-tenure system under which
they suffer, 'the vicious system of "tenancy in common"'.
According to Lockhart, this system encourages the Caribs to
produce only enough food and goods for their immediate needs
since any surplus would simply be divided communally. The
entirely 'natural' impulse to create surplus for the market and
therefore to enrich the individual is shown by the fact that
'many Caribs' plant crops outside the Reserve so that any
surplus generated will be individually owned.

This may not be an accurate description of how the
Carib land-tenure system actually worked at the time—certain
individuals or families were clearly able to gather rather
large amounts of land and, consequently, wealth: speaking
relatively. What is interesting, however, is that Lockhart is keen
to downplay the differences that might separate the Caribs from
the rest of the population of the island—differences that Bell has
sought to exacerbate. For Lockhart the Carib land-system is
'tenancy in common', a holdover from post-Emancipation
arrangements, not a modified continuation of aboriginal practice. The Caribs themselves belong to the 'peasant-proprietor
class', just like most Dominicans: in fact the terms 'indigenous'
and 'aboriginal' appear nowhere in the editorial, 'tribe' being
the one concession to a difference in social arrangements on the
Reserve.

As becomes clear in the latter part of the editorial, the governing ideology here is an incipient creole nationalism. The

Caribs cannot be seen in isolation, especially when they control such a relatively large portion of land on 'so small an island as ours'. Land is wealth, and to have land 'locked up in perpetuity as a tribal ranche' would prevent the full development of the island's potential.[68] That key group within nationalist ideology, the taxpayers, are introduced to suggest that the Caribs derive benefits from their citizenship in excess of their current contributions (though anyone on the Reserve reading Lockhart's editorial would probably have been surprised to hear about these supposed benefits).

As might be expected, underwriting Lockhart's creole nationalism is an implied possessive individualism. If the majority of *individual* Caribs want to keep *their* holdings in common, then that is a decision for them; but the 'industrious and energetic' individuals should be 'unshackled' so that they can develop their—and their share of the land's—potential. Little more than half a century after Emancipation, the key word here is 'unshackled', which lets Lockhart suggest that the Caribs themselves are effectively enslaved by the land-tenure system which has recently been confirmed by the colonial interests that Hesketh Bell represented. The colonial authorities would, in time, as we shall see, change their views, but Lockhart here articulates a nationalist position which has, in essence, remained unchanged for a century, although its articulation has not been possible in all political circumstances.

Alexander Lockhart's evident feelings about the social and racial exclusivity of colonial and white settler society in Dominica at the turn of the century were probably exacerbated by his equally evident but unacknowledgeable relationship to one of the grand settler families of the islands, the Lockharts of Geneva. Alexander was almost certainly the grandson of James Potter Lockhart (d. 1837), frequently President of the island assembly, but by means of an outside relationship with a slave woman, and therefore unrecognized. As Alexander made money, a reputation, and children, his white half-cousin, Acton Don Lockhart, presided over the slow decline of the Geneva plantation, in the south of

---

[68] The 'ranche' and the 'stock raising', featuring in a predominantly agricultural context, suggest that Lockhart is drawing on examples from other places, possibly Venezuela.

the island. Meanwhile another half-cousin, Acton's sister Minna, married a young doctor called William Rees Williams who had recently arrived from Wales, and set up house in Roseau. By the time of Alexander Lockhart's editorial, the Williams's young daughter, Ella Gwendoline, aged 16, was already getting ready to leave Dominica for England. More than fifty years later, this daughter would write a fictional evocation of her youth in Dominica, set back into her grandmother's time, in which the female narrator would recall a friendship (and later imply a sexual relationship) with a boy she refers to as Sandi, son of Alexander Cosway: 'Once I would have said "my cousin Sandi" but Mr Mason's lectures had made me shy about my coloured relatives.'[69]

Ella Gwendoline Rees Williams would return just once to the island of her birth, in 1936, as Ella Tilden Smith, a visit that produced the one significant piece of fiction written about the Carib Reserve, which I will discuss in Chapter 5: a story called 'Temps Perdi', published under her *nom de plume*, Jean Rhys.

PRESENT REPRESENTATIVES

1930 marks a turning point in modern Carib history, since that year saw what came to be known as the 'Carib War', the subsequent commission which resulted in the suspension of the chieftainship, and the arrival on the island of the first linguist to take an interest in the surviving Caribs—such an interest that he soon settled on the island. These stories will occupy Chapter 4. There are, however, two final visitors from before 1930 to take brief account of, a French geographer called M. Neveu-Lemaire, who visited the Caribs in 1921, offering a fair summation of the dominant views about them at that time, and a travel writer who uses a local white planter to give him the inside story on the Caribs—obviating the need to visit the Reserve himself.

Neveu-Lemaire is the first twentieth-century French writer to visit the Caribs, but he picks up a tradition that goes back into the seventeenth century, when the Caribs were targeted by French missionaries and, as might be expected, Neveu-Lemaire

[69] Jean Rhys, *Wide Sargasso Sea* (1997: 28); and cf. Hulme 1994*a*.

knows well the texts of Breton, Du Tertre, and especially Labat, whom—like Bonsal at the end of the previous chapter—he quotes from and refers to throughout his essay.

Although his visit was, Neveu-Lemaire says, the outcome of a 'lucky chance', his essay has scientific pretensions: it is certainly longer and more thorough than many. The question of Carib origins is dealt with at some length, as is the disposition of the indigenous Caribbean at the time of Columbus, and the fate of the Caribs over the colonial period. Carib diet is elucidated by learned reference to the Latin names of their foodstuffs; a register of deaths between 1917 and 1920 is analysed by age and sex; and a Carib vocabulary is reproduced, collected by Daniel Thaly between 1916 and 1918 from an old woman called Rosalie.[70]

However, the essay makes no claim to be an anthropological study: the stay on the Reserve seems to last no more than a day or two at the most and, if there is plenty of observation, there is precious little participation. The authority of Labat weighs heavy on Neveu-Lemaire's shoulders, and much of what he has to say concerns how the Caribs are not what they used to be: 'Today the surviving Caribs lack picturesque traits; through contact with black and white creoles they have adopted their clothes. . . . Carib women do not currently appear very coquettish and wear few ornaments, while at the time when *roucou* was their only covering they did not neglect their finery . . .' (Neveu-Lemaire 1921: 136)

Neveu-Lemaire also offers a particularly clear example of that disconcerting ability to combine a sense of the Caribs' decline from what they once were with an assurance of their unchanging character: 'Melancholy is the root of their character; their physiognomy carries the imprint of their sadness and their disdain' (136). His composite picture of Carib character traits is not convincingly consistent: 'They are vindictive, do not forget slights . . . are kind and generous to their friends and cordially practice the duties of hospitality' (136); 'Nonchalant by nature, the men spend whole days doing nothing . . .' (136); 'enterprising and war-like, vigorous rather than lazy . . .' (146).

---

[70] This vocabulary was, it seems, one of the last collected from a native speaker of the Carib language on Dominica. On Thaly, see above, p. 10.

The chief, Jules Corriette, is the only Carib mentioned by name and the only one apparently spoken with, although Neveu-Lemaire gives no indication of anything that Corriette might have said. Like so many other travellers, he is unimpressed by the Chief, partly because he dresses in the European manner, 'which takes away any possible cachet', partly because, since childless, he 'has not set an example in the conservation of his race', partly, it seems, because Neveu-Lemaire mistakenly thinks that the concept of the chiefdom was imposed by the British on the Caribs who therefore lack respect for their chief (140).[71]

Finally, in the early 1920s Archie Bell travelled to Dominica in the course of writing a book for one of the burgeoning sets of travel narratives that were so popular at the time, the 'Spell' series: this was *The Spell of the Caribbean Islands*. Like many of his predecessors, Archie Bell expressed a great interest in the Caribs; like many of them, also, he never ventured to the part of the island where the Caribs lived, having to be content with the one Carib he saw in Roseau on an errand: 'I endeavored to persuade him to talk with me, but he was shy, suspicious and somewhat surly, which no doubt is an inheritance' (Bell 1926: 307). He was regretting that the only Carib he had seen had a comparatively dark skin, when a Dominican planter assured him that this was the case with the majority. The planter gives him the inside story:

'Think of it,' he said, 'there were hundreds of thousands of Carib—perhaps millions—when the first Europeans landed on this side of the world. I have heard it said that there may be no more than fifty full-blooded Caribs remaining in the West Indies today. A large number of them were victims of the last volcanic eruption on St. Vincent's island. Their settlement was wiped out, and I understand that most of the remaining Caribs over there are half or quarter breeds. Probably more Caribs now live on Dominica than elsewhere. I know them well and have spent as much as two weeks among them, and I would say that there are not more than twenty-five full-bloods remaining. Why, even their present chief is part negro. Strange, but here is the passing of a once-powerful race and nobody seems to be sufficiently interested to

[71] Jules Corriette may have been the Coryet who was one of Frederick Ober's guides in the late 1870s.

make a careful and scientific study of them, although we know less of them than of almost any people on earth. I believe that they have not been photographed for scientific purposes, and not even the government library at Roseau has anything of interest about them. Of course it is well known that they are very shy with strangers and it would not be an easy thing to gain their confidence. But it could be done. They are suspicious of all strangers and, when one of their trusted friends brings a stranger, they become suspicious of him. But if anything is to be done, it must not be long-delayed, because one of these days, the last pure-blood Carib will die and their race will have become extinct. It seems that nobody cares much about them. Once I heard an English traveler ask the governor if it would be worth while for him to make the trip across the island to the Carib settlement. An emphatic *no* was the answer, and the administrator smiled at the suggestion'. (307–8)

4. Narrating the Carib War: Douglas Taylor and the Struggle over History (1930–1940)

> The general feeling seems to be that a white man who chooses to spend his time in the bush in the company of 'a lot of ignorant savages' instead of discussing cricket and local gossip at the club, can be up to no good. (Douglas Taylor)[1]

In the metropolises of the Western world, the news broke at the beginning of October 1930 that a serious riot had taken place in Dominica. Under the headline 'Starving Caribs' Attack on Roseau', the London *Times* carried a report from its New York correspondent of how refugees from Dominica, arriving in Port of Spain, Trinidad, had told of how 'Indians from the Carib Reserve, half-starving because of the loss of their crops in the recent hurricane, advanced on Roseau, the capital of Dominica on Monday, looting food stores as they went. They were met by constabulary who were forced to use their firearms. A number of the rioters and four constables were wounded, the latter seriously. Later, Marines and sailors from HMS *Delhi* helped to restore order and ration foodstuffs.' The *New York Times* told of how starvation had hit the island following a violent hurricane in early September: 'The rioting began in the Carib Reserve, the last stronghold of the descendants of an ancient race of warriors long opposed to the advances of the white man. Panic stricken and facing starvation, the Caribs advanced on the capital, Roseau. The chief of police and the constabulary left their barracks hurriedly to stem the advance.'[2]

---

[1] From a letter to M. W. Stirling, Head of the Bureau of American Ethnology (14 Nov. 1936), quoted *in extenso* below, p. 193.
[2] *The Times* (2 Oct. 1930), p. 11; *New York Times*, quoted in *Dominica Tribune* (18 Oct. 1930).

Just about the only accurate statement in these wild newspaper reports was that there had been a violent hurricane in Dominica in early September. Destructive of crops and houses, it had caused hardship throughout the island. However, two weeks later the Carib Reserve was slowly putting itself back together, as all Caribbean communities have had to do for many centuries—clearing wreckage, replanting, rebuilding. On the morning of Friday 19 September these activities were interrupted by a police raid. Five policemen—Corporal Sweeney, and Constables Joseph, Jacob, Greenaway, and Lake—came onto the Reserve at dawn, searched the house of James Lessainte, and arrested and handcuffed him after seizing tobacco and other goods. They then proceeded to the shop of Madame Titwa (Esther Frederick), whom they also arrested after finding rum in the grounds of her house. By this time a crowd had gathered, including the Carib Chief, Thomas John ('Jolly John'), who questioned the right of the police to be on the Reserve without his permission. A tug-of-war developed over one of the seized items between Constable Greenaway and one of the Carib men, Dudley John. One of the policemen, Joseph, shot Dudley John, and the other policemen—with the exception of Sweeney—fired into the crowd, hitting several other Caribs, before being disarmed, beaten, and run off the Reserve. Five Caribs were wounded by gunfire during the incident. Four were treated in Roseau hospital, where they had to be taken by boat: two died—Dudley John and Frederick Royer. Two policemen were treated for minor injuries at Marigot hospital, just beyond the Reserve.

Captain Branch, working on Hurricane Relief on the windward coast, came across some of his battered constables making their way to Marigot. He telephoned news of what had happened to Roseau, asking for twenty men from the Defence Force. The Administrator, Edward Carlyon Eliot, decided that tougher action was needed and—on the advice of the Chief Inspector of the Leeward Islands Police Force—asked the Governor of the Leeward Islands, based in Antigua, for a warship, reporting by telegraph that '4 Police Constables on duty at the Carib Quarter have been attacked and dangerously injured by mob'.[3] The Governor telegraphed for HMS *Delhi*, which came

[3] CO 152/417/10: 127 (in Capt. W. E. C. Tait, 'Letter of proceedings no. 11/30, 14th to 25th September 1930').

at full speed from Trinidad, and a contingent of marines was landed at Portsmouth and trucked over to Marigot. On Sunday night (21 September), the *Delhi* cruised down the windward coast shooting starshells over the Carib Reserve in a bizarre echo of the scene in *Heart of Darkness* where Marlow observes a French man-of-war shelling the bush:

In the empty immensity of earth, sky, and water, there she was, incomprehensible, firing into a continent. Pop, would go one of the six-inch guns; a small flame would dart and vanish, a little white smoke would disappear, a tiny projectile would give a feeble screech—and nothing happened. Nothing could happen. There was a touch of insanity in the proceeding, a sense of lugubrious drollery in the sight; and it was not dissipated by somebody on board assuring me earnestly there was a camp of natives—he called them enemies!—hidden out of sight somewhere.[4]

As a later commentator noted, without a trace of irony: 'This is one way of dealing with a grave situation when caught in its early stages, and will always pay handsome dividends when the Navy tackles the problem' (Agar 1962: 196).

On Tuesday Jolly John reached Roseau to report to the Administrator and was immediately suspended and arrested. Meanwhile local police with marines in attendance swept through the Carib Reserve searching houses and making more arrests: the *Delhi* steamed round to Roseau with seven Carib prisoners. Thomas John and six other Caribs were tried at the Circuit Court in early January 1931 for 'Assaulting certain members of the Leeward Islands Police and Rescuing from them certain goods seized under the Trade and Revenue Act'.[5] All six Caribs were acquitted unanimously of the charges by the local jury, but Eliot, the Administrator, refused to reinstate Jolly John.[6] In May a Commission of Enquiry was established by the Colonial Office 'to enquire into conditions generally in the Carib Reserve and into all circumstances connected with a disturbance there in September, 1930, with particular reference to any special privileges the Caribs may possess; and having due regard to the requirements of good Government in Dominica

---

[4] Conrad 1989: 28. I owe this point to Sue Thomas (1999: 149).
[5] 'The Circuit Court', *Dominica Tribune-Guardian* (10 Jan. 1931).
[6] 'The Famous Carib Case', *Dominica Chronicle* (24 Jan. 1931); 'The Carib Case', *Dominica Tribune-Guardian* (5 Feb. 1931).

generally' and 'to make recommendations for the future welfare of the Caribs'.[7] This brought to Dominica and eventually to the Carib Reserve itself two men who were 'visitors' in the most official sense of that word, His Honour the Chief Justice James Stanley Rae and Sir Sydney Armitage Armitage-Smith, KBE, CB, who constituted a Commission of Enquiry. However, Eliot made it plain to the Colonial Office that the man *really* responsible for the incident was a visiting Englishman, Douglas Taylor, who had stirred up trouble. Eliot was quietly relieved of his post shortly after the Commission reported. Taylor, however, settled on Dominica and became the leading twentieth-century expert on Carib culture, consulted by many post-war visitors up to the time of his death in 1980.

BACKGROUND TO THE INCIDENT AT SALYBIA

One question which would never be asked during the official Enquiry, but which certainly interested the local newspapers, was just why the police had chosen this moment to raid the Reserve. In Dominica there was widespread resentment about the high excise charges on alcohol. Wine and rum were cheap in Marie Galante and Martinique: contact with those islands from the Reserve was frequent. Eliot seems to have made smuggling something of a target. Early in his administration, he wrote to the Colonial Office about the 'three black spots' affecting island revenue: praedial larceny, smuggling, and rum-making:

Our Revenue Officers are locally recruited, as strangers could hardly live on the salaries paid, and, though I make no accusation of participation in profits, it is doubtful whether any customs official—with the exception of the Head of that Department—would expose a case of smuggling, neither has a single instance of such exposure occured since local officials held office. What has been done of late in this direction, is the work of the Police Force, recruited from other Islands, to whom rewards have been given for seizures, mainly on information obtained from informants.[8]

---

[7] Great Britain (1932: 2–3).
[8] CO 152/398 (Letter from E. C. Eliot, Administrator of Dominica (25 July 1925)).

Part of the confusion about what happened on that September morning seems to have arisen from the sheer unusualness of the events. Nobody quite knew how to behave: there was no accepted narrative, either for policemen or for Caribs. Chief Inspector Edward Bell, with thirty-one years' experience in the Leeward Islands Police Force could remember no previous raid being made in the Carib Territory.[9] Bell also said, revealingly, when pressed as to whether Captain Branch should have been present for the raid: 'It would be difficult to say that had Captain Branch been there there would have been no trouble, but there would certainly have been a more intelligent account of what happened.'[10] Two factors seem to have coalesced. In the first place there was a denunciation of some kind from within the Reserve itself. Details are not easy to reconstruct, but a faction associated with the 'retired' chief, Jules Corriette, and which may have included the Lessainte (Licente in the Commission Report) initially arrested, but never charged, seems to have informed the police of a recent consignment of goods arrived at Madame Titwa's.[11] During the Commission's hearings, the Caribs' attorney asked Captain Branch, who had authorized the raid, whether the informant was 'a friend of the Corriette faction'? The question was disallowed.[12] Within the Dominican colonial administration, there seems also to have been a rancorous conflict about the proper attitude to take towards the Caribs, a conflict which had been simmering in the previous months. Somebody—perhaps Eliot himself—saw this report of smuggling as the opportunity he had been waiting for to bring matters to a head and even, perhaps, to abolish the Reserve entirely.

By 1924 Jules Corriette had apparently become a powerful and wealthy man who had made himself unpopular on the

---

[9] CO 152/425/1: 231 (Evidence of Edward Bell, 19 May 1931). NB: references to the 262 pages of evidence taken by the Commission of Enquiry are identified by pagination as well as description.

[10] CO 152/425/1: 235 (Evidence of Edward Bell, 19 May 1931).

[11] The Commission Report speaks of 'an informant' (Great Britain 1932: 10).

[12] CO 152/425/1: 205 (Evidence of J. R. A. Branch, 18 May 1931). On the land dispute behind this factionalism, see Owen (1974: 166).

Reserve.[13] As a result of complaints about him, Eliot had in February of that year read to his Council a minute he had written after his visit to the Carib Reserve on various matters, 'especially in regard to the relations between the Caribs and their Chief, Corriette Jules'. Eliot had decided 'that no sufficient cause had been shown for removing Jules from office'; but that in the event of his resignation or death, rather than appoint a successor, there should be a 'Head Man' who would be responsible to the Government Officer for such things as the upkeep of roads: 'The Caribs should be informed that if they fail to keep up their roads etc. the Government would throw open the reserve. There did not appear to be any reason why they should be exempted from taxes other than the Road and Boat Tax.'[14]

On 24 April 1926, the Official Gazette of the Dominica Presidency published a bulletin from the Administrator's Office to the effect that the Administrator had, subject to the approval of the Secretary of State for the Colonies, appointed Thomas John, alias Jolly John, to be the 'Head Man' of the Caribs in place of Jules Corriette, 'who has been retired' (quoted in Aspinall 1928: 154). In his evidence before the Commission of Enquiry, Thomas John said that Corriette had been 'deposed': '[The Caribs] did not want Corriette because he used to make them pay taxes and take them to Law also they did not like Corriette's wife who was a mixture between a black woman and a Carib.'[15] The Administrator's memory of events has a slightly different spin:

---

[13] The unpopularity goes back at least as far as 1916, when twenty Caribs signed a petition drawn up by William Davies which complained about Corriette's behaviour and asked for his deposition (Dominica, G.O. 316, from Mr Wm Davies, 15 Feb. 1916 (LH)). This apparently followed hard upon Corriette being given responsibility by the colonial administration for such matters as the recording of births and deaths and the reporting of non-attendance at school; in other words his incorporation. A follow-up letter by Davies in July conveyed further Carib anger at Corriette. Davies had his own agenda, which comes out towards the end of this letter: 'What is ridiculous about the appointment is that there is nothing peculiar for the Chief to adjudicate. There are not any customs peculiar to Caribs which a magistrate or judge could not unravel. These men are all Dominicans and the sooner they are merged in the general population the better' (Dominica, G.O. 1199, from Wm Davies, 4 July 1916 (LH)). See above, Chapter 3, p. 130, for the continuity of Davies's views on this matter. Davies's views, so at odds with Hesketh Bell's, had come by 1930 to be accepted as *de facto* colonial policy, although only Eliot matched Davies in the querulousness of his tone towards the Caribs.

[14] CO 74/41 (19 Feb. 1924).

[15] CO 152/425/1: 152–3. (Evidence of Thomas John, 13 May 1931). John's evidence was translated from creole by Frederick Augustus Piper.

In 1929 [*sic*, i.e. 1926] I found that the time had come to remove from office the old Carib chief. He was entering on his dotage and was unduly under the thumb of his wife, a negress, who was endeavouring to bring members of her own family and her negro friends into the Carib Reserve. With the unanimous approval of my Council I recommended to the Colonial Office that this chief should be superannuated on a small pension. This was approved by the Secretary of State. I then visited Salybia (the Carib settlement) to depose the chief and to ascertain the wishes of the Caribs regarding the appointment of a successor. I found that the man that they chose, by a considerable majority, was a man of straw whom they wanted simply because he was a nonentity, who could be controlled at the will of the people. . . .

I told the Caribs that while I would accept their nominee as the headman of their tribe and spokesman for the community, I could not approve or recommend to the 'Big Chief in England' that he should be made chief, and given the Stick and other badges of office, until I was satisfied that their selection was a good one. (Eliot 1938: 225)

Eliot's account suggests some of the anomalies of the Carib situation. At least as far as the Administrator is concerned, it is he who has the power to remove Carib chiefs from office and to approve the nomination for a new chief. The Caribs themselves are merely to be consulted. A chief 'controlled at the will of the people' might be thought to have had a certain democratic resonance, but Eliot was clearly looking for something else: perhaps a chief controlled at the will of the Administrator. However, the Colonial Office paper quoted earlier makes it clear that Eliot's decision to downgrade the post of chief to head man had been taken before Jolly John's election and was a political, not an *ad hominem* decision. What is striking about Eliot's behaviour from this moment onwards is his deep antagonism towards Thomas John, who would belie Eliot's assessment of him as a 'man of straw' by proving an active advocate for the Caribs, cannily bypassing the Administrator and directing himself straight to London—the 'offences' Eliot would eventually cite as the reason for not lifting John's suspension after he was acquitted in the Roseau trial.[16]

[16] Eliot had been Administrator since 1923 and therefore probably the author of the remark quoted by Archie Bell at the end of the previous chapter. Thomas John founded the modern council system, selecting four men to give him advice (though more recently the councillors have been elected) (CO 152/425/1: 155 (Evidence of Thomas Jollie John to Commission, 13 May 1931)). He also received strong support

In June 1927 Thomas John drew up a petition about the Carib situation addressed directly to the King (George V). I will quote it in full:

A petition to His Most Gracious Majesty the King from His Loyal Carib sujects in His Island of Dominica. May it please Your Majesty; we, the Loyal and obedient Carib subjects of Your Most Gracious Majesty pray for your kind consideration on our behalf.

Most Respectfully showeth That Your Majesty's petitioners since at the beginning of the reign of our Vice Chief 'Mr Jules Corriett' who has been retired sometime ago use to suffer a lot of trouble and dissatisfaction and up to now it has been the worse.

His Honor, the Administrator of the Colony is not in our favour and he is by all means trying his very best to reclaim our sovereign right. He wish to put us just like civilian. He wish to take up our road of our Reserve. In fact he wish to put new rules over us, which is altogether different from those, which we did receive from Administrator Bell in the year 1902.

Thomas John, whom he did appoint as headman for us, has applied several time for little reward from him, and he refuse him.

That your petitioners are 500 in number of which 250 are pure Carib descendant and our number is still increasing. The rest are not pure Carib but they are native born.

We most humbly beg His Most Excellent Majesty pardon and excuse, some of us are poor, so poor, that we cannot even maintain our young little one. Considering how poor and hard up we are we humbly pray His Most Gracious Majesty with our utmost fidelity veneration and respect to grant us our Reserve once more and to allow us to follow our ancient rules as in the time of Ti Francoise our Ancient Chief. We profoundly and humbly beg His Most Gracious Majesty to appoint Thomas John for our Chief and to increase his fee and authority. A sum of ten shillings monthly is mention for him but we consider this to be immoderate as he is serving us faithfully from the time of probation till up to now and we Most Humbly beg for His Majesty's help.

And Your Majesty's Humble petitioners,

As in duty bound, will ever pray.[17]

from other Caribs at the time of the Enquiry and in subsequent years when a petition in favour of his restoration carried 159 Carib signatures (CO 152/425/1: 171 (Evidence of Nelson Lucien to Commission, 14 May 1931); CO 152/425/1: 167 (Evidence of Fan Fan Bruney to Commission, 13 May 1931); and CO 152/462/6 (22 Jan. 1936)), although he did have a rival in the late 1930s called Felixien Daroux.

[17] Petition and accompanying documents are in CO 152/406 and 407 (1927).

The key phrase here is 'just like civilian'. Whereas Corriette, it seems, was willing to act at least in part as an agent of the colonial government, continuing the process of bringing the Caribs into the national body, Thomas John had a strong sense of Carib difference, based firmly on the fact that the Caribs were not 'civilians'.[18] In North American Indian terms, Corriette was a modernizer, Thomas John a traditional leader—with his notion of tradition defined by reference to the time of the Ancient Chief, Ti Françoise, who lived just the other side of the perceived moment of cultural decline in the second half of the nineteenth century with the disappearance of the Carib language, the final conversion to Catholicism, and the formalization of Carib lands into a Reserve authorized by the British state. Arguably, of course, the 'sovereign right' that John defends from the Administrator is not very sovereign if it owes its status to 'His Most Gracious Majesty'. Nevertheless, the very use of the petition direct to the King is a political move of some skill in the context of insular politics. The dominant note, as with the letters to Hamilton forty years previously, is that of poverty: 'poor, so poor'.

Thomas John enclosed this petition in a letter he sent to a correspondent in Sheffield, England, one E. A. Iliffe, along with a request to put it into correct English and to forward it to the King. Iliffe did neither. Instead he sent the petition and letter to the Secretary for the Colonies, L. C. M. S. Amery, along with a letter of his own in which he explained that as a schoolboy and a philatelist he had come into contact with Thomas John and they had corresponded quite regularly. However, 'I ceased owing to the excessive demands he made, having asked me to send him several things which were quite beyond my means.' Iliffe clearly had no idea what to do with the petition and so was sending it to the Colonial Office: 'You will doubtless be more conversant with the affairs of the Island than I, & it would seem that either

[18] At the Commission hearings, several of the Carib elders suggested that Corriette had been an exception in sending cases to the Magistrate's Court for settlement rather than trying to resolve disputes himself (CO 152/425/1: 166 (Evidence of Fan Fan Bruney to Commission, 13 May 1931); and 171 (Evidence of Nelson Lucien to Commission, 14 May 1931)). Corriette seems to have seen himself as occupying an official position within the colonial administration, and this may have alienated him from the majority of Caribs, in the face of a younger and more aggressive political leadership.

the Caribs have some grievance to rectify or that this Thomas John is trying to work things for his own ends.' The Colonial Office forwarded the petition to Dominica so, eleven months after starting its long and circuitous journey, it arrived in Roseau, some twenty miles from its starting point. There it was received and acknowledged by Major Peebles, the Acting Administrator, who turned Thomas John from 'Head Man' into 'Chief'—possibly exceeding his authority, and seems to have at least given the Caribs grounds for believing that he was acceding to some of their requests, even in the later account of Peebles' meeting with the Caribs offered by Captain Branch in his evidence at the District Court hearing in December 1930.[19]

Eliot clearly resented the way in which, 'in the usual native manner' (1938: 226), his absence had been taken advantage of by the Acting Administrator, Peebles, recommending to the Governor of the Colony, and thence to the Colonial Office, that Jolly John should be made Chief. To add insult to injury, Eliot returned from leave to find that he had been left to carry out the investiture. He asked the Colonial Office to reconsider, but was 'commanded' to carry out the order. His resentment was undoubtedly a factor in subsequent events, which he saw as full justification for the way in which the Colonial Office had ignored his advice and insisted on the appointment of a man whom he described as 'useless and dangerous' (228)—though it is hardly obvious how someone can be a dangerous man of straw. Eliot liked Dominica as little as its inhabitants liked him. He later wrote of how the zest had gone out of him by this stage in his career, leaving him 'too fully conscious of the Lilliputian nature of the inhabitants' (228), one of whom, nevertheless, a girl less than half his age, he married.[20]

In August 1930 Thomas John pressed home his moral advantage in two ways. Perhaps noting yet another of Eliot's absences, he wrote to the Administrator asking that the Caribs should be exempted from paying taxes. However, this time, the Acting

[19] CO 152/41710: 70–71 (Précis of evidence of J. R. A. Branch, Dec. 1930).
[20] Eliot spent a lot of time away from the island he was supposedly administering. In 1925 Reginald St-Johnston was asked to 'act' for six months prior to taking up a post in St Kitts, in order to see if he could sort out the colony's tangled finances (St-Johnston 1936: 92–3).

Administrator was the island's treasurer, Baynes, an Englishman, who spoke in his master's voice, writing back to say that the payment of taxes was the duty of every citizen and that the Chief should use his influence to get his people to obey the law: 'Instead of helping the Government you have been setting a bad example to the Caribs by defying the law and the Government Officer.' Baynes concluded: 'I have now explained to you what your duties as Chief should be, and I hope that no more complaints will be made of your conduct towards any Government Officers charged with the carrying out of the law, as otherwise His Majesty the King's Government in Dominica may consider it necessary to remove you from the position of Chief.'[21]

But John had already sent a second petition to London (dated 10 August 1930):

WE, Thomas John, Chief of the Caribs, and all the Caribs of Dominica greet and express their loyalty to His Most Gracious Majesty George V, King of Great Britain, of Ireland and the Dominions and Colonies over Seas, Emperor of India, and humbly submit to His Majesty's Gracious consideration, this our petition.

WE beg His majesty graciously to grant us:—

1. The restoration of our ancient rules and privileges, where perpetual continuance was graciously accorded us by Her late lamented Majesty Queen Victoria and which have unlawfully and unjustifiably been taken from us since the year 1926.

By our ancient rule and privileges, is meant that within the boundaries of the Carib territory the lawfully elected Carib Chief should have power to administer law and justice over the Carib people and that there should be no interference on the part of the British local authorities except at the Chief's express request or at the majority of the Carib people. MOREOVER, that the Carib people living peacably in the Carib territory should never become liable to any forms of taxation, other than the duty of keeping open some part of the road within their territory, except by their majority consent or approval.

2. That the Government grant of ten shillings a month at present made to the Carib Chief be raised to a sum compatible with the upkeep of dignity and honour of his position.

WE would bring to His Majesty's notice that a protest and petition made by us some time ago to His Majesty's Secretary of State has remained unanswered and unacknowledged.

---

[21] CO 152/425/1: 259 (Exhibit 'B': Letter from T. E. P. Baynes to Thomas John, 26 Aug. 1930).

FINALLY, we would submit to His Majesty's gracious consideration that we, the Carib people, have since the beginning of the British rule in this island always lived as peacable and loyal subjects of His Britannic Majesty, that since the beginning of recorded history these islands have always been our home, and that today, living on a small section of territory in this island we, the last of our race, are, through lack of recognition, absence of means of communication and marketing, reduced to a state of poverty in which we can only face extinction, we are convinced that the submission of these facts will suffice to persuade His Majesty of the urgency of taking such measures as will ensure us, His Majesty's loyal Carib subjects, the proper respect, recognition and protection worthy of His Majesty's Government.[22]

As the language of this petition suggests, a further and ultimately influential player had entered the stage that summer, an English modern languages graduate and budding amateur anthropologist called Douglas Taylor, who was on a world tour with his wife and child. After spending a few weeks on Dominica, one or two of them on the Carib Reserve, Taylor returned to Europe. From Nice he wrote to a Cambridge friend, the anthropologist Noel Teulon Porter, an important letter which I quote at considerable length:

I have just returned to France from the West Indies where I spent some time amongst the Caribs of Dominica (not to be confounded with the Dominican Republic or Santo Domingo). I am writing to you, as the only person I know interested in such matters , to ask if you would be willing to help me to preserve the Carib race, of whom only four or five hundred remain, and who are rapidly becoming extinct in the pure form owing to the local government's trying to ride over the privileges accorded them by Queen Victoria.

Dominica is an island belonging to the British Leeward group, situated 15° N by 61° W between the French islands of Guadeloupe and Martinique, which I also visited. It is the most mountainous and the most wild of the Antilles, about 10 miles by 20, and the only place on earth where pure Carib blood survives. They probably owe this continued existence to the fact that there are no proper roads across the island, whose greater part is still uncultivated and covered by virgin forest.

The Caribs now live in a legally defined Reserve of ample dimensions on the windward and most savage part of the island, under the

[22] CO 152/425/1: 262–3 (Petition of Thomas John to King George V, 10 Aug. 1930).

nominal rule of their Chief. There is no village as we understand it, the houses which are well built of hardwood in a style of their own raised on stakes, and *scrupulously* clean, being scattered over miles, each one being surrounded by plantations of coffee, cocoa, vanilla, nutmeg, breadfruit, tania, dachine, limes, etc. and the whole intervening countryside being covered with bay trees. About ten miles inland starts the forest, from which they get their hardwoods, seman, balata, ceder and gommier this latter being used for the making of the native boats, gommiers, which they sell for 25/– the current price at Fort de France being 18 pounds, (a good boat takes several men several weeks to complete). This together with Carib baskets and limes is their only way of getting money. The only means of communication with the port of Roseau is by sea, in these same gommiers, which means an absence of several days from the Reserve, and considerable danger in the channel of Martinique. Salybia, (the Carib Reserve) does not possess either doctor or priest the nearest being about 3 or four hours walk entailing the crossing of a river impassible in the heavy rains.

The Caribs themselves, of whom there must be at least 250 *quite pure* (the chief himself puts it at 400 out of a total of 500, but I think he is optimistic) are small and wiry, the women sturdy and well formed; olive to light copper skin through which the blood shews red, high cheek bones, slightly slanting eyes, broad flat foreheads with tendency to recede towards the top, coarse black straight hair, hands and feet small, the latter with very high arches. A peculiarity is that men and women have little or no hair on the face and body. In character, they are much less exuberant than the blacks, almost melancholic, soft voiced and *extremely shy* with strangers. Their language is almost extinct, only the old men remember some of it, the current language is Creole French and of course the young ones learn a certain amount of English in school. The rest of the population of the island, black and white, look upon the Caribs much as we look upon the gypsies,—as a lazy good for nothing lot. In point of fact they are not lazy but as long as they stay on the reserve, they can only work for themselves. I think this suits their temperament best, and it is sure that if they went to town or to work on the big plantations the race in it's pure form would soon be extinct. As it is, many of the girls leave to marry half-casts or niggers, and the chief himself has a pretty half Carib wife.

They are at present very unhappy because the government (the administrator is a man called Eliot) is trying to starve them into absorption with the nigger population. They want on the one hand to levy taxes on boats etc, and on the other hand to bring the Caribs under the jurisdiction of the local coloured magistrate in Rosalie—the nearest village out of the reserve. The shop keepers in Roseau,—a days journey by boat or through the jungle on foot, now refuse to buy their bay leaves, and give less and less for the baskets. (A Carib basket is the local form of luggage throughout the West Indies; made to be carried on the head, it is about 3 ft. long by $1\frac{1}{2}$ broad by 3 ft. tall, very light and water-proof, made of the bark of a tree called 'la rouman' double lined, i.e. one basket made to line another with plantain leaves between the two; the design is in black, red brown and white. Each one takes about two days to make—after the preparing of the bark—and they sell if lucky, after carrying them to market, for 2/– a piece. Could they be sold in England in quantities to make export worth while?

I enclose a copy of a petition to the King written by the Carib chief. You will see that his complaints are rather on the score of prosperity than health. But in my opinion one of the most important things is to preserve the health of the Carib infants a great many of whom suffer from mal-nutrition, which produces a disease called locally 'chaws' and which results in a bleeding from the genital organs. Anthropologists and ethnologists like yourself would find a great many things to interest you among these people, and I think it is worth while doing something to ensure the continuation of the race.

Is it worth while sending this petition? Could a campaign be started in the *Times* (letters) or in some other papers? The chief's idea is that if he came to Europe and could tell people about the Caribs he could raise enough to start a little local industry for the extraction of bay essence and bay rum. Or they might sell some produce in Europe.[23]

Taylor did not choose his correspondent wisely. Although Porter did forward John's petition and Taylor's letter to the Colonial Office, and did venture to wonder what had happened to the first petition, he contextualized his remarks with some judiciously obsequious statements:

Loath though I am to trouble you or your Department I feel that I owe it to myself as well as those more intimately concerned to make some slight effort to discover the rights and wrongs of the case herein propounded. I shrewdly suspect that, as in most things of the sort, there will only be found enough of both to balance and cancel each other! . . .

[23] CO 152/418/2 (Letter from Douglas Taylor to N. Teulon Porter, 25 Sept. 1930). At the time of writing Taylor would have been still unaware of the events on 19 September on Dominica.

I am not suggesting for a minute, as my Correspondent seems to, that we should keep this or any other tribe in its aboriginal purity simply as a museum specimen so to speak, especially, as seems to be the case with the King at any rate (who has evidently married outside his tribe) against the will of those people.[24]

Perhaps unsure as to Porter's reliability in this affair, Taylor—now back home in Germany—wrote in October directly to Buckingham Palace, enclosing another copy of the petition which he hoped to have put before the King's eyes, 'this more especially as the Chief particularly desired it, several petitions addressed to Your Majesty's Secretary of State through the Administrator of the island, Mr Elliot [*sic*], having, it appears, gone unanswered'.

In conclusion may I say that this race, which peopled at their discovery all the islands south of Haïti, is represented today only by some four hundred pure blooded members living on an isolated reserve in the island of Dominica. The latter's survival seems probably due to their isolation and special privileges, which have rendered the need of money minimum, emigration from the reserve unnecessary, and reduced the opportunities for intermarriage with the negroid imported population. It seems desirable, and practicable to preserve the loyal sentiments of this interesting people together with their race integrity; and that without change of policy (the status quo is all they desire) and at but a nominal cost.[25]

After the September incident a good deal of the correspondence in the Colonial Office files is taken up with formulating replies to letters from defenders and advocates of the Caribs. The Colonial Office wrote back to Porter informing him of the recent 'disturbances', a letter he passed on to Taylor. Meanwhile Taylor had had news of what had happened from Percy Agar in Dominica, in a report which did not exactly tally with the story the Colonial Office was circulating.

Having become embroiled in the controversy surrounding the Carib War, Taylor wrote again to the Colonial Office to explain his interest and to establish his credentials which—with an eye

---

[24] CO 152/418/2 (Letter from N. Teulon Porter, 9 Oct. 1930).
[25] CO 152/418/2 (Letter from Douglas Taylor to King George V, 17 Oct. 1930). This letter was also presumably written without knowledge of the events of 19 September.

to what would impress the Colonial Office—put his rowing achievements at Cambridge before his degree in Economics and Modern Languages. The son of a Batley woollen manufacturer, Taylor had apparently not been forced to earn a living: study in Heidelberg and Paris had followed Cambridge: 'Since then I have devoted myself exclusively to the study of literature and anthropology, and have made a hobby of travel.' He continued:

During my stay in the West Indies last summer, where I travelled with my wife and child, I visited Martinique, Guadeloupe, and Dominica, to which last island I was drawn especially by the existance there of the last surviving Caribs. My interest in these latter was, during the whole of my stay, social, and in no wise political. The Chief, who offered me his hospitality during my stay in the Reserve, told me his troubles and shewed me a petition he had written, asking me to transmit it to H.M. the King, on my return to Europe. I undertook to do this, my only other part in the whole affair being that I pointed out to him certain mistakes of English which could only have led to ridicule or miscomprehension or both, and which he corrected under my guidance. I am not aware of having in any way caused him to change the sense of what he had written, or of having put any ideas seditious or otherwise into his head. I think you are entirely cognizant of the rest of my part in this affair.[26]

Taylor's letter (sent from Mittenwald, Germany) may have been written because he got wind from friends in Dominica of a letter Eliot had sent to the Governor of the Leeward Islands in Antigua (and on thence to London), giving his rather different account of Taylor's visit:

Mr. Douglas Taylor arrived in Dominica from Martinique about the end of July 1930. He called at the Government Office in Roseau and interviewed one of the Clerk's [*sic*] as to the means of reaching the Carib Reserve. Mr. Taylor did not ask for an interview with the Acting Administrator—Mr. Baynes.

Mr. Taylor left for the Carib Settlement early in August and spent some period, probably from one to two weeks, with the Carib Chief.

Mr. Taylor brought a letter of introduction from Martinique to Mr. Percy Agar, a coloured gentleman who owns the estate of La Haut, near Roseau. Mr. Agar is the correspondent referred to by Mr. Douglas

[26] CO 152/418/2 (Letter from Douglas Taylor, 23 Jan. 1931).

Taylor as 'an Englishman, resident in Dominica' in his letter to the Colonial Office of the 13th November. Mr. Taylor brought with him, on his return to Roseau from the Carib Quarter, the petition of Thomas John, the Carib Chief, dated the 10th August. Mr. Taylor showed this petition to Mr. Agar, and informed the gentleman that he would take the petition to Europe and forward it to the Colonial Office.

Mr. Taylor also brought with him to Roseau a Carib girl named Vina Huggins, about 16 years old. Mr. Taylor took this girl with him to the Paz Hotel in Roseau. The Manager of the hotel however refused her admittance with Mr. Taylor. Mr. Taylor took the girl with him to Martinique and subsequently to Guadeloupe. The girl was sent back to Dominica early in October. Mr. Taylor telegraphed to Mr. Agar from Guadeloupe asking him to meet the girl, and to send her back to her parents in the Carib Reserve. Bishop Moris states that the Salybia Parish Priest, Father Barreau, publicly chided the parents for having temporarily sold this young girl to Mr. Taylor. This matter was not however reported to the Acting Administrator.[27]

In a covering letter Eliot adds that since the petition was prepared while Taylor was at Salybia, 'and as Thomas John is not sufficiently educated to have drafted this document there is, I submit, strong presumption that the petition was drafted by Mr. Taylor'. Furthermore, Eliot says, 'I am forced to the conclusion that Mr. Douglas Taylor badly advised the Carib Chief, and has been largely instrumental in fermenting and fostering the spirit of unrest in the Carib Quarter which culminated in the unfortunate fracas of the 19 September.'[28] In other words, the Caribs, like most natives under British tutelage, are perfectly happy until some outsider comes and stirs them up, 'fermenting . . . the spirit of unrest'—a peculiarly apt (if unintentional) figure of speech given that the disturbance focused on the smuggling of rum.[29]

[27] Father Barreau had been the priest at La Soie since early in the century and an influential figure on the Carib Reserve.

[28] CO 152/418/2 (Letter from the Administrator, Dominica to the Governor, Antigua (with enclosure), 3 Jan. 1931). This seems to have become the official wisdom. Helen Cameron Gordon, who as Lady Russell wandered around the West Indies during the Second World War and who presumably moved in government circles in Dominica, notes curtly of the Caribs: 'In former times their overlord had the title of King, until a busybody arrived amongst them to awaken race consciousness by instructing them in their own folk-lore and traditions: propaganda intended to make them restless and troublesome to the rest of the community and the Government' (1942: 69).

[29] When he gave evidence to the Commission of Enquiry, Thomas John said of the Petition: 'I was the author of this petition. No one told me what to put in it.

Meanwhile, Taylor was pressing the Carib case hard with the Colonial Office:

From personal acquaintance with most of the Caribs in the quarter, I believe them to constitute a peaceable, loyal, and in every way desirable element in the island's population, and in direct contrast to the rather brutish character of some of the negro population of the other, or leeward side of the island . . . [F]rom my knowledge of them, it is incredible to me that they should have attacked the negro police unless these greatly exceeded their duty.[30]

Eliot seems not to have been entirely honest in his official statements about the Carib Reserve. In January 1931 Hesketh Bell wrote from his retirement home in Cannes to Grindle, Chief Secretary in the Colonial Office: 'I have had a long screed from Eliot of Dominica on the subject of the trouble with the Caribs. I don't think he is very sympathetically inclined to these people and seems to have absorbed some of the Creole prejudice against them.' And he quotes from Eliot's letter: ' "If it were not for reasons of sentiment I think the Reserve might be thrown open in a few years time, and sufficient land allotted to each family. They are bound to become absorbed in the native population before long." '[31] Given Eliot's clear *lack* of sentiment towards the Caribs, his own view is unmistakable. Bell's view, however, had not changed: 'I think that most people who are interested in ethnology would view with sorrow the disappearance of this last surviving remnant of the virile and often heroic race which Columbus found in possession of the Lesser Antilles when he discovered the islands.' His main theme is also the same. He recalls how he did all he could to discourage the Caribs from intermingling with the Creoles 'and to induce them to preserve their interesting individuality':

They are my own words' (CO 152/425/1: 160 (Evidence of Thomas John, 13 May 1931)). Comparison of the two petitions might suggest that this is an outrageous claim, but it should be remembered that Jolly John's evidence was being translated by an interpreter from patois. The first petition was, arguably, his best effort in writing in a second language he did not fully master. The second petition was *translated into* that second language by a native speaker and therefore is likely to represent John's intentions more clearly than the first effort.

[30] CO 152/418/2 (Letter from Douglas Taylor, 3 Dec. 1930).
[31] CO 152/418/2 (Letter from Sir Hesketh Bell, 22 Jan. 1931).

The Creoles from the neighbouring districts have always tried to get a footing in the Reserve. We always drove out the trespassers but found it difficult to deal with the cases where the young men of the tribe took wives or mistresses from among the Creoles and produced half-breeds from them. But in spite of these influences the number of pure bred Caribs has not sensibly declined during the past 20 years, and Eliot puts them down at about 100 . . . On the other hand it appears that the whole population of the Reserve has risen from about 400 to nearly 600 and that people who have no real right in the Reserve have been allowed to remain there and to cultivate land.

The Reserve was granted on the understanding that it was to be for the benefit of Caribs of more or less pure descent. Exemption from direct taxation was also granted on the same principle. Intermarriage or concubinage with Creole negroes and negresses from neighbouring districts has been going on for many years without interference from the government and, as it would be very difficult now to turn out of the Reserve all the half-breed children born of such associations, the only thing to be done is to see whether means cannot be adopted by which the interests of the pure-bred remnant can be better protected.

I suggest that the supervision over the Carib Reserve and its inhabitants should be far more effective than it has been in the past. During the last 25 years half-breeds and three-quarter-breeds have been allowed to enjoy privileges and immunities which they should not have been allowed to have. Although the Caribs have been permitted to have a 'Chief', chosen by themselves, the man has had no real or legal authority, and his stipend of £6 a year has merely been a sort of tacit acknowledgment of him by the government.

I venture to suggest that the Reserve and the rights of the Caribs should now be placed on a proper footing. 'Occupancy rights' should be granted only to pure-bred Caribs and to the *existing* half-breeds. No other person, save those already possessing and occupying dwelling in the settlement should be permitted to live and cultivate land in the Reserve. Only pure-bred or half-bred Caribs should be exempted from taxation.

In future any man or woman bringing into the settlement, as husband, wife or paramour, a person not a pure-bred Carib, should lose his or her privileges and be required to leave the Reserve. All the existing children, who are not pure-bred or at least half-bred Caribs, should, on attaining the age of 21 years be required to leave the settlement.

The Chief should be a pure-bred Carib, elected by the pure-bred Caribs only, and approved by the government. He should be paid a salary of at least £50 a year so that he may value his position and be anxious to carry out the wishes of the government. He should be given such authority over all the inhabitants of the Reserve as may be expedient . . .

The continued survival of this interesting remnant of the Carib islanders will, I think, depend almost entirely on the degree of attention which the Dominica administration will give to the matter.[32]

Bell is writing twenty years after his last direct contact with Dominica, and at a moment when he clearly felt that the measures he had put into place were in danger of being undermined by the indifference, and even active hostility, of the current Administrator. Nevertheless, it is striking how his benevolence, given a slight twist by his impatience, turns into a frighteningly disciplinarian stance. The 'pure-bred remnant' needs protecting against itself and its desires, since it clearly cannot recognize its own best interests; and this can be done only through more effective 'supervision', which will involve expulsions of those deemed not pure enough, even if they were born and bred on the Reserve. At best, this is a call for crude social engineering. In a letter written in 1931, it runs the risk of being associated with calls elsewhere for more drastic eugenic solutions. Although Bell is quite willing to envisage an increase in the authority (and salary) of the chief, he understands the chief's role as carrying out 'the wishes of the government'. Autonomy this is not.

REPORT OF THE COMMISSIONERS

The local newspapers in Dominica had called for a Commission of Enquiry soon after the shooting incident, although what they really wanted, no doubt, was an enquiry into the Administrator's behaviour rather than the Caribs'; and so, in early February 1931, they welcomed the call in the House of Commons by Sir Robert Hamilton for an enquiry that would look into the status of the Carib Reserve, the position of the Carib Chief, the economic position of the Caribs, the actions of the police, and the actions of the Administrator.[33] The Colonial Office wanted

---

[32] Letter from Sir Hesketh Bell to Gilbert Grindle (10 May 1931) (copy in BP4).
[33] *Dominica Tribune-Guardian* (26 Mar. 1931). Sir Robert W. Hamilton, Liberal MP for the Orkneys and Shetland, was the son of the Sir Robert Hamilton who had produced the 1894 report on Dominica.

an enquiry for the simple reason that the jury had unaccount-
ably failed to convict the Caribs as charged.[34]

His Honour the Chief Justice James Stanley Rae, Attorney-
General to the Leeward Islands, and Sir Sydney Armitage
Armitage-Smith, KBE, CB, a prominent British civil servant,
arrived in Dominica in early May 1931. They sat in open session
in Roseau for nine days and examined twenty-seven witnesses.
They visited the Carib Reserve on the 22 and 23 May, finally
leaving Roseau on the 27th. Their report was written in Antigua
in July, presented to the British Parliament in December and
published the following year (Great Britain 1932).

The report begins by offering a short 'Historical Account of
the Caribs', very different in content and tenor from that offered
by most twentieth-century travellers. Although the Caribs are
allowed to have 'gallantly resisted' European attempts at settlement on their islands, the Commissioners mostly eschew any
romantic nonsense. The Carib practices of killing and devouring enemy men and marrying enemy women are asserted as
facts, along with the pointed reminder that those who employ
the term 'of pure blood' should do so with caution in the light
of the evidence of admixture for many centuries (3). But the
main point of the brief history lesson is to dispute the argument
made by the Caribs' counsel at the beginning of their trial that
the Caribs were 'subject only to the suzerainty of the Crown
and not amenable to the ordinary jurisdiction of any local court'
(4). Such a claim, if given credence, could clearly have put the
aboriginal cat among various settler pigeons around the world,
and the Commissioners were extremely keen to scotch the idea;
although also clearly so anxious about the feasibility of the
claim that their researches generated a vast correspondence
between the Colonial Office and the Foreign Office. The key
document in this claim was the Treaty of Aix-la-Chapelle
(1748), in which Britain and France agreed to leave Dominica
to the Caribs, a fact which is mentioned in many historical
accounts of the Caribs, including those written by, for example,

---

[34] As an official noted: 'It is clear that the result of the trial can only be regarded
as highly unsatisfactory from a Government point of view, and that in view of the
inferences which will be drawn from the acquittal of the accused, if for no other
reason, it is absolutely essential to hold a thorough enquiry' (CO 152/425/2 (Note
dated 30 Jan. 1931 signed by Mr Bowyer)).

Hesketh Bell.[35] However, for the Commissioners, the crucial fact is that the Caribs were not signatories to the Treaty themselves and so, presumably, cannot be judged harmed in legal terms by the non-compliance of the signatories: 'This observation is necessary in order to dispel the wholly erroneous conception of a definite status accorded to the Carib people by international treaty, the facts being that the arrangement by which France and England abstained from claiming Dominica expressed merely their inability to conquer some particularly savage tribes, which clung by force, so long as they were able to do so, to independence' (4). The legal nails thud into the coffin of this spurious Carib argument: no recognition of a Carib state, no independence conferred by the Treaty of 1748, no acknowledgement of right to independence, no such right conferred, no immunity from taxation ever granted. The absence of a treaty signed by the Caribs conferring the island of Dominica to Britain is not remarked; nor is the legality of the British conquest questioned.

The matter of taxes and licences proved a veritable can of worms. Basically, the Carib position was that they had traditionally not paid taxes or, if some of them had done so, they had merely been a few coerced individuals. The position of the authorities, upheld by the Commissioners, was that the Caribs should always have paid taxes and, if they had not done so, it was because of the dereliction of the inspectors, or because, in the case, say, of the horse tax, Caribs did not usually own horses. For the Caribs, not paying taxes was clearly a potent symbol of their autonomous status on the island. Edward Green, who had

---

[35] 'By the treaty of Aix-la-Chapelle . . . Dominica was apportioned to neither British nor French, but was specially set apart as a neutral island for the sole benefit of the Caribs. It was stipulated that no European nation should make settlements there, and a native chief was to be recognized as master of the island . . . Dominica, however, was much too fair and desirable a possession to remain efficiently protected by the provisions of the Treaty of 1748, and the French soon unofficially commenced to resume their small trading stations and plantations on the leeward coast . . . Under the pretence of enforcing the provisions of the Treaty and of protecting the rights of the Caribs, the English would land and burn the plantations of the French. If fortune favoured the interlopers, the rights of the Caribs were speedily lost sight of, and the British filibusters would retain possession of the French estates. The Caribs would find that the nationality of the trespassers was the only difference in the case, and the English took up the aggressions where the French had left them off' (Bell 1902: 8–9).

been Government Officer for the Eastern District until 1924, tes-
tified to the official position that the Caribs were liable to all
taxes, except boat taxes: 'The Caribs had to obey the Laws of the
Colony just like any other person.' Though he did admit that
Judge Pemberton thought that the Caribs should be left to themselves: 'He has peculiar views that the Magistrate has roped them
in and that in former years they were free from taxation.'[36] The
older Caribs tended to agree with Pemberton's version.

After an account of 'the facts with respect to the Incident,
which are undisputed' (8), the Commissioners dealt with what
they identified as the two main issues: how far the authorities
were justified in their proceedings with respect to the searches
and arrests, and how far the police were justified in using their
revolvers.[37] On the first matter, the authorities were slapped on
the wrist for the practice of issuing search warrants in blank to
Inspector Branch, who passed them on to Corporal Sweeney,
who had a constable fill them in once the actual searches were
under way. The Commissioners mildly opined 'that when a
written authority is applied for it should contain, so far as
possible, the designation of the person or persons and place
or places to be searched' (13).

As far as the shooting was concerned, the Commissioners
began by noting that they found the evidence of the Caribs 'generally unreliable' and the evidence of the police 'often unreliable
and nearly always conflicting' (13)—not a promising start since
those two groups made up the entirety of the eyewitnesses. Corporal Sweeney had claimed that no shots were fired in the yard,
and that the police only opened fire on the Caribs after two
warning shots had been fired in the air once they realized they
were being pursued and attacked. Despite this, Dr Armour, who
met and treated the policemen as they were leaving the Reserve,
told the Commission of Enquiry that Sweeney had told him 'that
he did not get beaten in the yard because the people knew he
did not give orders to fire and it was Joseph who lost his head
and fired'.[38] However, the Commissioners fairly rapidly reached

---

[36] CO 152/425/1: 217 and 219 (Evidence of Edward Richard Green, 18 May
1931).

[37] This section of the report is reprinted in *WM* 286–91.

[38] CO 152/425/1: 209 and 254 (Evidence of Thomas Richard Sweeney, 18 May
1931; and evidence of Reginald Armour, 27 May 1931).

a conclusion to the effect that 'an attack had been launched against the Police before any shot was fired' (15). Having exonerated the policemen from initiating the violence, the Commissioners then rejected the policemen's claim that the first shots fired were into the air as warnings and criticized Inspector Branch for sending an armed search party into the Reserve without the direction and support of a commissioned officer (16). However, the fundamental conclusion remained: 'The moral responsibility for the death of two persons and the wounding of three others rests primarily on the Caribs who feloniously resisted lawful action by the Police. Secondarily the responsibility rests on the Carib Chief who made no attempt to control the mob' (17). The Commissioners also vindicated the action of the Administrator in calling for the warship and its marines.

The long final section of the report, 'Measures for the Amelioration of the Social and Economic Conditions of the Caribs', begins with an account of the Commissioners' visit to the Reserve. They travelled by motor-launch from Roseau to Portsmouth, by road to Hatton Garden, and the following morning on horseback to Salybia.[39] They gave a brief account of the government school and of photographic sessions with children and adults: 'The women very readily responded to our invitation and showed obvious pleasure in displaying the long tresses of bluish-black hair which they regard with legitimate pride as a distinctive characterstic of their race' (23). A meeting with the community followed, the day ending with a visit to Madame Titwa's yard, 'the *locus* of the regrettable incident of the 19th September last' (23).

The Commissioners' conclusions were negative in tenor. Repeating their misgivings about ' "pure" Carib blood', they stressed the extent to which the Caribs 'have almost entirely lost the qualities and characteristics which distinguished their ancestors', apart from their addiction to strong liquor (an ancient custom authorized by a quotation in French from Père Labat):

They have no folk-lore, no songs or music, no dances or customs, no costume or ornament to distinguish them from other inhabitants of Dominica.

[39] This section of the report is reprinted in *WM* 291–8.

No inscriptions, carvings, or relics could be pointed out to us in the Reserve.

They have become part of the Roman Catholic community.

For the once famous Carribean [*sic*] race the past is lost, forgotten, never to be recovered.

Under these circumstances the sentimental desire expressed in some quarters to conserve the racial individuality of the people commands a less ready sympathy than would otherwise be the case, and gives to the most impartial observer a sense of unreality and pretence. (24)

Perhaps surprisingly, at least from an early twenty-first-century perspective, this opinion was partly based on Thomas John's own lengthy evidence at the beginning of the hearings. Presumably in answer to questions (not marked on the record) by the Carib's attorney, C. E. A. Rawle, John stated:

There are no traditions handed down from father to son and the present Caribs know nothing of the Ancient customs and habits of the Caribs; the present Carib mothers sing the everyday Dominican songs to their infants; we dance when we are happy but only dance the Dominican dances; we do not dance Carib dances and we have no special Carib dress, we have no Carib ornaments and the only ornaments we wear are those purchased in the shops of Dominica. There are no special customs or ceremonies on births, marriages or deaths. There are no carved ornaments. Sometimes we discuss our ancient history. I do not remember any ancient occurrence in Carib history and there is no Carib poetry left.[40]

Those repeated negatives seem to admit in trumps the sense of cultural loss so often perceived by outsiders; though they may also speak eloquently of a very *different* sense of what constitutes culture: after all, there is little doubt that—despite the Commissioners' scorn (and perhaps the occasion of it)— Thomas John was a forthright spokesman for his community, in which he enjoyed great support.

As for the political status of the Reserve, the Commissioners recommended the appointment of a Government officer 'charged specifically with the care of the Carib people'. A chief could be democratically elected, subject to the approval of the Government, by whom he would be appointed; but he would

---

[40] CO 152/425/1: 1 (Evidence of Thomas Jollie John to Commission, 13 May 1931) (given via the interpreter, Frederick Augustus Piper).

only be able to advise the Government officer: 'No power, authority, or jurisdiction whatever should be given to the Chief ... The present Head Man or "Chief" under suspension is wholly unfitted for the discharge even of such limited duties as those which we have suggested above' (26–7). Eliot's attempt to downgrade, or degrade, Carib leadership was confirmed and even taken further, although no such Government officer was ever appointed. The Commissioners concluded that the real choice for the Caribs lay between 'squalid isolation', trying to pretend that they were beyond the law, and closer contact with their neighbours, which would teach them to understand 'the nature of their citizenship' (27).

Fundamentally the Report was a whitewash. The fact that six Caribs had been tried and acquitted in a Roseau court was entirely set aside by Rae and Armitage-Smith; in fact the trial was never even referred to in their Report. The Caribs, and especially Thomas John—'the Carib "Chief"' as they ostentatiously referred to him, always remembering the inverted commas— were retried and found guilty; the policemen more or less exonerated—the question of disciplining them in any way never arose; and the Administrator, E. C. Eliot, was regarded as justified in his actions. His plan to abolish the Reserve was not pursued, but the policies recommended by the Commissioners would clearly lead to its demise in due course.

The Caribs' counsel, Cecil Rawle, had written to the Aborigines Protection Society after the visit of the Commissioners, anticipating that 'the findings of the Commission will protect the Police in respect of the shooting incident complained of, but will nevertheless prove very helpful to the Carib Indians by suggesting practicable schemes for ameliorating their conditions of living'. Despite this rather optimistic forecast, the Caribs were not happy with the Report. In response to a further letter from the Caribs in June 1932, asking for the reinstatement of their Chief and the return of his insignia, the APS wrote to the Colonial Office, which dismissively referred them back to the Report, helpfully including details of price and availability.[41]

---

[41] (Letter from C. E. A. Rawle to AS&APS, 29 May 1931; Letter from H. Beckett to AS&APS, 1 July 1932 (APS/GN 294 (Dominica 1930–2, Disturbances).

Shortly after Elma Napier and her husband arrived in Dominica in 1932 and took up residence at Pointe Baptiste, just north of the Carib Reserve, they were visited by Thomas John: 'When at last our uninvited guest had revealed the purpose of his call he asked us to protest to the Aborigines Society against the rude things said of him in the official report on the Carib incident of 1930 about which, at that stage, we knew absolutely nothing' (Napier MS: 89–90). Mrs Napier soon returned the visit, writing a short piece for the *Guardian Weekly*. Her account of the 1930 incident is drawn from the Commission Report, but her portrait of Jolly John and his house revealing:

A milder-mannered chief of native tribe than Thomas Jolly John it would be hard to imagine—not unintelligent, but seemingly so devoid of personality that one wonders how he got himself elected. His wife and child are beautiful, the woman with long plaits of the destroyer of the devil—namely, straight black hair (what stress one lays on straight hair, living among negroes). Theirs is a new house, set starkly upon a hillside, the timbers and shingles not yet weathered to a uniform grey. Inside the one room (with alcove curtained off for sleeping), the walls are papered with an incongruous assortment of cigarette cards and holy pictures. There are three books on the table—the Bible in English, a Petit Larousse Illustré, and an agricultural handbook. Over the doors hang little charms, strips of stuff binding crossed sticks. 'I am making my new house for foreigners to sleep in,' says Thomas Jolly John, as we drink coconuts together; 'it would be nice if you could give a little present'. (Napier 1933)[42]

LOCAL OPINION

To some substantial degree the events recounted in this chapter—and, in a different register, those in the next—need understanding against the background of larger currents within West Indian history. The late 1920s and early 1930s saw a number of movements in the direction of political, social, and cultural self-assertion: the early stirrings of what would soon become a demand for West Indian independence. The first

[42] Elma Napier (1892–1973) went to Dominica with her second husband, Lennox, in 1932. She wrote two novels and two books of memoirs, and contributed to English journals during the 1930s and 1940s. As representative for the northeastern district on the Legislative Council from 1940 to 1951, she was one of the first women active in West Indian politics.

real signs of cultural nationalism are usually dated from the literary and cultural magazines founded around this time, such as *Trinidad* (1929), *Cosmopolitan* (Jamaica, 1929), *Beacon* (Trinidad, 1931), and *Forum Quarterly* (Barbados, 1932). The accompanying political expression would find its manifesto in C. L. R. James's *The Case for West Indian Self-Government*, published by the Hogarth Press in London in 1933.[43]

At the political level there had already been some small movement towards representative government in a number of the islands. On Dominica, there were signs of the emergence of a new political class, with its most dynamic member the Trinidadian-born lawyer, Cecil Rawle, who was to act as counsel for the Caribs during the Commission of Enquiry. In general terms this emerging group belonged to the professional *gros bourg*, the increasingly prosperous descendants of the 'mulatto ascendancy', although the group included at least one fully creolized 'white'—Ralph Nicholls, son of the Dr Nicholls who had so impressed Froude. Locally notorious both for his lack of colour prejudice (he actually *married* his coloured mistress) and for his working-class sympathies, Ralph Nicholls would go on to co-found the Dominica Trade Union with Christopher Loblack in 1945.[44] Other witnesses at the Enquiry who spoke in favour of the Caribs, such as H. D. Shillingford and Reginald Armour, usually belonged to this group, some of whom were acting as Unofficial Members of the Legislative Council at the time. The group continued to own, edit, and write for the island's newspapers, and therefore to represent and guide local opinion. The first crack in Crown Colony government had come in 1925, with local elected members—including Rawle and Shillingford—able to act in an advisory capacity. The campaign for better political representation continued through groupings such as the Taxpayers Organization (1927) and the Constitutional Reform Association (1931), all of which had very much the same membership. As the Dominica Taxpayers Reform Association, the group would convene the West Indies

---

[43] First published in Nelson, Lancashire, in full, in 1932, as *Captain Cipriani*; then by the Hogarth Press in 1933 as a long pamphlet, *The Case for West Indian Self-Government*. Extracts are reprinted in James (1977: 25–40).

[44] Ralph Nicholls was portrayed as Uncle Rufus by his cousin, Phyllis Shand Allfrey, in her novel *The Orchid House* [1953].

Conference of 1932 in Roseau, lamenting the 'arrogant and calculated contempt of popular desires and opinions' displayed by the British colonial regime in the West Indies.[45] So the trial of the Caribs and the subsequent Commission of Enquiry took place against a backdrop of substantial political agitation on the island.

From the start local opinion was critical of the government's response. In the *Dominica Tribune-Guardian* on 27 September 'Fiat Justitia' gave a summary of events in four succinct columns. On the actions of the HMS *Delhi*, the columnist noted drily: 'A demonstration of force was made by the warship at the Carib Reserve, on the night of the 21st instant, and the Caribs have, no doubt, been duly impressed'. Additional policemen landed from Antigua 'in full war kit including steel helmets to the amazement and amusement of the inhabitants of Roseau'. The same columnist's comments a fortnight later were even more forthright. Responding to a misleading report in the *Trinidad Guardian* that the *Delhi* had been sent to quell looting following food shortages, 'Fiat Justitia' stated that 'The HMS *Delhi* was summoned from Trinidad not to control food distribution, but on a Fool's errand by some panic stricken Official who had lost his sense of proportion. She was brought here to subdue a phantom enemy.' The column ends: 'The Caribs are the last surviving members of a dying race; they are ignorant, illiterate, timid, and poverty-stricken. They have moreover been hard hit by the recent hurricane. As a community they need assistance and protection. The *Delhi* demonstration was a senseless act of aggression towards Carib women and children and we shall be surprised if its causes and effects are not queried when the House of Commons reassembles.'[46]

When J. B. Charles—representative for the district of Dominica that included the Carib Reserve, and father of recent Prime Minister, Eugenia Charles—was called to give evidence to the Commission of Enquiry, he was full of resentment about the way in which the Administrator had acted: 'In my opinion the *Delhi* was not necessary. In my opinion the landing of the marines and the cost of sending up the police from St. Kitts

---

[45] See Lewis (1969: 102 and 427 n. 9); Honychurch (1995: 162–3).
[46] *Dominica Tribune-Guardian* (11 Oct. 1930).

should be paid by the person sending for them.'[47] On 10 January 1931 'De Omnibus Rebus' called in clear terms for a change of Administration.

In their reporting of the trial in which the Carib defendants were acquitted, what all the local columnists dwelt on was the blatant contradictions in the police testimony. 'Fiat Justitia' summed up: 'The verdict of the jury was not only popular, but was merely an acceptance of the directions on the facts of the learned Judge who somewhat reluctantly but nevertheless unequivocally and fearlessly in keeping with the sworn testimony before him indicated to the jury that the Police witnesses were untrustworthy.'[48]

Inasmuch as a division of opinion can be seen in the papers of the Commission, now lodged in the Public Record Office in London, it lies between the colonial authorities (mostly white, mostly non-resident or only temporarily resident on Dominica) and the Dominicans (mostly not white). As we have seen in earlier chapters, opinion about the Caribs does not always divide this way, with the *gros bourg*, in particular, developing a nationalist opinion opposed to special treatment for the Caribs. Violence, and the trials that follow, however, can cause seismic—if temporary—shifts of opinion; and Dominican voices spoke firmly in support of the Caribs throughout the hearings, although that support could always be seen—from a Carib point of view—as ambivalent: given because the Caribs were, after all, Dominicans, fellow islanders with whom *gros bourg* interests could be identified, at least at this moment when the two groups had a clearly common enemy in the oppressive colonial administration.[49] There was no significant Dominican association with

---

[47] CO 152/425/1 (Evidence of J. B. Charles, 19 May 1931).

[48] *Dominica Tribune-Guardian* (5 Feb. 1931).

[49] On the Dominican background for this period, Honychurch (1995: 156–72). H. D. Shillingford, a landowner from Hatton Garden, close to the Carib Reserve, went further in his evidence, revealing a rather astute sense of the key underlying issues: 'I do not think that it would be right to divide the land among the Caribs who now have rights. They hold the land now in common. Also if the land was divided per capita some would get good land and others bad land; also they have their cultivations scattered all over the Reserve . . . I see that if you define the privileges you must define the Caribs. It is a matter for the Caribs to decide who to let in and who not to do so' (CO 152/425/1: 242 (Evidence of Howell Donald Shillingford to Commission, 20 May 1931)).

that administration, at least as far as this incident was concerned: the police involved belonged to the Leeward Islands Police Force and only one of the five black policemen on the initial raid was Dominican. The white officers, Branch and Bell, were British, as of course were the Administrator, E. C. Eliot, and the Treasurer, Mr Baynes. (Two significant outsiders, Douglas Taylor and the ex-Administrator, Hesketh Bell, opposed the colonial viewpoint; and at least some of the misunderstanding about taxes, which lies behind the incident, seems to be due to the more sympathetic view of the Caribs taken by Major Peebles, who acted for Eliot during at least some of the Administrator's absences.)[50]

Ralph Nicholls's attitude towards the Caribs—ignorant but sympathetic—was probably typical of the *gros bourg* group at this time:

I have never been to the Carib Reserve. It is very difficult to get there and entails many days absence from Roseau to get there. I am particularly interested in them. I see a lot of them in town. I have always been interested in them. As a Dominican I am interested and proud of them. This is the general feeling of 99% of the people in Dominica. Strangers coming into the island take a great deal of interest in them and are keen to know all the history concerning them. My late father also took a great interest in them ... They are the remnants of the occupiers of the country which we have taken away from them and have been driven to a section of the country where the lands are poor and unproductive. This is why I say that they ought to be freed from direct taxation.[51]

Other versions of what had happened that day in Salybia had also been expressed, even if they had not appeared in the public realm. A telegram had been sent by concerned Dominicans to the Aborigines Protection Society in London. These Dominicans were the Unofficial Representatives of the

[50] Major Herbert Walter Peebles (1877–1955) was Commissioner and Treasurer of Montserrat from 1922 to 1929 and Administrator of St Vincent from 1929 to 1933. He served as Acting Governor of the Windward Islands in May and June 1930 and for several years was also Chief of Police in Dominica, where he was responsible for the clearing of the ground then used for the Roseau market, which is now known as Peebles Park. (With thanks to Lennox Honychurch for this information.)

[51] CO 152/42511: 238–9 (Evidence of Ralph Edgar Alford Nicholls to Commission, 20 May 1931).

Legislative Council—all members of the same *gros bourg* group discussed above:

Five Dominica Caribs shot by police nineteenth September two dead outcome alleged attempted resistance seizure goods on unlicenced shop in Carib reserve stop Caribs claim exempted direct taxation stop Caribs were unarmed stop Warship Delhi dispatched punitive expedition twentyfirst whole Carib community terrified fled into woods with babies still there stop Carib chief held prisoner now released on bail charged obstructing police stop independent enquiry into necessity shooting and subsequent treatment Carib imperative stop Caribs destitute consequent recent hurricane stop illiterate and last remnants of their race letter follows.[52]

The letter that followed (31 Oct. 1930) spelled out their concerns in some detail, combining a sceptical view of the actions of the colonial administration with a condescending approach to the Caribs. The concluding paragraph reads:

The Caribs are timid, illiterate, ignorant, poverty-stricken country-folk, and they deserve the special protection of the Government. They complain (a) that at a time of distress and destitution, caused by the hurricane which Dominica experienced on the 1st. September last, they were entitled to expect a measure of hurricane relief rather than a Police raid on the Reserve: (b) That the policemen concerned were motivated by the hope of a reward which they usually receive out of fines in revenue cases, rather than by the prevalence of any lawlessness or illicit trading within the Reserve: (c) That the authority under which the police purported to act was illegal, being equivalent to a general search warrant signed in blank by the Treasurer, the names of the parties against whom such authority to search was directed being filled in by the Police themselves after it was issued in blank, and without the knowledge of the Treasurer: (d) That the Coroner's Jury, as selected by the Police, for the Inquests touching the said deaths, contains an undue proportion of ex-policemen, and that the circumstances will militate against the expression of a true and proper verdict; and that the holding of the said Inquest has been unduly delayed: (e) That the show of force by the 'Delhi' was harsh and unwarranted, and inflicted much unnecessary hardship on Carib women and children, innocent of any allegation of criminality; And (f) that the liberties which they have enjoyed as a community from time immemorial are now endangered owing to the fact that the Government has in the past neglected to

---

[52] Undated copy in CO 152/417/10 (Magistrate's Court, 10 Nov. 1930).

safeguard their privileges by legislation, and now appears desirous of repudiating official assurances hitherto made verbally to the Caribs, and accepted by them in good faith.[53]

The writers' opening self-identification—'We the Elected and Nominated Unofficial Members of the Legislative Council of the Presidency of Dominica of the Leeward Islands, British West Indies'—goes a long way towards indicating the *gros bourg* position: this is not power speaking. They are officially Unofficial; the Legislative Council only has an advisory role to the President; the President is subordinate to the Governor of the Leeward Islands; who is appointed by the Colonial Secretary. The letter outlines the kind of case that would be made in favour of an official enquiry, and the kind of case that Rawle eventually made out in front of the Commission. As with other Dominican documents—such as Alexander Lockhart's article considered towards the end of the previous chapter—the attitude towards the Caribs themselves is not unsympathetic, but does largely describe them within the familiar post-Emancipation discourse about the peasantry: 'timid, illiterate, ignorant, poverty-stricken country-folk', the one concession to their difference being, on this occasion, the recognition of their 'immemorial' exemption from taxation.

THE CAPTAIN'S STORY

The papers gathered together by the Commission of Enquiry are especially useful for the evidence they offer of early attempts to describe what actually happened on that September morning, of the struggles of the people on the ground to construct a satisfactory narrative to deal with this 'disturbance' in the colonial order. The very presence in this case of the official narrative as produced by a Commission of Enquiry is itself evidence that these early narratives struggled unsuccessfully, which is precisely why they are of interest for cultural criticism.

Perhaps the most telling account of the events was that produced by Captain W. E. C. Tait of HMS *Delhi* when he reached Roseau on the morning of the 20 September. Tait is

[53] Six signatories, including F. Rose, H. B. Shillingford, J. B. Charles, R. E. A. Nicholls, and Cecil Rawle (APS/GN 294 (Dominica 1930–2, Disturbances)).

self-evidently dependent in the first part of what he writes on what he has been told. His source, as he says, is Chief Inspector Bell, but Bell knew only what he had been told by Inspector Branch, and Branch only what he had pieced together from the stories of the policemen involved. So what we see in Tait's narrative is the police story at a relatively early stage of its elaboration, a privileged site for the observation of narrative production:

The Dominica Police Force consists of 39 men, all blacks, with two white officers, and early on the morning of Friday 19th September, one corporal and four constables were sent into the Carib Reservation to seize a large consignment of liquor that was known to have been smuggled into the island and to arrest those men on whose property the liquor should be found. The Caribs had taken advantage of the disorganisation produced by the recent hurricane and the dispersal of the police on relief work, to smuggle on a large scale.

The liquor was found and arrests made, but on coming out of the hut a large crowd armed with sticks and stones barred the way of the police. On the appearance of the corporal the crowd shouted to him to put the liquor down and release the prisoners. This he refused to do and ordered the crowd to get out of his way. At this moment the Carib Chief himself appeared and asked to see the corporal's warrants. These were shewn him. He then, in front of the crowd, told the corporal to put the liquor back in the hut and release his prisoners at once. The corporal, knowing he could get his prisoners again at any time, consented to release them but said he must take the liquor. Thereupon the Caribs shouted the more, and started to throw stones, sticks and anything they could lay their hands on. Seeing now that their only road was completely blocked by a menacing and infuriated crowd and that the Chief was not even attempting to control his followers, the police drew their revolvers and fired in the air. This further enraged the people, more stones were thrown and a Carib with a shot gun opened fire on the police. The corporal and constables then fired on the mob. Two Caribs dropped at once, how many were lightly wounded may never be known. A momentary passage was left in the crowd by this action, and dropping the rum jars each of which weighed 40 lbs, the police passed down it presenting their revolvers at the Caribs. There was now three miles to go along a rough path to the end of the Reservation and the police had a yelling furious mob behind them throwing missiles of all kinds. Only a few rounds of ammunition had been taken out and these were soon expended in an endeavour to keep the crowd back. When the Caribs saw the constables were no longer dangerous they drew in closer, pelted them more than ever and belaboured them with heavy poles. Every now and then one policeman would fall to the ground and was jumped on by the crowd and kicked till rescued by his comrades. Finally all arrived somehow near the Reservation limit, here the Caribs completely surrounded the police, got them down, jumped on their stomachs, kicked their heads and faces, took away their revolvers and warrants and anything else they fancied, and then pushed and kicked them more dead than alive over the boundary. Such treatment would probably have killed white men, but being blacks, the corporal recovered sufficiently to tell the tale to Captain Branch, the District Superintendent of Constabulary who quickly arrived on the scene.

Captain Branch immediately telephoned the news through to Colonel Bell at Roseau who in consultation with the Administrator decided this was no ordinary outrage and that strong and instant measures must be adopted, and that immediate naval assistance must be sought.[54]

Tait's narrative is absolutely seamless: the Caribs act as a 'mob', large and co-ordinated; the policemen act with impeccable propriety, firing warning shots first and only shooting to kill when their lives are threatened. Tait's report also makes clear that it was he—the person with least experience of the local situation— who suggested to Bell that a demonstration using searchlights and star shells 'might have a salutary effect'; Bell agreeing that it 'would shew them that the Government was in earnest and really did mean business'. What it meant in practice was that the entire community dispersed, making it extremely difficult to make arrests over the next few days.

Tait's visit to Dominica lasted five days. He sailed up and down the coast off the Carib Reserve, flashing his lights and exploding his shells, and spent the rest of the time either in the roadstead at Roseau or in the Administrator's house. This brief acquaintance with the place did not prevent him having an opinion about the Caribs and what he called 'the problem of their future'. From his remarks on the matter, it sounds as if his opinions concurred with—and were perhaps derived from— those of Eliot. He notes, for example, that while to that date there had been no police station on the Reserve, 'it is probable that a station will be established there after this'. As indeed it

[54] CO 152/417/10: 127–8 (in Capt. W. E. C. Tait, 'Letter of proceedings no. 11/30, 14th to 25th September 1930').

soon was. Looking into his crystal ball, he did not see much future for the Caribs, although his predictions were at least in part based on the faulty assumption that 'the Carib Chief and some of his principal followers are likely to spend the next few years in gaol': 'Considering these points it seems more than possible that the Caribs will have to submit to all the laws which govern the rest of the community and that therefore their independence in name, even if sentiment preserves it for them, will in course of time mean nothing at all. This riot of Friday 19th September may mark the beginning of the end.'[55]

We have now seen a number of different accounts of what happened in the Carib Reserve on 19 September 1930, from the dramatically ill-informed newspaper reports to the relatively sophisticated narratives produced by different parts of the colonial bureaucracy. Behind the latter, as the previous section showed, are many other accounts—less sophisticated, often partial or incomplete, often conflicting—that have been generated at different stages of the containing process, but then consigned to the archives without ever becoming part of the public record. Underlying my approach to this material has been a concern for questions of narrative, for the way in which this story gets constructed and told. Narrative produces causality, and a constant feature of most of the longer stories about the 'incident at Salybia' is a concern for who is responsible or (ultimately the same thing) where the story begins.[56]

What is most striking in all the narratives presented in this chapter is the assigning of the role of initiator: this 'actant'—to use the narratological word—is the crucial agent in colonial narratives of this kind, because the person who begins the story is usually the one held legally or morally responsible. So here, in all the narratives, the Caribs are the initiators, most clearly in Eliot's brief telegraphic version (above, p. 156), where the police

---

[55] CO 152/417/10: 131–2 (in Capt. W. E. C. Tait, 'Letter of proceedings no. 11/30, 14th to 25th September 1930'). The 'salutary effect' is also referred to by Hesketh Bell (the sight of the warship 'being a salutary proof of the power that lies in the background' (1946: 75)), and by the Governor of the Leewards: 'This harmless procedure undoubtedly had a salutary effect' (St-Johnston 1936: 102). If three such eminent officials were agreed that something was so good for Carib health, the Caribs were probably justified in running for cover.

[56] Cf. Hayden White's landmark essay (1980).

constables are merely 'on duty' and have been quite mysteriously attacked for no apparent reason. There are two tropes at work here: negative causality—the lack of apparent reason for this attack by a 'mob'—with its implication that savages attack simply because they are savages; and the trope of self-victimization: the colonial authorities—like the settlers before them—never do anything to provoke attack: they are initially passive and only react to aggression. This is how official discourse tends to work in other places, but it is a specially prominent feature of colonial narratives.[57]

In these stories there are two sets of beginnings. The shooting of the Caribs by the policemen is incontrovertible, so it cannot be allowed to stand as the beginning of anything—because then it would be without justification. It needs to be preceded by a tightly drawn web of actions, all of which lead inevitably to that shooting. So—looking back to Tait's report—the story needs to be read backwards from the sentence 'The corporal and constables then fired on the mob'. 'Mob' plays an important role here in de-individualizing the Caribs, blurring them into a singular and threatening mass, so that the shots were fired into this 'mob' without the intention of injuring or killing any *individual* Caribs. The 'then' in that sentence is both a linguistic shifter and a mark of causality. It is immediately preceded—reading backwards—by a Carib firing a shotgun, more stones being thrown, warning shots being fired by the police, the inaction of the Carib chief, the actions of a menacing and infuriated crowd, and the throwing of sticks and stones. In other words—now reading forwards—there is a gradual escalation of violence which leads to the police shooting in self-defence. The 'beginning' marked by the shots has now been sufficiently embedded within a causal network to stifle, contain, and displace the violence that left two Caribs dead.

The other 'beginning' concerns the beginning of the story itself: where exactly does one start in order to narrate these events? The usual technique within colonial discourse is what

---

[57] An offhand example comes in the memoirs of a Navy Captain serving in the Caribbean at the time: 'the few surviving native Carib Indians . . . were difficult to handle at the best of times. On one occasion, in 1930, native disturbances became so serious that . . .' (Agar 1962: 195). Captain Agar's account is somewhat undermined by his memory that five policemen had been killed in riots.

might be called 'normalization', going about one's proper and lawful business: four constables 'on duty'. In Tait's letter, however, that beginning is finessed by another characteristic linguistic device. The police have been sent onto the Carib Reserve to seize smuggled liquor. The presence of smuggled liquor, at least in such large quantities, is itself explained by the disorganization produced by the hurricane, which has resulted in the 'dispersal' of the police on relief work. The Caribs had 'taken advantage' of this disorganization. It is difficult to plumb the ignorance suggested by this remark. The Caribs were not perhaps as 'disadvantaged' by the hurricane as everyone else? They were not also busy repairing their houses and gardens? The aftermath of a hurricane provides good sea conditions for small boat sailing? The true beginning of the narrative is therefore the hurricane, that archetypally Caribbean phenomenon which has always served to disrupt European order, a beginning which is echoed in those early newspaper reports. What this unlikely beginning obscures is that liquor has been smuggled into the Carib territory of Dominica for at least two centuries, and that this was the first *ever* police raid on the Reserve. In the light of this knowledge, the crucial phrase in that opening paragraph becomes 'that was known to have been smuggled', an example of the importance of the dead bat of the passive voice in official colonial discourse—the voice of naturalization, here presumably used to protect an informer. Tait had clearly mastered the genre of the official report, his task perhaps made easier, like that of other 'visitors', by his absence from the events reported, his ignorance of the area involved, his failure to talk to anyone other than colonial officials, and his absolute trust in the truth of what he was told. It was hardly his fault that so much of the story unravelled in the months that followed.

THE WRITINGS OF DOUGLAS TAYLOR

Between 1930 and 1934, in the aftermath of the Carib War, Douglas Taylor made several short visits to the island and to the Carib Reserve. These visits did not pass unnoticed—as Eliot's memorandum to the Colonial Office shows—but no obstructions seem to have been put in his path. In 1936 he arrived for a longer stay, but after a few months was already boiling over with frustration. In a letter to M. W. Stirling, Chief of the Bureau of American Ethnology, Taylor recalled his visit to Stirling in June of that year, during which Stirling had offered him assistance in carrying out his research among the Caribs:

While I came to look for primitive custom and tradition among the latter, I have encountered, with a vengeance, primitive predjudice [*sic*] and jealousy among the West Indians of position; and am today compelled to appeal to you to corroborate, in as far as you feel justified in doing, the authenticity of the work I have been doing in this island.

The general feeling seems to be that a white man who chooses to spend his time in the bush in the company of 'a lot of ignorant savages' instead of discussing cricket and local gossip at the club, can be up to no good. Ethnology, for the average West Indian, white or colored, either does not exist, or is 'damn foolishness'. Then, an injudicious though perfectly truthful statement in an earlier article of mine (to the effect that a police inspector responsible for the killing of two Caribs had been censured and transferred, only to be brought back to Dominica some time later) having reached the eyes of 'those in authority', local government circles started a regular campaign of defamation of character against me. As my own friends here only laughed at these reports, and assured me that this was a part of 'local custom', I did not worry. Then the Administrator sent for me and asked, in a very tactful way, when I should have finished what I was doing in the Reserve as he was afraid of 'something happening' to me for which the government might be held responsible, and as they had only three policemen up there . . . Moreover, he said, the Reserve was intended for Caribs only. I pointed out that nothing had been said to numerous negros living there and contaminating the Carib stock, whereas I was a visitor, there for the sole purpose of gathering information. He answered that he knew there were negros there and felt it was a fact to be regretted, and that the police (also negro) had been instructed to stop such infiltration. Since then two of the policemen have had children with Carib girls!

Taylor spent time in Roseau writing up his notes, and was preparing to return to the Reserve when the Administrator (Henry Bradshaw Popham) sent for him again 'and intimated, in the most round-about terms imaginable, that if I did not soon get out, I would be kicked out of the island. When I mentioned my intention of going back to the Reserve, he practically forbade me to go near the Caribs. As he refused to make any formal accusation, but talked vaguely of "certain reports" and "accumulated evidence", I am at a loss to know what it is all about.'[58] Taylor eventually settled in Dominica in 1938, buying the small Bellevue Estate. As resident of the island he became perhaps too familiar a figure on the Carib Reserve to be considered a visitor in the sense of the word being employed here, especially after he established a family with a Carib woman. However, between 1930 and 1938 he visited the island about six times, spending periods from between one day and several weeks with the Caribs, and so can count as a visitor during these years.[59]

Like Hesketh Bell before him, Taylor's first impressions were of cultural degeneration: 'Though they have become a tame and in many ways uninteresting lot, they still have a certain interest as being the last direct descendents of Columbus's first found "Americans." '[60] Elsewhere he calls them 'my poor little group of Caribs' and fears as early as 1939 that he has completed 'just about all that can be done among this remnant of Island Karib'.[61] The first piece Taylor wrote on the Caribs was an

[58] BAE (Letter from Douglas Taylor to M. W. Stirling, 14 Nov. 1936). Stirling usually lent a sympathetic ear to Taylor's complaints about the authorities in Dominica, but it should be noted that he felt himself obliged to make 'a few emendations' to the section of Taylor's 1938 article dealing with the recent 'Carib War'—'because of our official governmental status' (BAE: Letter from M. W. Stirling to Douglas Taylor, 24 Sept. 1937). In Colonial Office papers, Taylor is referred to as the 'erratic ethnologist': there was clearly serious consideration given as to whether it would be possible to expel him (CO 152/462/6). The Governor of the Leeward Islands, Lethem, summed up in a long letter to the Colonial Office in this same file: 'The whole matter presents the usual feature of a pseudo-scientist indulging in an ill-proportioned and gullible enthusiasm for an ethnological relic with an added feature that his personal morals have invited unsavoury comment' (21 Aug. 1936).

[59] Although the division is not watertight, I have considered Taylor's early pieces for the *American Anthropologist* (1935, 1936), his more popular piece for *Natural History* (1941), and the letters he wrote between 1930 and 1938, as his writings as 'visitor'. His scholarly work then falls into several categories: the ethnography of the Dominican Caribs (1938, 1945, 1946a, 1946b, 1948 (with Moore), 1949, 1952); supplemented by the work on the Black Caribs of British Honduras (1951); studies of Caribbean languages, including Island Carib but with an increasing attention to forms of creole (1956, 1956 (with Rouse), 1958, 1961, 1963, 1977, 1980 (with Hoff)—in addition to about seventy-five other articles.

[60] BAE (Letter from Douglas Taylor to Editor, *National Geographic Magazine*, 19 July 1934).

[61] BAE (Letters from Douglas Taylor to M. W. Stirling, 21 Sept. 1934 and 26 Oct. 1939). His many articles on the Island Carib subsequent to 1939 rather belie this last statement.

article he offered to the *National Geographic* under the title 'The Last of the Caribs': the *National Geographic* was not interested. He then wrote two introductory pieces for the *American Anthropologist* (1935, 1937) before completing his lengthy and still valuable paper for the Bureau of American Ethnology in 1938.[62]

Taylor's early writings on the Caribs poise themselves— like so many of their predecessors—on the brink of the precipice of total cultural loss: '[A]t last their course is run, and they are fast disappearing. Of their story little is known and less written; and it is with the purpose of recording before it becomes too late, something of this vestige of a once virile and powerful people, that my own attempt at knowing them has been made' (1938: 109). However, the ethnologist's task is justified by things not 'being so irremediably lost as some people seem to believe' (1935: 265), a tart reference to Rae and Armitage-Smith and their oracular pronouncements about Carib cultural decline made on the basis of a two-day visit to the Reserve. By contrast Taylor plays down his own ethnographic authority. What he has gathered are 'meagre scraps, gleaned by me in the course of about half a dozen visits of from one to five days' (1935: 265); with the clear implication that if such brief visits can produce this much, then serious study could produce much more—a promise that Taylor's career was amply to fulfil.

From the beginning, Taylor's language was that of preservation and mediation. The pathetically unsuccessful letter to his friend Porter (quoted above, p. 166) asks him 'to help me to preserve the Carib race', as if a couple of white men can suddenly have an immediate impact on a historical process under way for nearly five centuries. Taylor knows well enough that, according to the old stories, the Dominican Caribs are an admixture of old Caribs and old Arawaks, yet he has no compunction about distinguishing between the 'pure Carib blood' and the mixed race produced from interbreeding with the black

[62] J.-P. Delawarde's ethnographic snapshot of the Carib Reserve (based on two months' research in Dominica in 1936, with a week on the Reserve) was also published at this time (1938). Taylor's generally favourable but slightly condescending comments on it are contained in his correspondence with Stirling (BAE: Letter from Douglas Taylor to M. W. Stirling, 6 Jan. 1939).

population: 'Interbreeding and the dying out of the old ways seems to be inevitable; but it might be possible by encouragement and judicious help to stem the tide' (Taylor 1935: 272). The racial sterotyping is overt ('the bolder, more hot-blooded negro's relatively greater success as a lover' (1938: 114)), with the 'tide' an embedded reference to Lothrop Stoddard's influential racist tract, *The Rising Tide of Color Against White World-Supremacy*, published in 1921. Nevertheless, that hasty letter, bristling with urgency and advocacy, sketches out something of the future history of Carib relations with the outside world: baskets were eventually sold—without success—in England in the 1970s, under the auspices of the eccentric Carib enthusiast, Christopher Robinson; and the idea that the chief should come to Europe foreshadows the moment of global awareness of indigenous rights and claims associated with 1993, the United Nations Year of Indigenous Peoples, which took many indigenous leaders, including the Carib chief, to places such as Geneva, Ottawa, and New York.

In 1940, with Europe at war, Taylor wrote his most popular and personal account of the Caribs in an article which appeared in *Natural History*, the magazine of the American Museum of Natural History in New York, under the somewhat inappropriate title 'Columbus Saw Them First.' Rather like Hesketh Bell's draft chapter (see above, p. 142), Taylor's piece works through a series of imaginative reconstructions. It begins by recalling in the third person the appearance to Columbus on 3 November 1493 of the four islands he named Dominica, María Galante, Guadeloupe, and La Desirada. Switching century and perspective, Taylor then in the first person speaks from the point of view of the island inhabitants:

Again it is Sunday, November 3, and now, from the only spot where a single native 'Indian' may yet be found in the entire island chain from Florida to the delta of the Orinoco, I am looking out across the timeless Atlantic where Spanish ships were spied by some long-forgotten ancestor of the men and women around me here today . . . Here, in the last Carib Reserve, the records of bygone days are enhanced by many living traits. It is not hard to retrace the centuries in imagination and reconstruct a scene we might well have witnessed, had we, as unobtrusive strangers, visited this coastal strip in the days before the Conquest. (1941: 40–1)

Something like this imagined scene is reproduced in the dramatic photograph which opens the article (fig. 9). Down below present-day Caribs in their Sunday best stand around talking after the morning's church service, while on the hill above Salybia two young Caribs in fifteenth-century costume look out across the bay to where, 447 years earlier, they might have caught sight of Columbus's fleet. Meanwhile, to the left, empty hands on hips, stands the unobtrusive stranger, watching Caribs, bay, and church: *witness* to the changes wrought by history, changes which he now in imagination shepherds the reader through.

The first part of the article is dominated by the construction 'had we . . . we should have . . .', as Taylor takes the reader on a tour of Carib life four and a half centuries ago: 'Had we arrived in the evening, when men and women were home from

FIG. 9. 'A CARIB COVE: picturesque Salybia Bay on the British island of Dominica in the Lesser Antilles, showing the boulder-strewn strand where fishing boats are beached through rough surf'. (The opening illustration to Douglas Taylor's essay in *Natural History*, 48 (1941), p. 40; photograph by H. M. and E. L. Ayers. Museum of Natural History, New York.)

their various occupations, we should have been welcomed by the one whose duty it was to receive strangers.' From a passing hunter, 'had he unexpectedly chosen to be communicative, we might have learned much of what the forest meant to the men of his race' (42). The reader is part of that first person plural, but on a path chosen by Taylor and with his voice to translate and interpret the sights and sounds and words of this recreation of 1493, as we become ourselves, as readers, unobtrusive strangers awarded impossible access to a pre-contact world.

Gradually this literary technique fades from the essay to be replaced by a more conventional third-person account of Carib life under the general headings, 'Two languages in each family', 'Medicine men', and 'Trade' (46–7). The last three sections then deal with the history that connects 1493 with 1940, the pristine view from the hill with the present realities of church and social structure below: 'Outside influences on the Carib', 'The retreat before civilization', and 'Intermarriage' (48–9). Here the story is entirely one of Carib decline: the abandonment of native crafts, the deforestation of the north windward, the impoverishment of the soil, the increased contact with 'town' leading to drunken binges, and—most important of all—the loss of the language: 'And so it is that the Island Carib of today knows little about his own culture and nothing about our culture except, as it were, through Negro eyes' (49). Predictably—by now—the final sign of decline is the lack of compunction shown by the Caribs for 'interbreeding': 'Out of 400 inhabitants of the Reserve today, 300 are at best, as they themselves admit, "*bâtards Caraïbes*" (half-breed Caribs)' (49).

PICTURING THE CARIBS

Most visitors to the Caribs from Frederick Ober onwards have gone armed with a camera: indeed I suggested at the beginning of this book that the camera was in many ways the emblem of 'the visit' as I was defining that activity. Douglas Taylor was a keen photographer of the Caribs. His first unpublished article was accompanied by fifteen photographs taken on one of his early visits to the Reserve; and eighteen different photographs were published with his BAE article in 1938. He also commissioned and presumably directed the taking of the fifteen photographs by H. M. and E. L. Ayers which—together with six pencil sketches by Hester Merwin—accompanied the article in *Natural History* (1941); and the National Anthropological Archives at the Smithsonian Institution has a further thirty-five of the Ayers's photographs (ignoring duplicates), unattributed to them.[63] These seventy-two photographs, taken by three collaborating photographers over a period of no more than eight years, offer a different angle of insight into just what is regarded as valuable within 'the visit'.

Taylor's fifteen photographs taken on his early visits to the Reserve fall into well-established categories. Almost all are of large family groups, some seated in the style of the school photograph, and given titles such as 'Mother and five smaller children of mixed blood', 'Family group: mother and five smaller children of mixed blood', 'Family group, not necessarily all from same mother' (see fig. 10). There are only four of individuals: Jolly John—the only named individual, and three Carib girls aged fifteen, thirteen, and twelve. A note at the bottom of Taylor's list reads: 'The individual figures are the best examples I could obtain of full-blooded types.'[64] The seven photographs in his second *American Anthropologist* article are simply labelled 'Island Carib types' (1936: plates 14–15).[65]

Interestingly, the pictures in the *Natural History* article act as an undertow against the current about cultural decline present in the narrative itself and in Taylor's earlier photographs. Out of the twenty photographs and drawings (excluding the scene-setting shot already discussed), ten feature individual full body or face only portraits of individual Caribs. Eight are named, suggesting an engagement with the social reality of Carib society in 1940 that goes beyond its depiction as the endpoint of

[63] Douglas Taylor, Photographs of Carib Reserve, 1930–34. Department of Physical Anthropology: Caribs, Photo Lot 8, Box 9: Taylor Collection, National Anthropological Archives, Smithsonian Institution. It is impossible to be sure about who took all the photographs in this collection, but two of the photographs in the *Natural History* article (Taylor 1941) attributed to the Ayers form part of the Taylor Collection. On the history of pictorial representations of the Caribs, see Honychurch (1997b: 56–9).

[64] BAE (Letter from Douglas Taylor to Editor, *National Geographic Magazine* (19 June 1934)).

[65] Delawarde's contemporary piece has nineteen photographs, mostly labelled 'type caraïbe' or 'type bâtard' (1938: pls. VI–VIII).

FIG. 10. 'Family group: mother and five smaller children of mixed blood'. (Photograph by Douglas Taylor. Bureau of American Ethnography (Taylor to *National Geographic*, 1934, no. 6). National Anthropological Archives, Smithsonian Institution.)

cultural degeneration. One of the only two unnamed portraits is the only picture that seems to *support* the narrative account: 'A CARIB YOUTH who, like three out of every four in the last remaining Carib refuge, is of mixed descent.' The remaining photographs include two family groups, one in front of 'their *typical* thatched dwelling', another '*representative*' of the only American Indians to be found in the Caribbean (emphasis added on both occasions); six pictures showing native craft skills—basketry, sail-making, canoe construction; and, in some ways most interesting of all, a group photograph showing 'DOUGLAS TAYLOR, the author, standing between "Jolly John," the chief who recently died, and Jimmy Benjamin' (*WM* 308). No longer the 'unobtrusive stranger', Taylor emerges here as an individual sharing the same frame with and looking in the same direction as the man whom he elsewhere calls his 'host, guide, and sponsor in the Reserve' (1938: 152).

FIG. 11. 'Jimmy Benjamin, About 52 Years Old' (photograph by H. M. and E. L. Ayers. National Anthropological Archives, Smithsonian Institution, 07102400).

The vast majority of the photographs in the Taylor Collection in the Smithsonian Institution are also of named individuals. These are high quality and effective photographs, evincing a sympathetic engagement with the individuals portrayed. There is no indication that they were chosen to 'represent' or 'typify'

Fig. 12. 'Jimmy Benjamin, About 52 Years Old [Profile]' (photograph by H. M. and E. L. Ayers. National Anthropological Archives, Smithsonian Institution, 07102300).

the Caribs, but they probably do reflect Taylor's (and perhaps the Ayers' own) sense of the uncontaminated stock. There is just a hint, especially in the combination of full-face and profile photographs (figs. 11 and 12), of a documentary record being compiled.[66] Taylor—like Bell before him—was also, and with the same difficulty, collecting anthropometrical measurements.[67] It is also impossible to ignore the rather different set of photographs all called 'Portrait of Martine, 16 years old', the Carib woman—Martine Benjamin—Taylor was soon to set up home with on Dominica.

[66] Cf. Green (1984: 33); although Taylor's photographs had no scientific pretensions.

[67] He undertook these between 1938 and 1941, and later prepared a paper with Georg Neumann which was never published (see Taylor 1952: 267n. 1).

5. The Return of the Native: Jean Rhys and the Caribs (1936)

> This feeling I have about the Caribs & the Carib Quarter is very old & very complicated . . . When I try to explain the feeling I find I cannot or do not wish to . . . (Jean Rhys, 'Orange Notebook')[1]

Jean Rhys's *Wide Sargasso Sea* is by some distance the best-known literary text associated with Dominica. Like much else in Rhys's writing, the association is not direct. In *Jane Eyre*, from which Rhys takes the character of Bertha, the madwoman in the attic, the West Indian episode, narrated by Rochester, is set in Jamaica. The first part of *Wide Sargasso Sea* follows this setting, although many of the topographical details draw on Rhys's memories of her grandmother's plantation house at Geneva, in the south of Dominica: 'I tried to write about Geneva and the Geneva garden in *Wide Sargasso Sea*' (1981: 33). However, when Antoinette (Bertha) takes her unnamed husband (the Rochester figure) back to her own mother's island for their honeymoon, they land at a place called Massacre, the name of the village just north of Roseau that lies at the foot of the hill where Rhys's parents had their own small plantations during her childhood.

'And who was massacred here? Slaves?' [asks 'Rochester']
  'Oh no.' She sounded shocked. 'Not slaves. Something must have happened a long time ago. Nobody remembers now.' (*WSS* 55)[2]

'Nobody remembers now' is, as I suggested in the first chapter of this book, a fairly accurate summary of the state of knowledge, even on Dominica itself, about Carib history in the middle

---

[1] p. 52 (quoted in Angier 1990: 33). For an explanation of the references to Rhys's manuscripts, see the note on Manuscript Collections at the beginning of the List of References. The implications of Rhys's Caribbean connections are now being fully and sensitively explored: see e.g. Raiskin 1996, Savory 1998, Thomas 1999.
[2] Quotations from *Wide Sargasso Sea* (*WSS*) come from the 1997 Penguin edition.

of the nineteenth century, when Antoinette speaks these words according to the internal chronology of the novel. But 'remember' can be an ambiguous word. Antoinette does not say that she does not *know* what happened, or that nobody *knows*, just that nobody 'remembers'; which may imply that people *know* perfectly well what happened, but that nobody *cares* to remember, nobody is willing to make the effort of memory that would bring those past events into the present, into public consciousness, into a conversation with a puzzled newcomer, a European visitor, who shows some interest, too much interest, the wrong sort of interest, in the island's history. Antoinette knows enough to say that it was not slaves who were massacred; 'Rochester' (henceforward just Rochester)—like most newcomers to the islands in the post-Emancipation period—is all too ready in Antoinette's eyes to condemn the slave-owners, so massacres of slaves must not form part of the island's history. Whether Antoinette 'knew' what had actually happened at Massacre must remain a moot point. Rhys certainly knew, and that knowledge is intricately connected with her 'old' and 'complicated' feeling about the Caribs, a feeling she could not or did not want to explain, any more than Antoinette wanted to explain just who had been massacred at Massacre. Only once did that 'complicated feeling' confront the Caribs themselves, a visit to the Reserve that took place in 1936, during Rhys's one brief return to the island of her birth. Out of that visit came her long story, 'Temps Perdi', only published in 1969, but possibly written, or drafted, soon after the visit.[3] That story will be this chapter's main point of reference.

Another of Rhys's stories, 'The Imperial Road', also deals with that return, in ways I will be concerned to associate with 'Temps Perdi'. In the opening lines of 'The Imperial Road' the narrator looks at the Dominican mountains and exclaims on their beauty to a young man standing beside her on the deck of the ship. He politely asks if she has visited Dominica before. 'I was born in Roseau,' she says. 'His expression changed at once. He gave me a strange look, contemptuous, hostile.'[4] The

---

[3] Henceforth *TP* (Rhys 1987: 256–74).
[4] 'The Imperial Road' (henceforth *IR*) is due to be published (Rhys 2000) in a slightly different version from the one discussed here. Another draft of this story is called 'The Return of the Native'.

narrator's claims to 'native' status are constantly rejected by black Dominicans.

From the start of this book it has been apparent that outside attitudes towards the Caribs have been inseparable from attitudes towards the majority Afro-Dominican population. Rhys's position is different from many visitors in two respects. She writes fictional texts, even though these often draw very directly on her own experiences, especially in the later stories. And she returns in 1936 not just as somebody who *happened* to be born on the island, but belonging to a Dominican family whose history stretches back into the nineteenth century and whose members were still actively involved in local politics at the time of her return. The complexity of that sense of family and the ambivalence inevitably associated with a native returning will form the themes of this chapter.

MASSACRE

The first major English settlement in the West Indies was undertaken by Thomas Warner on St Kitts in 1625. As well as his legitimate children, Warner had a son with a Carib woman slave from Dominica, whom he recognized, gave his name to, and raised in his own house in Antigua with his other children. After Thomas Warner's death, his (third) English wife was hostile to this half-Carib son, who eventually left Antigua to live with his mother's people on the leeward coast of Dominica. 'Indian' Warner, as he was often known, was an important figure in the complicated and shifting alliances of the mid-seventeenth-century Caribbean. He was evidently trusted by the Lords Willoughby, father and son, who took him to England and made him Governor of Dominica; he was captured and imprisoned by the French; and he incurred the hostility of other English colonies, especially that of Antigua. He seems to have been an effective leader of the leeward Caribs on Dominica, but no friend of the windward Caraïbes, allies of the French.

Towards the end of 1674, Philip Warner, Indian Warner's half-brother and Lieutenant Governor of Barbados, arrived in Dominica with 300 men. Together with Indian Warner and sixty leeward Caribs, they attacked and killed a number of windward

Caraïbes, several of them under a flag of truce. According to the deposition of William Hamlyn, commander of an Antiguan sloop that had been pressed into Philip Warner's service and eye-witness to the events, whose account is followed here: 'After the dispute was over, Col. Warner invited Thomas Warner and his Indians, to the number of 60 or 70 men, women and children, to an entertainment of thanks, and having made them very drunk with rum, gave a signal, and some of the English fell upon and destroyed them.'[5] This was the massacre that gave Massacre its name: the killing by English soldiers of a group of Caribs led by a half-English 'musteech', the killing by brother of brother.

When Philip Warner returned to England in June 1675, he was imprisoned in the Tower and 'charged with the murder of his brother Thomas Warner, an Indian, and the destruction of other Indians, His Majesty's friends' (*WM* 102–3). The West Indian colonists rallied to Philip Warner's cause. Indian Warner's English parentage was denied, he was alleged to be in the pay of the French, he was accused of reverting to savagery, and—worst of all—he was said to have 'often dealt treacherously, pretending friendshipp, but proving an absolute enemy, not only to this Island [Antigua], but to our whole nation' (*WM* 97). Philip Warner was sent to Barbados for trial, judged by his peers, and acquitted.

In coming back to her mother's island Antoinette is risking, as she no doubt knew, the claims of a putative brother, supposed product of the profligate seed of a West Indian patriarch, honoured—as Cosway is in the novel, and as both Warner and Rhys's own great-grandfather were in fact—by the kind of marble tablet which ensures that everybody does remember who they were.[6] The story of the Warner brothers is perhaps too close

---

[5] *Calendar of State Papers*, 1675–6, pp. 175–6, quoted from *WM* 101–2. *Wild Majesty* collects together various documents relevant to Indian Warner's story. See also the account in Boucher (1992: 67–83) and the essay by Marina Warner (1997).

[6] Sir Thomas Warner's marble tombstone still stands in the churchyard at Old Roadstead, St Kitts. Jean Rhys's great-grandfather, James Potter Lockhart, was commemorated with a marble plaque in the Anglican church in Roseau until it was destroyed in the 1979 hurricane (Oliver 1927: 11). It is perhaps emblematic of changing times that, while Lockhart's plaque was destroyed, Indian Warner (now more usually Carib Warner) has been commemorated by a mural in Massacre painted in 1993 by Dominica's best-known artist, Earl Ettienne.

for comfort for Antoinette to tell Rochester. But if she will not tell the story of white planters and their half-caste children, cast out but seeking recognition, then Daniel Cosway, the occupant of the Indian Warner position within the novel, will seek to make it known to Rochester, the new master. To Rochester's standard English obsessions with slavery and voodoo is added the suspicion that what he calls 'the secret I would never know' (*WSS* 141) is actually the secret of his wife's relationship to this threatening figure on the margins, who insists on using the Cosway name. ' "They call me Daniel," he said, still not looking at me, "but my name is Esau" ' (101), cunningly playing the card that will worry Rochester the most: the suggestion that he, Daniel, is the first-born (like Indian Warner) and might therefore have a claim on the wealth that Rochester—who is only in this colonial place because he is a second-born son—hopes to inherit through his wife. Doubtless Daniel/Esau would appreciate a ' mess of pottage. His parting shot—' "You are not the first to kiss her pretty face" '—also suggests that Rochester will always be coming second, even in sexual matters.[7] With respect to the 'reality' of Daniel's claims, Rhys cleverly leaves the question open: when Rochester tells Antoinette that he has been to see Daniel Cosway, she replies that he has no right to that name (106) but, earlier, talking about Sandi, Alexander Cosway's son, she has revealed that Mr Mason had made her 'shy about my coloured relatives' (42). However, what Rochester never even suspects is that the secret he would never know might have something to do with the Carib threads in the island history, which Antoinette keeps to herself. Even at the time of their greatest happiness on the island they appear divided by language: 'Every evening we saw the sun go down from the thatched shelter she called the ajoupa, I the summer house' (74)—Rochester using the English word, Antoinette the Carib.

As the previous paragraph suggests, in terms of its sources and references *Wide Sargasso Sea* is an extraordinarily impacted novel. If the allusion to the Carib massacre casts a shadow on Antoinette's homecoming too dark for her, and perhaps even for

---

[7] On the figure of Daniel Cosway, see also Gregg (1995: 108–15), and Thomas (1999: 171–2).

Rhys, to penetrate, then a more proximate source—and therefore reference—is Rhys's own 'homecoming' to Dominica with
her own (relatively) new husband, Leslie Tilden Smith.[8] From
the somewhat scanty evidence available, it seems that Rhys was
deeply marked by her return to Dominica for two months in
1936, a return not just to the island itself but to family and to
memories and to family memories. The West Indies of her childhood had never been entirely absent from Rhys's writing, but it
now assumed a more important place, especially in the note-
book she called 'Creole', in which she began to collect West
Indian material, some of which would find its way into *Wide
Sargasso Sea*—an early version of which may have been written
as early as 1945. She also planned a novel to be called *Wedding
in the Carib Quarter*, wrote many of her childhood memories
of Dominica into the 'Black Exercise Book', and produced at
least the first version of several stories drawing on those early
memories, particularly 'Pioneers, Oh, Pioneers' (briefly discussed earlier, in Chapter 3).[9] However, the events of those few
weeks were more directly fictionalized in two stories. One of
these, 'Temps Perdi', puts Jean Rhys firmly into the ethnographic tradition under analysis here, while the other, 'The
Imperial Road', suggests her deep connectivity to many aspects
of Dominican history and politics.

JEAN RHYS AND DOMINICA

Ella Gwendoline Rees Williams had been born in 1890 in
Dominica, the daughter of William Rees Williams, a Welsh
doctor who had come to the island in 1881 and Minna Lockhart, who belonged to the third generation of a plantation-
owning family, originally from Scotland. The Lockharts were
centrally involved with the fraught history of the island sketched
in Chapter 4, where Acton Don Lockhart, one of Rhys's uncles

---

[8] Rhys had married Tilden Smith in 1934, although they had been together for
several years. She had previously been married to Jean Lenglet. For biographical
details, see Angier 1990.

[9] On the first version of *Wide Sargasso Sea* and on *Wedding in the Carib Quarter*,
see Rhys's letter to Francis Wyndham of 22 July 1962 (Rhys 1985: 213); and cf.
Angier (1990: 371, 372, 435). The 'Black Exercise Book' (*BEB*) forms part of the
Rhys collection at the University of Tulsa.

(*c*.1858–1922), appeared as Froude's guide: he later proved to be one of the colonial administration's strongest supporters, a support that Hesketh Bell continued to enjoy. The Lockharts owned Geneva, a genteelly fading plantation in the south of the island, a remnant from an earlier historical period, but still—especially in its house—a symbol of privilege and social standing. Rhys's father, William Rees Williams, a recent arrival from Wales, bought his own estates and seemed to want to relive that life of privilege, high above the town, perhaps emulating the established Dr Nicholls. Unfortunately, Rees Williams was a doctor in that town, and his absence generated complaints amongst his patients and in the local press.[10] Rhys's most vivid childhood memories, detailed in the autobiographical memoir *Smile Please*, are of her family house in Roseau, of Geneva, and of her father's plantation at Bona Vista in the hills beyond Massacre (1981: 21–6, 33–41). After the sale of the plantations, Dr Williams became more active in local politics: he was still attacked in the press as a government lackey, but seems to have earned some kudos as Chairman of the Roseau Town Board. Like Rochester, Dr Williams was a second son who had made his way in the world partly through marriage. However, unlike Rochester, he married up the social scale, securing himself a place in the colonial élite a notch or two higher than his professional capacity would have guaranteed.

Gwen Rees Williams, as she then was, had left Dominica in 1907 just before her seventeenth birthday. She had lived through seventeen years in Dominica's history, her adolescence coinciding with the period of Hesketh Bell's dynamic administration: she was 12 when he had sent off his report on the Caribs to London, nearly 16½ when he left the island for Uganda.

In 'Temps Perdi' the narrator speaks of 'a book I once read, pictures I once saw' (*TP* 268), locating her fascination with the Caribs in childhood but not in any personal knowledge or

---

[10] In 1885 the *Dominica Dial* wrote: 'it is somewhat remarkable that this officer can find time to devote no inconsiderable amount of attention to agricultural pursuits at Bona Vista. Dr Williams is constantly absent from town, and there have been cases within our own knowledge where his services have been urgently required by patients who were cheeringly told that they would find him at Bona Vista, two hours good riding distance away' (5 Sept. 1885; quoted in Thomas 1996a: 7).

recollections: her experience is as bookish and remote as if she had been born in the Swiss Geneva which gave the Lockharts' plantation its name. Indeed, Gwen Rees Williams might have seen a few Caribs in Roseau but she had never travelled to the Carib Reserve.

At the beginning of the third part of a story that moves from London to Vienna to Dominica, the narrator explains that 'temps perdi' is a creole phrase without the expected literary resonance, meaning simply 'wasted time', a phrase often applied to attempts to tame the wilderness of Dominica:

There are places which are supposed to be hostile to human beings and to know how to defend themselves. When I was a child it used to be said that this island was one of them. You are getting along fine and then a hurricane comes, or a disease of the crops that nobody can cure, and there you are—more West Indian ruins and labour lost. It has been going on for more than three hundred years—yes, it's more than three hundred years ago that somebody carved 'Temps Perdi' on a tree near by, they say. (267–8)

The narrator of 'Temps Perdi' expresses a desire to visit the Carib Quarter in the face of indifference from her curiously unnamed and ungendered companion ('Nobody else seemed to want to visit the Carib Quarter' (269)) and opposition from the black overseer: ' "There is nothing to see in the Carib Quarter," Nicholas insisted. . . . But I wasn't so easily put off. All my life I had been curious about these people because of a book I once read, pictures I once saw' (268). Eventually she convinces her companion to make the long trip on horseback from the 'Temps Perdi' estate, with a teenager called Charlie as their guide.

THE PHOTOGRAPH

That 'book I once read, pictures I once saw' makes another appearance in Rhys's work, in one of two passages from her earlier novel, *Voyage in the Dark*, which cast intertextual light on 'Temps Perdi'. Like the other story I will later suggest as intertext ('The Imperial Road'), the first of these passages was offered and withdrawn: initially incorporated into the harrowing final part of *Voyage in the Dark*, Rhys's third novel (published in 1934, but drawing on the unpublished *Triple Sec*, written as early as 1914) before she had removed it while revising the novel's ending, with some reluctance, on her publisher's insistence.[11] In *Voyage in the Dark*, Anna Morgan, a young white West Indian woman living in London and earning a precarious living as a chorus girl, rapidly descends from being mistress to a prosperous business man to a life on the verge of prostitution. The novel originally ended with her death, following an abortion, and the final pages consisted of a stream of consciousness largely made up of fragmented memories, some of them of her early years in the West Indies. One segment, the first, reads like this:

Smile please the man said not quite so serious
 He dodged out from behind the black cloth
You tell her to madam
 He had a long black-yellow face with pimples on his chin he dodged in again under the black cloth
 I looked down at my legs and the white socks coming half-way up my legs and the black shoes with a strap over the instep and the doll in my lap it could say Maman Papa and shut its eyes for Dodo.
 Show her the picture-book Aunt Jane said
 Now smile darling Mother said look at the pretty picture and smile
 The trees in the picture were so tidy and the little girl so round and plump and the wall so high and you kept wondering what was beyond it and you couldn't imagine anything
 Now the man said from behind the black cloth
 Now keep quite still Mother said
 I tried but my hand shot up of its own accord
 Oh what a pity she moved now it'll have to be done all over again
 I began to cry
 Now now now the man said
 A big girl like you I'm ashamed of you Mother said just one second and you are ten years older Meta was fanning her with a palm leaf to keep the flies away and she was too young to die Meta said with tears running down her face but I was only thinking of my white dress and the wreath I would carry.[12]

---

[11] Cf. Angier (1990: 294–5); Kloepfer (1989: 75–8).

[12] The typescript of the original ending to *Voyage in the Dark* is quoted from Nancy Hemond Brown's transcription (Brown 1985; this quotation 45–6). There are disagreements both as to which version Rhys 'really' preferred and as to which is superior. It seems that she chose to leave the revised ending in place when *Voyage in the Dark* was republished because she already planned to use some of the material from the original ending in her autobiography (JRC: Letter to Oliver Stoner (15 Dec. 1969)).

We are justified in thinking of this as Rhys's own memory—or at least one she claimed—by the fact that the expunged passage appears many years later, in slightly shortened form, as the opening paragraphs of her autobiographical memoir, *Smile Please*, published just after her death in 1979 (1981: 1). Like 'Temps Perdi', the passage turns on the relationship between movement and photograph, memories of an embarrassing moment tinged with sadness and death.

Earlier in *Voyage in the Dark*, Anna Morgan, shut up in her cold English room, had recalled Dominica and thought about the Caribs:

> 'And drift, drift
> Legions away from despair.'

It can't be 'legions.' 'Oceans,' perhaps. 'Oceans away from despair.' But it's the sea, I thought. The Caribbean Sea. 'The Caribs indigenous to this island were a warlike tribe and their resistance to white domination, though spasmodic, was fierce. As lately as the beginning of the nineteenth century they raided one of the neighbouring islands and kidnapped the governor, his wife and three children. They are now practically exterminated. The few hundreds that are left do not intermarry with the negroes. Their reservation, at the northern end of the island, is known as the Carib Quarter.' They had, or used to have, a king. Mopo, his name was. Here's to Mopo, King of the Caribs! But, they are now practically exterminated. 'Oceans away from despair . . .' (1982: 90–1)

It is an odd moment, which begins with two lines remembered from a song; moves into correction of the quoted lines; continues into stream of consciousness: legions—oceans—sea—Caribbean—Caribs; switches into an unlikely direct quotation from what sounds like a popular history or travel-book; and ends with a gloss, an added memory, and a return to the starting point with the remembered lines corrected. As Mary Lou Emery suggests: 'What may appear to be subjective musings linking eccentrically one random thought to another actually juxtaposes an intensely private memory to a public statement, pointing away from the self to the system of language and its formal conventions' (1982: 421). In addition, Anna seems to suggest a certain identification, perhaps hinting at her suicidal state of mind. She picks up the phrase 'practically exterminated', a condition which distances the Caribs from despair, an extermination perhaps therefore to be desired;[13] although the presumed identification is also open to a more political inter- pretation since, if the few hundred Caribs that are left do not intermarry with the negroes, then that would also be true of the small white population to which Anna belonged. Mopo appears in no published book about the Caribs, and so is probably Rhys's invention. The nearest English word, 'to mope', means 'to yield oneself up to ennui, to remain in a listless, apathetic condition'.[14]

As Sue Thomas points out, Anna's recitation is part of a strategy for dealing with the despair over the excess femininity of her own writing by seeking distractions, in noises, objects, or—as here—in memory: 'The recitation from memory marks a return to the unquestioned colonial veracities of Anna'a origins—it is a writing (and an interpellation of her own ethnic identity) that consoles' (1999: 146). The Caribs—'remembered' in a sense, though of course never actually 'known'—are little more than a token of a memory which is at least hers, to which she belongs.

The narrator in 'Temps Perdi' is in a more privileged position than Anna with respect to knowledge of the Caribs, especially as a 'native' with access to information, but she is also both 'desirous of visiting' and in a social situation which requires her to justify that desire. She recalls what she knows about the Caribs, what she has remembered from the childhood book:

Whenever the Caribs are talked about, which is not often, the adjec- tive is 'decadent', though nobody knows much about them, one way or the other or ever will now. There are a few hundreds left in the West Indies, or in the world, and they live in the part of the island called Salybia. They had not intermarried much with the Negroes and still have smooth, black hair, small, slanting eyes, high cheekbones, copper-

---

[13] Cf. Rhys's memory of the picture of Mary Queen of Scots going to her exe- cution, which hung over the sideboard in the house in Roseau: 'Mary Queen of Scots was tall and stout, dressed in black velvet, her right foot eternally advanced, walking daintily to extinction. The crowd behind her was male, also dressed in black. I have often since seen their narrow eyes, their self-satisfied expressions' (1981: 24).

[14] Mapoia is the name of a Carib spirit (see *WM* 143); Morpo is the name of an area near Geneva, the Lockharts' plantation; Mopo, a historical African figure, plays a key part in H. Rider Haggard's novel about the Anglo-Zulu War, *Nada the Lily* (1892). On supposed Carib listlessness, see below, p. 284.

coloured skins. They make baskets, beautifully plaited, light and waterproof, dyed red and brown or black and white. The largest is the island's substitute for a trunk, the smallest would just hold a baby's shoe. Sometimes the baskets are made to fit one inside the other, like Chinese boxes.

The infrequent talk is presumably recalled from the early years of the century, before Rhys left the island. The baskets, a common sight in Roseau in 1936, as they had been thirty years previously, are a tangible sign of handiwork; yet the narrator is still 'tormented' with the fear that the childhood book has been imagined, and so brings out a special number of the French magazine *L'Illustration*, produced in November 1935 for the *Tricententaire des Antilles Françaises*, and shows the reprinted picture '*Homme Caraibe Dessiné d'après natur par le Père Plumier*': 'Bow and arrows in his right hand, a club in his left, a huge, muscular body and a strange, small, womanish face. His long, black hair was carefully parted in the middle and hung smoothly to his shoulders. But his slanting eyes, starting from their sockets, looked wild and terrified. He was more the frightened than the frightening savage.'[15]

This 1930s reproduction of an eighteenth-century French print is not offered as a 'real' Carib, just as the touchstone of a real memory, because 'We had a print very like this—perhaps it was the same one—in the dining-room at home.... And he always used to look so sad, I thought, when they laughed at him. With his wild, strained eyes and his useless bows and arrows' (269–70). Having reached the bedrock of her own adolescent fascination, the narrator is pushed by her partner onto less solid ground as historian:

'The original West Indian, is he?'

'Oh no, that's a Carib. The original West Indians were killed by the Spaniards or deported to Hispaniola—Haiti. Well, most of the men were. The Spaniards told them they were going to Heaven. So they went. Weren't they suckers? Then the Caribs, the cannibals, came from the mainland of South America and killed off the few men who were left.'

But that book, written by an Englishman in the 1880s, said that some of the women, who had survived both Spaniards and Caribs—

---

[15] *TP* 269; and see the illustration in *WM* 302.

people were not so thorough then as they are now—had carried on the old language and traditions, handing them down from mother to daughter. This language was kept a secret from their conquerors, but the writer of the book claimed to have learned it. He said that it was Mongolian in origin, not South American. He said that it definitely established the fact that there was communication between China and what is now known as the New World. But he had a lot of imagination, that man. Wasn't there a chapter about the buried Carib treasure in La Soufrière, St Lucia—one of the mouths of Hell, they say—and another about the snake god, and another about Atlantis? Oh yes, he had a lot of imagination. (270)

The net result of these paragraphs is to convey a good deal of information about the Caribs, most of which is undermined by its source of authority being thrown into doubt. They tell all that the narrator knows, but the suspicion grows—not least in her own mind—that it is all the product of a fervid English imagination and therefore not to be trusted. These paragraphs seem to be muddled recollections of Frederick Ober's *Camps in the Caribbees*, first published in Boston in 1879 but reprinted in Edinburgh in 1880, probably leading Rhys to the 'Englishman in the 1880s' since her father's or the library's copy would have been the Edinburgh edition. Ober's geological speculations about the Caribbean island chain lead him to connect 'these mountain-peaks with a submerged continent that extended over the vast space now occupied by the Caribbean Sea' and therefore ready to speculate 'that the "lost Atlantis" of the ancients is not a myth' (1880: 250). He also describes the Carib snake-god (154–5). There are various mentions of treasure, although not in St Lucia; and the 'soufrières' of both St Lucia and St Vincent feature in Ober's travels. He discusses the dual language system (100–2); and tells a story about how a Chinaman—'pure Mongolian'—had married a yellow Carib and how their children could not be distinguished from the Indian children around them (92).

EXCURSION TO THE CARIB QUARTER

Leslie and Ella Tilden Smith spent six of their eight weeks on Dominica at an estate called Hampstead on the north-east coast of the island, which Rhys describes in her one published letter written at that time (1985: 28–9). A little inland from Hampstead is an area called Temps Perdi (there are several in Dominica, including one close to Geneva), the name that Rhys gave both to the story under discussion and to the Dominican estate in the story that corresponds to Hampstead, from where she and her husband went south on an expedition to visit the Carib Quarter, as she calls it, a trip Leslie Tilden Smith refers to in an unpublished letter to his daughter:

But we had a good day for our excursion to the Carib quarter, which is very beautiful and, I thought, very interesting. The Caribs are more or less wild still and they have no regular village, living in little houses dotted around in the bush. But very bright, clean little places with gay gardens. We went into one or two and met the ex-'King', who owns the prettiest kitten I have seen in the West Indies and a very untypical old lady who had been children's nurse for seven years to a French family in Martinique and Paris! She remembered Jean's father and the famous Owen. She was the mother of a girl who, from the waist upwards, is one of the loveliest creatures I have ever seen, but her poor legs are shrunken and paralysed and she has to drag herself about on her hands. She is about 20. Quite cheery but a tragedy for all that.

We had five hours on horseback in the Quarter and were very tired, though nothing like so bad as when we 'crossed the island'.[16]

A surviving photograph shows Rhys and her husband setting off on horseback (fig. 13).

The story describes it this way: 'The day we went to the Carib Quarter the wind was blowing heavy luminous clouds across the sky, tormenting the thin crooked coconut-palms on the slope of the hill opposite the verandah, so different from the straight, healthy, glossy-green coconuts just around the corner of the road—tame trees, planted in rows to make copra' (*TP* 157).

The first person they meet at the edge of the Reserve is a black Dominican policeman, who guides them into Salybia, the main

[16] Letter from Leslie Tilden Smith to Phyllis Smyser, 25 May 1936 (JRC). 'Crossed the island' refers to the incident which became Rhys's story, 'The Imperial Road', discussed below.

FIG. 13. Jean Rhys and Leslie Tilden Smith, probably on the trip they took to the Carib Reserve, Dominica, 1936. (Photographer unknown. Jean Rhys Collection, McFarlin Library, University of Tulsa).

Carib settlement. Here they come to the clearing which contains a Catholic church and a police station:

In the station the rifles were stacked in a row, bayonets and all. The room was large, almost cool. Everything looked new and clean, and there was a circular seat round the palm tree outside.

'We had trouble here,' our policeman told us. 'They burnt the last station, and they burnt twenty feet off this one while it was being built.'

'Why?'

'Well, it seems they thought they were going to have a hospital. They had asked the Government for a hospital. A petition, you know. And when they found out that the Government was giving them a police-station and not a hospital, there was trouble.'

'Serious trouble?'

'Pretty serious. They burnt the first one down, and they burnt twenty feet off this one.'

'Yes, but I mean was anybody hurt?'

'Oh no, only two or three Caribs,' he said. 'Two-three Caribs were killed.' It might have been an Englishman talking. (272)

The ethnographic encounter always needs to be pristine: visitor sees Carib, often engaged in traditional pastime. Rhys's encounter, by contrast, is with a black policeman, who will act as intermediary, a policeman who is black (and therefore not Carib) but also a representative of colonial authority. Mimicking his colonial masters, the policeman 'might have been an Englishman'. Her companion in the story, husband in actuality, was of course an Englishman; and the comment serves to distance him too from any possible site of authority within the story. Indeed, Leslie's letter acts as a counter-text to 'Temps Perdi', with its collection of vapid tourist clichés ('very beautiful . . . very interesting . . . prettiest kitten') of exactly the kind that Rhys, as writer and as native, wanted to avoid.

In 'Temps Perdi' the policeman tells the narrator and her companion about a beautiful but disabled Carib girl whom they ought to take photographs of: 'She and her mother will be very vexed if you don't go' (272), the policeman says.

The girl appeared in the doorway of the dark little bedroom, posed for a moment dramatically, then dragged herself across the floor into the sun outside to be photographed, managing her useless legs with a desperate, courageous grace; she had white lovely teeth. There she sat in the sun, brown eyes fixed on us, the long brown eyes of the Creole, not the small, black, slanting eyes of the pure Carib. And her hair, which hung to her waist and went through every shade from dark brown to copper and back again, was not a Carib's hair, either. She sat there smiling . . . (273)

'She sat there smiling.' The Carib girl is compliant, she willingly smiles for the camera. At first sight she seems almost a counterimage to Rhys's memory of herself at the photographer's in Roseau, spoiling the photograph through her involuntary movements, although, if so, the girl has paid the price in her loss of mobility—traditional attribute of the Caribs, as it has been of her own mother ('in her youth she had lived in Martinique in service with a French family and then been taken to Paris' (273)). The girl's revenge is subtle. The visitors are there, like all visitors to the Reserve, to *see* the Caribs, to *see* the physical characteristics by which the Caribs are known as culturally different from the majority population of the West Indies. The girl is eager to oblige, but her eyes and hair are wrong, not Carib at all—though it is unclear what is 'not Carib' about the girl's hair.[17] Something of the story's ambiguity is suggested by the different readings that have been given of the girl's 'Caribness'. For Sue Thomas the mother/daughter pair is a sign of the narrator's splitting of 'pure' and 'mixed' Carib (1999: 201); for Howells the girl is '[m]istakenly identified as a "Carib"'— though what she goes on to say about the girl, that 'she is in fact the illegitimate daughter of an unknown Frenchman and a black Martinican woman' (1991: 142), is a complete misreading.[18] As so often, it is not a matter of 'identity' or 'mistake', but of expectations and perceptions: here the narrator's notion of 'purity', fed by eighteenth-century illustrations, is too stringent for any real bodies to match: 'We took a few photographs, then Charlie asked if he might take the rest. We heard his condescending voice: "Will you turn your side face? will you please turn your full face? *Don't* smile for this one." ("These people are quite savage people—quite uncivilized")' (*TP* 273).

The narrator's part in the photography is obscured by the first-person plural pronoun—it may have been her companion who took the photographs[19]—but in any case she quickly retreats to the role of third party as Charlie takes over, allowing her, the implication seems to be, some sense of identification with this 'savage' girl whose ready smile is now ordered to cease so that her face can reflect her people's lack of civilization. The true ethnographic distance no doubt lies between all visitors and all Caribs, but the female protagonist and writer here distances herself from Charlie's almost violent use of the camera as a weapon of cultural distinction—even if this move only serves to

---

[17] The best discussion of the story is Thomas (1999: 143–54); see also Savory (1998: 170–3); and Howells (1991: 141–4). The hair certainly has the requisite length and shininess: perhaps it is not black enough. Thomas reads the story in the light of the Commission report, which had scoffed at claims of cultural distinction, but admired the Carib women's 'long tresses of bluish black hair' (quoted above, p. 178).

[18] Howells assumes that the girl's mother is Martinican. Although the mother says that she had lived in Martinique in her youth, she clearly states that she had come back 'here' (i.e. to the Reserve) to see her own mother.

[19] Given Rhys's own legendary incompetence with everything mechanical, it would presumably have been Leslie who took any photographs on the occasion of their actual visit. The Executor's Archive contains more than fifty photographs taken in Dominica in 1936, but none that would correspond to the ones described in the story. There is a picture of two small Carib girls (fig. 14).

FIG. 14. Two Carib girls. (Photograph probably by Leslie Tilden Smith, Dominica, 1936. Jean Rhys Collection, McFarlin Library, University of Tulsa).

suggest a further symbolic level, with the Carib as metaphor for a violated creole self, the narrator's own.[20]

What happens here, I am suggesting, is that the economy of cultural difference, emblematically represented by that metaphorical snapshot of the encounter between distinguished visitor and Carib Indian, is disrupted when the narrator stands aside from the photographic session and lets us see, in her account, the implicit violence in the instructions to smile or not to smile, instructions with which Rhys too was once made to comply, and which she always remembered as a gesture of sexual violence. In memory she gendered a photographic convention as a refusal of her young girl's body to conform to the demand of the male photographer that it take up a particular position, that it compose itself, that it be silent and smile. That

[20] Cf. reference to full/profile at the end of Chapter 4. Rhys's deeply personal response to the Carib Reserve stands in stark contrast to the account given by Père J.-B. Delawarde after his visit that same year. Although he spent two months on the island and had 'many conversations' with Caribs, nothing is said about himself or his movements or the people he spoke to (1938: 167).

vivid memory of being photographed perhaps intersects and dislocates the conventional operation of cultural differentiation in 'Temps Perdi'. That the policeman should direct the white tourists to the beautiful but lame girl is, then, no accident. She is offered by the story's cultural intermediary (the local representative of colonial power) as the embodiment and representative of a doomed culture, broken by history, yet casting an elegiac glow as the final remnant lives out its last years, its way of life preserved by Hesketh Bell's administrative fiat, open now to the photographic gaze of the tourist. The narrator's personal construction as a 'native' allows a swerve away from the tourist visit, a genre identified with her companion and also with Charlie, who plays the part of local visitor, mimicking—to crude excess—the gestures of the metropolitan tourist.

The 'Carib Quarter' is the third part of the story 'Temps Perdi'. Like part two, 'The Sword Dance and the Love Dance', it seems to take the form of a memory recalled as a diversion from the neutrality of life in Rolvenden, a house on the east coast of England occupied by the narrator during a November of the Second World War. Putting bolsters along the window sills reminds her of how she used to keep the cold out in Vienna, precipitating the second part of the story. Remembering the story told by the Japanese officer, Matsu, of how he had been lost all day on the Inner Circle underground in London, the narrator imagines her own 'inner circle' of happy memories, from which she, however, will emerge as 'a savage person—a real Carib' (267)—leading into her memory of a trip to the Carib quarter.[21] All three parts of the story have their cultural encounters, of very different kinds. The third part is the longest and the one where the title of the story gets explained. The idea of 'the stranger', so important in Rhys's fiction, is key: in the first part she herself is the stranger, in part two Vienna provides a meeting ground for strangers, none of whom is at home and, as a result, none of whom seems to sense that sharp feeling of

[21] According to Rhys, her father said to her in 1906: 'Well, you are a bit of a savage, you know. That's why you're going to England' (quoted from the drafts of *Smile Please* by Angier 1990: 33). Her brother Owen's fictionalized version of their family history fantasizes a possible affair between his young sister and a half-Carib boy (Angier 1990: 30–3). The 'real savage' gets glossed in her description of the Carib in Père Plumier's illustration: 'wild . . . terrified . . . frightened' (269).

strangeness; and in part three, her unnamed companion is the stranger, to whose opinion the narrator is sensitive, although his approving remarks about the Dominican countryside still carry an echo of Rochester's in *Wide Sargasso Sea*: 'Beautiful, open, park-like country. But what an *extreme* green!' (271).[22]

Leslie's letter offers some indication of the kinds of choices Rhys made in putting together her story. His touristic eye makes no mention of the policeman or police station, and the *de facto* chief, Jolly John, is mentioned only for the prettiness of his kitten. The beautiful but paralysed Carib girl is the centre-piece of both accounts but, whereas for Leslie she is simply a Carib they happened to see, in 'Temps Perdi' she is the Carib whom they are almost *directed* to see by the black policeman. In other words the girl is offered as representative not by the story itself, but by the action of the policeman within the story: the process of representation is politicized. However, as always in Rhys's writing, nothing is quite that straightforward. In 'Temps Perdi', the policeman points to 'the king's house' and 'I thought "So there's still a king, is there?"' (*TP* 272); whereas Leslie's letter makes it clear that they did actually meet Jolly John.

THE IMPERIAL ROAD

'The Imperial Road' is the only other story that draws directly on Rhys's return to Dominica. It was due to appear in Rhys's last collection, in 1976, but was pulled out just before publication. When, shortly afterwards, Rhys offered many of her private papers and manuscripts for sale the catalogue listed the unpublished story with the notation: 'Miss Rhys has stated that her publishers declined to include this story in *Sleep It Off, Lady*, considering it to be too anti-negro in tone.'[23]

In order to get to Hampstead, Rhys and her husband had had to travel on a launch up the coast from Roseau to the town of Portsmouth, and then by car along a rough track. In the story— and I will try to hold on to the distinction between event and story, although, as with the third part of 'Temps Perdi', the story

---

[22] Cf. '"What an extreme green," was all I could say' (*WSS* 42).
[23] Quoted in O'Connor (1992: 404); cf. Hulme 2000.

is very closely based on an actual incident—when it is time to leave Hampstead, the narrator convinces her husband, in the story called Lee, that instead of returning to Roseau by the same route they should walk across the island on the old Imperial Road: 'I was perfectly certain that it must still exist,' she says (*IR* 11). As with the trip to the Carib Reserve, everybody else, husband included, is distinctly sceptical, but the narrator insists and gets her way, although they are persuaded to hire two guides. This is the narrator's account:

Everything went splendidly at first. I felt as if I were back in my girl-hood, setting out on some wonderful adventure which would certainly end happily and remembered all the old names, Malgré tout, Sweet River, Castle Comfort. On this side the names were Portsmouth, Hampstead and so on, the people Protestants of various sects, the language a sort of English.

Soon the road wasn't a road any longer but a steep, uphill track. It was very stony and then the first catastrophe happened. I stumbled over a sharp stone and when I [got up] I didn't seem able to walk, just limp painfully. (12–13)

Lee then hires a mule, which the narrator immediately falls off. The forest thickens and it starts to rain: 'The farther we went the more I reproached myself. The whole thing was my fault and Theodore and all the others had been right. There wasn't a vestige left of the Imperial Road' (15). Just as she thinks they are going to be abandoned by their two guides, the trees thin out 'and soon we emerged onto a very civilized scene, a close clipped lawn, a white house' (15). The place had, she says, been either bought or rented by an American couple, and the scene it presents is in sharp contrast to anything else in the story: 'In a large cool room a man in a spotless white robe was playing the piano and there was a woman, also in a spotless kimono with two long plaits of hair hanging down and with rather a pretty face' (15–16).

Their driver has come to meet them and so the misadventure ends comfortably enough, with champagne and chicken sandwiches back at their hotel in Roseau. But the mystery of the Imperial Road keeps the narrator awake:

'I have been thinking over things and do you know I'm absolutely certain that that wasn't the Imperial Road at all. It's quite impossible it should have disappeared without leaving any trace. That Martinique man [one of their guides] must have took us wrong.'

'You think so?' [her husband says]

'I'm quite sure of it. It was a large wide road. An engineer came out from England specially to build it and it took several years. It just couldn't be overgrown to that extent.'

. . .

I lay awake for a long time asking myself if I could conceivably have imagined this ceremony with the administrator in his best uniform, in gold lace, cocked hat and a sword (not [*sic*] I'm not sure about the sword, but I am about the cocked hat and uniform). The band played, the crowd cheered and he made a little speech declaring the Imperial Road across the island open to all traffic. I couldn't have imagined it and the Imperial Road couldn't have disappeared without a trace, it just wasn't possible. No Imperial Road or a trace of it. Just darkness, cut trees, creepers and it just wasn't possible. (17–18)

That is how the story ends.

There is one other mention of the Imperial Road in Rhys's writings, more lighthearted, less plangent than the treatment in her story. In 1949 the travel writer Alec Waugh published an essay called 'Typical Dominica', in which he discusses the Imperial Road.[24] Rhys read 'Typical Dominica' in Waugh's anthology, *Where the Clock Strikes Twice*, and wrote him a long letter, almost all of which is about the Imperial Road:

What happened, I wonder, to the 1st Imperial Road. That was nearly finished when I was a small child or supposed to be nearly finished. I can remember the opening ceremony. The administrator, whose name was Hasketh Bell, wore a cocked hat and cut a ribbon with silver scissors I think. Perhaps the next man disliked Dominica or the money dried up . . .

But about the Imperial Road. We tried the walk from Hampstead . . .

However, it was an awful walk. It rained all the time. A kind woman lent me a mule half way, and I fell off the first time there. Was a steep downwards bit of road.

---

[24] 'Typical Dominica' was first published in shortened form in an English magazine, before appearing in full in the English edition of his *Where the Clocks Chime Twice* (Waugh 1952: 46–79), but not in the US edition—*Where the Clocks Strike Twice* [1951]—which is otherwise (and apart from its title) identical. It also appears in his collection, *The Sugar Islands* (1958).

This Martinique guide swore. Why a Martinique man? I don't know. But the Dominica one said, 'Do not cry Madame.' The Dominicans can be very gentle. The country people mean. But the Martinique men are completely cynical. Did you notice?[25]

'Hasketh Bell' is of course Hesketh Bell, and Rhys undoubtedly remembered well the cocked hat and silver scissors (*WM* 256), emblematic of the flourish with which the Imperial Road was opened: Chapter 3 traced something of its unfulfilled promise as equally emblematic of how the imperial system failed the West Indies.

Rhys would have been familiar enough with the first couple of miles of the Imperial Road, here described in a piece Bell wrote for the journal of the West India Committee:

The Imperial Road may be considered to start from the Good-will Bridge at Roseau, and it follows, for the first two and three-quarter miles, the old track along the leeward coast. It passes through two large and valuable sugar estates that are being transformed into lime plantations. This section was reconstructed in a superior manner, and was metalled throughout. It is now an excellent driving road, and a good deal of wheeled traffic passes over it. For a considerable distance it is bordered by immense tamarind trees, and is a favourite afternoon promenade. The construction of this small length of driving road resulted almost immediately in the importation of a few carriages and a considerable number of bicycles. (Bell 1904*a*: 5)

It was this 'small length of driving road' that Bell was travelling in his carriage when he passed an embarrassed Gwen Rees Williams, as Jean Rhys then was, on a January afternoon in 1905, an incident Rhys recalls in *Smile Please*:

We had at that time a very energetic administrator called Mr Hesketh. That was part of his name anyway. . . . He improved the roads out of all knowledge and triumphantly carried through his better idea of an Imperial Road across the island so that the Caribbean and South Atlantic sides were no longer cut off one from the other. . . . He tried

[25] Quoted from Campbell (1979: 59) (the letter is in the Twentieth Century Archives at Boston University). Campbell's discussion of the letter refers to Rhys's husband as her brother, and puts the 1936 visit to Dominica in 1938. The letter is tentatively dated 'early 1950s' (62). Rhys lived at the return address on the letter to Waugh from early 1952 to late 1953 (Angier 1990: 465–7). It is not clear which of the two versions (story or letter) was written first.

to tackle the sewage problem but here even he failed. However he gave several prizes for the best-dressed mask at the yearly carnival and was a great patron of the local cricket club.

One day the rumour started that Mr Hesketh was going to give a fancy-dress ball for his little niece, who was staying at Government House with her father and mother. The rumour was true, it was to be a fancy-dress dance for children and the invitations were sent out. . . .

As soon as I got to Government House several people congratulated me on my dress. And Mr Hesketh came up and asked me to dance the first waltz with him. Among his other accomplishments he was a very good dancer indeed and like all good dancers he could make his partner feel she too was an expert. . . . I longed for that waltz to last forever, to skim forever round and round with Mr Hesketh's arm about me. I stopped being shy and managed to laugh and talk to him. I waltzed three times with Mr Hesketh and each time was better than the last and I was happier. I went home, I suppose, somewhere between twelve and one and looking at myself in the glass I knew that night had changed me. I was a different girl, I told myself that I would be just as happy the next day, now I would always be happy.

In the afternoons when I came home from school I often went for a ride. . . . So I was ambling along when I saw in the distance Mr Hesketh driving a small trap.

The moment I saw him I became very nervous. He was driving towards Roseau, I was riding away from it. We must inevitably meet. He seemed to be coming along very fast, I had no time to think what I should say, to prepare myself for the meeting as it were. Almost at once we seemed to be side by side. He took his hat off, waved it at me and called something. Overcome with shyness I turned my head away and pretended not to see him. Then he was gone and I rode on, knowing that I had behaved in a foolish, bad-mannered way. I tried to console myself by saying that no one had seen us, no one would ever know.

It was some days afterwards that my mother said to me 'Why were you so rude to Mr Hesketh?' I stared at her and said: 'Do you mean that he told you?'—'Oh, he made a joke about it,' said my mother. 'While we were playing croquet he asked me what he had done to offend you. He said that you met him on the Goodwill road and cut him dead. He was laughing.'

I could only say that I didn't mean to be rude. 'You are a very peculiar child,' said my mother. 'There are times when I am very anxious about you. I can't imagine what will happen if you don't learn to behave more like other people.'

I didn't answer this, I only told myself that never again would I like Mr Hesketh or think about him. I was also very miserable. (1981: 89–92)

The incident has all the power of a short story, although there is no reason to doubt its status as memory.[26] It reads very much like some kind of rite of passage, perhaps a sexual awakening of some sort.[27] Rhys had turned fourteen four months earlier: Bell, just turned 40, was old enough to be her father. Elsewhere in *Smile Please* she writes: 'I shut away at the back of my mind any sexual experiences . . . not knowing that this would cause me to remember them in detail all the rest of my life' (1981: 50)—just as she shut Bell out of her mind, only to remember him now, over sixty years later, as she dictates her memoirs.

'Mr Hesketh' represents an early avatar of that public, masculine, English world of business and civilization and officialdom, that Rhys and most of her heroines consistently falls foul of. As Administrator, Bell was the most important man in the small world of Dominica. Rhys's father, William Rees Williams, in his capacity as Chairman of the Roseau Town Board, had spoken one of the official addresses of welcome to Bell soon after he arrived in Dominica. When he left his previous appointment in Nassau, Bell had been seen off by a former Dominican President, Spencer Churchill, who was the husband of Jean Rhys's aunt, Edith Maxwell Lockhart. This is a tightly-knit white West Indian world in which there are not many people one can play croquet with.[28]

---

[26] Bell's sister Nell, brother-in-law Jack Scully, and small niece Marjorie (Medjé in Bell's diaries) spent a lot of time on Dominica during Bell's administration. Scully was one of the 'pioneers', who soon found that trying to grow cocoa high in the interior of the island was a sure way to lose money. The children's fancy-dress party that Rhys refers to seems to have taken place on 29 December 1904 (BP2 (29 Dec. 1904)).

[27] That awkward relationship between older man and young girl is frequent in Rhys's fiction, and is now usually traced back to the encounter with a 'Mr Howard' she wrote about in the 'Black Exercise Book' and which, as Teresa O'Connor (1986) and others have suggested, leaves its mark on much of Rhys's writing. In the earliest account of this incident Rhys gives her age as 14: 'How old are you? I'm fourteen—Fourteen he said fourteen—quite old enough to have a lover' (BEB 51).

[28] On Nassau: BP2 (18 Aug. 1899). The synopsis of Bell's diary for the week following the party reads in part, and perhaps coincidentally: 'I seriously consider the advisability of getting married and note the "pro" and "con". I describe my "ideal" ' —the only mention of this topic in his available papers (BP2 (6 Jan. 1905)).

So the Imperial Road existed for Jean Rhys because she had seen it opened and indeed been deeply and unforgettably embarrassed on it by the very man who was responsible for its existence. Not knowing that thirty years has been insufficient time for its completion now leads to embarrassment at the other end

FIG. 15. 'Dominica: Caribs on the Imperial Road', engraving by Thornton Oakley (in Amy Oakley, *Behold the West Indies*, New York: D. Appleton-Century Company, 1941, p. 276).

of the route. Although Rhys would not necessarily have known this, her story about the Imperial Road has a further connection to Hesketh Bell. The clipped lawn and white house, where she and her husband find their car awaiting them, was the estate called 'Sylvania', rented in the 1930s by a US couple called the Knowltons, but originally cleared and planted by Bell during his Dominican tenure of office. In 1936 the Imperial Road was drivable as far as Bell's old estate, but no further.

OUT OF THE SHADOWS

Wide Sargasso Sea, as one would expect, offers the most complex version of Rhys's return to Dominica, not least because of the way it also writes West Indian history into the margins of *Jane Eyre*. As so often, there are elements of Rhys's own family life in her heroine's—the Rochester figure is a version of Rhys's own father, a second son making his way in the world and marrying into an established creole family; Antoinette's convent days echo Rhys's own account of school, set back into the early days of Emancipation; the family memory of the attack on Geneva (Coulibri in the novel) is combined with the brief riot on the street where Rhys lived as a child (1981: 47).[29]

Wide Sargasso Sea's version of the history of the old white creole families of the West Indies is oblique: their decline is encoded in metropolitan betrayal, black hostility, and the take-over by new capital from England. To the extent to which Antoinette embodies some of the old creole values, in however confused a form, those values are forcefully removed from their home and taken prisoner in a cold and hostile land. The decline in the Lockhart family fortunes was less dramatic, if not entirely dissimilar. In *Smile Please* Rhys recalls that by the turn of the century, 'what with one thing and another' (35), the profits from Geneva were small. Well before the 1936 return, the male heir, Rhys's uncle Acton Don, had died (in 1922), followed a year later, through suicide, by his son. By 1936, '[w]here the house had been was an empty space' (37).

---

[29] I discuss some of the possible reasons for all this in an essay called 'The Locked Heart' (Hulme 1994a). Also, see above, pp. 104–6.

Some of the themes of 'The Imperial Road' had already appeared in *Wide Sargasso Sea*. At the beginning of the novel, Antoinette's family has few visitors, her mother suggests, because the road from the capital is bad and road repairing is 'a thing of the past' (*WSS* 5). The sign of indigeneity—of root-edness in an island—is the ability to walk across it, a question of local knowledge and physical adaptation. The Caribs and the black population have both. The white planters and their descendants had neither and were relatively immobile—until the roads were built. In a plantation enclave on the island, Antoinette and her mother are effectively imprisoned once their horse has been poisoned. They remain, again to use Antoinette's mother's word, 'marooned'—a term whose meaning in this context is almost exactly the opposite of its original meaning of an animal (and later a slave) which has *escaped* confinement.

Antoinette's nightmares are of walking in the forest, hearing heavy footsteps behind her and not being able to move, on the second occasion having a sinister man guiding her towards some steps (11 and 34). Interestingly, however, the passage in *Wide Sargasso Sea* most reminiscent of 'The Imperial Road' is the one in which Rochester is lost in the forest and needs to be rescued by Baptiste, one of the servants at Granbois. He has been fol-lowing a road; not, however, an 'imperial' road, but a cobbled French road, which leads to a ruined house. Baptiste comes to Rochester's rescue, but denies the existence of the road, just as the Dominicans had denied the existence of the Imperial Road to Rhys. Within the fiction, we know that Rochester has seen a road: the native denial is an insular closing of ranks against the outsider. Only outsiders are denied; Rhys has been denied; there-fore the experience must, it seems, be transferred to an outsider, an Englishman, although one with whom, perhaps tellingly, the reader begins, at this point in the novel, to have some real sym-pathy. The displacements are complex, perhaps too impacted to be disentangled. But the key would seem to remain that strong sense of returning as a *revenant*—not a native, not a foreigner, not English, not Dominican, not quite.

There is one last connection between 'The Imperial Road' and *Wide Sargasso Sea*. After the narrator in the story has hurt her foot, the walking party stops at a house to hire a mule. The woman of the house bathes the narrator's foot, but with evident bad grace, made apparent when she straightens up and says: 'I don't do this for *you*, for I know who you are and for one of your family I would do *nothing*. I do it for your husband for I hear that he's a good man and kind to all' (*IR* 13–14), sentences that echo the line of Daniel Cosway's letter to Rochester: 'I hear you young and handsome, with a kind word for all, black, white, also coloured' (*WSS* 61). Cosway is arguably buttering Rochester up: the novel has not given much evidence of his kind words to anybody at all. In the story, the directness of the address is quite shocking, the more so for being both unexpected and unexplained, the harshness of the words contrasting violently with the assumed humility of the gesture.

The coloured character in *Wide Sargasso Sea*, Daniel Cosway, is in many ways the hinge on which the narrative turns, in literary terms the Iago to Rochester's Othello, except in this case the supposed betrayal has been before the marriage, supposed evidence of a kind of moral laxity which Rochester is not averse to associating with tropical islands. Boyd—Daniel Cosway's 'proper' name, according to Antoinette, and therefore presumably his mother's name—is a name that appears in one other place in Rhys's writing, when Anna Morgan (in *Voyage in the Dark*) remembers reading on an old slave list from the Constanz estate:

Maillotte Boyd, aged 18, mulatto, house servant. The sins of the fathers Hester said are visited upon the children unto the third and fourth generations—don't talk such nonsense to the child Father said—a myth don't get tangled in myths he said to me . . .
  'All those names written down,' I said. 'It's funny, I have never forgotten it.' (1982: 45)

If it were possible to use *Voyage in the Dark* as a way of reading *Wide Sargasso Sea*, then Daniel Boyd is presumably Maillotte Boyd's son by Antoinette's father. Maillotte is the name of Christophine's friend in *Wide Sargasso Sea*, the mother of Tia. If this is Maillotte *Boyd*, then Tia is half-sister to Daniel, who is half-brother to Antoinette. Daniel's already important role in the novel would then be further accentuated: he would be the mediating figure in a *familial* relationship between Antoinette and Tia. Such readings may be impermissible by the norms of literary criticism. The point, however, is that Rhys's fictional universe encourages speculation on such matters through the hints and innuendoes it throws up about 'outside' relationships, forcing them to remain in a narrative penumbra that corresponds to their status on the island itself: as that exasperated outsider, Rochester, says, when he notes the resemblance between Antoinette and the servant-girl Amélie: 'Perhaps they are related, I thought. It's possible, it's even probable in this damned place' (*WSS*: 105).

The tone of that statement is echoed, at much greater length, in the letters Leslie Tilden Smith wrote to his daughter about some of the very real and demanding coloured figures who often crowded into the Paz hotel in Roseau in 1936: a set of Jean Rhys's illegitimate nephews and nieces by her brother Owen:

We were not altogether sorry to leave Roseau. Every beggar in the place—90% of the population—was at my heels—and her illegitimate relatives at Jean's. The latter perhaps the more trying. Ena, the most presentable, got an extra couple of quid by showing gratitude for her present. (If they knew all the circumstances—of course impossible to explain—and how poor their 'claim' is! Owen has got through nearly all of what money there ever was in the family, and Jean has had far less than any of them, while after the old doctor's death the family has united against her and for him. Why should she do anything?) Mona seems to have been insistent but colourless, but Oscar was downright beastly. He was rude; he said the money wasn't half enough to be any good; and he suggested giving it back as Jean was so poor. Jean marvellously kept her temper. 'No, Oscar,' she said, 'you can give it to your sister if it's no use to you. And you can go.'[30]

Owen's liaisons were firmly within the colonial tradition, certainly within its insular version, and also followed the well-known family example of James Potter Lockhart, Rhys's great-grandfather. In a passage of the 'Black Exercise Book' Rhys writes about her ambivalence towards this man, the

[30] JRC (Leslie Tilden Smith to Phyllis Smith, 19 Mar. 1936). Ena Williams has confirmed the broad outline of this account (interview with PH (22 Nov. 1990) and cf. Angier 1990: 356–7). Ena Williams is Owen's daughter with Mary Johnson; Oscar and Mona Williams his children with Teresa Hill, who was a servant at the Rees Williams's second estate, Amelia. Rhys's own account has three mistresses and four children (DPP 7), though she may have been confusing the children with the mistresses and the children's children with the mistresses's children: Ena Williams was 29 in 1936 and had a young daughter, Myrtle (cf. Frickey 1988: 5).

patriarch and slave-owner. She veers between pride and shame: 'But the end of my thought was always revolt, a sick revolt & I longed to be identified once and for all with the other side which of course was impossible. I couldn't change the colour of my skin' (*BEB* 30). However, one of the things she finds to say in his favour is that 'he was good to some of his mistresses presenting them with freedom, money and land . . . When my mother was left very badly off the descendent [*sic*] of one these who had prospered exceedingly wrote to her offering to lend her any money she needed—she refused the offer but said in a pensive way—"Cast your bread upon the waters for you will find it after weary days"' (30–1)—a biblical proverb seemingly designed to neutralize Hester's tart remark about the sins of the father in *Voyage in the Dark*.[31]

The story of the coloured Lockharts is difficult to reconstruct. What seems to emerge, however, is a parable of the slow decline of the planter class in Dominica: as the Geneva plantation becomes more and more difficult to work and less and less profitable, and those dependent on its rents fall slowly into genteel poverty, the coloured branch flourishes in trade and establishes itself as a political force. Theodore Francis Lockhart, presumably one of James Potter Lockhart's outside children, sat in the same House of Assembly (1852) as his half-brother Edward, Jean Rhys's grandfather.[32] Theodore's son, Alexander Lockhart, the prominent newspaper owner and politician, was nominated to the Legislative Assembly in 1887 along with Jean Rhys's two uncles, Norman and Acton Don Lockhart. In all probability it was Alexander Lockhart who offered to lend money to Rhys's mother sometime after her husband's death in 1910.[33]

[31] Quoted above, p. 232; and cf. what Antoinette overhears at her mother's marriage to Mr Mason: '"And all those women! She never did anything to stop him—she encouraged him. Presents and smiles for the bastards every Christmas"' (*WSS* 13).

[32] *Dominica Blue Book*, 1852: 74–5.

[33] The jovial and easy-going Uncle Bo in *Voyage in the Dark*—one of the few characters in Rhys's *œuvre* that Carole Angier finds difficulty in relating to a 'real' person—is called Ramsay Costerus ('With illegitimate children wandering about all over the place called by his name—called by his name if you please . . . The Costeruses seem to have populated half the island in their time it's too funny' (Aunt Hester says))' (1982: 55). One of Alexander Lockhart's middle names was Ramsey; and see above, p. 150.

At the 1932 conference to consider West Indian confederation and self-government, one of the first major signs of the impending demise of imperial rule in the West Indies, the white Lockharts—predictably—had no representative, while one of the Dominican delegates was Randall H. Lockhart, Alexander Lockhart's son, a prominent progressive voice—and the equivalent, if the Lockhart families are mapped onto the fictional Cosways, of the Sandi who taught Antoinette how to throw stones straight and with whom she has an affair (*WSS* 54 and 121).

THE POLITICS OF RETURN

In 1936 Jean Rhys had returned to a West Indies on the edge of political turmoil. A sugar-workers' strike in St Kitts the previous year had heralded a period of labour disturbances, with political overtones: this was the decade when the great trade union leaders like Grantley Adams (Barbados), Alexander Bustamante and Norman Manley (Jamaica) were coming to prominence. There had been riots in St Vincent and St Lucia before the end of 1935. Marcus Garvey's reputation was at its height: he would visit Dominica the following year, 1937, a visit arranged by a local supporter, the writer J. R. Ralph Casimir. The very month Rhys left England (February 1936), a prophetic volume called *Warning from the West Indies* had been published.[34]

As the previous chapter showed, Dominica had its own line in disturbances. A smuggling incident in the Carib Reserve had led to the death of two Carib men, shot by black policemen. A Commission of Enquiry had not helped matters and, as this 1935 newspaper article suggests, the Reserve was still being aggressively policed, a local view represented by Rhys in 'Temps Perdi':

What is happening in the Carib Reserve? Sometime last month the framework of the police station, which is being erected in the Reserve, was burnt down; whether it was accidental or not no one can tell. Since the occurrence the Caribs have received visits from both Inspectors of

[34] On Casimir, see André (1995: 22–5); *Warning from the West Indies* (Macmillan 1936 and cf. Hart 1993: 370); and cf. Bolland 1995.

Police, and a Corporal and three policemen have been stationed there, no doubt to see that the building goes on without any further interruption. The Police cannot be very popular in the Reserve, for the regrettable incident of September 1930, which engendered much ill feeling between the Caribs and the Police, is not yet forgotten. The Caribs say they asked for a hospital, and in stead are given a police station. This is asking for bread and being handed a stone with a vengeance.

Naturally they would have preferred the hospital, and there is very little use for the station in the Reserve if it is to prevent smuggling, as there are hardly any shops. The chief occupations of the remnant of this once renowned Caribbean race is canoe-building and basketmaking. There is no need for the Caribs to smuggle wood or reeds: there is plenty of that in the Reserve.[35]

The most significant political event during Rhys's childhood in Dominica had been the establishment of Crown Colony government, direct rule by Administrators appointed from the Colonial Office, such as Hesketh Bell. The first elections to the local legislature had not then taken place until 1925, with Dominica becoming around that time the regional centre for the discussion of constitutional change, in ways outlined in the previous chapter. However, in 1932 the elected members of the Dominica legislature—including Randall Lockhart—walked out, tendering their resignation, after refusing to sanction increased taxation unless the salaries of English government officials were reduced, a political gesture that was admired throughout the region.[36] To make up the required numbers in

[35] 'Whispers', *Dominica Chronicle* (30 Jan. 1935). Cf. the remarks of Reginald St-Johnston, Governor of the Leeward Islands at the time of the 1930 Carib War: 'The Caribs have since been more or less well-behaved, except for occasional fits of temper, which included the setting fire to a new police-station that it was decided only last year to build among them! I am all for maintaining the traditions of ancient races, and trying to save them from too much "civilization" where such is obviously going to do them harm, but there are limits to all things, and the "peace and good order" of a country has to be maintained' (1936: 103). Even after the Carib War and the more aggressive policing of the Reserve, visitors who, unlike Rhys, never made it to the north-east coast, could still peddle the oldest of stories, calling the interior of the island 'a mountain wilderness with two or three hundred of the native Carib—the Indians that Columbus found on the island—still living there undisturbed and practically without contact with the whites or their government' (Van Dyke 1932: 75).

[36] The resigning members were R. E. A. Nicholls, J. B. Charles, R. H. Lockhart, H. D. Shillingford, C. E. A. Rawle, and Capt. G. F. Ashpitel (*Dominica Official Gazette*, 55/43 (12 Sept. 1932), 178). The colonial official responsible for increas-

the council, the Administrator, W. A. Bowring, nominated two white planters as safe pairs of hands, one of them being Norman Lockhart, Rhys's uncle and manager of the Geneva estate for his family. Both were 'cut in the clubs', and soon afterwards Mitcham House at Geneva was burned down, destroying the house which Rhys was to celebrate as Coulibri in *Wide Sargasso Sea*.[37] That burning of the house, such a central event in the novel, probably carries in its depiction some of the tensions Rhys experienced on her return to the island just four years after her family had proclaimed their commitment to a colonial administration which now had perilously few supporters. Although the narrator of 'The Imperial Road' shows no sign of understanding it this way, the black woman's 'inexplicable' hatred for her family has a very recent and very precise explanation.

Much of what I have been discussing in this chapter adheres to the pattern, perhaps especially common in an island context, whereby an impoverished stranger comes from off the island, usually from 'Home', and courts and marries a local woman who, in narrative terms, is seen to represent the island itself. That story is fundamental to Rhys's work. It is the story of Thomas Warner, who takes a Carib wife from Dominica, and whose English son murders his half-Carib brother at the place thereafter named Massacre, an event Antoinette wants not to explain to her husband. It is the story of Mr Ramage, in 'Pioneers, Oh Pioneers'. It is the story of Rochester and Bertha Mason in *Jane Eyre*, doubled in *Wide Sargasso Sea* by the earlier arrival of Mr Mason to marry Antoinette's mother. It was the story of Rhys's own parents, her father an impoverished second son, like Rochester, who supposedly married her mother after

ing taxation (and defending the high salaries of colonial officials) was Sir Sydney Armitage-Smith, one of the Commissioners who had investigated the 'Carib War' two years previously (see Hughes 1952: ch. 2).

[37] On this period, see Honychurch (1995: 162–3); and Napier (MS: 31–3). According to a letter in the Colonial Office records, Norman Lockhart had been induced to come to the Government's assistance by his mother, who owned a majority share in Geneva (CO 152/438/9). The Geneva Estate was sold in 1949 and rebuilt, only to be burned down again during political disturbances in 1974, an incident which still resonates on the island (see White *et al.* 1976; Grell 1984; Nassief 1994*a* and *b*; Henderson 1994).

she nursed him back to health, the modern version of the colonial story in which the native woman warns her lover of an impending attack. And, crucially, it is the story of Rhys herself when she takes Leslie Tilden Smith back to Dominica, where she finally can be the native again, with him as the stranger, only to find how hard it is to occupy the position of a 'British native of Dominica' at the exact moment when the bankruptcy of the imperial ideal is becoming more and more apparent throughout the West Indies. To attempt to walk across the island was a desperate assertion of belonging, of being native, of doing something that only Dominicans could do, or would want to do, or would need to do. Yet the attempt is compromised from the start by being dependent on the Imperial Road, that failed dream of colonial modernization. The non-completion of the road undermines her claim to indigeneity as comprehensively as it had demonstrated the failure of the imperial project. Right at the end of her life, Rhys clipped from the *Dominica Star*, the local newspaper that Phyllis Allfrey sent regularly from the island, an article about a 21-year-old girl who had been lost in the tropical forest for days. The article ended: 'WARNING: Visitors should realise that the terrain of Dominica, though a pinprick on the map, is as vast as an African jungle when you get lost . . .' (Angier 1990: 651). In some ways this acts as a retrospective justification—it could have happened to anybody; but only if Rhys identifies herself as a *visitor*: no longer a native.

POSITIONING THE NATIVE

Coral Ann Howells offers a good reading of all three parts of 'Temps Perdi', along with an assessment of the narrator's position:

In order to see this story as counter-discourse, it is necessary to read its statement of resistance not in its historical catalogue of events but in its structure, for the decentred narrative may be seen to be both the result of subjection to colonisation and a challenge to it. In its series of anecdotes it dismantles imperialist fictions of centrality, insisting instead on the cultural relativity of values. This story contains a multiplicity of centres, suggesting that anywhere—England, Vienna, Dominica—is marginal to somewhere else and so can be denigrated when seen through a different frame of reference. The solid English house might be only a negative when looked at through the eyes of the Creole narrator; in Vienna, European culture was held in contempt by the Japanese, German culture looked 'provincial' to the French, while the Japanese were not taken seriously by the Europeans. In the shift to the Caribbean perspective, all European conquest is seen against the backdrop of a particular colonial society with its own history of slaughter and dispossession where imperialism itself might be emblematised by the Temps Perdi Estate. . . .

And what is the narrator's own position in this fabric of contradictory discourses? She aligns herself with the victims of history. Like the Caribs she is in hiding and like the Creole girl she is helpless and silenced. All she can do to register her dissent is to write up her patois message 'Temps Perdi' on the mirror in 'enemy territory' and hope that somebody might see it and be able to understand it. The very mode of resistance chosen shows a feminine preference for indeterminacy over imperial narratives of progress and mastery, in a story whose drifting meanings cannot be repressed or contained but continue to revolve after its ending. (Howells 1991: 143–4)

The acuteness of this reading is only slightly, if significantly, gainsaid by the misidentification, previously noted, of the paralysed young woman as 'the Creole girl'. The story's 'drifting meanings' are certainly not to be contained. However, identification and misidentification are at the heart of the story, as they are in a rather different sense in 'The Imperial Road'.

One constant of Rhys's self-identification and that of her fictional protagonists is that they are not English. Teresa O'Connor quotes a revealing passage out of one of Rhys's unpublished notebooks:

My relations with 'real' little English boys and girls (real ones) were peculiar . . .

I nearly always disliked them. I soon discovered the peculiarly smug attitude which made them quite sure that I was in some way inferior . . . If I said I was English they at once contradicted me—or implied a contradiction—No a colonial—you're not English—inferior being. My mother says colonials aren't ladies and gentlemen, etc., etc.

If on the other hand I'd say exasperated, 'All right then I'm not English as a matter of fact I'm not a bit. I'd much rather be French or Spanish. They'd get even more amazed at that. I was [a] traitor. You're British they'd say. . . . Neither one thing nor the other. Heads you win tails I lose—And I never liked their voices any better than they liked mine. (1986: 19)

The protagonist of Rhys's story, 'The Day They Burned the Books', has a conversation along these lines, which ends with her saying: 'It's much more fun to be French or Spanish or something like that—and, as a matter of fact, I am a bit' (Rhys 1987: 153). In her autobiography Rhys refers to her fascination with the possibility that her great-grandmother was a Cuban countess (1981: 34). These might all count as strategies of alternative identification; as might, in a different way, the interest Rhys took as a girl in Catholicism (79) or the way in which she transformed herself from Ella Gwendoline Rees Williams to Jean Rhys (a Scottish Christian name and the spelling of the patronym closer to the Welsh original). 'Names matter', as Antoinette says towards the end of *Wide Sargasso Sea* (*WSS* 117).

In that novel, Antoinette has a French mother, which explains her French name, insisted upon against Rochester's attempt to impose the lumpenly English 'Bertha'.[38] Earlier in the novel we get to see the formation of Antoinette's views. Her favourite picture is *The Miller's Daughter*, whose brown curls and blue eyes symbolize Englishness (18).[39] However, by now, after the break of Emancipation, it has become clear that the West Indian planters are not English: the English are the newcomers, like Mr Mason—'so sure of himself, so without a doubt English' (18). Antoinette is clearly no Miller's Daughter in appearance, but that disidentification with the English is less a matter of appearance than it is of place of birth and social standing. However, it is much less clear, to everyone concerned, just what identification should apply. The one that hurts, whispered by the freed blacks, is 'white nigger' (18).

Rhys herself left Dominica before twentieth-century political changes made the choices acute for white Dominicans. The examples of people like Ramage (turned into the central character of her story 'Pioneers, Oh Pioneers'), or to a lesser extent her brother Owen, demonstrated that there really was no posi-

---

[38] In *Jane Eyre* her name is Bertha Antoinetta Mason. Intriguingly, a Carib woman who gave evidence to the Commission of Enquiry in 1931 was called Antoinette Lockhart.

[39] The picture would have been based on Tennyson's popular poem, 'The Miller's Daughter' [1832], which describes an English rural idyll: the millstream, the quiet meadows, the smell of the meal-sacks (Tennyson 1987: i. 406–17).

tion—certainly no respectable position—within Dominican society that could be occupied by a white person not fully committed to imperial norms of behaviour. It was only in the 1930s that people such as Ralph Nicholls began openly to ally themselves with the political views of the 'coloured' population.

Returning to the island in 1936, Rhys had no easy position to occupy. She was a 'native', but out of touch; white and English-speaking, but ideologically out of sympathy both with the colonial regime and with the newer English settlers; a visitor, but associated by Dominicans with her mother's family's continued prominence in island affairs. As Howells suggests, Rhys aligns herself in 'Temps Perdi' with the victims of history, the Caribs, partly perhaps out of some deep psychological perception that she herself was truly a victim, but more specifically because her situation *on Dominica itself* was, she felt—from the relatively little she actually knew—analogous to that of the Caribs: belonging in a fundamental sense to the island, but despised by most of its inhabitants, powerless to alter perceptions, and part of a class (group) in danger of extinction. The imperative behind the narrator's unwillingness to recognize the paralysed girl as Carib lies, I would suggest, in Rhys's desire to be identified with her. The girl's long brown eyes and waist-length hair ('through every shade from dark brown to copper and back again' (*TP* 273)) could be read as a compromise form between Carib black hair and eyes, and Rhys's own light brown hair and 'eyes of no particular colour' (Rhys 1987: 20).

The identification is a form of abjection, a way of negotiating—psychologically and in a sense politically—the difficulties of return.[40] The movements of the visit become a complicated dance since Rhys's narrator is both a visitor, in a group that includes an English tourist and a condescending local, and—in imagination—the victim of that violent photographic act, which reads as a kind of visual rape: 'I shall be a savage person—a real Carib', she says (*TP* 267). There is of course no apparent sense in which the Carib girl perceives the taking of photographs

---

[40] The relevance of Julia Kristeva's concept of 'abjection' to the study of Rhys's work is finely brought out by Helen Carr in her reading of *Good Morning, Midnight* (1996b: 66–72).

as an act of violation: everybody photographs her, the pathos of paralysed beauty is irresistible, the payments received probably constitute her family's main source of income. But the moment resonates with the photographic session that Rhys remembered so well from her own childhood as a first violation: 'smile please . . . keep still'. The Carib girl 'sat there smiling', with an assortment of pictures of Virgins and saints smiling down from the walls. After the photographs have been taken, she still 'smiled contentedly . . . smiled again.' 'And all the Virgins and saints on the walls smiled at us too.' She smiles, as she moves, we are meant to conclude, 'with a desperate, courageous grace' (273). Rhys searches as ever for the courage and the grace, but the despair is always close to fixing the smile into a rictus.

Rhys's deeply personal involvement with at least the *idea* of Caribness as represented by the paralysed young Carib woman does not prevent her story from having a clear political dimension: Salybia is heavily policed, a black policeman acts as a semi-official guide. Yet the apparent visit to Jolly John, deposed Chief, which might have given voice to a Carib political position with respect to the 'trouble' is omitted from the story, leaving the politics as purely that of oppression, with the Caribs apparently behaving with all the vigour of the Virgins and saints on their walls.

In at least one respect, 'The Imperial Road' reinforces this identification. Setting out to walk from close to the Carib Reserve across what would have been old Carib trails to the nearest point of the Imperial Road, Rhys hurts her foot and cannot walk. She becomes temporarily immobile, has her feet bathed, and is carried on a mule—an almost religious sequence violently undercut by the hostile words directed towards her by the woman washing her feet. The attempt to walk across the island reads like a final claim to the status of native, an attempt so misjudged that it can only be rescued by embracing—at least in narrative terms—the *narratively* unmotivated venom that is directed towards her. This vilification is so complete and so unanswered that it gives both point and power to the story of 'The Imperial Road' and yet it was so discomforting that it ensured that the story remained unpublished for some twenty-five years after its final redaction.

The very struggles Rhys had to understand her identity, real and imaginative, with respect to Dominica and its various populations give her fictional work a complex power, both psychological and narrative, that puts it in a different category from any other writing considered in this book. These are the struggles of nativity; and the Caribs are both illuminated and overshadowed by having to play their part in Rhys's dramatic tableaux.

WEDDING IN THE CARIB QUARTER

Just before she died Rhys told the writer David Plante, who had been helping her with her autobiography, that she had something to give him, a present she accompanied with a typically elusive gloss:

'This is what I want to give you,' she said and handed me the sheet. 'It's the outline of a novel I wanted to write called Wedding in the Carib Quarter. I won't write it. Maybe you will.'

I asked, 'Will you sign it?'

She wrote on it, in large shaky letters that looked like Arabic script: 'Think about it. It is very important.' She gave it to me.

She said, 'Someone once told me that. I won't tell you who.'[41]

---

[41] Plante (1983: 57) (cf. the slightly different earlier version: Plante 1979: 284). In a letter to Francis Wyndham in 1962, Rhys mentions an unfinished novel, 'Wedding in the Carib Quarter', the manuscript of which 'disappeared *completely*' (1985: 213).

6. Travellers and Other Transients: Patrick Leigh Fermor and his Followers (1945–1998)

> One minute I was driving along a road where everyone was black, and then after an invisible barrier—there is no change of vegetation, no fence, no signboard—many of the people look completely different. Although some were very clearly of mixed race, many showed not the slightest sign of African descent. They had straight hair, pale skins and looked as if they could have come from some remote Indonesian island; often noticeable, too, was a Mongolian or Red Indian cast to their faces. (John Hatt, 'Dominica Done' (1993: 166))

When Jean Rhys spent those weeks in 1936 at Hampstead on the north-east coast of Dominica, a short distance from the Carib Reserve, she and her husband had few social relationships. However, a couple of places were 'visitable'—in the English sense of that word; and Rhys and her husband visited them, not altogether comfortably judging from her published letter on the subject:

The lady to the right (Calibishee) has already asked us to lunch and done her war dance at me. (Tomahawk in hand, smile on face). The lady to the left (Melville Hall) has also asked us to lunch. . . . The Calibishee lady is by way of being literary. She wrote a book which was offered to Hamish Hamilton and declined. The readers report (signed) was sent to her—so can you wonder that she had us to lunch double quick. I could see that she thought it was all my fault, because she was nice to Leslie and has already sent him a long novel to report on. ('I know it is *unpardonable* to bother a man on holiday but I should be so grateful if etc etc'). (Rhys 1985: 29)

The 'lady to the right' was Elma Napier, owner of the Pointe Baptiste estate, a not insignificant literary and political figure in her own right, and one who—as we saw earlier—had written her own account of the Caribs.[1] About twelve years after Rhys's visit, it was from Elma Napier's house that Patrick Leigh Fermor set out to visit the Caribs, with his companions, Joan and Costa. 'If you want to see the Caribs,' Napier has said to him, 'why don't you come and stay with me . . . ?' (Fermor 1984: 104), her words echoing Aspinall's 'those desirous of seeing the Caribs . . .', inscribed in his much-reprinted guide book, to which Fermor concedes himself 'heavily indebted' (12).

Fermor's account of his visit to the Carib Reserve was published in the *Geographical Magazine* in 1950, and later the same year, in a slightly longer version, it formed chapter 5 of his *The Traveller's Tree*, the best-known of all travel-books about the Caribbean, and the one which sets the terms for post-war descriptions of the Caribs. For those reasons it will be given some detailed consideration here as a way of introducing the main themes of this chapter, which will then be pursued via rather briefer references to more recent travel writers. Often reprinted, *The Traveller's Tree* has tended to function as a textual authority for those who have travelled in Fermor's footsteps, and echoes of his words can often be caught in more recent texts. Since Fermor himself was widely read in the seventeenth-century French missionary writings, being especially fond of Père Labat, *The Traveller's Tree* has become the conduit through which the old colonial verities have passed into contemporary accounts.[2]

ALMOST MANCHU SOLEMNITY

Appropriately enough, given the plethora of Oriental comparisons in Fermor's descriptions of the Caribs, his chapter on Dominica is constructed like a series of Chinese boxes. A thin outer box describes arrival in and departure from Roseau. Within that is an idyll at Pointe Baptiste, a happy week of resting, reading, and good company. Within that is the visit to the Carib Reserve. And within that is the long account

---

[1] For an argument that Rhys read and engages with Napier's writing, see Thomas 1996b. On Napier, see above, p. 181.
[2] Fermor read the six-volume French edition of Labat's *Nouveau Voyage* (1722), not the popular, short, English abridgement (1931).

of what the Caribs *were*, taken from Labat. Of the twenty-eight pages on Dominica, sixteen are given over to the Caribs, but of these ten retail Labat. Fermor is a fine writer, but the story he tells is the conventional one. The Arawaks lived 'an almost idyllic life' (109) until confronted by a 'terrible horde of newcomers' (110)—Caribs, not Spaniards. The Caribs then occupy a seventeenth-century ethnographic past: 'The first action of a Carib's day was ... Their only clothing was ... Their gift for passivity seems to have been limitless ...' (113–14).

Like Jean Rhys and Leslie Tilden Smith, Fermor and his companions travelled on horseback and approached the Carib Reserve from the north. Since they were continuing over the mountains and back to Roseau, they carried their baggage with them, or rather several porters carried it, the whole party headed by a local guide from Pointe Baptiste, René Williams. Fermor, with a keen eye for the ridiculous, notes that their 'caravan has assumed the portentousness of an expedition of Mungo Park into the jungles of Africa' (107).

In recent years travel to the Reserve has been made easy by a new road. For Fermor, though, the arduousness of the journey was still a factor, a difficulty of access which could itself become a metaphor for a movement back in time:

The road twisted as it climbed, and the thickness of the sodden leaves turned it into a dense and tortuous cavern ... The path grew level at last, and through a gap in the trees we could gaze from our lofty head-land into a deep gorge downy with tree-tops. .... All day long our path followed this long climb and fall. .... The road suddenly widened into a clearing, where a group of shingle huts lay back under the trees, and by the edge of the path a group of men were standing, as though they were expecting us. So sharp was the contrast of their complexion and bearing with those of the islanders, that I thought for a moment that they were white men. But they were Caribs.

We dismounted and walked towards them, and, as we met, hats were raised on either side with some solemnity. We all shook hands. This meeting with the last survivors of this almost extinct race of conquerors was as stirring and impressive in its way as if the encounter had been with Etruscans or Hittites. (107–8)

Fermor's learned comparisons show the extent to which this meeting (to use the relatively neutral term) is turned into an 'encounter', an occasion with resonance.[3] The Caribs are representatives of their race, one of history's great conquering races, and Fermor's historical consciousness endows them with significance on this score:

We were now able to see that they were either ivory-coloured in complexion or a deep bronze, with features that were almost Mongolian or Esquimaux except for the well-defined noses. Their straight black hair was cut across their foreheads in a fringe. They had a dignity of presence that even their hideous European rags could not stifle. A tall man in the middle, smoking a pipe and equipped with an elaborate walking stick, took charge of us with a diffident, almost Manchu solemnity. This was George Frederick, the king or chief of the Caribs, and the elders that surrounded him were members of the Carib Council. He led us up a steep path, through the leaves to a little green glade in front of his own shingle hut, where we sat down under a mango tree, and leaned our backs against a half-excavated canoe. (108)[4]

It is interesting to compare this with Hesketh Bell's account of his encounter with the Carib chief half a century earlier. The formal greeting and Carib demeanour are unlikely to have been significantly different, but the tone of the description has shifted dramatically. Although well disposed to the Caribs, Bell had clear expectations of feathers and red paint. Fermor is less disposed to pass judgements, and his only negative comment—on the 'hideous European rags'—seems contradicted by the photograph of the chief (*WM* 325). 'Rags' may here be a relative term: George Frederick does not look badly dressed, but he is certainly not wearing the latest Lillywhites safari jacket. Perhaps as historical 'remnants', the Caribs are seen as necessarily wearing rags.

Expectations of chiefly demeanour have clearly changed. For Bell, the very term 'Carib king' seemed an oxymoron, so manifestly did the holder of that office fall short of a European sense of royalty. For Fermor, the chief's diffidence lends him the true dignity of chiefdom, whatever the clothes he is wearing.

---

[3] On the tradition of the 'arrival scene', see Pratt (1992: 78–81).

[4] George Frederick was not 'officially' recognized by the colonial administration, though this seems not to have worried Fermor. Frederick was formally invested, after a favourable report by the local social welfare officer, in June 1952, and the staff and sash of office, confiscated in 1930, were restored.

Manchu—added to Etruscan and Hittite—intensifies the sense of antiquity, but also adds, alongside Mongolian and Esquimaux, to the particular history of American Indian groups like the Caribs, lending them the dignity of their own historical connections, retracing their supposed migratory paths from Old World to New. For Bell and others, this can mark a contrast, a falling away from the achievements of the past to the squalidness of the present. Ultimately Fermor sees no future for the Caribs, either, but they are allowed to retain some dignity, although arguably it is the writer rather than his subjects that is aggrandized by the comparisons *he* is able to make, and which would mean nothing to *them*.[5]

The pre-Columbian exploits of the Caribs are summed up through the conventional tropes, slightly leavened by the elegance and wit of Fermor's writing:

They made short work of their unwarlike forerunners. They massacred and sometimes devoured the men, and married the women; some of them taking root, while the others moved off, rapidly eating and marrying their way through the Windward and Leeward and Virgin Islands, and into the greater Antilles. They never, as far as I can gather from the chroniclers, settled permanently in the western Caribbean. Cuba and Jamaica escaped them altogether, and Hispaniola and Puerto Rico lived in dread of their frequent invasions, but did not have to endure them as a permanent evil. Perhaps their arrival in these regions coincided with the advent of the Spaniards, or perhaps they preferred the forests and gorges of the Lesser Antilles to the sierras and savannahs of Borinquen. Or they may have felt that the time had come to pause and, as it were, digest their conquests. They became static. (110–11)

The language of movement and stasis has always entrapped the Caribs. Like the other great polarities of Western thought, civilization/savagery has a ready-mapped place for American Indians. Yet the underlying contrast between the settlement of the city, with its agricultural hinterland, and the threatening, nomadic—and often pastoral—hordes has never been quite as secure as the other dichotomies. Christian imagery is itself ambivalent. Abel was of course the pastoralist, Cain the tiller

---

[5] Fermor's language, with its evocative historical associations performs what Dean MacCannell calls 'sight sacralization', a marking or framing of what is to be seen, which is to be met with a corresponding 'ritual attitude' (1976: 42).

of the ground, until his fratricide resulted in him becoming a fugitive and wanderer, but also the builder of a city, in the land of Nod (Genesis, 4: 16–17). In early Christianity, the city was often rejected as an emblem of this-worldly concerns, with pilgrimage and wandering regarded as hallowed activities. Augustine's *Civitate Dei* was in part an attempt to synthesize this pastoral Christianity with an imperial tradition for which the city was the central idea.[6]

When those dichotomies were mapped onto indigenous populations—as they almost always were—they became even less secure. Within colonial discourse the indigenous Caribbean population was divided into female and male, settled and nomadic, pacific and aggressive. Christian imagery supplied the lamb and the wolf, which helped confirm the cannibal trope. However, the Caribs had obviously *settled* certain of the islands, troubling the dichotomy, and leading Fermor here to essay the vegetative 'taking root', before deciding on the more reptilian pause for digestion. 'Static' is nicely chosen. Unlike its near synonyms—settle down, feel at home, become established—it turns the positive pole of the dichotomy into a negative: what is by nature mobile has lost its impetus, run out of steam.

With Labat as his constant companion, Douglas Taylor's 1938 treatise to hand, and presumably well briefed by Elma Napier on recent events, Fermor is able to give a fairly sympathetic and not inaccurate account of Carib history in the colonial period, although one still cast—as almost all have been—as a narrative of inevitable decline:

There are, in these few miles of mountains and forests, scarcely five hundred of them left, and of these many have a small amount of African blood. In the whole world there are now only about a hundred pure-blooded Caribs left, and the little rearguard is growing smaller every year. They are a doomed race lingering on the shores of extinction, and in a generation or two, unless some miracle of regeneration and fecundity intervenes, the black tide will have risen and swept them off the face of the earth for ever. (118)

This chapter will have to return to confront the language of 'pure' blood and 'doomed' races, a language which still

---

[6] For a longer analysis of the relevance of these ideas to early European colonial thought, see Hulme 1994*b*.

dominates discussions of indigenous peoples. With respect to Fermor's metaphors, let me just notice how closely—in even such a liberal and well-disposed visitor as Fermor—the 'black tide' again echoes the title of Lothrop Stoddard's infamous *The Rising Tide of Color Against White World-Supremacy* (published in 1921), part of the inter-war white paranoia about Western global domination being threatened through the breeding habits of the non-white races.[7]

With Jean Rhys and Douglas Taylor, Patrick Leigh Fermor completes the trio of mid-century writers of distinction who have left written records of their visits to the Caribs. In the last half-century visitors have increased several hundredfold (though many 'visit' for minutes or hours rather than days or weeks) and writers perhaps tenfold or more. Five categories of writers can be identified, though the categories are hardly watertight. Four anthropologists have visited the Caribs for substantial periods of time and written Ph.D. theses which have been drawn on for published articles (Eugene Banks, Nancy Owen, Anthony Layng, Lennox Honychurch), and a sprinkling of scientists have also visited.[8] 'Official' visitors have in this period tended to come from or on behalf of agencies offering support to the Caribs, rather than—as with the 1932 Commission—from disciplinary organizations. Travel writers can then be divided, roughly, into two categories: those writing articles which form part of the growing tourist literature about the Caribbean; and, more important for my purposes, those writing books, usually, on the Fermor model, about the Caribbean islands or some group of them (Quentin Crewe, Henry Shukman, Lucretia Stewart, to mention only three of the most recent)—mostly English-speaking, although one of the most

[7] See Douglas Taylor's reference to the same text (above, p. 196).
[8] See the References under these four names for details. Owen (1981) is the most personal of the accounts, but argues in effect that the author was *not* a visitor but a temporary resident who internalized Carib beliefs. Lennox Honychurch belongs to a separate subcategory as a Dominican with a close knowledge of Carib lifeways before he undertook his professional training in anthropology and museum ethnography at the University of Oxford. There was also a French *maîtrise d'Anglais* on the Caribs, Hamot-Pézéron (1983), published as Pézéron (1993). There is a rich body of anthropological work about the Vincentian Caribs and the Black Caribs in Central America: e.g. Gullick (1985); Gonzalez (1988); Kerns (1983).

intruguing is Jean Raspail, the French writer, who will feature prominently in this chapter. The book writers tend to stay longer, but not always. The fifth (catch-all) category writes particularly about the Caribs though not principally about associated visits—such as the present writer; or make films about the Caribs.[9]

All these categories are drawn on in this final chapter, but the organizing themes are those of chiefly encounter; visible differences; purity of blood; decline and loss; survival and assimilation; and tourism. A final section looks at a new and different kind of visitor.

MEETING THE CHIEF

Fermor's 'encounter' with George Frederick stands as an intriguing modern attempt to convey something of the dignity intrinsic to the position of chief, a successor perhaps to Samuel Purchas's note 'wilde majesty' inserted alongside John Layfield's seventeenth-century description of a Dominican Carib chief in a rich crimson robe, with a Spanish rapier by his side, and a brass lion on his breast.[10] In the modern era, however, the norm has been to mock Carib chiefs' supposed 'pretensions' to kingship, pretensions which in fact belong to the observers who endow the inappropriate title of 'king' the better to demonstrate that there is nothing properly king-like in the demeanour of its possessor. At the beginning of the century, Symington Grieve writes of King Ogis [Auguste François], with his Queen, Crown Prince, Prime Minister, and Advisory Council, vocabulary which, apart from being entirely inappropriate since the chieftainship is not hereditary, is bound to sit comically alongside the photographs of poverty-stricken life on the Carib Reserve (Grieve 1906: 90).

---

[9] I should make it clear that although I have been a visitor on a number of occasions, most recently in 1994, I have undertaken no ethnographic fieldwork in or detailed study of the Carib Reserve itself. The major film about the Caribs is Teuscher 1983.

[10] Purchas (1905–7: xvi. 55). This note provided the title for *Wild Majesty*. Note that Carib ideas of 'majesty', at least at this period, have to do with appropriating external symbols rather than with conforming to anybody's idea of what might look 'authentic'.

Frederick Ober set the tone with his comic remarks about the ancient king, Old George, tottering along the path (above, p. 66), but the best fun can be had when the false majesty of the Carib king can be shown up by the presence of the real thing. A pseudonymous newspaper article written in Dominica in 1936, as part of a series of memories of momentous occasions, recalls 'the day the Prince of Wales came to Dominica', referring to the visit of the Prince of Wales in 1920:

Many happenings took place on the occasion. I will only mention one of the most notable ones. It was on the 'Bell Jetty' a few seconds after His Royal Highness had landed ... At the end of the jetty the notabilities of the town and a delegation of Caribs from Salybia, had been awaiting the arrival of the Royal Heir.

'I am very pleased to meet you,' said the Prince to old Coriette, the Carib Chief who for the occasion had put on a long black coat and set a silk top hat on his supple black hair. The old chief who up to that moment had remained as mute as a River Mulet, said very politely to His Highness 'Moin pas ka parlé anglais.' (I do not speak English). 'Oh, pardon me, chief,' said His Royal Highness in excellent French. 'Je suis heureux de faire votre connaissance. Comment allez vous?' The poor old chief with a very unhappy smile, replied very politely to the Prince: 'Poince, moin déja di ou moin pas ka parlé anglais.' (Prince I am sorry, but I have already told you that I cannot speak English.) At that moment a bystander ... was heard to utter in a voice full of sincere admiration: 'Ah! Ah! Ah! Ah! Ah! The man is well educated eh!' Little he knew that His Royal Highness who is a great linguist, spoke French to perfection.

Now the Prince looked at the old chief with a smile. Then his face grew quite serious, nearly sad. I suppose he was then thinking: 'This old man, with a frock-coat and a top-hat out of fashion. This is what civilization has made of one of the last sons of a noble race that used to fight bravely from the Green Island of Sunset to the coast of America in open boats. Not even a crown made of hawk or parrot plumes on the forehead. No bow and arrows. No ancestral pride displayed as such was the case with the North American Indian tribe of Canada that made me one of them by naming me "Chief Morning Star." A winter frockcoat and an old top hat from Piccadilly!'. ('Chi lo sa' 1936)[11]

---

[11] A more directly condescending reference to this event is in a 1937 guide book, which says, with reference to a visit to what it calls 'Caribland', and speaking in the guide-book imperative addressed to the second person: 'When you reach this primitive settlement you will be all diplomacy: these Caribs have their own ruler

In the mind of this empire loyalist, there is no contest here between 'His Royal Highness' and the 'poor old chief' who welcomes him to Dominica. Not only does the noble Prince obligingly speak French when he hears Corriette's words, but he speaks Corriette's language 'better' than the chief himself, as Corriette is left not understanding what is said to him in French. That a local cleverclogs should assume that the failure is the Prince's only heightens the pleasing irony of the situation, as far as the writer is concerned. Even the Chief's compliance is turned against him in the internal monologue attributed to the Prince by the percipient writer on the basis of his serious face: no feathers, no arrows, no ancestral pride.

There are, however, ironies here that escape the writer. To begin with, his linguistic point only makes sense from the perspective in which the Dominican patois spoken by Corriette is a decadent version of the French so purely articulated by the Prince. If patois is given its position as a language, then the interchange becomes a polite misunderstanding in which neither party triumphs over the other. By putting his thoughts into the imagined and unspoken words of the Prince, the writer attests to his belief in the identity of their outlooks, an attestation challenged by what is clearly his own—rather than the Prince's—obsession with the Chief's clothes: not only a frockcoat and a top hat, but a *winter* frockcoat and—most shocking of all—an *old-fashioned* top hat. To lose own's ancestral pride is bad enough; but to be out of fashion to boot . . . The empire loyalist suffers most from his own words, his insular priorities on display. The contrast with the Canadian Indians is the writer's final flourish: here is something like true, if now powerless, majesty recognizing its modern superior through a respectful naming ceremony. The writer (like his Prince, presumably) fails to reflect on the fate of a previous white man honoured with the Indian name of 'Morning Star'—George Armstrong Custer. The last laugh probably belongs to the Canadian Indians.

and go their own way without molestation by the British king across the seas. They will even proudly tell you that when Edward VIII—then Prince of Wales—came to Dominica in 1920 their own king paid a formal call on the man who was to rule the British Empire for a few months. King of Caribs and Prince of Wales met as man to man' (Parmer 1937: 97).

In the last half-century there have been three Carib chiefs who between them have served thirty-three years in the post, leading their community through some massive changes. Germandois Francis was the first chief who had to deal with visitors on a regular basis: many written interviews with him were published, and he appeared on the British television programme, 'Tonight', interviewed by Alan Whicker in 1964. In such circumstances it is not surprising that a tone of briskness soon replaces Fermor's sense of awe. Francis was also the first Carib leader actively involved in national politics—initially as a firm supporter of the Dominica Labour Party's modernizing programme and later as a prominent participant in the march against Chief Minister Le Blanc's Seditious Publications Act in 1968, a key event in the island's history.

Several of Francis's interviewers will appear later. But to demonstrate the change of tone apparent at this time, here is Charles Graves, a travel writer who never stopped anywhere for very long and was clearly not about to be awed by anything. Note how he also echoes Aspinall's 'those desirous of visiting the Caribs':

If you want to visit the Caribs personally, you follow the so-called Transinsular Road, by way of Pont Cassé, towards the airport, then stop at Hattan's Corner. At a nearby cottage an elderly negress will order you a driver and jeep to cross the river and then bump upwards through the forest, along execrable roads, for about forty minutes. The first Carib huts then come into view. The Caribs have much paler skins, and they wave and smile as they stop washing clothes in the stream, to greet you as you pass. If lucky, you will be given an audience with François Mon Droit, wearing his sword and red and green sash. He is only in his thirties, and receives a Government grant of sixty BWI dollars a month from the local government. (Graves 1965: 139)

And that's about it. Execrable roads, pale skins, clothes in stream, young chief with sash, salary, and misspelled name.

Other chiefs have often fared no better. Jacques-Yves Le Toumelin visited Dominica in May 1955 on board his yacht *Kurun*, which he had earlier sailed around the world. Leaving *Kurun* in Prince Rupert Bay, he travelled across the island and was taken into the Reserve by its parish priest, Father Visonneau, a journey still involving a difficult walk south from Pagoua Bay. Le Toumelin quotes extensively from Père Labat and Bryan Edwards, giving the conventional picture of Carib savagery and cannibalism, a picture which purports to describe the 'real' Caribs of the pre-Columbian Caribbean, and has next to nothing to say about the intervening five hundred years. When the previous paragraph has quoted Edwards on young Carib boys being annointed 'with the fat of a slaughtered Arrowauk', the meeting that follows is bound to seem bathetic, an impression Le Toumelin reinforces by quoting Fermor's sentence about Etruscans and Hittites, and commenting: 'Heck! I must admit that the Carib women Father Visonneau and I met before entering the Settlement provoked no such comparisons in my mind. They talked and looked like any other native women' (Le Toumelin 1963: 130).[12] Eventually they work their way to the Chief's house:

One of these huts, no less dilapidated than the rest, housed the Carib 'King'. We found him, the victim of a sprained ankle, lying on his bed and looking rather the worse for wear. However, he welcomed us with great courtesy and consented to pose for his photograph just as he was, in pyjamas. King of the Caribs . . . ! Though his niece proudly showed me his sceptre, a silver-topped cane made of some rare wood surmounted by a silver crown, he seemed a trifle self-conscious about his title and, as Father Visonneau told me, had said to him once, when they were alone together: 'It is you who are King of the Caribs, Father, not I.' (1963: 136)

The last sentence is open to more than one reading. Certainly Father Visonneau belongs to a long line of outsiders, mostly priests, who have been seen, by themselves, by others, and perhaps on occasions by the Caribs themselves, to have wielded considerable power and influence during their time as residents on or close to the Reserve. Some of this aura also attached to Douglas Taylor, who was reported by a reseacher for the 1948 film, *Christopher Columbus*, to have become 'the "uncrowned King of the Carib reserve" ': so much so that he '*permitted* the Caribs to take part in the film, re-enacting the roles which their ancestors had played'.[13] However, it may sometimes have been

[12] I have been unable to locate an original French edition of this book.

[13] My emphasis. ' "Christopher Columbus" Discovers the New World Again— On the Screen' (production notes to *Christopher Columbus* [1948]: 2). The Caribs were re-enacting their ancestors' roles in much the same way as mountainous Dominica was re-enacting a pancake-flat Bahamian island (cf. *WM* 317–22).

in the Caribs' interest to deflect attention away from the actual chief, who—at least in earlier days—seems to have acted with quiet effectivity rather than with the flamboyance that visitors usually expected. Whatever Visonneau's motive in retailing that story to Le Toumelin, it is telling that he does not even mention the chief's name, allowing his sprained ankle and pyjamas to symbolize a house-bound ordinariness at odds with any lingering expectations of 'wild majesty'.[14]

In 1983, journalist and travel writer Anthony Weller and his unnamed companion went to meet the chief, Hilary Frederick:

He was glad to see us, he said, if we would tell the truth about the Caribs. The Caribs had never been cannibals, he insisted; whoever had made up that story, centuries ago, was a cannibal himself. No, the Caribs had never kept slaves. . . . How many pure Caribs remained? we asked. He shrugged. Perhaps 20 or 30, no more. He did not look at us as he spoke, except when he smiled, and we were never able to determine how much of his false history was deliberate misinformation and how much was wishful thinking. (1983: 73)

No awe here, indeed little sign of respect or even politeness on the part of the intrepid Western reporter. Whether one considers the two hours or so that Weller has spent on the Territory by this point, or the few days that he subsequently stays, more than a hint of arrogance might be detected in the tone. There are important questions to be asked about Carib versions of Carib history, but they are not addressed by the wilful assumption of deliberate misinformation and wishful thinking. Weller confidently produces the 'true' history that the Carib chief ignores: 'The Caribs settled Dominica perhaps as many as a thousand years ago. They were a tall race, and they came from the banks of the Orinoco River in South America and conquered the docile, smaller and lighter-skinned Arawaks . . . The defeated Arawak men were eaten . . . and the women and children who were not eaten were taken into the tribe . . . The Caribs ate and married their way up through the Antilles' (1983: 76).

The Chief is not only ignorant of his people's history, he cannot even see them properly, or at least count them: 'We were

---

[14] The chief was probably Simon John, who served for a short time in the early 1950s.

to find that the chief's estimate of the number of pure Caribs
was inexplicably low. There are certainly more than 100 left,
and they are by no means all old' (76). The Western eye can see
these things, even if—no doubt inexplicably—genetics is unable
to give an account of lineage in which the notion of 'purity'
could make any sense at all.

But the most striking aspect of modern responses to the Carib
chiefs remains the persistence with which the figures are read in
terms of royalty, whether or not that association is positive for
the writer, and whether or not the chief is seen to merit the association. Fermor comes closest, of the writers looked at so far in
this chapter, to writing about the Carib chief on something like
his own terms, as a leader of his community, although even he
uses the periphrasis, 'presided over by a sort of elective voivode
with the style of king' (1984: 118), a description that would
seem to cover most possibilities.

Jean Raspail's response indicates how an embrace of the idea
of Carib monarchy can just as easily miss the point as a casual
dismissal of the idea. Writing in 1980, he recalls his first
encounter with a Carib chief in 1964: 'This was going to be the
first king I'd ever met. That he was a king of the Savages, a
Carib cacique, didn't alter, as far as I was concerned, the almost
religious solemnity with which I anticipated this visit. I am a
subject without a king, a soul wandering in the shadows of
democracy in search of dead loyalties' (1980: 46). He addresses
this king in his imagination, recalling in graphic detail the
history of the Caribs—for fifty years you ate priests at every
meal, he says, with a modicum of exaggeration: 'I pay homage
to your appetite' (48).

For all his bluster, Raspail has a sharp understanding of his
own moves. He knows very well that he is responding to a
stereotype:

The king was every inch a Carib. A good ten years older, he still looked
just like his photograph. I knew just who he was. He featured in the
anthropometric archives of all the institutes of ethnology worthy of
the name: 1.6 metres tall, average male build for his race, yellow skin
slightly bronzed, small and slanting eyes, with the mongoloid fold,
straight black hair (but combed, with a parting on one side), full
cheeks, a straight nose, little body hair, even, as I also knew, on the

private parts, and a full and fine set of teeth . . . and his blood group O, typically Amerindian. Francis Fernandois 1st was very far from knowing as much about me, it was still very much the white man's manners, bad manners, no equality, the measurers should go and have themselves measured by the Greeks every now and then! I was sorry that he'd been pigeon-holed in that way . . .

He found it hard to understand why I was there. My arrival didn't correspond at all with the usual protocol attached to visitors. Hearing a car he had quickly assumed his best commercial, most profitable, pose, with sceptre and in front of the piano, the dollar-a-photo pose; included in the price was even advice to the tourists on the best angle, the right distance, and desirable lens. And lo and behold, instead of the sheep rushing from the minibus—which in those days used to stop for at least a minute, but since then . . . he found himself looking at somebody who was taking his time, was expressing his intention of spending the night on the reserve, and even invited him to supper. (53–4)

Raspail proceeds to take a banquet out of the Daimler in which he has arrived.[15] Raspail's exaggerated—parodically exaggerated—respect for royalty provides the standard by which the chief is judged: judged to have sold himself to the touristic impulse for a quick photograph, incapable of recognizing when he sees it the true devotion of a genuine lover of the monarchical principle who wants to spend some time in his company.

What Raspail wants to know about, he says, is 'the past' (55). It is for that reason he has come: 'To verify one of my beliefs: there is no survival without consciousness of the past' (56). The response is not encouraging:

The king scratched his head. Visibly, trying to please me, he tried. But, equally visibly, he dried . . . Finally he came up with something:

—The old folk used to say to my father's father that the Caribs had conquered the island of Haiti . . .

I told him that Haiti meant 'the big land' in Carib. He didn't know. He asked me:

---

[15] There are severe limits to the seriousness with which this picture should be taken—tourist minibuses were not whizzing through the Carib Territory in 1964; the chief was called Germandois Francis; none of these events was mentioned in the first account Raspail wrote, shortly after the visit; he transposes the events of the 1930 'war' onto 1964, with the Dominican police attacked by Caribs with bows and arrows—but the attitude it encapsulates is intriguing.

—Are they all dead over there too?
I told him they were. (56)[16]

The depth of Carib ignorance—and the relative extensiveness of
Raspail's historical knowledge—is paraded over the next few
pages, without the terms of and possible reasons for the contrast ever being explored. Germandois knows nothing of the
past—he is, in Raspail's terms, 'at the trough of the wave' (56),
a wave that has risen again by the time of Raspail's second visit
to a Carib chief in April 1979, shortly after the election of the
most influential of post-war Carib leaders, Hilary Frederick.
Again, by pretending that the Carib chief is in fact a 'king',
Raspail can play off supposed expectations of grandeur against
the 'reality' of Caribbean rural poverty: 'The palace. Concrete
shack, corrugated iron roof, progress. A table and chair at the
entrance and on the table several piles of papers and a modest
array of pencils and ball-point pens: a start at administration.
A cautious entry for the Carib nation into the modern era.' Still,
he remembers Frederick's predecessor posing for photographs
and demanding payment. 'This one didn't pose and didn't
ask for anything, except interest in and sympathy for his
people'(62).

When he asks Hilary Frederick what difference Dominica's
impending independence will make, the answer is that the
Caribs have been independent for 2,000 years, an answer that
resonates with Raspail:

Here we have a dying people, who have lost their history, their culture,
their language, their religion (except for the imported one), and who
remember nothing, a people who possess only modesty and silence,
whose only concern, after the conquest, amounts to the rudiments of
everyday life: birth, sustenance, death, while the rest of the world gets
its fill of all the contemporary rages, and who have clearly been able
to survive in a name alone, with no surrounding content, which therefore only represents the merest abstraction: 'The Caribs have been
independent for two thousand years . . .'! (64)

The 1970s were the most fraught decade in Dominica's history.
After the collapse of the short-lived West Indian Federation,
Dominica had become effectively independent in November

[16] Cf. Germandois Francis's conversation with Alan Whicker, which took place
in the same year (*WM* 335–6).

1967 with the attainment of Associated Statehood, with total control of all aspects of its own government except external defence and some aspects of external relations. The popular Dominica Labour Party had won a landslide victory at the general election, with Edward Le Blanc becoming the Chief Minister. Appropriately enough, given Dominica's long record for outspoken, not to say vitriolic journalism, the DLP shot itself in the foot in 1968 with the publication of a draconian Seditious and Undesirable Publications Act, which served only to galvanize a previously divided and fragmented opposition into a new grouping which eventually became the Dominica Freedom Party, the party which, with Eugenia Charles at its head, would govern the island between 1980 and 1995.

The 1970s was a decade marked by violence, previously rare on the island. A white visitor was shot dead during Carnival and a retired Canadian couple were murdered in their home. The government blamed the so-called Dreads, a heterogenous group influenced by the Black Power movement, by Rastafarianism, and by various 'alternative' philosophies, who had established several communities in the forests. Le Blanc was soon replaced by Patrick John, who combined leftist rhetoric with a fascistic attitude towards law and order. He promulgated the passage of the Prohibited and Unlawful Societies and Associations Act, usually known as 'The Dread Act', which in effect gave any citizen the right to kill anyone they suspected of being a Dread whom they found on their property. A Dread was popularly thought to be anyone with long hair, especially locks. John founded a full-time Defence Force in 1975, with himself as Colonel, a force which killed a couple of supposed Dreads but otherwise tended to operate as John's private army. Throughout the decade there were also a number of long-running strikes and states of emergency which had sapped the civil foundations of Dominican society.

Patrick John acted quickly to terminate the association with Great Britain, an outcome which was foreseen by the legislation establishing statehood, although nobody had envisaged termination taking place in such difficult circumstances. Few people on Dominica opposed independence in principle, although there were long and difficult discussions about the constitution and the exact form of government. Formal independence came in

November 1978, just a few months before Raspail's visit to Hilary Frederick. Patrick John's period of office as Chief Minister had been marked by an extraordinary association with crooks and mercenaries. As Prime Minister of the fully independent country, he would soon become embroiled with a dubious scheme backed by a Texan businessman for a Free Port Zone in the north of the island which, along with increasing domestic unrest, would lead to his removal in June 1979.[17]

So Raspail was visiting at a very difficult time. The young Chief who impressed him at this moment had had an unusual background. Because the family was in financial difficulties, Hilary Frederick's father had asked a visiting US anthropologist, Arthur Einhorn, to take his son to the USA to be educated. This had nearly happened once before: one of Douglas Taylor's ideas was to provide what he called 'a good and thoroughly Indian education for one or two of the few full blooded Carib children'. After a visit to Washington in May 1934 he wrote to the Bureau of American Ethnology to ask for advice about an Indian school, preferably 'in a community where there is some racial or linguistic affinity with the Caribs (the Seminoles?)'. Taylor was willing to finance such an education. His aim, he wrote, 'was to fit the boy to become a worthy Chief of his own people, & who might subsequently protect them from the incursions of negro blood & customs & the consequent disappearance of the race'.[18] Three days later he wrote again to reiterate the point: 'Personally I should be more satisfied if the young man could get his education along with other Indians—and away from negro influence.'[19] But nothing seems to have come of the idea.

Hilary Frederick lived for five years, 1972 to 1977, with Einhorn's family in New York State, where he attended high school and the local college where Einhorn taught. The timing proved auspicious. Einhorn was, in any case, a well-respected expert on Iroquois culture with good contacts amongst Native

[17] On the political background in Dominica, see Honychurch (1995: 253–73); André and Christian 1992; Higbie 1993.

[18] BAE (Letter from Douglas Taylor to J. N. B. Hewitt, 3 June 1934).

[19] BAE (Letter from Douglas Taylor to J. N. B. Hewitt, 6 June 1934). The reply from the BAE suggested the Bacone School as the most likely and suggested that Taylor get in touch with John Collier, the American Commissioner of Indian Affairs in Washington (Letter from M. W. Stirling to Douglas Taylor, June 1934).

Americans, and so Frederick got to visit many reservations, such as the Onondaga, Seneca, and St Regis. 'One of the conclusions he came to,' reported Einhorn, 'was that a lot of the problems Indians were having in intercultural relations were similar to the Carib problems in Dominica.'[20] The late 1960s and 1970s saw the burgeoning of the American Indian Movement (AIM) as part of the general radicalization of US culture. Frederick's years in the USA exactly coincided with what Ward Churchill has called the 'bloody wake of Alcatraz' (1995). After the long occupation of Alcatraz Island by the San Francisco Bay Indians of All Tribes coalition (1969–71), the 1970s were punctuated by a violent state repression of American Indian activism, leading to the occupation of the symbolic site of Wounded Knee, South Dakota, in 1973 and the shoot-out at Jumping Bull's compound in 1975, which left two FBI agents and an American Indian dead—and Leonard Peltier imprisoned for life just as Hilary Frederick returned to Dominica.[21] These events must have had a tremendous impact: Frederick learned about the larger American Indian context within which the position of the Dominican Caribs could be understood; and also learned something about practising radical politics in changing times.

Despite being away from the Carib Reserve for five years, and despite still being a very young man, Frederick clearly returned to Dominica with his stock high. As the earlier example of Jolly John suggests, the Carib community seems always to have valued outside experience among their leaders; and Hilary Frederick was swept into the role of chief in 1979. Frederick's infusion of AIM-influenced radicalism, adapted for local circumstances and sometimes referred to as 'Caribism', probably marks 1979 as a major turning point in modern Carib history, although the two previous chiefs, the brothers Faustulus and Mas Clem Frederick (not closely related to Hilary) had already made some of the contacts with outside agencies which would flourish in the 1980s.

[20] Arthur Einhorn, reported in Pound (1983: 7aa). On North American Indian movements of the time, see Hertzberg 1971. Interviewed for Philip Teuscher's film (1983), Arthur Einhorn mentions that Hilary Frederick's father, Andrew, had maintained a long correspondence with Clinton Rickard, a Tuscorora American Indian activist.

[21] On these events, see Matthiessen 1992.

FIG. 16. 'Vote Hilary Frederick', poster produced during Carib chief election campaign, Dominica 1994.

The rise of Caribism also has its roots in various decoloniz-ing processes of the 1970s. For the first time significant atten-tion was paid to Caribbean literature from outside the region, and there was a marked increase in interest in Caribbean archaeology and therefore the pre-Columbian history of the area. In Dominica itself, a pioneering radio series—later turned into a book—told its inhabitants the story of their island, with a crucial place for the Caribs; and Carib children attended secondary school for the first time to find that a new series of school texts had 'Caribbeanized' the curriculum.[22]

Save the Children and Canada Plenty, two Non Governmental Organizations (NGOs) began to play important roles on the Reserve around this time, funding various projects including the construction of a cultural centre, the inauguration of an oral history and documentation project, and the establishment of links with other indigenous groups, especially in the Caribbean region. The older generation's strongest memory was of the 1930 'Carib War', which had taken place when many of them had been young men and women: as a result that incident came to loom large as a key moment in recent Carib history, a kind of Carib Wounded Knee, as Honychurch has suggested, appropriately enough given Hilary Frederick's knowledge of the 1973 occupation of that site.[23] Shortly after Frederick became chief, an unusual visitor to the Carib Territory, Yusuf M. Hamid, prepared a presentation to be given by the Chief to an NGO conference on 'The Rights of Indigenous People and their Land' held in Geneva in September 1981 and subsequently published in London by the UN organization EAFORD (The International Organization for the Elimination of All Forms of Racial Discrimination). *The Caribs and their Colonizers* (Frederick 1983) is a well-researched and scholarly paper, especially as regards the long-running dispute over the boundaries of the 1903 Reserve, but it also argues a strong Carib position with respect to sovereignty, a position that was unlikely to endear the Caribs to the new Freedom Party government on the island.

That imbrication of the Carib Reserve into the world of international indigenism has ended, probably for ever, the isolation in which the Dominican Caribs had largely lived since the middle of the eighteenth century. However, the political upheavals of the early 1980s ensured that the imbricating process was distinctly precarious. The new Freedom Party government, which took control of Dominica in the 1980 elections, was not especially sympathetic to radical Caribism, and Hilary

---

[22] The 1974 radio series became Honychurch 1995.
[23] Honychurch (1997b: 236). The only monument raised by the Caribs themselves is a small one on the site of the 1930 killings, a monument that is not shown to tourists.

Frederick's first term as chief ended under a cloud of financial scandal in 1984. However, the policies of his successor, Irvince Auguiste, were not significantly different from Frederick's and, after Auguiste's two terms, from 1985 to 1995, Frederick was elected for a second time, giving the Caribs a significant level of political stability for the last twenty years of the century.

Hilary Frederick and Irvince Auguiste have both been active and mobile chiefs, spending significant amounts of time building links between the Caribs and indigenous organizations in the Americas and worldwide. Both have become fluent speakers on public platforms and in the media, representing their community's interests and lending a Carib accent to larger causes.[24] As always, the chief has been sought by visitors for interview and comment—but in recent years the number of interviews has grown rapidly. Some visitors take the opportunity to listen and convey what is said to them. Quentin Crewe met Hilary Frederick in 1986 while Frederick was an opposition MP and gives an extensive, though not uncritical account of Frederick's words: 'It was at once apparent that Hilary was much aggrieved at the treatment that he felt the Caribs receive from the Government. As is the way with minorities, he believed that their problems were the result of a conspiracy' (Crewe 1987: 116). He then talked to Auguiste, the Chief:

He, too, felt that the Caribs were underprivileged in many ways and again felt it was a conspiracy on the part of the government. Above all, he was convinced that the Reserve was originally bigger than it is now. 'I have asked to see the original document, but all they will show us is a copy. How do we know if it is genuine? Our old people remember that the boundaries were set much further north and much further south.' I promised to look into the question with the Public Records Office in England. (117)

He did too, although he found that the 1903 map corresponded almost exactly to the present boundaries of the Reserve.

Visiting in 1990 José Barreiro, an academic and activist of Cuban Taino descent, who edits the journal *Native Americas*, allows a large percentage of his article to consist of the words

---

[24] A new chief, Garnette Joseph, was elected in 1999. A long-time activist and member of various Carib cultural groups, Joseph is unlikely to change the general lines of Carib policy established by his two predecessors.

that Auguiste and others speak to him, explaining Carib practices, Carib positions, Carib strategy for the future. As a fellow Native American who has visited the Reserve on several occasions and been involved in various projects there, Barreiro is perhaps treated differently from most visitors: he is noticeably involved in group discussions. However, he also writes very differently from most earlier visitors, saying little about himself or his reactions, and never taking advantage of the moment of writing to offer an authorial perspective that goes significantly beyond the content of his discussions.

In the same year, by contrast, Robert Booth, from *National Geographic*, gave a fine example of how careful editing can keep the writer ahead of his subjects. Interviewing Auguiste, he includes substantial direct quotation from the answers and yet, by bringing forward to the end of the section about the Caribs a comment from Dominica's President, interviewed in the *next* section, manages to completely undercut the Chief's words:

'Descendants of African slaves are today doctors and lawyers. We need Carib doctors and lawyers, and we need our own secondary schools if our children are to remain Carib. Most of all we need our own financial institutions so Carib people can use their land, which is held in common, as collateral for loans. We could then begin to build an economic base.'

What are the chances of such autonomy?

'I might not see it,' [Auguiste] admitted, 'but I'm thinking of my children. There are laws to preserve the wildlife of Dominica. Surely the native people of Dominica should be preserved.'

It may well be too late, according to Dominica's president, Clarence A. Seignoret, a cordial, powerfully built man of 71 who is himself the grandson of a Carib.

'They've lost their language,' he told me. 'Apart from a few of the old ones, there are no pure-blooded Caribs. They are already integrated into Dominican society. At this point I truly feel it is better for them.' (Booth 1990: 108)

VISIBLE DIFFERENCES

For Fermor, George Frederick and the other members of the Carib Council are representatives of their community in both senses of the word: they have been accepted by the Caribs as their political representatives, but their demeanour is also allowed to stand as representative of the history and present status of the Caribs. For other writers, particularly those who are fixated on the Carib chiefs as 'royalty', these functions are often divided, with other figures offered as symbolic representations of 'Caribness': not infrequently (as we saw earlier with Ober and others) a semi-naked woman washing herself or her clothes in a stream.

Le Toumelin, for example, leaves the pyjama-clad Chief with his sprained ankle and walks back towards Pagoua Bay: 'As we crossed the river at the north-west boundary I caught a final glimpse of the last of the Caribs—some young women standing, naked to the waist among the rocks in the sparkling stream, silently washing their clothes' (1963: 136). This image, so persistent in travel accounts, connotes innocence and sexual attraction—two of the staple ingredients of descriptions of 'natives'; but also suggests, in its distance from modernity and in its subjects' defencelessness, that the 'masculine' fighting spirit of the Caribs has been reduced and domesticated. 'The last of the Caribs' is a resonant phrase, inevitably rhyming with 'the last of the Mohicans'. All Le Toumelin is saying, at one level, is that these are the last Caribs he sees as he leaves the Reserve, but the rhyme turns the young women into symbols, a symbolization that, appropriately enough, one might think, robs them of the voices that always accompany the collective washing of clothes. It is as if the seriousness of the symbolic moment demands a silence adequate to the void of history into which the indigenous tribe is supposedly about to fall. Hence the doom-laden conclusion with which Le Toumelin takes his leave: 'Thus the proud warrior race is quietly dying out in this sun-drenched corner of Dominica, where the ocean winds sigh and wander in the massive gloom of the primeval forest' (136).

Carleton Mitchell sailed through the Caribbean islands in his yacht *Carib* shortly after the end of the Second World War (1947), and wrote articles for the *National Geographic* which formed the basis of his *Islands to Windward: Cruising through the Caribbees*, which first appeared in 1949 (with a second enlarged edition in 1955). He and his wife spent some time on the west coast of Dominica and once travelled as far as Marigot where they hoped to see some Caribs, but failed. This failure did not prevent the usual paragraph of historical summary along with the pronouncement that Dominica was a fitting home for the last of the race that had once dominated the islands: 'Its fastnesses provided the shelter necessary for survival, and even the diluted remnants live in savage simplicity' (Mitchell 1955: 95). When he returned in 1965, travelling in the thirty-eight-foot ocean cruise-racer, *Finisterre*, he chose to travel up the island chain from Grenada, 'planning to retrace the island-hopping migration of the Caribs' (1971: 12).

This time a visit to the Caribs is at the top of the agenda for the Dominica leg. Mitchell and Winfield Parks, the *National Geographic* photographer, travel by Land Rover with a local guide, Alford Benoit, fording a river, negotiating a swamp by means of a road of tree trunks, and crossing their fingers that rain does not make the final part of the trail impassable.

My first glimpse of a Carib was of a girl, no more than five years old. Clutching a bottle filled from a stream, she stopped as we paused alongside. Her long hair was as black and smooth as Chinese lacquer, and her coppery features had a definite Mongolian cast. . . .

Not far beyond we came upon a woman washing her family's clothes in a pool under a small waterfall. When she looked up, I was startled by her appearance: I had not expected to find pure types, but rather 'Black Caribs,' descendants of runaway Negro slaves and Indians. But here I saw slanting eyes, high cheek bones, straight hair, and parchment-yellow skin. To me, it was a scene from the Far East. She might have been Korean or Vietnamese. (96)

As so often the washerwoman acts as a boundary marker, as an unthreatening and usually erotic welcoming party, and as evidence of an authentically pre-modern existence. Meanwhile, the litany of Asian comparisons—Chinese, Mongolian, Korean, Vietnamese—once again makes in trumps the point that at least some of these people have a real purity, untouched by African admixture. Being described as 'Korean or Vietnamese' by an ex-US Navy officer in 1965 might not have been taken as unalloyed good news, had Mitchell thought to share his perceptions with the objects of them.

A final symbolic figure is provided in Anthony Weller's account, which dates from 1983. Weller begins his piece by gathering most of the old tropes together for an impressive reunion:

On a wild island of legendary beauty, along a steep coast of palms facing the Atlantic, the last indigenous race of the West Indies has made its final home. Once conquerors and roving seamen, now farmers, the Caribs will vanish within a century, doomed by intermarriage. Yet here on Dominica, the last dim echoes of their past may be heard, a past of war canoes sailing up the islands, of a population that once numbered in the millions, of annihilation by the Europeans—and eventual shelter on these eight miles of rough coast. (1983: 71)

Ethnographic writing often traps its subjects in a different time, denying their coevalness with the observer and writer by suggesting that they belong to an earlier stage of human development and therefore do not properly share the writer's 'present'.[25] Weller's language, controlled by the master trope of 'remnant', operates to similar effect, but by different means: 'last . . . final . . . once . . . vanish . . . doomed . . . last . . . dim . . . past . . . once . . . annihilation . . . shelter'. The Caribs are allowed a present existence, but it is merely a weak echo of the time when they were truly themselves. In a sense, Weller draws out the implications of Fermor's classical analogues of an epic past underlined by a miserable present.

As with many visitors, Weller actually wants it both ways. The changes have been dramatic and devastating; but 'the few roads are rugged and empty' and 'the sense of isolation and secret grandeur is overwhelming', contributing 'paradoxically to the impression that little has changed here in 500 years' (71). The roads may be empty—but 500 years ago there were no roads; indeed the road through the Reserve was completed only about ten years before Weller's visit. He may not have realized it, but he was among the first writers to arrive by road, hitching a lift on the back of a truck.

The ease with which Weller reaches the Carib Reserve is therefore in marked contrast with Patrick Leigh Fermor's horseback journey in the late 1940s, but the arrival scene has some similarities:

Then, abruptly, the road curved once again, and small houses began to appear on the hillsides in clusters or set along the road. Behind each house, a smaller structure issued smoke. The scents of cooking reached us, and we realized that we were among the Caribs at last, but as our

[25] See the study by Johannes Fabian (1983).

truck hurried on, we saw no one. And then behind us a man stood diminishing in the road, barely visible in the twilight, waving and smiling curiously at us. He looked oddly dignified, barefoot and bare chested, wearing only long trousers: his skin was copper, and he had the blackest hair imaginable. Then he was gone as the road descended, and the truck stopped to let us clamber out. (71)

As with Fermor, the event is quotidian, but the descriptive language produces a symbolic 'encounter', though not this time with the chief. Darkness is falling so everybody is indoors. However, the absence of people connotes the announced theme of disappearance. The visitors have hurried to get there, but they are in danger of being too late. As they sit in the back of the truck, looking behind them, a suitably resonant position for Western visitors, they suddenly see a man in the road, 'diminishing . . . barely visible'. The 'encounter' turns into a 'farewell'. There is acknowledgement in the 'waving and smiling curiously at us'—though considerable ambiguity as to whether the smile manifests the man's curiosity or whether Weller considers the smile a curious example of the genre, or indeed whether he considers it curious that the man should smile at all. The man's dignity is similarly odd—'oddly dignified'— though here it must be the writer's sense of what constitutes dignity that is put into question by the man's bearing. As with Fermor, a demeanour more often associated with the 'highly born' of the Old World is glimpsed in the rags of a Carib. Here, indeed, there is only one item of clothing to give a precarious respectability to the bare feet and bare chest. As the truck moves downhill, the framing road surface moves up his body. He, after all, is absolutely still; but for Weller the man 'was gone' as suddenly as he had appeared, leaving behind him the indelible image of 'the blackest hair imaginable': the true mark of Carib authenticity—but really the traveller's sign to himself of the supposed authenticity of his experience.

'Difference' may be a fashionable term for discussions of cultural or ethnic identity, but the indigenous peoples of the Caribbean have been seen as 'different' ever since Columbus noted them in 1492 as 'neither black nor white' (see Hulme 1994*b*). To a remarkable extent, that tripartite distinction has governed perceptions for five centuries, but in the last hundred years—in common with the experience of many Native Americans in the USA—the crucial distinction has been between Indian and black. One of the determinants of American Indian identity has been white racism in the Americas: some American Indian groups have only been able to survive at all by distinguishing themselves from black populations, distinctions made as sharply as they *had* to be made rather than as sharply as the Indians themselves necessarily *wanted* to make them. That would be true, for example, of the Powhatan Indians of Virginia, whose struggles in the middle part of this century to have themselves classified as American Indian were struggles against the determination of white Virginian bureaucrats to classify them as 'coloured'.[26]

This has been a factor in the Caribbean too. Visitors—whether tourists or anthropologists—are still largely whites for whom the distinctiveness of the Caribs depends on their perceived difference from the surrounding African-descended population: 'The physical appearance of this disappearing race is remarkable. They are people of average stature, small-boned, with long, delicate hands and feet, perfectly straight hair, and a physiognomy somewhat like that of the northern Chinese. They are particularly proud of their small eyes, which slant slightly' (Smith 1961: 51). 'Remarkable' is a word that makes sense only in the context of a particular set of expectations. After all, to look like the northern Chinese is hardly in global terms a claim to singularity. But for Bradley Smith, travelling through the West Indian islands in 1956, the encounter with this 'disappearing race' clearly comes as a major surprise. Truly remarkable, it must be said, is Smith's determination to eliminate all traces of perceived modernity: 'Although there have been many changes in the way Caribs live since the time they repulsed the early explorers on the beaches, none of the changes is visible to the visitor today' (50–1). As long as the visitor does not look at the clothes the Caribs wear or the tools they use or the furniture in their houses, or the animals in their yards. . . .

---

[26] See Rountree (1990: 219–42); on the similar case of the Lumbee, see Sider 1993; and more generally, Forbes 1990 and 1993; and Snipp 1986.

Difference is not always coded in visual terms. At least one traveller—the young trombonist, Henry Shukman—feels the difference rather than seeing it:

There is a peace in the air, a sense of harmony, that you feel nowhere else on the island. Everything is neater, the gardens, the plantations, the houses, no matter how small and how patchy their construction. Everything is well tended. And everyone is friendly. They stop whatever they are doing and ask your name and talk. Then you sit together a while talking little, or not at all, wondering if this is your cue to leave, when silence is in fact a vestigial Amerindian tradition, whereby two strangers should sit in one another's company a decent length of time before venturing to speak. (Shukman 1993: 115–16)

Travel writers never see themselves as tourists. They have different interests and different agendas. They may not behave very differently from tourists, but they are sometimes sharply aware of the difficulty of their position. This is Amryl Johnson, for example, a black Trinidadian who has lived in England since she was 11 and who returned to the Caribbean in 1983 and 1984 in order, in her own words, to appease the ghosts that haunted her. Like many others, her visit to the Carib Territory is brief, but the tone of her writing is unusually anxious and awkward, with some efforts at empathy—'What must it feel like to be gawked at all the time?'; an unusual confession of ignorance—'I could not say how many of the people in the reserve were of pure Carib descent'; and some of the usual search for traces of the 'pulse which sang of warriorhood', as if the response to invasion of one's lands somehow defined the entry for ever more in the great encyclopaedia of nations. But then something different begins to happen:

We drove slowly through the Carib Reserve. I was like a tightrope walker edging my way along one of those eroded, rusty spokes. Blindfolded. If I fell, I would do my best to hang on. I had not set out to look for anything more profound than a basic understanding. Almost by accident, somehow, I could feel myself close to the hub. I was arriving. I was getting there. History had come alive, been lifted off the page into the shape of a reality. The spectres had been given some form of substance. (Johnson 1988: 240)

There is no attempt at conversation, no pretence at anything other than a slow drive through the Carib Reserve. Yet there is a disturbance to the narrating self, which feels on edge, close to the hub . . . It is not clear quite what this hub is. Perhaps some of the unease comes from the fact that the writer might have expected the spectres she encountered to be the ghosts of slavery, but she finds a different and unexpected history which 'lifts off the page' to become reality once she enters the Reserve. Unlike all the other examples I have looked at so far in this chapter, Johnson is black and a woman. Both descriptions are arguably relevant to the *difference* of her writing, to the admitted disorientation, to the odd mixture of connection and distance, to the refusal of poise.

PURE BLOOD AND MIXED

Of overwhelming interest in recent years, just as it was at the end of the nineteenth century, has been the question of purity of blood: for most visitors the discourse of race is still securely in place. In a very few cases this interest might have a scientific dimension, but for the most part it is a matter of visible physical characteristics: skin colour, shape of face, type of hair. These elements—when light, oriental, and straight, respectively— provide the reassurance that visitors need of Carib distinctiveness. Their relative absence is seen as a mark of decline, of absence of purity: 'cultural surrender' in the words of one recent visitor (Tree 1998: 105).

In a related concern, visitors have been obsessed with numbers: the number of inhabitants in the Reserve, which has steadily increased since the turn of the century; and the number of supposedly 'pure' Caribs, a number that fluctuates wildly according to the purely subjective criteria of what constitutes 'purity'. Few aspects of racial thinking illustrate its ridiculousness as patently as its arithmetical pretensions. Harry Luke, the genial and well-informed British Council representative, who visited the Reserve in the late 1940s, around the same time as Fermor, had the decency to sound slightly baffled: 'In 1903 the pure Caribs were estimated at 120 out of the total of 400; a Commission which investigated conditions in the Reserve in 1931 put them at 170. Taylor goes no higher than 100, but George Frederick, the headman of the Carib Council, told the present writer . . . that he thought 200 would be nearer the

mark' (Luke 1950: 130–1). In the 1950s Bradley Smith estimated about 600 inhabitants, twenty-five 'of "red" descent'
(1961: 49); in the early 1960s Le Toumelin had 1,000 inhabitants, 'at the most 200 . . . of pure blood' (1963: 126); in the
early 1970s Wolfe had a total of 1,500, fewer than a hundred
pure-blooded (1970: 34).

During the 1960s there were two scientific visits—one English,
one French—to study the Caribs through blood groups.[27] To an
unscientific eye, the resulting analyses seem flawed by unexam-
ined preconceptions (and confidence in the French team is not
increased by the transcription of the name of their Dominican
co-worker, Dr D. C. Shillingford, the island's Chief Medical
Officer, into Chilling-Rathford, who sounds like a mad scientist
played by Vincent Price in a Hammer horror film). The main pre-
conception lies in the categories of 'pure' and 'mixed', which are
absolutely pre-given: 'We have tried to estimate the degree of
racial mixing in each individual tested, and we have been led to
classify our sample into three categories: I.—Supposedly pure
Caribs. II.—Carib-Black mixes. III.—Other mixes' (Chilling-
Rathford 1966: 324). The scientists were clearly 'led' to their
classification by the usual subjective assessment of facial and
other physical features. The scientific analysis of blood groups
does not *provide* a distinction between 'pure' and 'mixed': that
pre-given distinction provides the parameters through which the
blood group analysis results are then interpreted.

Often, there is no need for scientific testing. Shortly after
Dominica became an independent associated state in 1967, the
Scandinavian writer, Kjeld Helweg-Larsen, having already inter-
viewed Douglas Taylor, was taken by the new British governor,
Geoffrey Guy, to meet the much-interviewed Carib Chief,
Germandois Francis:

He was clean and neatly dressed and I was studying his face well, there
could not be any mistake, this young man seemed to be a hundred per
cent pure Carib Indian with no mixture of blood since the time the
islands were discovered by Columbus. . . .

I was also introduced to the Chief's father, and studying the old
man's face there could be no discussion—here was another pure Carib.

[27] Harvey *et al.* 1969; Cabannes and Schmidt-Beurrier 1966; and Chilling-
Rathford 1966.

As Mr. Taylor had said to me, 'You just have to take one look at the present Carib Chief or his father and you will realise that this people could never have mixed blood with any other races whatsoever.' (Helweg-Larsen 1967: 155)

Just one look. The whole of a people's history in just one face, at least when scanned by eyes that know, imperial eyes with 20/20 historical vision.

The Caribs themselves—like most surviving American Indian groups since 1492—have incorporated Africans and Europeans into their kinship groups without apparent strain, and certainly without consideration of blood or genetics. The division between 'pure' and 'mixed' Caribs has often been an issue on the Reserve, but it is not clear that the Caribs mean the same thing by the division as outsiders such as Hesketh Bell. For outsiders, the division was—and is—a matter of blood and therefore appearance. For Caribs, the key question is one of residence: 'black' or 'creole' means someone not born on the Reserve and not descended from someone born on the Reserve, with the collective memory going back several generations. This would mean that Caribs and outsiders would not always concur on who counted as 'pure' Carib. The supposed 'tradition' of a Carib woman having to leave the Reserve if she sets up house with a non-Carib male seems only as old as the Reserve itself, and is in any case the simple consequence of a patrilocal norm common throughout the island. According to Honychurch, the Caribs regard it as the social custom but hold it in no special regard as a particularly Carib tradition (Honychurch 1997b: 154). Jolly John spoke strongly in 1931 about not allowing intermarriage, but by that he clearly meant 'a Carib marrying a non-Carib out of the Reserve', not a Carib marrying a mixed-blood resident of the Reserve.[28] For the most part, it would seem that where distinctions are now made on the Territory itself, they either distinguish between 'pure' Caribs who have established family connections and 'half-Caribs' who are the children of one parent from outside the Territory, or—as has happened on occasion—the language of blood has been adopted from the

---

[28] CO 152/42511: 163 (Evidence of Thomas Jollie John to Commission, 13 May 1931).

colonial discourse that introduced it in establishing the Reserve in the first place.

However, it was in the interest of everyone concerned—the Caribs themselves and the Afro-Dominican majority who were taking over the island at the time of independence—that the language of race was not enshrined within the laws of the new state of the Commonwealth of Dominica. To this end the Carib Law act offers a careful definition of who has the right of residence on the Reserve (and not who has the right to call themselves Carib). Under 'The Carib Reserve, Act no. 22 of 1978' 'a person shall be deemed to have a right of residence in the Reserve if— (a) he was born in the Reserve; (b) at least one of his parents is a Carib; (c) he has lawfully resided in the Reserve for a period of 12 years or more' (Dominica 1991: 51–2). With this law in place, the Caribs themselves have fundamental control over the question of just who can call themselves 'Carib'—a matter still of considerable tension in the North American Indian situation thanks to the continued deployment of degree-of-blood requirements imposed for access to federal services in the USA. Although not well known enough to be widely referred to, Carib practice is close to the procedures recently adopted by the Oglala Lakota on Pine Ridge, where the crucial factors for Oglala identity are now residency on the reservation, affinity to, knowledge of, and service to the Oglala people (see Jaimes 1992). At the same time the Carib Reserve was *granted* to the Caribs, to be held by the Carib Council in trust for the community as a whole, at least ensuring Carib control over its future.[29]

ELEGY FOR A DYING RACE

When it loses, as it soon will, what remains to it of its integrity, this race will belong only in history. (Delawarde 1938: 204)

These Caribs are the last remnants of a once-proud warrior people. They lost their own indigenous culture long ago. A whim of the island's

---

[29] The new Carib Reserve Act (Dominica 1991) made minor amendments to the original 1978 Act (Dominica 1978); in other words the new government simply accepted the boundaries that Bell had established, despite continuing Carib claims that these boundaries misrepresented an original grant, often dated back to the time of Queen Charlotte.

erstwhile British colonial rulers enabled them to survive as a group. Now, through continuing intermarriage, they are gradually losing the last *visible* signs of their Indian origins. It can only be a matter of time before those too are irretreviably lost. (Sütterlin 1991: 28; my emphasis)

The narrative of purity is a narrative of loss and therefore inevitably a narrative of death; which means, as has been apparent from the very beginning of this book, that the appropriate genre for the visiting writer to adopt is that of the elegy. However, where identity is troped as *visible*—through physical characteristics—survival is possible beyond death, as trace. Maurice Barbotin, the curé of Grand-Bourg, on the small French island of Marie-Galante, ends his discussion of the history of the indigenous settlements on that island with a paragraph on Carib traces, what Jean Raspail calls, in discussing the passage, '[t]he silent language of the face . . . When memory has died, at least that language remains' (Raspail 1980: 83).

In our time there is no longer a single Carib of pure race on Marie-Galante, but in several families of the region where they had their last carbet you can still find undoubted traces of their mixed race, traces that are getting weaker more and more quickly. I used to know an old woman who died about twelve years ago, who told her troubles to me: 'My mother was the very stamp of a Carib, with beautiful, black, shiny hair, it was my father who was a negro and gave me this horrible head of hair'. (Barbotin 1976: 118)

Raspail has encountered Père Barbotin by following what he calls a 'Carib trail' to Marie-Galante: 'Amazing, this line of Catholic priests without whom the Carib memory would be lost' (1980: 80). He points out that Houël, a French Governor in the seventeenth century, treated with the Caribs, leaving them the north and north-east of the island, with the result that the censuses only took account of Indians living in the south, and cannot therefore be taken as accurate indicators of the overall indigenous population of the island: 'This division of the island is still quite perceptible today. Until recently the circular road was just a badly made track in the north between Vieux-Fort and Grand Bassin. Houses are scarce and date from the last century. No mill except the one in Cambrai. An almost non-existent network of interior roads. And even today, no drivable road leads to the beach at Coq where the Carib cacique of Marie-Galante lived until . . .' (1980: 82). Raspail leaves the answer hanging, although an earlier visitor suggested that there were certainly Caribs in the area as late as 1816 (Montlezun, 1818: ii. 143–5).

Jean Raspail's first two books about the Caribbean, *Secouons le cocotier* and *Punch caraïbe* were published in 1966 and 1970 (and combined in 1973). *Bleu caraïbe et citrons verts* (1980) recounts a fresh visit but also reworks earlier material.[30] Raspail visits the Carib Reserve on Dominica, but what he calls his 'Carib trail' also takes him through Guadeloupe, Marie-Galante, and Haiti as well as Nancy, Lausanne, and Rotterdam. It begins with a Caribbean warclub or *boutou*, bought at dead of night off a Haitian *houngan*[31] and ends in the Grenadine islands.

Raspail is, it should be explained, the pre-eminent modern author of 'last man/woman' stories, and the Caribbean provides him with a rich source. In *Bleu caraïbe et citrons verts* he mentions police reports from Haiti in 1862 about the Viens-Viens of La Selle, supposed descendants of the Taino; and he is disappointed only to see the fresh grave of Anna, last of the Lucayans, in the Caicos islands ('She was the last survivor of her people') (1980: 27).[32] This 'last of' trope was extensively discussed in Chapter 3 as a late nineteenth-century phenomenon: it is still alive and well and extremely visible, which is more than can be said about the 'last man/woman' themselves, who has always already just died, shortly before our intrepid reporter arrives on the scene.[33]

[30] Respectively, 'Let's Shake the Coconut Tree', 'Caribbean Punch', and 'Blue Caribbean and Green Limes'.

[31] Raspail claims that this weapon was identified by Edgar Clerc in Guadeloupe as dating from the 6th cent., though such precise dating of stone weapons is usually impossible.

[32] These stories have long circulated in the Bahamas. Stewart Culin begins his 1902 account of a journey to Cuba in search of surviving Indians with a story heard from an Englishman he meets on the steamer to the effect that survivors of the original Lucayans are still living 'in primitive savagery' on the island of Little Abaco in the Bahamas (1902: 185). That such a possibility could even be mooted for such a small island suggests what psychic investment there has been on the part of some outsiders in the idea of such survival.

[33] Raspail has written about the Patagonians in a similar way (1988). His best-known novel, the deeply racist *The Camp of the Saints* (1995), deals with the invasion of Europe by the Third World.

As I will suggest in more detail later in this chapter, questions of cultural survival have to be dealt with carefully in the Caribbean: it is, after all, common to see history books airily discussing the complete extermination of the indigenous population of the islands in the years immediately after 1492. The historical record is still far from complete, and in places like Cuba there are indigenous communities which are only today coming into the knowledge of anthropologists. Above all, what counts as indigenous is constantly under discussion and revision. However, none of this matters to the 'last man' stories, whose whole *raison d'être* is the supposed pathos of the last survivor of a race, the last speaker of a language, with nobody to communicate or mate with, dying alone.

A sub-set of these stories take place in the 'lost valley' where, hidden from history, an indigenous group has survived beyond the reach of European weapons and disease. Frederick Ober has a good example in his *Camps in the Caribbees*. He tells of how in May 1877 he was camping in the Dominican rainforest above the Carib territory with his guides Meyong and Coryet, sheltering in the cave which supposedly had held the wife of the governor of Antigua, kidnapped by Caribs some two centuries earlier—and released unharmed. Suddenly the figure of an old man staggers into the firelight and is given food and rum. Meyong and Coryet recognize him as 'a crazy chief' who fled to the mountains fifty years earlier after 'refusing to submit to English rule': 'He had been insane for many years' (1880: 149). He speaks only Carib. The following night he leads them through the deep forest to an old maroon village. From this place, Ober reports, he pays occasional mysterious visits to 'a gloomy gorge, into which he would not allow us to penetrate' (153). The guides relate to Ober the story that the old man has a beautiful granddaughter, only survivor of the family he took with him to the forest: 'they described her as being as beautiful as the old man was ugly, which was saying a good deal'; but they never lay eyes on her, 'nor did we even obtain conclusive proof of her existence' (153). The crazy chief's granddaughter remains a haunting figure, however, for Ober: a pure Carib, speaking only the language of her ancestors, having no knowledge of the Europeans who had conquered Dominica, a fantasy figure whose avatars he and others would create in their novels, the *properly* fictional version, so to speak, of that imaginary figure—the Indian of 1492—whose shadow late nineteenth-century US anthropology spent so much time chasing.[34]

Raspail has his own version of this story. Crossing Dominica, he stops to pick up a young white hitchhiker who has just emerged from the forest. Raspail's map shows the central northern part of the interior as uninhabited and roadless, but the young man has a hand-drawn map with a path and some instructions about crossing seven rivers and following the course of the eighth to a hamlet which, he says, acts as an outpost for a maroon community. This young man has been there on the instructions of a friend, who had lived in the hamlet two years, to find the girl whom his friend had promised to come back for, and to tell her that he was not going to. The girl, already nursing the friend's baby, had not been pleased. She was called Arouague, the young man says, prompting Raspail to ascertain that, yes, she had long straight black hair and bronze skin, and needing him to explain to the young man that she was an Arawak, original inhabitant of the island, long before the Carib invaders arrived. 'Mon Dieu' is the young man's only comment. Man of the world that he is, Raspail is sympathetic: 'I imagine that having held her in his arms and penetrated her belly, she, Arouague, the last link in her race, he was now undergoing the new sensation of having fulfilled a kind of religious rite' (Raspail 1980: 33). Raspail undertakes to give the good news to the father, in a flat in Nanterre, but he cannot be found.

However, Raspail's most powerful Carib story begins in an unusual place, a striptease bar in the red light district of Lausanne, where he has gone to relax after giving an exhausting lecture. He gazes in fascination at the stripper:

Men don't usually fix their gaze on the flare of the nostrils, the fold of the eye-lids and the lobe of the ear when looking at a totally naked and superb body on a cabaret stage. Especially when she arches that supple caramel-skinned body towards the horizontal during the performance of a difficult *limbo*, the point of her breasts brushing the

---

[34] Ober wrote two striking fictional versions of this archetypal story, *Under the Cuban Flag* (1897) and *The Last of the Arawaks* (1901): cf. Hulme 1997*a* and 1997*b*. Douglas Taylor was sceptical about Ober's story, having spoken to some of the older Caribs who knew nothing of the 'crazy chief'—or weren't telling (1938: 10–11).

burning stick held out twenty centimetres off the ground, while she, with only her feet on the ground, slides and slithers underneath like a snake. (84)

From her skin colour and her creole accent, Raspail deduces the stripper's origins, but he wants her to explain them spontaneously to him. Calling her over to his table, he leads the conversation delicately in the right direction, complimenting her on her almost straight mirror-black hair and the elegant angle of her eyelids, but refraining from mentioning the feature that he calls her 'originalité première', her 'ravishingly small and round bottom, discreet and fleshy at the same time' (87). She asks: 'You find me different, don't you?' and then speaks the words he has been waiting for. 'Kallinago? Do you know what that is? . . .', she asks, using the old female form for 'Carib'. 'My mother was a pure Kallinago. I was born near the village of Pistolet, at the tip of Grand Vigie' (88). Raspail tells Rose of his researches. Of how the official censuses of Guadeloupe mention no Caribs after 1730, of how nobody on the island has any memory of a reserve, but how—in Guy Lasserre's monumental thesis on the geography of Guadeloupe—he had finally found the evidence: 'Because Grand Vigie was an Indian reserve. But its birth, life, and death passed completely unnoticed. It's impossible to know how, after 1730, the surviving Caribs on Guadeloupe had obtained, or submitted to, isolation in a land grant situated to the north-east of the community of Anse Bertrand, on the dry limestone plateau of "Hautes caraïbes" at the tip of Grand Vigie' (90). He sketches from memory the 1884 map that Lasserre had found. 'Rose picked up the pencil: "We lived in one of those houses. There, there was a pond, and there a big carved stone"' (91). Raspail recalls reading Lasserre's description: 'In 1960 . . . all trace of human habitation had disappeared. Just some patches of old crops and charcoal broke the undergrowth of logwood and acacia. Near one of the clearings we found the one *métis* with obvious Carib traits that we'd laid eyes on in Guadeloupe. A triangular house covered with straw recalled the *mouinan* or Carib carbet. There, perhaps, are to be found the last traces of a civilisation' (91, quoting Lasserre).

Seven years after Lasserre had written these words in 1961, Raspail had gone—he tells Rose—to that same spot in a vain attempt to find some sign of the *métis* with Carib traits. He braves, he says, the possible charges of excessive romanticism or of artificial tragedy: 'Why not simply admit that there was something extraordinarily moving, on that vast plateau swept by a strong trade wind, to roar out a call for the last of the living. In vain . . .' (92). Nobody would have replied, says Rose, because that *métis*, Nestor by name, brain-damaged by nature, had died several years previously: 'The village idiot!', groans Raspail, 'Landed with a ridiculous name. He was the incarnation of the the "last trace of a civilisation"' (92). But there is something else that Raspail wants to explain to Rose, a strange story unearthed by another scholar working in the colonial archives:

In 1882, the last descendants of the Caribs at the tip of Grande Vigie had addressed a plea to the French government in which they complained that the land of their reserve was constantly being transgressed. Ten names followed this desolate text, most signed with a cross . . . The only response that these unfortunate people received was the removal of the topographical map of the reserve by the master of works, L. Bon, two years later, in 1884, to the sole benefit of the metropolitan sugar companies who were exploiting the neighbouring plots of Habitations Pistolet and Berthaudière. The arbitrarily drawn line of 500 yards only included rocky undergrowth unsuited to agriculture and ratified the arbitrary expropriation of nearly the entirety of the reserve, almost 2,000 acres of good sugar-growing land. (93)

Rose recalls her mother, how little she had talked of the past but how melancholy she had been; how she knew nothing of the Caribs on Dominica, just across the channel; how, when she learned of Nestor's death, she had spoken of 'the last of the warriors'; how from that moment she had begun to hate her husband (94–5). As the night comes to a close, Rose asks not to be left alone and leads Raspail to a small hotel nearby. After making love, she says to him, 'Jean Raspail, one day you will make for me a little Kallinago baby' (96). He leaves quietly in the morning while she pretends to sleep.

Raspail can no doubt be seen—and no doubt wants himself to be seen—in the great tradition of Julien Viaud (Pierre Loti), as he tells of fucking the beautiful young body of the dying race with a suitable tinge of Old World melancholy in his voice. In his extraordinarily popular *Le Mariage de Loti*, first published in 1880, Loti describes his 16-year-old Tahitian lover, Rarahu: 'She was a touching and sad little personification of the Polynesian race, which is dying out in contact with our civilization and our vices, and before long will be only a memory in the history of Oceania'.[35]

Like Loti, Raspail's writing often demonstrates a rather loose relationship to historical facts. The whole story of the 'last man' should also be put in proper context. The last Carib on Guadeloupe is not the last of a species in any proper biological sense, and not even the last Carib man any more than Rose's mother is the last Carib woman. It can hardly be repeated too often that the language of race underpinning such rhetoric has no scientific basis. Physical features anyway bear an uneven relationship to genetic inheritance. The complex history of the Caribbean since 1492 means that most, if not all, surviving indigenous communities were deeply mixed, both with other Indians, as well as with Africans and to some extent Europeans, and had often moved, or been moved, from the island of their birth.

But the story of Rose rings true. Lasserre's book certainly exists and contains the map that Raspail refers to. Indigenous communities surviving deep into the colonial period, and even up to the present day, have certainly been written out of mainstream Caribbean history. The story of the reserve at Grand Vigie sounds like so many other stories of indigenous dispossession all over the Americas: small native communities tolerated until their land is required by colonial concerns. Rose's mother's ignorance of the Caribs on Dominica, just a few miles away across the sea, is a poignant reminder of how European colonialism destroyed a Caribbean way of life which had been so dependent on inter-island communication.

SURVIVAL, ASSIMILATION, ETHNOGENESIS

One final example of this narrative of decline comes from Alan Whicker's pioneering documentary programmes for the BBC's *Tonight* programme in the 1960s. Whicker included a series on the Caribbean, one ten-minute segment of which recorded his

[35] Loti (1976: 117); and cf. Rennie (1996: 206–10).

visit to the Carib Reserve in Dominica. Many of the tropes will by now be recognizable. The difficulty of the journey is emphasized—'expedition into the remote territory . . . almost inaccessible', although the traditional horses have now been replaced by a Land Rover. The Caribs are seen as living out a 'tragic destiny . . . doomed to extinction':

what is perhaps the most lonely and tragic destiny in the world, for they are the last of their race, the rearguard growing smaller in numbers each year of a doomed people, listlessly awaiting extinction. Soon these bewildered descendants of the warriors who defied Columbus will have retreated from their wretched and pathetic today, and faded away to join their forebears in the valhalla reserved for them in the history books, leaving only their sea, the Caribbean.[36]

Alan Whicker's half-scripted words probably do not merit too close a scrutiny; but they do clearly demonstrate the ludicrousness of some of the descriptions that the Caribs are made to bear. Just how many hours of each day, how many days of each week, how many weeks of each year, how many years of each century is it possible to spend 'listlessly awaiting extinction'? How does even the perceptive visitor distinguish the listless awaiting extinction from the listless waiting for the next bus?

By the 1960s, however, when these words were broadcast, the penny seems to have dropped that the Carib 'remnant' was hanging around rather a long time, 'lingering'—in Fermor's classic phrase—'on the shores of extinction' rather *too* long in fact; malingering, indeed; outstaying the welcome of history; making the story untidy. There have been a number of suggestions, at least from the 1930s onwards, that the 'black tide' might not be coming in quite quickly enough for some people's taste. We already saw in Chapter 4 that certain forces within the colonial administration were interested in the 1930s in eliminating the special status of the Reserve. The renewed attention given to the Caribs after the 1930 killings strengthened that sense, but at the same time contributed to the interest that outsiders showed in precisely that *special* status.

---

[36] WM 332. Transcribed from the original recording, which was first transmitted on BBC1 on the evening of 10 April 1964, and then formed part of 'Whicker's World: A Caribbean Compilation', broadcast on BBC2 on 5 February 1966, just as Queen Elizabeth II began an extensive tour of the area.

Between 1930 and 1967, the official British attitude to the Caribs seems to have been unwavering. In July 1944 Charles Whitaker, US Vice Consul in Grenada, visited the Caribs as part of an Anglo-American Caribbean Commission, with Douglas Taylor as his guide and main source. Whitaker's conclusion was that

[t]here is probably little to be said in favour of keeping the Carib race as a distinct entity, and there are possibly numerous advantages to be derived from having these people gradually melt into the population as a whole. Under the present Carib system any Carib who builds a house on land in the reservation has possession of the land in the neighbourhood of that house . . . He can move to new land at will. Usually he does move after a few years. This system does not encourage the pride of individual ownership, for the Carib cannot be assured of the possession of his land, not can he leave it to his offspring.[37]

However, this regrettable exception to the laws of possessive individualism and personal inheritance, the pillars of Western civilization, was due to disappear soon: 'The British policy towards the Caribs seems to be to let them mix with the rest of the population and, as a race, become extinct as soon as possible.'

In 1962, the anthropologist Raymond T. Smith, working under the auspices of the University of the West Indies, conducted a brief study of the Reserve and submitted a report to the authorities in which he went a long way towards recommending assimilation:

One alternative to the continuation of the present system would be for the Government to begin immediately to treat the Caribs like anyone else in Dominica. This would involve a partition of the Carib lands and the abolition of special chieftaincy and special exemption from boat tax. In place of the Carib Council a local authority or a series of local authorities could be established, and I assume that there is provision in the local government system for the nomination of persons such as school-teachers or the priest to serve on village councils, along with the elected members. Of course local authorities so constituted would have to raise revenue which means levying a tax of some kind.

---

[37] Smithsonian Institution, National Anthropological Archives, Division of Ethnology Manuscript Pamphlet File: f. 110 Carib Indians (Report (no. 37) from American Consulate, St George's, Grenada (31 July 1944)).

This would be unpopular but it is essential to begin at some time if the vicious circle of dependency is to be broken, and adequate measures will have to be taken to see that the money so raised is well spent. (Smith 1962: 7)

Geoffrey Guy was the British Administrator during the period, shortly after Smith's report, when Dominica was changing its status from colony to independent associated state, the first step in the process of decolonization. In 1967 the Scandinavian writer, Kjeld Helweg-Larsen, gave a very clear account of Guy's views:

What was once the last stronghold of a fierce cannibal tribe—as the warriors were in the old days—was now obviously the home of a dying and vanishing tribe, the charming, peaceful Caribs we had just visited in their Reserve. The Administrator told me that the Government's policy is directed towards absorbing the Caribs into the life of Dominica. It would not be desirable to have them survive as a separate people in, so to speak, an ethnic museum. There are many of Carib blood and appearance who live outside the Reserve and who follow lives of the same pattern as everyone else in Dominica. There are no distinct customs which the Caribs have in their Reserve nor do they have a separate language any longer; their distinguishing characteristics are their physical appearance and their living on land that was once set aside for them as a Reserve. By building roads and schools, the Government hopes that agriculture of a higher standard will be encouraged and that in a few years any distinction between Caribs in the Reserve and people outside will disappear. (1967: 159)

Indeed Guy made his views clear to the Caribs themselves in a letter to the chief, Germandois Francis, at around the same time:

It is the intention of this government that Caribs should ultimately be treated in the same way as every other person who resides in Dominica. They should have the same rights and privileges, the same duties and obligations as everyone else. The Caribs should be subject to the same laws as other people, administered in the same courts and they should pay the same taxes. The benefits of a full village council organization are available for the area, as soon as the Caribs wish for them. (Quoted in Owen 1974: 100)

The Colonial Office was doubtless trying to clear up the Carib 'anomaly' before passing effective power over the island's internal affairs to the Dominicans. The Caribs themselves used the handover as an opportunity to flex their muscles, attempting to expel several non-Caribs from the Reserve, only to find that the new regime was going to speak and act even more firmly than the colonial power, informing the Carib Council that what it was proposing to do was 'against the law of Dominica, the English law and the Human Rights Resolution of the United Nations'.[38] At the same time, following Raymond Smith's earlier recommendation, the government tried to push the Council up to eight members, three nominated by the government, a move that the Caribs successfully resisted. This would have been the first move towards turning the Carib Council into the same kind of village council as exists elsewhere in Dominica, thus eliminating one significant mark of Carib difference (Owen 1980: 268–9).

'To treat Caribs like anyone else in Dominica'. A certain discourse of human rights can be heard in Smith's phrase, along with a trace of resentment that the Caribs have had *special* treatment—and therefore that the rest of the population of the island has been in some sense discriminated against. In an independent country, with that majority population now in control, the situation was bound to change, although in fact the years since independence have seen an uneasy compromise punctuated by moments of crisis.

Guy's invocation of the inappropriateness of the 'ethnic museum' indicates the way in which the 1932 Commission of Enquiry set the terms of the British policy of assimilation.[39] Assimilation is of course not an actively destructive policy: it merely refuses to recognize more cultural difference than it has to, refuses to give political form to those cultural differences, and waits—more or less patiently—for its policy to bear fruit as the cultural differences disappear. It is not difficult for a state to adopt such a policy: after all, it has to commit itself to equal

---

[38] Owen (1974: 101); and cf. Gregoire *et al.* (1996: 153–4).

[39] See above, Chapter 4, p. 179. Basil Cracknell, who visited in the early 1970s, also quoted the 1932 Commission of Enquiry's conclusions as the touchstone, and found 'that at last the Caribs are taking this message to heart. Soon, the Caribs will be fully integrated into the wider community, but for the time being their almost miraculous survival adds a colourful and fascinating dimension to Dominican life' (1973: 59).

treatment for all its citizens. But to do so is to adopt a particular theory of cultural identity based on the 'objective' assessment of what counts as cultural individuality: below a certain—though usually implicit—threshold, a group or community, even if self-defined as significantly different, is judged to have failed the test of *sufficient* cultural difference. However, a different paradigm has recently been developed by anthropologists, one which gives more attention both to ethnic self-definition and to the invention and reinvention of cultural groups over time.[40] The concepts associated with this paradigm—terms such as ethnogenesis and tribal zone—are particularly appropriate in the Caribbean where all indigenous groups have had to cope with vertiginous changes if they were to survive at all.[41]

'Invention' is in many ways an appropriate word to describe how Carib ethnicity came into being in the first place: the product of forced but imaginative adaptation to the changes consequent on the European invasion and colonization of the Caribbean islands. Politically, the argument from ethnogenesis can cut both ways, as the word 'invention' suggests with its implications of either 'fabrication' or 'imagination', putting the emphasis—according to analytical preference—on either the inauthentic or the postauthentic.[42] Much recent writing has focused on the ways in which communities have been imagined, putting the emphasis, properly enough, on both nationalism and ethnicity as cultural *processes*. But it should also be stressed that in the earlier model, which is sometimes seen as a bastion of 'authenticity' against the supposed fabrications of postmodern theory, the conventional classifications are no less precisely inventions: cultural units such as 'Carib', defined by anthropology as existing at the moment of contact or earlier, are them-

[40] Cf. e.g. the distinctions made by Les W. Field (1994) between what he identifies as the 'cultural survival position' and the 'resistance school' and by John H. Moore (1994) between 'cladistic' and 'rhizotic' theories of historical relationship to antecedent groups.

[41] For the 'tribal zone', see Ferguson and Whitehead, eds. 1992. For new ethnohistorical work on the Native Caribbean, see Sued Badillo 1992; Hulme 1993; Honychurch 1997b; Baker 1988; and the papers collected in Whitehead, ed. 1995.

[42] The distinction is made by Anderson (1991: 6). On the 'invention' debate, see Desai 1993. For the 'inauthenticity' and 'postauthenticity' contrast, see James Clifton, ed. (1989); and James Clifford (1988).

selves fictions rather than simple observations of fact, even if fictions which demonstrate the power of colonial classifications to call their inventions into being.

As might be expected, professional anthropologists have been more alert than other visitors to changing notions of cultural identity. E. P. Banks's work in the early post-war period operated with a traditional sense of cultural loss, very much along the lines of Douglas Taylor's pioneering studies. More recently, the specific question of ethnicity has been discussed by Nancy Owen, Anthony Layng, Patrick Baker, and Lennox Honychurch. Owen did research on the Carib Reserve in the early 1970s, Layng in the mid-1970s and early 1980s. Baker was also in Dominica in the early 1970s (though not on the Reserve), with a return visit in 1984, after which he wrote an article on Carib ethnogenesis. Honychurch, a Dominica resident, spent extended time on the Territory in 1995–6.[43]

If invention is seen as the opposite of the ideal of cultural authenticity, then the Carib Reserve, its chief and its council can be derided as merely 'early twentieth-century creations' which disguise the fact that its inhabitants are 'almost completely creolized' (Lowenthal 1972: 181–2). This view depends upon the idea of a cultural authenticity located at some moment in the past, traditionally—in American cases—before 1492. Even Nancy Owen accepts without evidence that 'the aboriginal Caribs comprised a distinct ethnic group' (1974: 18), seemingly, as with the traditional picture of the indigenous Caribbean, back-projecting the seventeenth-century French accounts into the pre-contact era. For others, such as Patrick Baker, 'When we talk of the Carib we employ a European fiction' (1988: 394), recognizing the processual nature of identity as a cultural constant kept in the foreground by the ravages—material and ideological—associated with colonial contact. It has, however, proved very difficult to deploy this kind of language without being taken as undermining claims to cultural authenticity.[44]

---

[43] My references here are chiefly to Owen's doctoral thesis (1974), plus two articles drawing from it (1975, 1980); Layng's book (1983), based on his doctoral thesis (1976), plus two articles drawing from it (1979–80, 1985); Baker's article (1988), with some references to his book (1994); and Honychurch's doctoral thesis (1997*b*).

[44] Cf. the instructive debate about Hawaian identity between Joyce Linnekin and Haunani-Kay Trask: Linnekin 1983; Trask 1991, 1992; cf. Tobin 1994.

Baker's analysis of Carib ethnogenesis is valid in broad terms; and in any case, an increasing suspicion of the over-rapid identification of archaeological remains with ethnic groups has, at least in theory, made historians more chary of speaking confidently about 'the Caribs' when discussing the pre-contact period.[45] The problem—and Baker falls into this trap—comes when writers suggest that 'creation' or 'invention' is exclusively the explanation for certain forms of ethnicity (usually the ones previously identified as 'primitive') rather than merely being an aspect of *all* forms, since ethnicity should be seen, by definition, as a fully social and intercultural phenomenon. If, then, all ethnic identities are seen as essentially invented, or at least negotiated, then the Carib case becomes a specific instance of a general rule instead of an example of the culturally inauthentic.

Frederik Barth's insight into ethnicity—summarized by Nancy Owen as 'the ethnic boundary which defines the group, not the cultural stuff that it encloses' (1974: 15)—lends itself to a consideration of the question of the territorial boundary, now widely recognized as crucial to any consideration of Carib identity.[46] From within this perspective, the Caribs are sometimes seen as offering a particularly clear opportunity to study a case of the extreme situation: an ethnic group whose *only* identity lies in the physical boundary that marks the limits of the community. Leo Despres, Layng's supervisor, sums this up best in his foreword to Layng's book, in commenting on his student's ethnographic focus on 'the last remnant of those warlike American Indians who once occupied most of the islands of the Eastern Caribbean':

And what a pitiful remnant they are: without a language of their own, without a distinguishable phenotypical appearance, without manifest evidence of genealogical relationship, or a characteristic set of religious practices, without even a distinctive presentation of self in the usual range of social encounters, in short, without any apparent basis for their categorical differentiation these so-called Caribs, or at least a significant number of them, claim primordial attachments. On the face

---

[45] For a useful overview, see the work of William Keegan (1994, 1996*a*, 1996*b*); and cf. Jones (1997).

[46] Barth's work (1969) is conventionally seen as a turning point in studies of ethnicity. Despres's work on ethnicity (1975) is clearly a major influence on Layng.

of it, the claim is preposterous. (Despres, in Layng 1983: p. xiv (and quoting p. 1))

Resisting the undoubted temptation to make a citizen's arrest on the grounds of impersonating American Indians, Layng studies the political strategy of a community whose only ethnic difference is supposedly to be found in their *claim* to be different. In terms of rhetoric and vocabulary, it is perhaps surprising how the language of anthropology can repeat the language of its dreadfully unscientific predecessors, with Despres's string of 'withouts' embedded in a long history of classical and Renaissance negativity in the description of 'primitive' or utopian communities (see Levin 1972). 'Remnant' is, as we have now seen *ad nauseam*, the word that is umbilically attached to 'Carib' in modern times: 'pitiful' and 'so-called' are just condescending. Physical appearance and cultural traits are, it should be said, not to be wiped out of the story quite so easily. Baker does it too: 'they have lost most of their traditional manufacturing specialities, such as their basketry and boat-building' (1988: 392). One does not have to be committed to a culture-trait approach to point out that basket-making still flourishes, with Carib basketry instantly recognizable and highly regarded, and that boat-making, while not as common as previously, is still recognized as an important Carib skill (see Honychurch 1997*b*: 112–39).

But, on this understanding of modern Carib society, as developed by Layng and Baker, the articulation of ethnic identity is largely a matter of political strategy. There are gains to be made—probably economic—through the maintenance of a territorial boundary which gives preferential access to land (the argument goes), and so an ethnic identity is constructed on that territorial basis. Owen suggests it has been in the interests of the Caribs to emphasize three traits in particular: racial features, the chieftaincy, and legends (1974: 58–73). She also suggests that provoking conflicts over land is an effective way of maintaining ethnic identity. The extent to which these strategies are deliberate or spontaneous is left unclear, but the instrumentalist language of post-Barthian sociological theories of ethnicity tends to talk of 'manipulation'. Owen's focus on 'conflict', often over land, and often involving non-Caribs, leaves open the possibility of unconscious strategies, even if the issue is not pursued.

Anthony Layng takes the instrumentalist view much further than Owen. For Layng, the Caribs are not distinctive either culturally or physically, but do constitute a 'minority group' (Layng 1985: 213). In other words he moves away altogether from a discussion of ethnicity. He gives a definition: 'The Caribs are not a racial minority (although they claim to be); they are, more meaningfully, a territorial minority. Viewing this population as a territorial minority rather than as a racial minority is not only more accurate, but it is also more conducive to an understanding of their political and economic behaviour' (1985: 217). Layng thinks that the land will run out and that Carib farmers will not be able to purchase land outside the Territory because they are not eligible for bank loans without the deeds to the land they already cultivate. So he predicts that early in the next century (that is, this current century) the Caribs will voluntarily relinquish their reservation status and consequently their minority status (1985: 218–19). At least for Layng the behaviour of the Caribs is rational, even if their rationality involves a collective deception of some kind—which does not fool the anthropologist. For others, this cohesion based on territory is 'entirely artificial', a mere 'common interest which connects some individuals to others, despite a lack of common origin or traditions' (Thomas 1953: 59): in implicit contrast, therefore, to more *authentic* forms of ethnicity. Honychurch has a more subtle understanding of the process, recognizing that the Caribs are 're-inventing' within the parameters they have been given: 'As the twentieth century has progressed, a double and complementary movement has evolved which at first may appear paradoxical: the Caribs do not cling to their Reserve to protect their identity; rather the need to maintain the Reserve fosters that identity . . . The symbol of the Reserve transcends, but at the same time is sustained by its utilitarian value as a place for subsistence and shelter' (Honychurch 1997b: 156).

The most difficult period in the relationship between the Caribs and the post-colonial national government probably came in the years 1984 to 1987. In 1980 the Freedom Party had come to power in Dominica under the leadership of Eugenia Charles, with a mandate to create stability and unity in a divided society, a task not made easier by the coup attempt of April 1981 and by the prominent and controversial role that Charles played as Chairman of the Organization of East Caribbean States, strongly supporting the US invasion of Grenada in October 1983. Firm measures had brought the Freedom Party some significant successes, so it was probably not surprising that it responded to signs of financial irregularities in the Carib Territory by preventing the chief, Hilary Frederick, from standing for re-election at the end of his first term of office in 1984.

Frederick's tenure had seen a marked increase in the number of outside organizations working on the Territory, during a period when the national government had had a series of more pressing matters to deal with. However, under the new chief, Irvince Auguiste, the Caribs continued to press their case for better living conditions and greater autonomy, and to develop the cultural institutions that would be so important in recreating a strong sense of Carib identity. Once again it was the thorny question of the Territory itself, and who has a right to live there, that brought matters to a head in 1987. After a further attempt at the expulsion of non-Carib squatters, Eugenia Charles spoke of 'apartheid' and the Minister for Legal Affairs, Brian Alleyne, accused the Carib chief of trying to create a 'state within a state' (Gregoire *et al.* 1996: 157–8). Alleyne further accused the NGO, Save the Children, of 'fomenting discord and racial disharmony in our country' (159), exactly the word that Administrator Eliot used in accusing Douglas Taylor of responsibility for the 1930 Carib War—or rather the word that Eliot was looking for when he came up with 'fermenting'. This moment coincided with the visit to Dominica of Christopher Robinson, a visitor who had a significant impact on the lives of the Caribs over a number of years. Robinson was an English enthusiast who had raised money for the Caribs and who wanted to establish a trust to help them with various projects of his own devising. Unfortunately one of his pet ideas was to prevent Carib 'disappearance' by encouraging the intermarriage of 'pure' Caribs, a eugenic scheme that, however well meant, could not but appear deeply racist. Robinson, a true innocent abroad, was not even savvy enough to keep his views quiet, as a result of which he was deported from Dominica in 1987.[47]

Despite the publicity that these skirmishes attracted, the real threat to the Caribs from the Freedom Party government came out of its ideological commitment to the values of the free market and possessive individualism. At a time when the country was undergoing a process of radical financial restructuring under the aegis of the IMF and the World Bank, and when the whole region was in the grip of a further outbreak of anti-Cuban paranoia, the Carib Territory, 3,700 acres held in common, could hardly but be seen as a communitarian—and therefore potentially communist—anomaly within a sea of privatization. Although the Caribs themselves had always resisted attempts to change the status of the Territory, there had equally well always been calls for financial measures to enable Caribs to borrow money to invest in farming equipment—since the land was not available as collateral. A minority of Caribs have probably always seen the breakup of the Territory and the allotment of land into individual ownership as the best resolution to this dilemma. Predictably, this was also the policy of the Freedom Party, a policy which for a while had the crucial support of a Carib MP, Ann Timothy. Ultimately, however, the government did not want to grasp such a potentially difficult nettle, and the threat passed with Timothy's defeat in the 1990 General Election before being laid to rest—at least for the time being—with the coming to power of the United Workers Party government in 1995.

TOURISM

There is a sense in which the period covered by this book is co-terminous with Caribbean tourism: Frederick Ober wrote tourist guide books, and my touchstone has been Algernon Aspinall's suggestion from 1907 about how to 'visit the Caribs'. However, until the early 1970s tourists to Dominica, let alone to the Carib Reserve, were few and far between. Although figures are not available, the number of tourists visiting the Reserve has increased dramatically from a very low base in the

---

[47] See Pattullo 1992; and see below (p. 307) for the Robinson Trust.

1950s, the two crucial factors being the overall increase in tourist volume to the Caribbean and the provision of a road linking the Carib Territory to the towns of Portsmouth and Roseau.

Dominica has occupied an interesting position in tourist development. During the 1960s and 1970s, when cheaper air travel opened up the Caribbean islands to mass tourism, Dominica was almost completely ignored. It offered no white beaches and, anyway, gained an unenviable reputation for violence. For a number of years, tourist books would warn people off Dominica. However, even at this early stage, a far-sighted report on possible development strategies for tourism (by the London firm Shankland Cox and Associates) had recommended that the island should look to its strengths rather than attempting to follow the examples of Barbados and St Lucia: 'We have concluded, therefore, that the most important tourist attraction the island has to offer is the entire unspoilt advance of mountainous forest and coastline when these are made suitably accessible' (Dominica 1971: 79). Despite the unspoken tension between 'unspoilt' and 'suitably accessible', this recommendation effectively sketched out what slowly became the island's fundamental tourist strategy, consolidated in its promotion of the title 'Nature Island'.[48] As the tourist cycle leaves other islands struggling, and as notions such as 'ecotourism' and 'alternative tourism' gain ground, Dominica's tourist industry has grown at a significant but manageable pace, despite the looming threat of a massive cruise-ship invasion and the increasing danger that tourism will be seen as a panacea to replace the declining banana industry.[49]

'Alternative tourism' became an important concept after extensive discussions at the conferences at Zakopane (Poland) and Tamanrasset (Algeria) in 1989 sponsored by the International Academy for the Study of Tourism. There is little consensus as to the precise meaning of the term, and of its offshoots

[48] See the lavishly illustrated book of that name, Dominica 1989. Shankland Cox envisaged 5,200 tourist beds by 1990, a number that would inevitably have had a major impact of the 'unspoiled' nature of the island.

[49] Cultural studies of tourism include MacCannell 1976 and 1992. On 'alternative tourism', see Smith and Eadington, eds., 1992; and Young (1995: 189–222). On Dominica, see Weaver 1991; and Pattullo 1996.

'ecotourism', 'cultural tourism', and 'ethnic tourism', although all certainly imply smaller scale—as opposed to 'mass'—tourism, an emphasis on cultural or natural facets, and a retention of profits by the host country. 'Ecotourism', one commentator notes, 'has been touted as a form of sustainable development which could encourage capital investment while maintaining nature preserves, by making the preserves themselves commodities' (Bandy 1996: 544). The obvious paradox involved in the idea was understood early: 'At Zakopane in August 1989, the members of the Academy considered Alternative Tourism as a means to contribute to the 'sustainable development' of a society, whereas by October at the WTO meeting in Tamanrasset, Alternative Tourism had become co-opted as a way to ensure the sustainable development of tourism itself' (Lanfant and Graburn 1992: 112). With ecotourism the fastest growing sector of the tourist industry, and tourism about to become the largest global industry, the problems in store can easily be imagined.

As far as Dominica is concerned, the Kasterlak Report (1975) followed Shankland Cox in recommending a policy based on the island's environmental assets. The Report's specific proposals were rejected by the government of the day, but its philosophical perspective was adopted: 'Dominica's physical geography, hitherto maligned as a tourism liability, would henceforth be marketed as the major tourist asset of the island' (Weaver 1991: 420). Earlier visitors, such as Frederick Ober, could be seen as pioneer ecotourists, but sustained economic development obviously needs more than one visitor every two or three years, so steps were taken to provide a necessary infrastructure: the first National Park was established in 1975 (Morne Trois Pitons) and a new National Development Corporation was put in charge of tourism. In the early 1990s, the Dominican government's Division of Tourism had a Nature Tourism Project and was being funded by the Caribbean Development Bank to upgrade seven tourist sites—including the Carib Territory (Savarin 1994: pp. xi–xii).

The Shankland Cox report had adopted a low-key attitude to the Carib Territory:

The Carib Reserve has for many years been a source of interest because of the people—the last remaining Caribs. Inevitably, visitors expect to find manifestations of their culture in the villages, houses and way of life but these have long since disappeared. Only basket work and dug-out gommier boats now remain, neither of them exclusive to the reservation. The people themselves, have over the years, intermixed with other Dominicans so that few pure-blood Caribs remain. From many points of view, all these developments have been consistent with the more progressive tendencies to de-emphasise race as a factor in contemporary affairs. Nevertheless, it is likely to remain an important tourist attraction. (Dominica 1971: 86–7)

Ecotourism and ethnic tourism have often been closely related, as interests in indigeneous issues are often combined with environmental concerns. During the second half of the twentieth century archaeological finds in the Caribbean have pushed occupation dates back and have led to some new understandings of the complexities of Native Caribbean cultures, although the Caribs have sometimes been in danger of remaining outside these new understandings since they had not developed the complex forms of economic exploitation which supported the culture of the Taino chiefdoms, and because Dominica, in particular, was supposed to lack archaeological sites—a misconception which is slowly being laid to rest (see Honychurch 1997b: 25–7). But the absence of any kind of museum or cultural centre on the Carib Territory has led even well-disposed commentators to be blunt about the relative absence of things to actually *see* on the Territory: 'In short, the visitor . . . sees nothing that is unusual or distinctive which warrants his time and expense in going to the trouble of visiting the Carib community . . . This can be a point of disgruntlement and disappointment, because the tourist obviously is expecting to see something with a *unique difference*' (Einhorn 1972: 2).

To date, tourist development in the Territory has been minor. The distinctive Carib basketry is now entirely sustained by the tourist industry and roadside stalls provide stopping places for tourist buses. It has been estimated that 35 per cent of Carib households are at least partially dependent on income from basket-making, a skilled, time-consuming, and poorly paid occupation. There are several Carib guest-houses on the Territory, but practically nowhere, beyond the small local bars and shops, for tourists to stop for refreshment. Ever since the opening of the road in the 1970s, ideas have been floated for cultural centres of one sort or another which would provide a focus for visitors.

The presence of tourism—or even the thought of tourism—seems to sharpen the issues and clarify views about authenticity and exploitation. The simplest view is that the Caribs are demeaned by tourism: here the image of tourism is the bus passing through the Territory without stopping, the tourists literally looking down on the Caribs. Zenga Longmore, from just such a bus, writes:

I can't think of a more humiliating experience for any person to endure than to have gaping tourists swishing past in a gleaming coach, pointing and laughing at everything you do.

'They didn't want a main road through their reservation, they preferred living in the forest, but we built one all the same, and now the reservation is one of Dominica's main tourist attractions.'

The coach driver smirked as though to say, 'That's got them on the jugular!' (Longmore 1990: 150)[50]

Predictably, Jean Raspail took a no-nonsense view of the possible benefits of tourism for the Caribs long before mass tourism got anywhere near the Territory:

if I were king of the Caribs, I would know very well what to do: I would have a folding costume drawn up by a theatrical designer, I would construct a fake village of straw huts grouped around a totem pole, in the style of that colonial Exposition where the great, aging Lyautey became a circus showman, I would undress my people, I would hang feathers from their behinds, I would organise sacred dances every day at pre-arranged times, and I would earn lots of money from the Caribbean cruise ship tourists, who would be delighted to finally discover something new. I would do all that, because I know how well it works. I used to know the great Sioux sachem of Niagara, a capitalist who rules over a tribe of millionaires disguised as savages: he sells tomahawks which are delivered to him by ten-ton lorry, and camps out in fair weather for reasons of business, having taken care to check in his Cadillac.[51]

[50] There is the occasional refusenik: Jack Grout, noting that the surviving Caribs are 'parked in a reserve', declines the offer of a visit, 'in no way tempted to go to look at human beings as if they were wild animals in a zoo'. His local driver is astonished, saying that the other tourists always want to go to see the Caribs (1970: 109).

[51] 1973: 149–50. Caribs now largely control the production of tourist postcards representing Caribs: all are in 'traditional' dress, usually with bows and arrows.

Raspail puts his finger on the tourism of the gaze. What tourists actually come to see is the Caribs themselves, to see precisely how *different* the Caribs are, or, more precisely yet, to see that the Carib skin is yellow and not black. The comparisons that litter travellers' descriptions vary in detail—Mongolian, Chinese, Indonesian, Korean, Vietnamese—but never in direction: 'many showed not the slightest sign of African descent' (Hatt 1993: 166; and cf. Urry 1990).

To put this somewhat crudely: if your appearance is what brings tourists, then you have not generated any useful source of income since tourists can look, from the bus, without stopping and, beyond a few roadside stalls, there are no stopping places anyway. You have been commodified, but you are not benefiting from any exchange. The Carib response to this dilemma has been to raise funds to create a Model Village which would recreate the kind of indigenous community that visitors want to see: a version of pre-Columbian life, with traditional agricultural practices, far removed from the intensive banana production that now characterizes Carib life. This village would depict the life-style of the Caribs 500 years ago and create significant employment through the showcasing of traditional crafts. It would also house a museum, souvenir shop, guesthouse, and bar: 'The main objective of the project is to develop a tourism product around indigenous resources that will ensure job creation as well as a viable tourist attraction that is in keeping with Dominica's tourism strategy . . . The project involves the development of a Carib Cultural Village as a tourist attraction.'[52]

Cultural Villages are now common in the Americas, usually under the control of Native American communities—a fact which alters the politics of the construction and of the exchange

This is how the Caribs prefer to be represented and these representations are, it seems, what tourists prefer to buy. Dressed in grass skirts and beads, a Carib is the central image on Dominica's National Development Corporation home page.

[52] *National Development Corporation Report*, 1987: 1.1 (quoted in Honychurch 1997*b*: 169); cf. 'Carib Council holds first-ever tourism consultation', *New Chronicle* [Dominica], vol. 85 (2 July 1993); and see Lee (1996: 25), reporting a conversation with Hilary Frederick. The plan for a model village has a long history, probably going back to Arthur Einhorn's 1972 plan, with the International Labour Organization producing another, more ambitious, in 1982 (see Einhorn 1972 and Layng 1983: 62).

involved without removing some of the issues of representation which are associated with the idea. Such maintenance
and preservation of ethnic forms for the entertainment of
ethnically different others is certainly open to criticism: it
constitutes what Dean MacCannell calls 'a final freezing of
the ethnic imaginary', with the implication that a social dialogue
comes to an end once commodification has fetishized the cultural representation.[53] Any exchange is, at a social level, likely
to be non-existent, while the Caribs act themselves, or some
ersatz representation of 'how they used to be', in exchange for
money.

MacCannell has offered a determinedly negative reading of
what he variously calls 'staged authenticity' or 'reconstructed
ethnicity':

Enacted or staged savagery is already well-established as a small
but stable part of the world system of social and economic
exchanges. Many formerly primitive groups earn their living by charg-
ing visitors admission to their sacred shrines, ritual performances,
and displays of more or less 'ethnologized' everyday life. The
commercialization of ethnological performance and display, co-
developed by formerly primitive peoples and the international tourism
and entertainment industries, is potentially a long-term economic
adaptation . . .
But on witnessing these displays and performances, one cannot
escape a feeling of melancholia; the primitive does not really appear
in these enactments of it. The 'primitivistic' performance contains the
image of the primitive as a dead form . . . The image of the savage that
emerges from these ex-primitive performances completes the postmodern fantasy of 'authentic alterity' which is ideologically necessary
in the promotion and development of global monoculture. The 'primitivistic' performance is *our* funerary marking of the passage of savagery. In the presence of these displays, there is only one thing we can
know with certainty: we have witnessed the demise of the original form
of humanity.[54]

Visiting writers certainly find it easy to make fun of such displays: 'On my way home I stop at a café where a Carib cultural
group is performing for a bus-load of French tourists. The

[53] Nobukiyo Eguchi quotes this phrase in a discussion of the Carib situation
(1997: 365).
[54] MacCannell (1976 and 1992: 158–71; quotation at 1992: 19).

Caribs are dressed like a cross between cowboys and Indians; their yellow cotton loincloths are trimmed with nylon fringe. Underneath they're wearing Lycra bicycling shorts. Most of their songs are calypsos' (Tree 1998: 106).

Interestingly, however, what ethnic tourism promotes—the restoration, preservation, and fictional re-creation of ethnic attributes—is very similar to what ethnic separatist movements themselves want to stress: their own difference, which is usually being eroded by the forces of modernity; which is why the cultural village idea has gained Carib support. In the post-colonial period a Carib cultural revival, with oral history and documentation projects under way, and contacts in place with other indigenous groups, has established the platform for such a village as a serious ethnographic construct.[55] Of course, the irony of the cultural village as a post-colonial artefact is that whereas it allows for—and indeed encourages—the kind of cultural invention (or reinvention) that theorists such as Jim Clifford have applauded in similar contexts, the expectations that such a village would have to meet are those that belong to the world of 'alternative tourism': expectations of 'authenticity' and 'purity' and 'survival', expectations that are associated with earlier and more obviously imperial models of cultural identity. The Caribs would be acting out for visitors a version of themselves and their own history which would need to recognize and respond to, even if it tried ultimately to contradict, the expectations that tourists would bring with them: and these would continue to be, for the foreseeable future, expectations of visible indigenous difference.

On a social level, such a village is probably difficult to defend. MacCannell sees this kind of project as simply fuelling the postmodern fantasy of 'authentic alterity' which is ideologically necessary to the promotion and development of global monoculture. He sees it therefore as embodying a kind of alienation, with—extrapolating to this case—the Caribs having to perform their ethnicity, turn it into a commodity, act out a version of themselves in a living theatre, which for MacCannell

---

[55] The Karifuna Cultural Group has been in existence since 1979; WAIKADA (Waitukubuli Karifuna Development Agency) since 1992. On these and related developments, see Gregoire and Kanem 1992.

clearly involves a loss of soul. On this reading nothing is less authentic than the performance of authenticity.[56]

However, the language of 'invention' and 'ethnogenesis' makes it clear that such a description of the model imaginary village should imply no betrayed essence. Indeed, if ethnic identities are indeed negotiated and constructed through the interplay of self-knowledge and communal understandings, it is important to recognize that that process does not—to coin a phrase—occur under historical circumstances of the partici-pants' own choosing, and those circumstances include the extreme economic and social pressures facing most indigenous communities in the Americas. On the one hand, created in the context of tourism needing to be embraced as economic saviour, such a village would have to provide a 'text' still legible to yet another set of visitors; on the other hand, the village might provide the space in which the Caribs could at least tell their own version of their history.

From one perspective, culturally and racially the Caribs are irremediably *mixed*: in that they are no different from the rest of us, products of the colonial processes that have shaped the modern world. But not every community is faced with the pos-sibility of *trading* on aspects of its identity in order to seek eco-nomic survival. At the end of the day, it is easy for cultural critics to patronize self-commodification but, as the Caribs face the new millennium, the possibilities seem stark: the yellow of bananas is a national choice, the black choice if you like; the only other trading route is to sell the yellowness of their skins to international tourism. But what have they got to complain about?: they are absolutely free to choose.[57]

NEW VISITORS

Although the last 120 years have seen a good variety of differ-ent kinds of visitors to the Carib Territory—and an even greater

[56] Unlike some indigenous groups, Dominican Caribs do not have a history of travelling in ethnographic showcases round the various World's Fairs—although that very first ethnographic display involving Native Americans should be recalled, along with its 1936 equivalent (above, p. 8).
[57] For a development of this theme, linked to a reading of Olive Senior's poem, 'Meditation on Yellow', see Hulme 1999a. On the political economy of the small Caribbean islands, see Grossman 1998.

variety of associated writing—I have found it possible to speak about the period under the general sign of 'the visit'. That word's centre of gravity has been associated with tourism and sightseeing, although it has had occasional connotations of the disciplinary visitation and more frequent connotations of intellectual curiosity. This last section asks whether there are signs of new kinds of visitors in this post-colonial age.

Dominican independence has itself led to certain real changes effecting the Caribs, and has been associated with other, more global developments. For one thing, the geography of power has changed substantially. In 1930 the Carib chief sought to bypass the outpost of British imperial authority in Roseau in order to speak directly to the sovereign political power in London. Today there are many more axes to be considered. Political power on the independent island now lies in Roseau, and any Carib claims for self-determination would be asserted against an Afro-Dominican government which—unlike the colonial regime—bears no responsibility for taking Carib land, a fact that marks the Carib case as very different from that of their North American cousins. Economic power still largely lies elsewhere but it is wielded by the USA and the European Community rather than by Britain itself.

The Caribs are happy to present themselves as acting in their country's interests, while Dominica is happy to use the Caribs as an important symbol of Dominicanness. As one of the Caribs' leading cultural figures, Garnette Joseph (elected chief in 1999), said in 1990: 'We are ambassadors of our country; when we perform out there, many people are surprised that there are still Carib Indians around; we promote Dominica a lot and that is our way of helping to build the tourist industry and showing off our cultural heritage.'[58] That is not to say that relationships between the Caribs and the majority population are always comfortable: land in particular is still a delicate issue. But the road system has certainly brought the Caribs into the nation in the sense that Caribs can travel to Roseau and other Dominicans to the Territory much more easily than used to be the case. No Dominican could now, as Alexander Lockhart once did,

---

[58] *New Chronicle* (5 Jan. 1990).

write a travel piece about the Caribs. Since Dominican independence, however, visitors from off the island have been getting more and more varied in their origins, purposes, and methodologies—giving the Caribs ever more to cope with. In particular, the last twenty years have seen an increase in the number of visitors who have been to the Carib Territory in order to offer assistance of some kind to the Caribs.

One of Jean Raspail's 'last man' stories has the last male Carib on Guadeloupe dying in the 1950s without even being aware of the Carib community a handful of miles across the sea in Dominica. That kind of isolation was a feature of the 'colonial' moment, what seemed to so many observers like the slow and lingering death of the scattered remnants of a culture. A striking change in recent (post-colonial) years, and one with the greatest potential impact on Carib ethnicity, is the growth in contact with groups outside the island: the roads that have brought more visitors have eventually allowed two-way traffic, enabling the international contacts that have allowed the Caribs to adopt additional Caribbean, Native American, and indigenous identities. If in 1930 London was the centre of the imperial world for colonized peoples such as the Caribs, today the post-colonial map of significant places would include, apart from Roseau and London, places like Akwesasne or Regina as symbolic of Carib links with Native American organizations on the American mainland, and Geneva as meeting-place of the United Nations Working Group on Indigenous Peoples.

So, over recent years, larger Caribbean and American networks have been established, involving the Caribs in receiving visitors in a slightly more formal but certainly more reciprocal way than the previous norm; and also involving at least some of them in their own visits to other places. Save the Children did valuable work of cultural revival in the 1980s, and has been followed by a Dominica-based NGO, Development Alternatives International Ltd., which from 1989 has sought 'to document the history and lifestyle of the Caribs from the Caribs' own perspective'. A major cross-sectional survey of Carib households was carried out by means of a questionnaire in 1990, conducted by Canadian researchers.[59] But in terms of indigenous politics

---

[59] The quotation is from Gregoire *et al.* (1996: 112). On Save the Children, see Duque Duque 1985.

the key visit was probably that by a group from the Saskachewan Indian Federated College in Regina, Canada, directed towards assistance in training and research, but also responsible for initiating the Caribbean Indigenous Revival conference of 1987 in St Vincent, and the formation in 1988 of the Caribbean Organization of Indigenous People—which held a further conference on the Carib Territory in Dominica in 1996, the first time that representatives of a number of Caribbean indigenous communities had visited Dominica.[60]

Indigeneity is also now an international issue. The Caribs have rarely featured on that international map, but their position on Dominica is inevitably effected by the substantial discussions that have taken place over the last fifty years (and more intensively since 1990) under the auspices of the United Nations and the International Labour Organization, in which definitions of indigeneity and aboriginal rights have edged international law closer to accepting the usage 'indigenous peoples', with the term 'people' having the weight it is given in chapter XI of the UN Charter. Indigenous *peoples* would have at least a claim to become self-determining nations in international law; and the constituent members of the World Council of Indigenous Peoples certainly make these kinds of *national* claims. At its strongest, indigeneity is an avowal of ethnic distinctiveness and national sovereignty based on the historical claim to be in some sense the descendants of the earliest inhabitants of a particular place. These are unfashionable claims, and their terms can all easily be put under erasure by cultural criticism; but they cannot—should not—be ignored.[61]

Four final visitors, or would-be visitors, will suggest something of the range that the Caribs will have to cope with in future years—beyond the tourists and travel writers, who are not likely to diminish in number. At least two recent visitors have been involved in collaborative projects with Carib groups. In the mid-1990s, Aragorn Dick-Read, an artist and sailor from Tortola in the Virgin Islands, spent much time on the Carib Reserve working with Caribs, especially the artist Jacob Frederick, to

---

[60] See Caribbean Indigenous Revival 1987; Mackenzie and Logan 1985; Palacio 1992; and Forte 1998.
[61] See Gray 1996; Wearne 1996.

bring to fruition the Gli Gli Carib Canoe project. A large traditional Carib canoe, made from a gommier tree, was to be sailed down the Caribbean islands to Guyana with aim of promoting indigenous cultural awareness in the region. The tree was felled in December 1995 and built over the course of 1996 by three specialists in traditional canoe-building, Etienne Charles, Hyacinthe Stoute, and Prince Hamlet. The two-month voyage took place in the summer of 1997, with a multinational crew of twenty-two, including eleven Caribs. At a time when fairly large-scale tourism has brought more visitors spending less and less time, the Gli Gli project exemplifies the possibility of collaborative work over a significant period of time, involving extended stays and numerous visits.[62]

A different kind of collaborative project was initiated by a visit from Mary Walters, a Scottish arts producer, in July to September 1993, to put on training workshops in photography, involving a dozen Caribs in producing a self-documentation project which has since been exhibited in the UK and in Dominica, suggesting some even wider connections. For example, some of the material was exhibited in Portree on the Isle of Skye during the annual Scottish Fotofeis, where the exhibition leaflet introduces the Carib people of Dominica as linked to other indigenous groups in the region 'by a fierce sense of survival which is currently nourishing a renewed cultural identity', terms which were likely to resonate in the Scottish highlands and islands in the late twentieth century.[63]

These kinds of projects should not be idealized. They are still likely to impose their initiators' views—the Gli Gli project, for example, never broke away from the idea that the designation 'Carib' identifies a single dispersed group in the southern Caribbean; and problems of finance are still likely to dog attempts to set up any kind of permanent archive or exhibition space—so that the photographs resulting from the self-documentation project have to remain in storage. But the projects need to be recognized as offering the beginnings of a new

[62] See Gli Gli 1997.
[63] 'The Carib People of North East Dominica: Yet We Survive', An Tuireann, Portree, Isle of Skye (5 October–5 November 1994).

kind of visit, looking much more like the very commonest meaning of the word: 'to call upon as an act of friendliness'.

Both these projects have received some funding from the C. T. Robinson Trust, a charitable fund established through the terms of the will of Christopher Robinson, a Carib enthusiast who had given financial assistance to various Carib projects during his lifetime.[64] As I bring this book to completion in the autumn of 1999, the Robinson Trust has for the first time officially notified the Carib community in Dominica about its existence, asked for requests for funding to come from individual Caribs or from the Carib community, and awarded a grant of some £20,000 for the purchase of a bus to take Carib children to secondary schools. A board of trustees (to which I belong) will continue to assess the applications, make awards, and monitor the uses to which the money is put. In all probability I will soon visit the Carib Territory in yet another version of 'the official capacity'.

It is tempting to end on the ironical note of the authorial visit, but I shall try to deflect some of the irony by ending on a visit which will probably not happen. In October 1992, the Human Genome Diversity Project gained an anthropological dimension with a conference which began the task of identifying the indigenous populations most worthy of genetic study—out of the 7,000 or so believed to exist throughout the world. The two overall criteria it worked with were to strive for a representative sample and to choose populations that could help answer major historical questions. The report in *Science* on the groups chosen was headed 'A Few of the Chosen', with the implication that these lucky people were about to have their 'mysteries' solved. Given that one of the questions to be addressed is whether any particular group is 'a relatively unmixed "remnant" of a much larger ancestral population' (Roberts 1992: 1301), it is no surprise that the Caribs featured on the preliminary list of 722 'chosen'. However, the Cordillera

---

[64] The trust is formally called the H. E. and C. T. Robinson Charitable Trust for the Lokono Indians of St Cuthbert's, Demerara, Guyana, South America, and the Carib Indians of the Reservation of the Comonwealth of Dominica, the Windward Islands, Eastern Caribbean, and is administered by a Board of Trustees based at Hadens Solicitors, Lichfield.

Peoples' Alliance has called for a halt to this aspect of the HGDP: 'Instead of spending $20 million for 5 years to collect our blood, tissues, and hair, this money can be used to provide the basic social services we need to be able to survive, and to protect our rights as indigenous peoples' (Tauli-Corpuz 1993). In common with other indigenous groups, the Caribs are currently withholding their co-operation.[65] When some visitors can be turned away, then perhaps the unequal power relations that have characterized the contact between the Caribs and their visitors over the last century and a quarter have finally begun to shift.

---

[65] See Wilkie 1993; Cunningham 1998; and 'Carib Council puts Genome programme on hold', *New Chronicle* [Dominica], 85 (23 July 1993).

Afterword

> I remember a far tall island
> floating in cobalt paint
> The thought of it is a childhood dream
> torn by a midnight plaint
>> (Phyllis Shand Allfrey, 'The Child's
>> Return')[1]

This book has an Afterword rather than an introduction because I wanted the book's narrative to reflect as closely as possible the narrative of its composition. Like, I suspect, many books, *Remnants of Conquest* seemed to write itself: not, unfortunately, in the sense of doing its own research and composition, but inasmuch as the decisions about its shape and content seemed somehow inscribed on that stone I have been touching throughout, leaving its author simply to translate those inscriptions into something resembling a coherent story. That is the story the reader has been reading. My own reflections, as author and first reader, follow in their place—as after-thoughts, after-words—rather than assuming a false introductory position as if they had somehow been in my mind all along, during the ten years in which this book has been slowly writing itself. That is not of course to imply that I did not have intentions in writing the book nor that I am not responsible for the decisions that have given the book its final shape.

I hope that *Remnants of Conquest* makes a contribution in four overlapping areas. To begin with, it aims to take travel writing seriously as an object of scholarly attention. To that end I have tried to bring techniques of literary analysis to travel writing, have researched travel writers whose work has previously been given little attention, and have tried to understand the body of modern travel writing about the Caribs in Dominica by placing

---

[1] [1973], in Burnett (1986: 171).

it within various contexts. One of the obvious, but most difficult challenges, is to decide which contexts are of most importance. I have given particular weight to the late nineteenth-century contexts that produced the work of Frederick Ober in the USA and Hesketh Bell in Britain, because of their key significance as founders of the modern discourse about the Caribs. But I have also chosen to emphasize the local context of the Carib Reserve itself, judging that that special place, much as its visitors might have wanted to see it as an island within an island, cannot be understood in isolation from Dominica as a whole.

The book's contribution to Caribbean studies is inevitably more tangential, dealing as it does with a very small minority population which occupies one small part of one small island in the Caribbean. Dominica's own history is hardly typical of the great Caribbean narratives founded on the slave trade, the development of plantation life, resistance and revolt, Emancipation, the evolution of a black peasantry, and decolonization and independence. Here I have to hope that the uncovering of some little-known stories from the archives will make a small contribution to a larger Caribbean history whose richness is still little appreciated.

I also regard *Remnants* as a contribution towards postcolonial studies, even if it may not look at first sight much like what usually appears under that rubric. The last chapter certainly makes use of the colonial/post-colonial contrast to gauge the significance of changes in the power relations affecting the Caribs. However, in terms of period *Remnants of Conquest* mostly deals with a resolutely colonial world: it is the perspective from which that world is approached which claims to be postcolonial in its assumptions, methodology, and politics. Most of what that might mean I prefer to leave implicit, saying only that 'postcolonial' is a necessary word because the 'colonial' is in various forms still an active global presence in the world. There is no brave new world visible yet: *Remnants* is therefore a work of disengagement, work necessarily in progress, incomplete. My impatience with the persistence of deeply colonialist assumptions in some of the modern travel writing I discuss will have been apparent—though not as apparent as it would have been had I not toned most of it down.

I assume, as should already have become obvious, that there is postcolonial value in particular forms of archival and historical specificity which take seriously and in detail themes that have usually been dealt with through generality. *Remnants* makes no contribution to postcolonial theory, but I would like to see it as a contribution to postcolonial scholarship and postcolonial criticism—perhaps thereby doing something to broaden the desperately narrow parameters of postcolonial studies as it is currently constituted.

The final area in which I hope *Remnants* contributes is in the study of indigeneity, not a topic that always sits easily with notions of the postcolonial, to put it mildly. As I made clear in the first chapter, this book does not offer a modern history of the Caribs, nor does it adopt an indigenous perspective: its interest is in the written traces of contact between the Caribs and their visitors. However, the material in Chapter 6 should have demonstrated that indigeneity is becoming a contested terrain of some significance, so I hope that a brief history of one of its modern sites will contribute towards an understanding of why indigenous claims might be important and why theories of indigeneity might usefully imbricate the political work of indigenous groups with broader postcolonial concerns. My future work will attend in a more theoretical manner to the intervention of indigeneity in postcolonial studies.

Acknowledgements

This book has taken a long time to research and write, probably too long. One advantage of taking such a long time is that I have had many opportunities to exhaust many audiences and individuals with rehearsals of the book's materials and ideas. In the process I have accumulated many debts, which I here acknowledge as fully as I can, basking as I write in the warm memories with which they are associated.

Some of the material in this book first appeared in other places: 'The Rhetoric of Description: the Amerindians of the Caribbean within Modern European Discourse', *Caribbean Studies*, 23/3-4 (1990): 35-50; 'Dancing with Mr Hesketh: Jean Rhys and the Caribs', *Sargasso*, 7 (1990): 18-26; 'Making Sense of the Native Caribbean', *New West Indian Guide*, 67/3-4 (1993): 189-220; *Elegy for a Dying Race: The Caribs and their Visitors*, 'Discovering the Americas', Working Paper no. 14, College Park: University of Maryland, 1993; 'The Re-invention of the Caribs (1878-1908)', in *Wolves from the Sea: The Anthropology of the Native Caribbean*, ed. Neil L. Whitehead (Leiden: KITLV, 1994), 113-38; 'Survival and Invention: Indigeneity in the Caribbean', in Laura García Moreno and Peter C. Pfeiffer, eds., *Text and Nation: Cross-Disciplinary Essays on Cultural and National Identities* (Columbia, SC: Camden House, 1996), 48-64. Some of the research used here was undertaken in the course of preparing *Wild Majesty: Encounters with Caribs from Columbus to the Present Day*, ed. Peter Hulme and Neil L. Whitehead (Oxford: Clarendon Press, 1992). All such material has undergone substantial revision.

Conferences and symposia at which some of these ideas have been presented and discussed are as follows, with acknowledgement of their helpful environments: 'Cultural Difference', University of Wales College of Cardiff (1991); 'Colonial Discourse/Postcolonial Theory', University of Essex (1991); Inaugural Conference of the European Society for the Study of English, University of East Anglia (1992); 'Transatlantic

Encounters: The "Discovery" of the Old World and the New',
Vanderbilt University (1992); 'The Anthropology of the
Caribbean: The View from 1992', University of Leiden (1992);
'New Approaches to the Teaching of English', University of
Salamanca (1992); 'The Caribbean Between Empires', Prince-
ton University (1994); 'Possible Pasts: Critical Encounters in
Early America', University of Pennsylvania (1994); 'A View of
Our Own: Ethnocentric Perspectives in Literature', Universiti
Kebangsaan Malaysia (1994);'Text and Nation: Cultures in
Conflict', Georgetown University (1995); 'Staging History: The
Indigenous and the European View', Haus der Kulturen der
Welt, Berlin (1998); 'Borders and Crossings', Magee College,
Derry (1998); 'Islands: Histories and Representations', Univer-
sity of Kent (1999); 'Trading Places', University of Queensland,
Brisbane (1999).

For further opportunities to present and discuss some of the
ideas that have gone into this book I would also like to thank
the following institutions and individuals: English Department,
University of Puerto Rico, 1989 (Lowell Fiet); Department of
Spanish, University of Indiana, 1990 (Gordon Brotherston);
Departments of History and Anthropology, Rice University,
Houston, 1990 (Patricia Seed and Michael Fischer); Department
of Art History and Theory, University of Essex, 1992 (Valerie
Fraser); Department of Spanish and Portuguese, University of
Maryland, 1992 (Saúl Sosnowski); Departments of English and
History, Rutgers University, 1993 (Myra Jehlen); Department of
Spanish, Montclair State College, 1994 (Jo Anne Engelbert);
Latin American Centre, Princeton University, 1994 (Arcadio
Díaz Quiñones); Center for Latin American and Iberian Studies,
Vanderbilt University, 1994 (Simon Collier); Department of
Anthropology, University of Wisconsin-Madison, 1994 (Neil L.
Whitehead); Department of Comparative Literature, University
of Wisconsin-Madison, 1994 (Keith Cohen); Department of
History, Rice University, 1994 (Patricia Seed); Program in
Theory, Tulane University, 1994 (Dan Balderston and John
Rouse); Centre for English Studies, University of London, 1995
(Warren Chernaik); Departments of English and Spanish,
Georgetown University, 1998 (Henry Schwarz and Veronica
Salles-Reese); Department of English, University of Casablanca
Ain Chok, 1998 (M'barek Rouwane); Department of English,

University of Queensland, Brisbane, 1999 (Helen Tiffin); Department of English, University of Wollongong, 1999 (Paul Sharrad and Cath Ellis); Department of English, ANU, Canberra, 1999 (Jacqueline Lo).

Research for this project was funded by the British Academy, the Rockefeller Foundation, and the University of Essex Research Endowment Fund via the Department of Literature. All are warmly thanked.

Research was undertaken at the following libraries, with thanks for the unfailing help of their librarians: Albert Sloman Library (University of Essex); American Museum of Natural History (New York); American Philosophical Society (Philadelphia); Australian National University Libraries (Canberra); Beverly Historical Society (Beverly, Massachusetts); Bishop's House, Roseau (Dominica); British Library; Cambridge University Library; Library of Congress (Washington, DC); McFarlin Library (University of Tulsa); McKeldin Library (University of Maryland, College Park); National Library (Canberra); Public Library Roseau (Dominica); Rhodes House Library (Oxford); Smithsonian Institution (Washington, DC); University of Birmingham Special Collections. The Albert Sloman Library at Essex, its librarian, Robert Butler, and its Inter Library Loan service, deserve special thanks; as does Terry Barringer of the Royal Commonwealth Society Collection.

This book is a product of the interests developed and fostered at the University of Essex, where colleagues and students have been extraordinarily supportive, among them Francis Barker, Elaine Jordan, Leon Burnett, Jonathan White, Jeff Geiger, Catherine Hall, Matthias Röhrig-Assunçao, Jeremy Krikler, Colin Samson, Andrew Canessa; and the students following the MA in Postcolonial Studies.

Much of the writing of the first draft of the book took place during a valuable year at the University of Maryland, College Park, on a Rockefeller Foundation Visiting Fellowship in the Department of Spanish and Portuguese. Thanks here to Kathryn Karam, Phyllis Peres, José Rabasa, Sangeeta Ray, Brian Richardson, Henry Schwarz, Bill Sherman, and Saúl Sosnowski.

The very last stages of the writing took place at the Centre for Cross-Cultural Research at ANU in Canberra. For arranging my visit, I would like to thank the ex-Director, Nicholas Thomas, and the Acting Director, Iain McCalman. For last-minute ideas and materials, thanks also to Richard Grove, Barry Higman, and Paul Turnbull.

On a number of visits to Dominica, I was helped in innu-merable ways by Lennox Honychurch, Patricia Honychurch, Sara Honychurch, Janet Higbie, Hilary Frederick, Irvince Auguiste, Garnette Joseph, Gregory Rabess, Patrick Henderson, Alick Lazare, Brian Alleyne, and Zena Tavernier. Other Dominica and Rhys scholars have been wonderfully generous with materials and responses: Polly Pattullo, Michel-Rolph Trouillot, Arthur Einhorn, Sue Thomas, Judith Raiskin, Elaine Savory, Francis Wyndham, Carole Angier, Helen Carr, Teresa O'Connor, Nora Gaines, Lori Curtis, and Lisa Paravisini-Gebert.

Others who have helped, and whom I would like to thank, are Sidney Mintz, Irving Rouse, Richard and Sally Price, Desmond Nicholson, Homi Bhabha, Marina Warner, Louis James, Amy Birge McKain, Rolena Adorno, Jeff MacKinnon, Robert Stam, Arcadio Diaz-Quiñones, Raymond T. Smith, Phillip Morris, and Maximilian Forte.

For reading and commenting on the first draft of the book I would like to give particular thanks to two anonymous OUP readers, and to Catherine Hall, Arthur Einhorn, Polly Pattullo, Lennox Honychurch, Tim Youngs, and Susan Forsyth.

At OUP Mary Worthington and Matthew Hollis sped the book's progress with efficiency and good humour.

Some people are just always there, either virtually or in person, with encouragement, ideas, or another bottle of wine. Through-out this long haul, always there have been Francis Barker, Gordon Brotherston, Catherine Hall, Gesa Mackenthun, Bill Sherman, Jonathan White, Neil Whitehead, Tim Youngs, and Susan Forsyth: such friendships might not themselves have improved the book, but they have certainly sustained me through its writing. As this book goes to press, Francis Barker's death begins to cast its shadow over the years to come. Susan Forsyth gets a further message where it belongs, at the begin-ning of the book, as well as this one, at its end.

Appendix: Original Language Quotations

CHAPTER 1

p. 8 Hos nullus est qui videat, quin scalpi sibi horrore quodam prae[lig]cordia fateatur: adeò atrox tartareusque est illis à natura & immanitate insitus prospectus à meipso, & reliquis qui unà mecum pleruquè ad illos intuendos Methymnae[lig] confluxerunt, coniecturam facio. (D'Anghera 1587: 15)

p. 8   Au poète des Antilles, Daniel Thaly, ami des
              derniers Caraibes.

A une exposition, à Fort-de-France, je vis, objets inoffensifs pour pavillon, numéro résigné d'attraction, ceux qui un jour—tête arrogante à plumes de perroquet, corps embrasé par les grains du *roucou,*—avaint fièrement décoché de leurs sveltes pirogues, les flèches trempées dans le suc mortel du mancenillier, les écumeurs de la mer qui porte leur nom: les Caraïbes.

Les rares et pauvres descendants qui étaient là—parvenus jusqu'à nous commes les survivants sur le radeau d'un triste naufrage—n'étaient même pas de la Martinique, on avait dû les dénicher dans la voisine Dominique. Un homme en canotier les avait amenés ici, glabre face de brique, oeil doux derrière les lunettes, et ce fut beau d'apprendre que ce berger était un poète—le poète des Antilles—comme si la poésie seulement savait encore offrir, dans un monde acharné à se détruire, un reste d'amour à une semence moribonde.

Cheveux lisses en toile cirée—contraste peu commun, dans le mousseux moutonnement des têtes des noirs tout autour—, pommettes saillantes en des faces d'olive—mystères des affinités raciales: n'est-ce pas parmi les Lapons que j'ai vu des traits semblables?—, les derniers Caraïbes restaient là sans sourire et sans orgeuil, taciturnes.

Exposés à toutes les impertinences des regards, dociles à tous les déclics de Kodaks, ceux qui avaient été si ombrageux et se tapirent en forêt dès que, de la mer, pointèrent, arbres jamais vus, les pennons des caravelles de Colomb.

On pensait, en les regardant, au cobra contemplé dans un Zoo, derrière la vitre qui rend stérile toute velléité de venin.

Vitre de ces survivants, le temps: les deux ou trois siècles d'arquebuses européennes qui ont suffi à en finir la race, à en édulcorer la cruauté.

Et aux descendants de cannibales qui, pour donner de la trempe à leur courage, ceignaient leur corps d'un cilice de fourmis carnivores, maintenant il ne restait même pas le stoïcisme de cet oiseau d'Amérique dit *quetzal* qui, mis en cage, se suicide. (Fiumi 1938: 80–1)

p. 26 Sólo bajo una forma simbólica hubiese podido el poeta expresar su amor a la patria y protestar contra el modo injusto e insolente de regirla. La palabra *patria* sonaba como un grito insurrecto en el oído de los gobernantes ... Bien sé yo que esto obedecía a la idea que los versos encerraban. Se veía en ellos un símbolo en el que los indios siboneyes representaban a los cubanos oprimidos, y los indios caribes a los injustos opresores. (quoted in Vitier 1970: 158)

p. 26 Lo he mandado llamar a Vd. para advertirle que si desea continuar escribiendo sobre siboneyes vaya a hacerlo a los Estados Unidos. Aquí somos españoles y no indios; ¿está usted? todos españoles. (quoted in Vitier 1970: 159–60)

CHAPTER 3

p. 123 Il m'a dit: Père, c'est moi-même qui, il y a deux ans, ai obtenu directement du roi d'Angleterre une pension de 200 francs pour le vieux sorcier. J'en ai bien regret. (Suaudeau 1927: 53)

p. 152 Aujourd'hui les Caraïbes survivants manquent de pittoresque; en contact avec les créoles blancs ou noirs, ils en ont pris les vêtements ... Les femmes caraïbes ne semblent pas actuellement très coquettes et portent peu d'ornements, tandis qu'à l'époque, où le roucou était leur unique vêtement, elles ne négligeaient point les parures ... (Neveu-Lemaire 1921: 136)

p. 152 ... la mélancolie est le fond de leur caractère; leur physionomie porte l'empreinte de la tristesse et du dédain. Ils sont vindicatifs, n'oublient pas les injures ... ils sont bons et généreux pour leurs amis et pratiquent cordialement les devoirs de l'hospitalité. D'un natural nonchalant, les hommes passent des journées entières à ne rien

faire . . . (136–7); entreprenante et belliqueuse, vigoureuse bien qu'in-
dolents. (146)

p. 153 Corriette est un homme qui paraît moins âgé que ne l'indique
son acte de naissance; il est malheureusement vêtu à l'européene, ce
qui lui enlève tout cachet. Ce chef n'a pas donné l'exemple de la conservation de la ace, en épousant une femme noire, dont il n'a d'ailleurs
pas eu d'enfants. (140)

CHAPTER 6

p. 257 C'était mon premier roi que j'allais rencontrer. Qu'il fût roi
des Sauvages, cacique caraïbe, ne changeait rien, pour ma part, à la
solennité quasi religieuse que j'escomptais de cette visite. Je suis un
sujet sans roi, une âme errant dans les ténèbres démocratiques à la
recherche des fidélités mortes. (Raspail 1980: 46)

p. 257 Je rends hommage à votre appétit. (Raspail 1980: 48)

p. 257 Caraïbe, le roi l'était jusqu'au bout des ongles. Vielli de dix
bonnes années, il ressemblait trait pour trait à sa photo. Car je con-
naissais tout de lui. Il figurait dans les archives anthropométriques de
tous les instituts d'ethnologie dignes de ce nom: 1,60 m, taille masculine moyenne de sa race, teint jaune légèrement cuivré, yeux petits et
bridés, avec le repli mongoloïde, cheveux noirs et raides (mais coiffés
avec raie sur le côté), les joues pleines, le nez droit, la pilosité peu
developpée, même dans les parties intimes et cela je le savais aussi, y
compris le nombre et la qualité de es dents . . . et la classification de
son groupe sanguin, groupe o typiquement amérindien. Il était loin,
Francis Ier Fernandoir, d'en connaître autant de moi, c'était encore
manières de Blanc mauvaises manières, sans égalité, les métreurs
devraient bien aller de temps en temps se fair métrer par les Grecs!
Qu'il fût fiché de la sorte m'avait chagriné. . . .
Il avait du mal à comprendre ce que je venais faire là. Mon
arrivée ne correspondait pas du tout au protocole habituel des
visites. Entendant une voiture, il avait aussitôt pris la pose, la plus
rentable, la plus commerciale, avec sceptre et dessus de piano,
la pose à un dollar la photo; pour le prix, il conseillait même aux
touristes le meilleur angle, la bonne distance et l'objectif souhaitable.
Et voilà qu'au lieu des moutons pressés de minibus—lesquels, à
l'époque, s'arrêtaient au moins une minute, car depuis . . .—il se trou-
vait devant quelqu'un qui prenait tout son temps, manifestait l'intention de passer la nuit dans la réserve, et même l'invitait à souper.
(Raspail 1980: 53–4)

p. 258 Vérifier l'un de mes credo: il n'y a pas de survie sans conscience du passé. Minorité ou majorité, le nombre importe peu, c'est la mémoire qui compte. (Raspail 1980: 56)

p. 258 Le roi se grattait la tête. Visiblement, pour me faire plaisir, il cherchait. Mais, tout aussi visiblement, il séchait . . . Enfin le roi trouva quelque chose:
—Les vieux disaient au père de mon père que les Caraïbes avaient conquis l'île de Haïti . . .
Je luis dis que Haïti signifiait la 'grande terre' en caraïbe. Il l'ignorait.
Il me demanda:
—Est-ce qu'ils sont tous morts là-bas aussi?
Je répondis que oui. (Raspail 1980: 56)

p. 259 Le palais. Case en dur, toit de tôle ondulée, le progrès. Une table et une chaise dans la pièce d'entrée et sur la table divers papiers *classés* et une modeste batterie de crayons et de stylos à bille: un début d'administration. Timide entrée de la nation caraïbe dans l'ère moderne . . . Celui-ci ne posait pas et ne réclamait rien, que de l'intérêt et de la sympathie pour son peuple. (Raspail 1980: 62)

p. 259 Voilà un peuple moribond, qui n'a plus d'histoire, plus de culture, plus de langue, plus de religion qu'importée et qui ne se souvient de rien, un peuple qui n'est que modestie et silence, dont le seul souci, depuis la conquête, se résume à l'élémentaire quotidien, naître, se nourrir, mourir, tandis que le reste de l'univers s'emplit de toutes les fureurs contemporaines, et dont on s'aperçoit qu'il a pu survivre au seul nom d'une idée, avec rien du tout autour, qui ne réprésentait donc rien d'autre qu'une abstraction: 'Les Caraïbes sont indépendants depuis deux mille ans . . .'! (Raspail 1980: 64)

p. 274 Nous avons essayé d'estimer le degré de métissage pour chaque individu prélevé et nous avons été amenés à classer notre échantillon en trois catégories: I.—Caraïbes supposés purs. II.—Métis Caraïbe-Noirs. III.—Autres types de métis. (Chilling-Rathford 1966: 324)

p. 276 Quand elle aura perdu bientôt ce qui lui reste de son integrité, cette race n'aura plus de place que dans l'histoire. (Delawarde 1938: 204)

p. 277 Le langage muet des visages . . . Quand de le mémoire tout est perdu, il reste au moins ce langage-là . . . (Raspail 1980: 83) *p. 277* De nos jours il n'y a plus un seul Marie-Galantais de pure race caraïbe, mais dans plusieurs familles de la région où ils avaient leur dernier carbet on retrouve des traces indubitables de leur métissage, traces qui s'atténuent de plus en plus vite. Ainsi j'ai connu une vieille femme décédée il y a une dizaine d'années, qui me confia ses peines: 'Ma maman était une griffe à Caraïbe, elle avait de beaux cheveux noirs glacés, c'est mon papa qui était un Nègre qui m'a donné ces vilains cheveux là ça.' (Barbotin 1976: 118)

p. 277 Etonnante, cette lignée de prêtres catholiques sans qui le souvenir caraïbe serait perdu. (Raspail 1980: 80)

p. 277 Cette division de l'île est encore tout à fait perceptible de nos jours. La route circulaire n'était il y a peu qu'une mauvaise piste au nord, entre Vieux-Fort et Grand Bassin. Les habitations sont rares et datent du siècle dernier. Pas un moulin sauf celui de Cambrai. Un réseau routier intérieur presque néant. Et encore aujourd'hui, aucun chemin carrossable ne conduit à l'anse Coq où résidèrent les caciques caraïbes de Marie-Galante jusqu'en ... (Raspail 1980: 82)

p. 280 J'imagine que de l'avoir tenue dans ses bras et d'avoir pénétré dans son ventre, elle, Arouague, dernier maillon d'une race, il lui venait après coup la sensation nouvelle d'avoir accompli une sorte de rite religieux. (Raspail 1980: 33)

p. 280 Ce n'est pas l'usage masculin de fixer son attention sur les ailes du nez, le pli des paupières et le lobe d'oreille d'une superbe créature entièrement nue sur la scène d'un cabaret. Surtout lorsqu'elle cambre jusqu'à l'horizontale son corps souple à peau de caramel pour le difficile exercice du *limbo*, la pointe de ses seins effleurant la baguette enflammée tendue à vingt centimètres du sol, tandis que, ses pieds reposant seuls à terre, elle se glisse et se love comme un serpent sous l'obstacle. (Raspail 1980: 84)

p. 281 J'affectai de découvrir l'oblique élégant de ses paupières mais me gardai de la moindre allusion à son originalité première: Rose était douée d'un ravissant derrière rond, discret et charnu à la fois. (Raspail 1980: 87)

p. 281 Vous me trouvez différente, n'est-ce pas? ... Vous savez ce que c'est Ma mère était une pure Kallinago. Je suis née près de l'habitation Pistolet, à la pointe de la Grande Vigie. (Raspail 1980: 88)

p. 281 Car la Grande Vigie était une réserve indienne. Mais sa naissance, sa vie et sa mort passèrent totalement inaperçues. Impossible de savoir comment, après 1730, les Caraïbes survivants de Guadeloupe avaient obtenu, ou subi, l'isolement dans une concession située au nord-est de la commune de l'Anse Bertrand, sur le plateau calcaire et sec des 'Hautes caraïbes' de la pointe de la Grande Vigie. (Raspail 1980: 90)

p. 281 Rose s'empara du crayon: 'Nous habitions l'une de ces maisons. Là, il y avait une mare, et là, une grosse pierre taillée'. (Raspail 1980: 91)

p. 281 En 1960... toute trace d'occupation humaine a disparu. Seules quelques clairières à vivres et à charbon de bois trouent le taillis à campêches et à acacias. Près de l'une de ces clairières, nous avons rencontré le seul métis à traits caraïbes évidents qu'il nous ait été donné de voir en Guadeloupe. Une case triangulaire couverte de chaume rappelait le *mouinan* ou carbet caraïbe. Là se trouvent, peut-être, les ultimes traces d'une civilisation... (Raspail 1980: 91, quoting Lasserre 1961: p. 270)

p. 282 Pourquoi ne pas admettre simplement qu'il y avait quelque chose d'extraordinairement émouvant, sur ce vaste plateau balayé par un alizé violent, à hurler l'appel du dernier des vivants. En vain... (Raspail 1980: 92)

p. 282 L'idiot du village! Doté dun nom ridicule! Telle fut l'incarnation de 'l'ultime trace de civilisation'. (Raspail 1980: 92)

p. 282 En 1882, les derniers descendants des Caraïbes de la pointe de la Grande Vigie avaient adressé une supplique au gouvernement français, dans laquelle ils se plaignaient qu'on violât sans cesse le territoire de leur réserve. Dix noms suivaient ce texte désolant, pour la plupart signés d'une croix... La seule réponse qu'obtinrent ces malheureux, ce fut justement la levée du plan topographique de la réserve par le conducteur de travaux L. Bon, deux ans plus tard, en 1884, au seul bénéfice des compagnies sucrières métropolitaines qui exploitaient les domaines voisins des Habitations Pistolet et Berthaudière. La ligne des 500 pas, arbitrairement tracée, n'englobait plus que du taillis rocheux impropre à la culture et scellait l'expropriation arbitraire de la quasi-totalité de la réserve, soit près de 2 000 hectares de bonne terre à canne. (Raspail 1980: 93)

p. 282 Ma mère apprit sa mort six mois plus tard. Elle dit seulement: 'le dernier des guerriers'. (Raspail 1980: 95) *p. 282* Jean Raspail, un jour tu me feras un petit garçon kallinago. (Raspail 1980: 96)

p. 292 C'est donc un intérêt commun qui lie les uns aux autres des individus sans origines ni traditions communes. (Thomas 1953: 59)

p. 298 ...si j'étais roi des Caraïbes, je saurais très bien ce que je ferais: j'aurais une belle tunique drapée dessinée par un deécorateur de théatre, je construirais un village bidon de paillotes groupées autour d'un totem, dans le style de cette Exposition coloniale où le grand Lyautey vieillissant devint un montreur de cirque, je déshabillerais mon peuple et je lui collerais des plumes dans le derrière, j'organiserais des danses sacrées tous les jours à heure fixe, et je gagnerais beaucoup d'argent avec les touristes des croisières abtillaises, ravis de découvrir enfin quelque chose de nouveau. Je ferais tout cela, car j'en sais le résultat. Je connais le grand sachem des Sioux du Niagara, un capitaliste qui règne sur un tribu de millionaires déguisées en sauvages: il vend des tomawaks qu'on lui livre par camion de dix tonnes, et campe sous la tente à la belle saison pour les besoins du bizenesse, en prenant soin de laiser sa Cadillac au vestiaire. (Raspail 1973: 149–50).

p. 298 A l'arrivée des Européens, l'île (ainsi que les autres petites Antilles) était peuplée par les Caraïbes. On peut encore y voir les derniers descendants de cette population, parquées dans une réserve. Jean-Pierre nous propose d'aller leur rendre visite, mais nous déclinons cette offre, nullement tentés d'aller observer des êtres humains comme des bêtes sauvages au zoo. Nous ne manquons pas de le dire à notre chaffeur, très étonné de cette réaction: 'Les autres touristes, eux, vont toujours les voir', nous déclare-t-il. (Grout 1970: 109)

Chronology

Dates	Carib Territory	Dominica	Visitors to Carib Reserve or Dominica
1800–1900	*c.* 1845: P'tit François, Chief *c.* 1860: Wakanik (Popote), Chief *c.* 1880: George, Chief *c.* 1880–1884: Joseph François, Chief *c.* 1884–1908: Auguste François (Ogiste), Chief 1890s: Bruni Michelle—rival chief	1882–9: John Spencer Churchill (President) 1889–94: George Ruthven Lehunte (President) 1895–9: Philip Arthur Templer (Administrator) 1899–1905: Henry Hesketh Bell (Administrator) 1905–13: William Douglas Young (Administrator)	1877: Frederick Ober 1887: W. A. Paton (D) 1887: J. A. Froude (D) 1887: W. S. Birge 1888: A. H. Verrill 1891: Frederick Ober 1893: Robert G. C. Hamilton 1895: C. A. Stoddard (D) 1899: Hesketh Bell
1900–30	1908–26: Corriette Jules, Chief	1914: Edward Rawle Drayton (Administrator) 1915–19: Arthur William Mahaffy (Administrator) 1919–23: Robert Waller (Administrator) 1923–30: Edward Carlyon Eliot (Administrator)	1902: A. H. Verrill 1903: Hesketh Bell 1906: Symington Grieve 1907: Frederick Treves (D) 1912: 'Vaquero' 1912: Stephen Bonsal 1921: M. Neveu-

Dates	Carib Territory	Dominica	Visitors to Carib Reserve or Dominica
			Lemaire 1922: Archie Bell (D) 1930: Douglas Taylor 1930: Capt. W. E. C. Tait
1931–59	1926–41: Thomas John (alias Jolly John), regarded by Caribs as Chief. Officially 'Head Man' from April 1926; then Chief until suspended by E. C. Eliot in 1930 1941: Five-man Carib Council instituted by government 1941–52: George Frederick, unofficial head man 1953: George Frederick officially Chief after staff and sash restored 1953–6: Simon John, Chief	1931–3: Walter Andrew Bowring (Administrator) 1933–7: Henry Bradshaw Popham (Administrator) 1938–45: James Scott Neill (Administrator) 1946–52: Edwin Porter Arrowsmith (Administrator) 1953–9: Henry Laurence Lindo (Administrator)	1936: Douglas Taylor 1936: Jean Rhys and her husband, Leslie Tilden Smith 1936: J.-B. Delawarde 1944: Charles Whitaker 1946: Harry Luke 1947: Carleton Mitchell (D) 1948: Patrick Leigh Fermor 1948: Alec Waugh 1950–51: Eugene Banks 1953: Léon Thomas 1955: Jacques-Yves Le Toumelin 1956: Bradley Smith

Dates	Carib Territory	Dominica	Visitors to Carib Reserve or Dominica
	1956–9: Whitney Frederick, Chief		
1960–97	1959–72: Germandois Francis, Chief 1972–5: Mas Clem Frederick Chief 1975–9: Faustulus Frederick, Chief After 1979 chiefs elected by registered voters for five-year term 1979–84: Hilary Frederick, Chief 1985–94: Irvince Auguiste, Chief 1994–9: Hilary Frederick, Chief 1999– : Garnette Joseph	1959–65: Alec Lovelace (Administrator) 1960–1: F. A. Baron, United People's Party (Chief Minister) 1961–7: E. O. Le Blanc, Dominica Labour Party (Chief Minister) 1965–7: Geoffrey Colin Guy (Administrator) 1967: Dominica becomes associated state 1967: (March–November) Geoffrey Colin Guy (Governor) 1967–78: Louis Cools-Lartigue (Governor) 1967–74: E. O. Le Blanc, Dominica Labour Party (Prime Minister) 1974–9: Patrick	1962: Raymond T. Smith 1964: Carleton Mitchell 1964: Charles Groves 1964: Jean Raspail 1965: M. R. Cabannes 1967: Kjeld Helweg-Larsen 1968: Linda Wolfe 1968: R. G. Harvey 1970 and 1971–2: Nancy Owen 1972: Basil Cracknell 1974–5: Anthony Layng 1979: Philip Teuscher and Greg Pettys 1979: Jean Raspail 1979, 1980, 1982: Anthony Layng 1982: Suzanne Hamot-

Dates	Carib Territory	Dominica	Visitors to Carib Reserve or Dominica
		John, Dominica Labour Party (Prime Minister)	Pézéron
			1982: Christopher Robinson
		1978: Dominica gains full independence	1983: Anthony Weller
		1979–80: Oliver Seraphim, Deb-Lab Party (Interim Prime Minister)	1983: Amryl Johnson
			1985: Georg Sütterlin
		1980–95: Eugenia Charles, Dominica Freedom Party (Prime Minister)	1986: Quentin Crewe
			1987: Christopher Robinson
			1988: Zenga Longmore
		1995– : Edison James, United Workers Party (Prime Minister)	1990: Henry Shukman
			1990: José Barreiro
			1990: Robert Booth
			1991: Georg Sütterlin
			1992: John Hatt
			1993: Mary Walters
			1994: Lucretia Stewart
			1994: Aragorn Dick-Read
			1995–6: Lennox Honychurch
			1996: Simon Lee
			1998: Isabella Tree

Biographical Notes on Visitors

The primary focus in this book has been on those writers who set foot on the Carib Territory. Nevertheless, since the differences in the writing of those who 'visited' in the strict sense of the word and those who wrote from a distance (usually Roseau) are often imperceptible, these Biographical Notes have been extended to all those who have been granted, or have granted themselves, an element of authority as 'visitors'. (I have excluded those visitors about whom I only know their piece of writing about the visit.)

Sir Sydney Armitage Armitage-Smith (1876–1932): a British civil servant who dealt principally with matters of finance and currency before he was appointed, as a safe pair of hands, to form part of the 1932 Commission of Enquiry. His early death, shortly after his return from Dominica, occasioned some comment in the island.

José Barreiro (1948–): born in Camagüey, Cuba, he now teaches at Cornell University and is editor-in-chief of Akwe:kon Press and author of the novel *The Indian Chronicles* (1993).

Archie Bell (fl. 1900–30): having begun his writing career with the engagingly titled *Cattle (The Human Species)* (1903), he went on to write several of the 'Spell' series apart from the one on the Caribbean Islands (1926): The Holy Land (1915), Egypt (1916), China (1917), Ireland (1928). He also wrote *Sunset Canada, British Columbia and Beyond* (1918).

Sir Henry Hesketh Joudou Bell (1864–1952): born at Chambery in the Savoie district of south-east France, Hesketh Bell was educated in Paris and Brussels before taking up a clerk's job in Barbados in 1882. This proved the first step on a long career in the Colonial Service, which took him to Grenada, the Gold Coast, the Bahamas, Dominica, and Uganda, ending as governor of Mauritius in 1925. He retired to the south of France but moved back to the West Indies in 1940. Apart from his memoirs, *Glimpses of a Governor's Life* (1946), he wrote *Obeah: Witchcraft in the West Indies* (1889) and several books of stories, including *The Witches' Legacy* (1893) and *Love is Black* (1911).

William Spoford Birge (1857–1925): born in Cooperstown, New York, he was a doctor resident in Provincetown, Mass., at the time of the publication of *In Old Roseau* (1900), although he travelled to the island in 1887. He also wrote *My Lady's Handbook: Health, Strength, and Beauty* (1915) and *True Food Values and Their Low Costs* (1916). He and his wife ran a sanitarium for the mentally ill.

Stephen Bonsal (1865–1950): a newspaperman, diplomat, linguist, soldier, and author. Written while he was international correspondent for the *New York Herald*, his *The Real Condition of Cuba* (1897) helped fuel support for the US invasion in 1898. His book on the Caribbean, *The American Mediterranean* (1912) was written just after he retired as a journalist. In the First World War he served in the American Expeditionary Forces, directing propaganda efforts to weaken the resolve of the soldiers of the Central Powers, and he was a key figure in the Armistice negotiations. His diaries of this period, *Unfinished Business, Paris Versailles 1919* (1944) won him the Pulitzer Prize.

Quentin Crewe (1926–1998): author of several travel books apart from *Touch the Happy Isles: A Journey Through the Caribbean* (1987), namely *In the Realms of Gold: Travels through South America* (1989), and *A Curse of Blossom: A Year in Japan* (1960), and many many books on food. One of his last publications was an autobiography, *Well, I Forget the Rest: The Autobiography of an Optimist* (1991).

Arthur Einhorn (1934–   ): the US anthropologist and ethnohistorian who hosted future Carib chief, Hilary Frederick, while he went to high school in New York State. Einhorn's own work has been chiefly on Iroquois history and culture. For many years Chair of the History Department at Lowville Academy, Einhorn was a frequent visitor to the Carib Territory between 1971 and 1981.

Frederic A. Fenger (1882–1970): apart from *Alone in the Caribbean* (1917), he was the author of *The Cruise of Diablesse* (1926) and *The Golden Parrot* (1921).

Patrick Leigh Fermor (1915–   ): after an active war career in Crete, Fermor became one of the leading travel writers of his generation. His book about the West Indies, *The Traveller's Tree: A Journey Through the Caribbean Islands*, won the Heinemann Foundation prize for Literature in 1950 and was followed by a series of what are now regarded as classic travel texts, including *A Time to Keep Silence* (1957), *Mani: Travels in the Southern Pelopponnese* (1958), *Roumeli: Travels in Northen Greece* (1966), and *A Time of Gifts* (1977). He also wrote a novel about the Caribbean: *The Violins of Saint-Jacques: A Tale of the Antilles* (1953).

Charles Graves (1899–1971): one of the most prolific and superficial of twentieth-century journalists and travel writers. Author of some sixty books apart from *Fourteen Islands in the Sun* (1965), including *Gone Abroad: A Lightning Tour of the Principal Cities and Watering Places of Belgium and Germany* (1932) and *The Rich Man's Guide to Europe* (1966). According to his wife's winningly titled memoir, *Married to Charles*, *The Times* called him 'the laureate of the pleasure resorts'.

Symington Grieve (fl. 1885–1930): a Scottish naturalist—President of the Edinburgh Field Naturalists and Vice-President of the Botanical Society of Edinburgh—whose other books include *The Great Auk, or Garefowl* (1885), *The Book of Colonsay and Oronsay; Forty-four Years of Research and Discovery in Early Scoto-Irish, Norse, Icelandic, and Danish History* (1923), and *Discovering About the Floating Power of Seaweed During 50 Years' Research* (1929). His *Notes upon the Island of Dominica* (1906) refer to a visit earlier that year.

Sir Robert George Crookshank Hamilton (1836–95): made his career as a civil servant with financial expertise, writing a standard work on *Book-keeping* (1868). After spells at the Board of Trade and the Admiralty, he was appointed permanent under-secretary in Dublin where he was an advocate of Home Rule. Removed from Ireland in 1886, he was Governor of Tasmania from 1887 to 1892, immediately before being appointed to head the Commission of Enquiry to Dominica.

Amryl Johnson (*c.*1960–): born in Trinidad and educated in England. Apart from *Sequins for a Ragged Hem* (1988), she is the author of three books of poetry, and now teaches creative writing.

Anthony Layng (*c.*1935–): Emeritus Professor of Anthropology at Elmira College, New York, where he taught for most of his career. His numerous visits to the Carib Territory produced a Ph.D. thesis, a book, and a number of articles.

Sir Harry Luke (1884–1969): born into a family of Hungarian descent (Lukàch), Harry Luke spent thirty-two years in the colonial service, much of the time in the Middle East. From 1913 (*The Fringe of the East*) he combined a career as a writer with his work in the colonial service. His autobiography (*Cities and Men* (1953–6)) was considered one of the best of the decade. After retiring from the service in 1943, Luke spent three years as chief representative of the British Council in the Caribbean. He travelled extensively during that time. After his return to England he wrote *Caribbean Circuit* (1950).

Carleton Mitchell (1910–90): born in New Orleans, Mitchell was a self-taught photographer and keen yachtsman, who became director of the US Navy Combat Photography Unit from 1942 to 1945. After the war, he established himself as one of the best US yachtsmen, winning many prestigious races and writing a series of articles and books about his travels: *Islands to Windward: Cruising the Caribbees* (1948 and 1955), *Passage East* (1953), *Yachtsman's Camera* (1950), *Beyond Horizons: Voyages of Discovery and Adventure* (1953), *Summer of the Twelves* (1959), *Isles of the Caribbees* (1966 and 1971), and *The Wind Knows No Boundaries: Cruises Far and Near* (1971).

Frederick Albion Ober (1849–1913): author, naturalist, historian. Born in Beverly, Massachusetts, Ober had an early interest in natural history: a boyhood collection of stuffed and mounted birds from New England impressed Alexander Agassiz of the museum at Harvard University. Ober first visited Dominica and St Vincent in 1877 to collect birds for the Smithsonian Institution. The popular success of his account of that visit, *Camps in the Caribbees* (1879) initiated his career as a writer of fiction, popular history, and travel and guide books. Later in life he had a second career in real-estate in Hackensack, New Jersey. For additional information, see Hulme 1997*a* (Appendix).

Nancy Owen (*c.*1945–) (now Nancy Owen Lewis): Dr Owen's fieldwork on the Carib Territory produced a Ph.D. from the University of Massachusetts and a number of scholarly articles. After holding positions in the District Attorney's Office and Municipal Court in Santa Fe, New Mexico, she is currently Director of the School of American Research at Santa Fe.

William Agnew Paton (1848–1918): born in New York. Author and publisher. Apart from *Down the Islands: Voyage to the Caribbees* (1887), also wrote *Picturesque Sicily* (1897), *The First Landfall of Columbus* (1907), and *Home Rule Ballads* (1907).

Sir James Stanley Rae (1881–1956): a prominent West Indian lawyer who ended his career as Attorney-General for the Leeward Islands (1931–7).

Jean Raspail (1925–): novelist and travel writer, genres which tend to blur in Raspail's hands. Travelled and wrote extensively about the Caribs in the period from the mid-1960s to the late 1970s: *Secouons le cocotier* (1966), *Punch caraïbe* (1970), *Bleu caraïbe et citrons verts* (1980). His anti-immigration novel, *Le Camp des Saints* (1973), was at the centre of US debates on the subject in the early 1990s. He is also consul-general in Paris to Orélie-Antoine I, self-proclaimed King of Patagonia.

Jean Rhys (1890–1979): born and brought up on Dominica, which she left in 1907, returning just once for a brief visit in 1936. Author in the 1920s and 1930s of a string of powerful novels, including *Voyage in the Dark* (1934) and *Good Morning, Midnight* (1939), she became famous only after the publication of *Wide Sargasso Sea* (1966). Echoes of her brief return to the island of her birth can be found in much of her later work, including the story 'Temps Perdi' (1967).

Christopher Robinson (1940–91): an egg-merchant by trade, Robinson developed an amateur enthusiasm for the Dominican Caribs, whom he supported financially both during his lifetime and after—by the establishment of a charitable trust. He visited the Carib Reserve twice, but was expelled from Dominica in 1987.

Henry Shukman (1962–): author, apart from *Travels with My Trombone: A Caribbean Journey* (1993), of *Sons of the Moon: Travels Among the South American Indians* (1990) and *Savage Pilgrims: On the Road to Santa Fe* (1996).

Bradley Smith (1910–): apart from *Escape to the West Indies* (1956), the author of *The Horse and the Blue Grass Country* (1960), *Spain, A History in Art* (1966), and *Columbus in the New World* (1962).

Raymond T. Smith (1925–): one of the foremost anthropologists to work in the Caribbean, Smith did his major fieldwork in British Guiana and Jamaica. He taught in Jamaica and Canada before joining the University of Chicago in 1966, where he taught until his retirement in 1995. Among his major publications are *Kinship and Class in the West Indies: A Genealogical Study of Jamaica and Guyana* (1988) and *The Matrifocal Family: Power, Pluralism and Politics* (1996).

Lucretia Stewart (1952–): journalist, travel writer, and novelist. Author of *Tiger Balm: Travels in Laos, Vietnam and Cambodia* (1992), as well as *The Weather Prophet* (1995); and of the novel, *Making Love: A Romance* (1999).

Captain (later Admiral Sir) William Eric Campbell Tait (1886–1946): a career naval officer who became Governor of Southern Rhodesia in 1945. He commanded HMS *Delhi* in the Caribbean in 1930.

Douglas MacRae Taylor (1901–81): born in Batley, Yorkshire, the son of a woollen manufacturer, he studied in Cambridge, Paris, and Heidelberg. Eventually settling in Dominica, he became the pre-eminent expert on Carib lifeways as well as a respected linguist. He taught at Yale during the 1960s and wrote the standard study, *Languages of the West Indies* (1977).

Sir Frederick Treves (1853–1923): best known as the foremost surgeon and anatomist of his day. Born in Dorset he was educated at William Barnes's school where he met Thomas Hardy, a lifelong friend. The textbooks on surgery that Treves wrote in the 1880s and 1890s were standard works in their field until after the Second World War. A later generation knows him better as the doctor who befriended Joseph Merrick, the Elephant Man: Treves's last book, *The Elephant Man and Other Reminiscences* (1923) is the source of all subsequent work on the topic. Shortly after his elevation to baronet (awarded for performing an appendectomy on King Edward VII two days before his coronation), Treves retired from surgery and spent the next twenty years travelling and writing about his travels. *The Cradle of the Deep* recounts his Caribbean voyages, probably undertaken in 1907. There is a recent biography: Stephen Trombley, *Sir Frederick Treves: The Extra-Ordinary Edwardian* (1989).

'Vaquero': pseudonym of author of *Adventures in Search of a Living in Spanish-America* (1911) and *Life and Adventures in the West Indies: A Sequel to Adventures in Search of a Living in Spanish-America* (1914). He seems to have been a British doctor who travelled in Central and South America and the Caribbean in the period 1900 to 1908.

Alpheus Hyatt Verrill (1871–1954): author, naturalist, explorer. Born in New Haven, he was the son of one famous naturalist and named after another. He was in Dominica for the first time in 1888, a visit he recounts in *Thirty Years in the Jungle* (1929), and was also resident there from 1903 to 1906. Throughout his life he was involved in many expeditions to remote parts of Central and South America, some of them in the employ of the Museum of the American Indian in New York. Amongst his many other books are *The Book of the West Indies* (1917), *Islands and Their Mysteries* (1920), *The Real Story of the Pirate* (1923), *The American Indian, North, South, and Central America* (1927), and *Strange Customs, Manners, and Beliefs; A Remarkable Account of Curious Beliefs and Odd Superstitions, Strange Ways of Living, and Amazing Customs and Manners of Many People and Tribes around the Earth* (1946). He also wrote an unpublished autobiography.

Alexander Raban (Alec) Waugh (1898–1981): a prolific novelist and travel writer. He wrote several books about the West Indies, including *The Coloured Countries* (1930), *The Sunlit Caribbean* (1948), *The Sugar Islands* (1958), and *A Family of Islands: A History of the West Indies from 1492 to 1898* (1964), as well as a novel, *The Fatal Gift* (1973), set on Dominica. His brief visit to the Carib Reserve is written about in his much reprinted essay, 'Typical Dominica', written in 1948 and first published in *Where the Clocks Chime Twice* (1952).

Anthony Weller (1957–): Canadian author of *Days and Nights on the Grand Trunk Road* (1997) and of two novels, *The Garden of the Peacocks* (1996) and *The Polish Lover* (1997).

Linda Wolfe (1939–): based in New York. Author, apart from *The Cooking of the Caribbean Islands* (1970), of *The Literary Gourmet* (1962), *Playing Around: Women and Extramarital Sex* (1975), *The Cosmo Report* (1981), *The Professor and the Prostitute and Other True Tales of Murder and Madness* (1986), and several novels, most recently *Love Me To Death* (1997).

References

MANUSCRIPT COLLECTIONS

Aborigines Protection Society, Rhodes House Library, Oxford: the APS amalgamated with the Anti-Slavery Society in 1909 and their papers are combined under the general class mark MSS Brit Emp S22.

Hesketh Bell: Hesketh Bell, Papers, Royal Commonwealth Society Collections (now at the University of Cambridge Library). Bell kept extensive diaries, scrapbooks and files. On his death the diaries were bequeathed to the British Library, where they will not be available for inspection until 2002; the rest of the material was left by his niece, Mrs Llewellin-Taylour, to the Royal Commonwealth Society Library on her death in 1968. The Library divided the material into eight: 1 Scrapbooks; 2 Synopses of diaries; 3 Notebooks; 4 Letters; 5 Files; 6 Pictorial; 7 Books; 8 Sundries. 'Scrapbooks' (BP1) contains many of the newspaper clippings quoted; 'Synopses of diaries'— often quite full and pertaining to the period August 1899 to December 1924—are referred to here simply as BP2, with date of entry; 'Files' (BP5) has material on the Caribs (A1 and A14) which Bell was collecting for his book. For a fuller description of the papers, see *The Manuscript Catalogue of the Library of the Royal Commonwealth Society*, ed. Donald H. Simpson (London: Mansell, 1975), 38–9.

The Chamberlain Papers, Special Collections, University of Birmingham: the papers of Joseph and Neville Chamberlain are referred to via the abbrieviations JC and NC.

Government Archives, Dominica: much local documentation was destroyed in the fire that burned down the Court House in 1979, the general destruction following Hurricane David (1976), and the construction workers' clear-out of archives prior to the refurbishment of Government House (1991). Most official documents are therefore quoted from secondary sources or from rescued originals now in the collection of Lennox Honychurch (via the abbreviation LH); with the exception of the *Dominica Blue Books*, which were consulted in the Royal Commonwealth Society Library (now at the University of Cambridge Library).

Frederick Albion Ober: Smithsonian Institution Archives, Washington, DC; and the George Newbold Lawrence (1806–95) Collection

(American Museum of Natural History, New York): Box Five, Correspondence (Frederick A. Ober, 1874–94).

Public Records Office, Kew, London: references to Colonial Office papers are via the abbreviation CO.

Jean Rhys: Jean Rhys Collection, McFarlin Library, University of Tulsa. References to the 'Black Exercise Book' are via the abbreviation *BEB*. Since the collection is undergoing rearrangement, classification numbers are not given. An associated collection in the same library is the David Plante Papers relating to the composition of *Smile Please*: references via DPP: folder number.

Douglas Macrae Taylor: Bureau of American Ethnology, General Correspondence, 1909–49 (Taylor, Douglas Macrae). National Anthropological Archives, Smithsonian Institution, Washington, DC. References are via BAE and date of correspondence.

NEWSPAPERS

Older Dominican newspapers—*Dominican, Dominican Dial, Dominica Guardian, Leeward Islands Free Press*—were consulted at the Newspaper Library of the British Library (Colindale); *New Chronicle* at the Public Library, Roseau.

BOOKS AND ARTICLES

N.B. Where material has been reproduced in *Wild Majesty: Encounters with Caribs from Columbus to the Present Day*, ed. Peter Hulme and Neil L. Whitehead (Oxford: Clarendon Press, 1992), this is signalled as [reprinted in *WM*].

A Collection of Plain Authentic Documents in Justification of the Conduct of Governor Ainslie; in the reduction of a most formidable rebellion among the negro slaves in the island of Dominica, at a crisis of the most imminent danger to the lives and properties of the inhabitants (1815), London: C. Lowndes.

Agar, Captain Augustus (1962), *Showing the Flag*, London: Evans Brothers.

Alegría, Ricardo (1978), 'Los estudios arqueológicos en Puerto Rico', *Revista Interamericana*, 8: 380–4.

Anderson, Benedict (1991), *Imagined Communities: Reflections on the Origin and Spread of Nationalism*, 2nd edn., London: Verso.

André, Irving W. (1995), *Distant Voices: The Genesis of an Indigenous Literature in Dominica*, Brampton, Ontario: Pond Casse Press.

——and Gabriel J. Christian (1992), *In Search of Eden: Dominica, the Travails of a Caribbean Mini-State*, Upper Marlboro, Md.: Pond Casse Press.

Angier, Carole (1990), *Jean Rhys: Life and Work*, Boston: Little, Brown & Co.

Anon. (1896), 'Jamaican Wooden Images in the British Museum', *Journal of the Institute of Jamaica*, 2/3: 303–4.

Armas, Juan Ignacio de (1884), *La fábula de los Caribes*, Havana: Imprenta Fenix.

Arrom, José Juan (1980), 'Mitos taínos en las letras de Cuba, Santo Domingo y México', in his *Certidumbre de América: Estudios de Letras, Foklore y Cultura*, Havana: Editorial Letras Cubanas, 56–73.

——(1986), 'Cimarrón: Apuntes sobre sus primeras documentaciones y su probable origen', in José Juan Arrom and Manuel A. García Arévalo, *Cimarrón*, Santo Domingo: Fundación García-Arévalo, 13–30.

Aspinall, Algernon (1914), *The Pocket Guide to the West Indies* [1907], London: Methuen & Co.

——(1928), *A Wayfarer in the West Indies*, London: Methuen & Co.

Atwood, Thomas (1791), *The History of the Island of Dominica*, London: J. Johnson.

Bacon, Edwin M. (1902), *Literary Pilgrimages in New England*, New York: Silver, Burdett & Co.

Baker, Patrick L. (1988), 'Ethnogenesis: The Case of the Dominica Caribs', *América Indígena*, 48/2: 377–401.

——(1994), *Centring the Periphery: Chaos, Order, and the Ethnohistory of Dominica*, Montreal and Kingston: McGill-Queen's UP.

Ballet, J. (1875), 'Les Caraïbes', *International Congress of Americanists*, 1: 394–438.

Bancroft, George (1840), *History of the United States From the Discovery of the American Continent* [1834], 7th edn., Boston: Charles C. Little & James Brown.

Bandy, Joe (1996), 'Managing the Other of Nature: Sustainability, Spectacle, and the Global Regimes of Capital in Ecotourism', *Public Culture*, 8: 539–66.

Banks, Eugene P. (1954), 'An Inquiry into the Structure of Island Carib Culture', Ph.D. thesis. Department of Anthropology: Harvard University.

——(1956), 'A Carib Village in Dominica', *Social and Economic Studies*, 5: 74–80.

Barber, James (1968), *Imperial Frontier: A Study of the Relations Between the British and the Pastoral Tribes of North East Uganda*, Nairobi: East African Publishing House.

Barbotin, Père Maurice (1976), 'Arawaks et Caraïbes à Marie-Galante', *Bulletin de la Société d'histoire de la Guadeloupe*, 11–12: 77–118.

Barreiro, José (1990), 'Carib Gallery', *Northeast Indian Quarterly*, 7/3: 47–55. [repr. in *WM*]

Barth, Fredrik, ed. (1969), *Ethnic Groups and Boundaries: The Social Organization of Culture Difference*, London: Allen & Unwin.

Bell, Archie (1926), *The Spell of the Caribbean Islands*, Boston: L.C. Page & Co.

Bell, Henry Hesketh (1893), *Obeah: Witchcraft in the West Indies*, 2nd. edn., London: Sampson Low, Marston & Co.

——(1899), 'Imperial Grant to Dominica: Scheme for Expenditure', CO 152/249 (Letter to the Governor of the Leeward Islands, 26 Oct. 1899).

——(1900), Letter to *The Times*, 20 Sept.

——(1902), *Report on the Caribs of Dominica*, Colonial Reports—Miscellaneous, no. 21, London: HMSO, Cd. 1298.

——(1903a), *Dominica. Roads and Land Settlement. Report on the Expenditure of the Parliamentary Grant in Aid*, Colonial Reports—Miscellaneous, no. 23, London: HMSO.

——(1903b), *Dominica: Notes and Hints to Intending Settlers*, [n.p.]. [copy in BP1]

——(1904a), 'The Imperial Road in Dominica', *West India Committee Circular*, 19 (28 June): 257–60.

——(1904b), 'Dominica: Ten Days in Dominica', in *The Book of the West Indies*, ed. Francis Dodsworth, London: George Routledge & Sons, 156–67.

——(1938), 'The Last of the Caribs', *National Review*, vol. 110, pt. 6: 227–34.

——(1946), *Glimpses of a Governor's Life: From Diaries, Letters and Memoranda*, London: Sampson Low, Marston & Co.

Beverly Historical Society (n.d.), 'Genealogical Record of the Descendants of Andrew Kimball Ober'.

Bieder, Robert E. (1986), *Science Encounters the Indian, 1820–1880*, Norman, Ohla.: University of Oklahoma Press.

Bigelow, Poultney (1901), *The Children of the Nations: A Study of Colonization and its Problems*, New York: McClure, Phillips & Co.

Birge, William S. (1900), *In Old Roseau: Reminiscences of Life as I found it in the island of Dominica and among the Carib Indians*, New York: Blanchard Press.

Bishop, Nathaniel H. (1869), *A Thousand Miles' Walk Across South America*, Boston: Lee & Shepard.

——(1878), *Voyage of the Paper Canoe: A Geographical Journey of 2500 Miles, from Quebec to the Gulf of Mexico, During the Years 1874–5*, Boston: Lee & Shephard.

Blumenbach, Johann Friedrich (1865), *The Anthropological Treatises*, trans. and ed. Thomas Bendyshe, London: Longman, Green, Longman, Roberts, & Green.

Bogdan, Robert (1988), *Freak Show: Presenting Human Oddities for Amusement and Profit*, Chicago: University of Chicago Press.

Bolland, O. Nigel (1995), *On the March: Labour Rebellions in the British Caribbean, 1934–39*, London: James Currey.

Bonsal, Stephen (1912), *The American Mediterranean*, New York: Moffat, Yard & Co.

Booth, Robert (1990), 'Dominica', *National Geographic Magazine* (June): 100–20.

Boromé, Joseph A. (1959–60), 'George Charles Falconer', *Caribbean Quarterly*, 6/1: 11–17.

——(1969), 'How Crown Colony Government Came to Dominica by 1898', *Caribbean Studies*, 9/3: 26–67.

——(1970), 'Origin and Growth of the Public Libraries of Dominica', *Journal of Library History*, 5/3: 200–36.

Boucher, Philip P. (1992), *Cannibal Encounters: Europeans and Island Caribs, 1492–1763*, Baltimore: Johns Hopkins UP.

Branch, C. W. (1907), 'Aboriginal Antiquities in Saint Kitts and Nevis', *American Anthropologist*, 9: 315–33.

Brantlinger, Patrick (1995), ' "Dying Races": Rationalizing Genocide in the Nineteenth Century', in Jan Nederveen Pieterse and Bhikhu Parekh, eds., *The Decolonization of Imagination: Culture, Knowledge and Power*, London: Zed Books, 43–56.

Brereton, Bridget (1997), *Law, Justice and Empire: The Colonial Career of John Gorrie, 1829–1892*, Kingston: Press University of the West Indies.

Breton, P. Raymond (1665–6), *Dictionaire Caraïbe–François*, 2 vols., G. Auxerre: Bouquet.

Brinton, Daniel G. (1871), *The Arawack Language of Guiana in its Linguistic and Ethnological Relations*, Philadelphia: McCalla & Stavely.

——(1876), *The Myths of the New World: A Treatise on the Symbolism and Mythology of the Red Race of America*, 2nd edn., New York: Henry Holt & Co.

Brooks, Van Wyck (1940), *New England: Indian Summer, 1865–1915*, New York: E. P. Dutton & Co.

Brown, Nancy Hemond (1985), 'Jean Rhys and *Voyage in the Dark*', *London Magazine*, 25/1–2, Apr./May: 40–59.

Bulkeley, Owen T. (1889), *The Lesser Antilles. A Guide for Settlers in the British West Indies, and Tourists' Companion*, London: Sampson, Marston, Searle, & Rivington.

Burnett, Paula, ed. (1986), *The Penguin Book of Caribbean Verse in English*, Harmondsworth: Penguin.

Bushman, Claudia (1992), *America Discovers Columbus: How an Italian Explorer Became an American Hero*, Hanover, NH: University Press of New England.

Buzard, James (1993), *The Beaten Track: European Tourism, Literature, and the Ways to 'Culture', 1800–1918*, Oxford: Clarendon Press.

Byres, John (1777), *References to the Plan of the Island of Dominica, as Surveyed from the Year 1765 to 1773*, London: S. Hooper.

Cabannes, M. R, and Schmidt-Beurrier A. (1966), 'Recherches sur les hémoglobines des populations indiennes de l'Amérique du Sud', *L'Anthropologie*, 70/3–4: 331–42.

Callcot, Wilfrid Hardy (1942), *The Caribbean Policy of the United States, 1890–1920*, Baltimore: Johns Hopkins Press.

Cameron Gordon, Helen (Lady Russell) (1942), *West Indian Scenes*, London: Robert Hale.

Campbell, Elaine (1979), 'Jean Rhys, Alec Waugh, and the Imperial Road', *Journal of Commonwealth Literature*, 14: 58–63.

Caribbean Indigenous Revival (1987), *Report on Conference of Indigenous Peoples: Caribbean Indigenous Revival, August 13–17, 1987*, Kingstown: n.p.

Carlyle, Thomas (1915), 'Occasional Discourse on the Nigger Question' [1849], in *English and Other Critical Essays*, London: J. M. Dent, 303–33.

Carr, Helen (1996a), *Inventing the American Primitive: Politics, Gender and the Representation of Native American Literary Traditions, 1789–1936*, Cork: Cork UP.

——(1996b), *Jean Rhys*, Plymouth: Northcote House.

Chamberlain, Joseph (1914), *Mr Chamberlain's Speeches*, ed. Charles W. Boyd, 2 vols., London: Constable & Co.

Chester, Grenville John (1869), *Transatlantic Sketches in the West Indies, South America, Canada and United States*, London: Smith, Elder & Co.

Chilling-Rathford [Shillingford] *et al.* (1966), 'Étude hémotypologique de la population indienne de l'île Dominique', *L'Anthropologie*, 70/3–4: 319–30.

Chi lo sa [pseudonym] (1936), 'When the Prince came to Dominica', *Dominica Chronicle*, 26 Sept., p. 7.

Churchill, Ward (1995), 'The Bloody Wake of Alcatraz: Political Repression of the American Indian Movement during the 1970s', in his *Since Predator Came: Notes from the Struggle for American Indian Liberation*, Littleton, Colo.: Aigis Publications, 203–44.

Clerici, Roger (1962), *Lionello Fiumi*, Paris: Pierre Seghers.

Clifford, James (1988), *The Predicament of Culture: Twentieth Century Ethnography, Literature, and Art*, Cambridge, Mass.: Harvard UP.

Clifton, James A., ed. (1989), *Being and Becoming Indian: Biographical Studies of North American Frontiers*, Chicago: Dorsey Press.

Clyde, David F. (1980), *Two Centuries of Health Care in Dominica*, New Delhi: privately printed.

Coleridge, Henry Nelson (1832), *Six Months in the West Indies in 1825*, 3rd edn., London: John Murray.

Columbus, Christopher (1989), *The Diario of Christopher Columbus's First Voyage to America: 1492–93*, ed. and trans. Oliver Dunn and James E. Kelley, Norman, Ohla.: University of Oklahoma Press.

Conrad, Joseph (1989), *Heart of Darkness* [1899], ed. Ross C. Murfin, New York: St Martin's Press.

Coombes, Annie (1988), 'Museums and the Formation of National and Cultural Identities', *Oxford Art Journal*, 11: 57–68.

Cooter, Roger (1984), *The Cultural Meaning of Popular Science: Phrenology and the Organization of Consent in Nineteenth-Century Britain*, Cambridge: CUP.

Cope, Edward D. (1883), *On the Contents of a Bone Cave in the Island of Anguilla (West Indies)*, Smithsonian Contributions to Knowledge 489, Washington: Smithsonian Institution.

Corbey, Raymond (1993), 'Ethnographic Showcases, 1870–1930', *Cultural Anthropology*, 8/3: 338–69.

Cracknell, Basil (1973), *Dominica*, Newton Abbot: David & Charles.

Crewe, Quentin (1987), *Touch the Happy Isles: A Journey Through the Caribbean*, London: Michael Joseph.

Crook, D. P. (1984), *Benjamin Kidd: Portrait of a Social Darwinist*, Cambridge: CUP.

Culin, Stewart (1902), 'The Indians of Cuba', *Bulletin of the Free Museum of Science and Arts, University of Pennsylvania, Philadelphia*, 3/4: 185–226.

Cunningham, Hilary (1998), 'Colonial Encounters in Postcolonial Contexts: Patenting Indigenous DNA and the Human Genome Diversity Project', *Critique of Anthropology*, 18: 205–33.

Currier, Revd Charles Warren (1902), 'The Carib Race in the West Indies', *Catholic World*, 75/448 (July): 433–40.

D'Anghera, Peter Martyr (1587), *De Orbe Novo*, ed. Richard Hakluyt, Paris: Guillaume Avrray.

——(1912), *De Orbe Novo: The Eight Decades*, trans. F. A. MacNutt, 2 vols., New York: Burt Franklin.

Darwin, Charles (1913), 'On the Extinction of the Races of Man' in his *The Descent of Man, and Selection in Relation to Sex* [1871], London: John Murray, 281–97.

Davies, John of Kidwelly (1666), *The History of the Caribby-Islands*, London: O. M. for T. Dring and J. Starkey [trans. of Rochefort 1658].

Davis, Dave D. (1996), 'Revolutionary Archaeology in Cuba', *Journal of Archaeological Method and Theory*, 3/3: 159–88.

Davis, N. Darnell (1888), *Mr. Froude's Negrophobia, or Don Quixote as a Cook's Tourist*, Demerara: Argosy Press.

Delawarde, R. P. J.-B. (1938), 'Les Derniers Caraïbes: leur vie dans une réserve de la Dominique', *Journal de la Société des Americanistes*, 30: 167–204.

Desai, Gaurav (1993), 'The Invention of Invention', *Cultural Critique*, 18: 119–41.

Despres, Leo A., ed. (1975), *Ethnicity and Resource Competition in Plural Societies*, The Hague: Mouton.

De Ville, James (1828), *Manual of Phrenology, as an accompaniment to the phrenological bust*, London: J. de Ville.

Dexter, Ralph W. (1966), 'Putnam's Problems Popularizing Anthropology', *American Scientist*, 54: 315–32.

Dilke, Charles Wentworth (1868), *Greater Britain: A Record of Travel in English-Speaking Countries during 1866 and 1867*, 2 vols., London: Macmillan & Co.

Dippie, Brian W. (1982), *The Vanishing American: White Attitudes and U.S. Indian Policy*, Lawrence, Kan.: University Press of Kansas.

Dominica (1971), *Dominica: A Tourist Development Strategy*, London: Shankland Cox & Associates.

——(1978), *The Carib Reserve*, Act. no. 22 of 1978.

——(1989), *Dominica: Nature Island of the Caribbean*, London: Hansib Publishing.

——(1991), 'The Carib Reserve', *Laws of Dominica*, ch. 25:31–89, Roseau: Government Stationers.

Dow, Mary Larcom (1921), *Old Days at Beverly Farms*, ed. Katharine P. Loring, Beverly, Mass.: North Shore Printing Co.

Drinnon, Richard (1980), *Facing West: The Metaphysics of Indian-Hating and Empire-Building*, Minneapolis: University of Minnesota Press.

Duque Duque, Cecilia (1985), *Consultant Report on the Cultural Revitalization Project in Dominica*, Bogotá: Save the Children Federation.

Du Tertre, R. P. Jean Baptiste (1667–71), *Histoire générale des Antilles habités par les François*, 4 vols., Paris: Thomas Jolly.

Edwards, Bryan (1819), *The History, Civil and Commercial, of the British Colonies in the West Indies* [1793–1808], 5 vols., London: G. & W. B. Whittaker *et al.*

Eguchi, Nobukiyo (1997), 'Ethnic Tourism and Reconstruction of the Caribs' Ethnic Identity', in Juan Manuel Carrión, ed., *Ethnicity, Race and Nationality in the Caribbean*, Río Piedras: Institute of Caribbean Studies, UPR, 364–80.

Einhorn, Arthur (1972), *Proposal for Development of a Carib 'Indian Village' and the Economic Development of the Carib Indian Reserve on the Island of Dominica, British West Indies.* Copy in the Public Library, Roseau.

Eliot, Edward C. (1938), *Broken Atoms*, London: Geoffrey Bles.

Ellis, Vivienne Rae (1976), *Trucanini: Queen or Traitor?*, Hobart: O.B.M. Publishing.

Emery, Mary Lou (1982), 'The Politics of Form: Jean Rhys's Social Vision in *Voyage in the Dark* and *Wide Sargasso Sea*', *Twentieth Century Literature*, 28: 418–32.

Fabian, Johannes (1983), *Time and the Other: How Anthropology Makes its Object*, New York: Columbia UP.

Falnes, Oscar J. (1937), 'New England Interest in Scandinavian Culture and the Norsemen', *New England Quarterly*, 10 (June): 211–42.

Fenger, Frederic A. (1958), *Alone in the Caribbean. Being the Yarn of a Cruise in the Lesser Antilles in the Sailing Canoe 'Yakaboo'* [1917], Belmont, Mass.: Wellington Books.

Ferguson, R. Brian, and Neil L. Whitehead, eds. (1992), *War in the Tribal Zone: Expanding States and Indigenous Warfare*, Santa Fe: School of American Research Press.

Fermor, Patrick Leigh (1984), *The Traveller's Tree: A Journey Through the Caribbean Islands* [1950], Harmondsworth: Penguin Books.

Fewkes, J. Walter (1891), 'On Zemes from Santo Domingo', *American Anthropologist*, 4/2: 167–75.

——(1903), 'Preliminary Report on an Archaeological Trip to the West Indies', *Smithsonian Miscellaneous Collections*, Quarterly Issue, 45: 112–33.

——(1904), 'Prehistoric Culture of Cuba', *American Anthropologist.*, n.s. 6/4: 535–8.

——(1907), 'The Aborigines of Porto Rico and Neighboring Islands', *Twenty-fifth Annual Report of the Bureau of American Ethnology*, 1903–4, Washington: Government Printing Office: 13–220.

Field, Les W. (1994), 'Who Are the Indians? Reconceptualizing Indigenous Identity, Resistance, and the Role of Social Science in Latin America', *Latin American Research Review*, 29: 237–48.

Fiumi, Lionello (1938), *Images des Antilles*, Paris: Les Éditions des Presses Modernes.

Fogelson, Raymond D. (1991), 'The Red Man in the White City', in *Columbian Consequences*, vol. iii: *The Spanish Borderlands in Pan American Perspective*, ed. David Hurst Thomas, Washington: Smithsonian Institution Press, 73–90.

Forbes, Jack D. (1990), 'The Manipulation of Race, Caste, and Ethnicity: Classifying Afroamericans, Native Americans and Red-Black People', *Journal of Ethnic Studies*, 17/4: 1–51.

——(1993), *Africans and Native Americans: The Language of Race and the Evolution of the Red-Black Peoples*, Urbana, Ill.: University of Illinois Press.

Forte, Maximilian C. (1998), '"The International Indigene": Regional and Global Integration of Amerindian Communities in the Caribbean', *http://pages.hotbot.com/current/mcforte/Intlindg.html* (accessed 4 Jan. 1999).

——(1999), 'Reviving Caribs: Recognition, Patronage and Ceremonial Indigeneity in Trinidad and Tobago', *Cultural Survival Quarterly*, 23/4: 35–42.

Fox Bourne, H. R. (1899), *The Aborigines Protection Society: Chapters in its History*, London: P. S. King & Son.

Frederick, Hilary (1983), *The Caribs and their Colonizers: The Problem of Land*, London: EAFORD.

Frickey, Pierrette M. (1988), 'The Dominican Landscape: In Memory of Jean Rhys', *Jean Rhys Review*, 3/1: 1–10.

Froude, James Anthony (1909), *The English in the West Indies, or The Bow of Ulysses* [1887], London: Longmans & Co.

Fryd, Vivien Green (1992), *Art and Empire: The Politics of Ethnicity in the U.S. Capitol, 1815–1860*, New Haven: Yale UP.

Geggus, David (1997), 'The Naming of Haiti', *New West Indian Guide*, 71/1 and 2: 43–68.

Gikandi, Simon (1996), *Maps of Englishness: Writing Identity in the Culture of Colonialism*, New York: Columbia UP.

Gladwin, Harold Sterling (1949), *Men Out of Asia*, New York: McGraw-Hill.

Gli Gli (1997), *http://www.delphis.dm/gligli/gligli.html*.

Goetzmann, William H. (1966), *Exploration and Empire: The Explorer and the Scientist in the Winning of the American West*, New York: Alfred A. Knopf.

Goldie, Terry (1989), *Fear and Temptation: The Image of the Indigene in Canadian, Australian, and New Zealand Literatures*, Montreal: McGill-Queen's UP.

Gonzalez, Nancie L. (1988), *Sojourners of the Caribbean:*

Ethnogenesis and Ethnohistory of the Garifuna, Urbana, Ill.: University of Illinois Press.

Gould, John M. (1877), *Hints for Camping and Walking; How to Camp Out*, New York: Scribner, Armstrong, & Co.

Graves, Charles (1965), *Fourteen Islands in the Sun*, London: Leslie Frewin.

Gray, Andrew (1996), 'Indigenous Peoples at the United Nations: The Declaration Reaches the Commission on Human Rights', *The Indigenous World 1995–96*, Copenhagen: IWGIA, 247–68.

Great Britain (1897), *Report of the West India Royal Commission*, London: HMSO, C. 8655.

——(1932), *Conditions in the Carib Reserve, and the disturbance of 19th September, 1930, Dominica* [Report of a Commission appointed by His Excellency the Governor of the Leeward Islands, July, 1931], London: HMSO. [excerpts in WM]

Green, Cecilia (1999), 'A Recalcitrant Plantation Colony: Dominica, 1880–1946', *New West Indian Guide*, 73/3 and 4: 43–72.

Green, David (1984), 'Classified Subjects. Photography and Anthropology: The Technology of Power', *Ten/8*, 14: 30–7.

Gregg, Veronica Marie (1995), *Jean Rhys's Historical Imagination: Reading and Writing the Creole*, Chapel Hill, NC: University of North Carolina Press.

Gregoire, Crispin, and Natalia Kanem (1989), 'Caribs of Dominica: Land Rights and Ethnic Consciousness', *Cultural Survival*, 13/3: 52–5.

Gregoire, Crispin, Patrick Henderson, and Natalia Kanem (1996), 'Karifuna: The Caribs of Dominica', in Rhoda E. Reddock, ed., *Ethnic Minorities in Caribbean Society*, St Augustine: ISER, 107–71.

[Grell, Oliver] (1984), *Land Settlement of Geneva Estate, Grand Bay*, Roseau: OAS and Government of Dominica.

Grieve, Symington (1906), *Notes upon the Island of Dominica (British West Indies) Containing Information for Settlers, Investors, Tourists, Naturalists, and Others*, London: Adam & Charles Black.

Grossman, Lawrence C. (1998), *The Political Ecology of Bananas: Contract Farming, Peasants, and Agrarian Change in the Eastern Caribbean*, Chapel Hill, NC: University of North Carolina Press.

Grout, Jack (1970), *Dans le sillage de la flibuste: Léopard Normand aux Antilles*, Paris: Arthaud.

Gruber, Jacob W. (1970), 'Ethnographic Salvage and the Shaping of Anthropology', *American Anthropologist*, 72: 1289–99.

Guitar, Lynne A. (1998), 'Cultural Genesis: Relationships Among Indians, Africans and Spaniards in Rural Hispaniola, First Half of the Sixteenth Century', Ph.D. thesis, History, Vanderbilt University.

Gullick, C. J. M. R. (1976), *Exiled from St. Vincent: The Development of Black Carib Culture in Central America up to 1945*, Malta: Progress Press.

——(1985), *Myths of a Minority: The Changing Traditions of the Vincentian Caribs*, Assen: Van Gorcum.

Haddon, Alfred C. (1901), *Head-Hunters: Black, White, and Brown*, London: Methuen & Co.

Hall, Catherine (1989), 'The Economy of Intellectual Prestige: Thomas Carlyle, John Stuart Mill, and the Case of Governor Eyre', *Cultural Critique*, 12: 167–96.

Hallowell, A. Irving (1960), 'The Beginnings of Anthropology in America', in *Selected Papers from the American Anthropologist, 1880–1920*, ed. Frederica de Laguna, Evanston, Ill.: Row, Peterson & Co., 1–90.

Hamilton, Robert G. C. (1894), *Report of the Commission (Appointed in September 1893), to Inquire into the Condition and Affairs of the Island of Dominica*, House of Commons, Sessional Papers, Cd. 7477, London.

Hamot-Pézéron, Simone (1983), 'The Carib Indians of Dominica Island in the West Indies', Maîtrise d'Anglais, Université de la Sorbonne-Nouvelle, Paris III.

Handler, Jerome (1978), 'The "Bird Man": A Jamaican Arawak Wooden "Idol"', *Jamaica Journal*, 11/3–4: 25–9.

Hart, Richard (1993), 'The Labour Rebellions of the 1930s', in Hilary Beckles and Verene Shepherd, eds., *Caribbean Freedom: Society and Economy From Emancipation to the Present*, Kingston: Ian Randle, 370–5.

Harvey, Penelope (1996), *Hybrids of Modernity: Anthropology, the Nation State, and the Universal Exhibition*, London: Routledge.

Harvey, R. G. *et al.* (1969), 'Frequency of Genetic Traits in the Caribs of Dominica', *Human Biology*, 41: 342–64.

Hatt, John (1993), 'Dominica Done', *Harpers & Queen*, April: 164–8.

Hawys, Stephen (1968), *Mount Joy*, London: Gerald Duckworth & Co.

Hearn, Lafcadio (1923), *Two Years in the West Indies*, New York: Harper & Brothers.

Heizer, Robert F. and Theodora Kroeber, eds. (1979), *Ishi the Last Yahi: A Documentary History*, Berkeley: University of California Press.

Helweg-Larsen, Kjeld (1967), *Pieces of Paradise*, London: Jarrolds.

Henderson, Thomas H. (1994), 'Hopelessness, Frustration Still Haunt Grand Bay', *The New Chronicle*, 14 Oct.

Herle, Anita, and Sandra Rouse, eds. (1998), *Cambridge and the Torres Strait: Centenary Essays on the 1898 Anthropological Expedition*, Cambridge: CUP.

Hertzberg, Hazel W. (1971), *The Search for an American Indian Identity: Modern Pan-Indian Movements*, Syracuse, NY: Syracuse University Press.

Heuman, Gad (1994), *'The Killing Time': The Morant Bay Rebellion in Jamaica*, London: Macmillan.

Hicks, Philip Marshall (1924), 'The Development of the Natural History Essay in American Literature', Ph.D. thesis, University of Pennsylvania.

Higbie, Janet (1993), *Eugenia: The Caribbean's Iron Lady*, London: Macmillan.

Higham, John (1970), 'The Reorientation of American Culture in the 1890s', in his *Writing American History: Essays on Modern Scholarship*, Bloomington, Ind.: Indiana UP, 73–104.

Hinsley, Curtis M., Jr. (1981), *Savages and Scientists: The Smithsonian Institution and the Development of American Anthropology 1846–1910*: Washington: Smithsonian Institution Press.

——(1990), 'The World as Marketplace: Commodification of the Exotic at the World's Columbian Exposition, Chicago, 1893', in *Exhibiting Cultures: The Poetics and Politics of Museum Display*, ed. Ivan Karp and Steven D. Lavine, Washington: Smithsonian Institution Press, 344–65.

Historic Beverly: Being an Account of the Growth of the City of Beverly from the Earliest Times to the Present (1937), Beverly, Mass.: Beverly Chamber of Commerce.

Holmes, W. H. (1894), 'Caribbean Influence in the Prehistoric Art of Southern States', *American Anthropologist*, 7: 71–9.

Holt, Thomas C. (1992), *The Problem of Freedom: Race, Labor, and Politics in Jamaica and Britain, 1832–1938*, Baltimore: Johns Hopkins UP.

Honychurch, Lennox (1995), *The Dominica Story: A History of the Island*, 2nd. edn., London: Macmillan.

——(1997a), 'Crossroads in the Caribbean: A Site of Encounter and Exchange on Dominica', *World Archaeology*, 28/3: 291–304.

——(1997b), 'Carib to Creole: Contact and Culture Exchange in Dominica', unpublished D.Phil. thesis, University of Oxford.

Horsman, Reginald (1981), *Race and Manifest Destiny: The Origins of American Racial Anglo-Saxonism*, Cambridge, Mass.: Harvard UP.

Howells, Coral Ann (1991), *Jean Rhys*, London: Harvester Wheatsheaf.

Huddleston, Lee Eldridge (1967), *Origins of the American Indians:*

European Concepts, 1492–1729, Austin, Tex.: University of Texas Press.

Hughes, Colin A. (1952), 'Politics and Constitution-making in the Eastern Group of the B.W.I., 1922 to the Present Day', Ph.D. thesis, University of London.

Hulme, Peter (1986), *Colonial Encounters: Europe and the Native Caribbean, 1492–1797*, London: Methuen.

——(1993), 'Making Sense of the Native Caribbean', *New West Indian Guide*, 67/3 and 4, 189–220.

——(1994a), 'The Locked Heart: The Creole Family Romance of *Wide Sargasso Sea*', in Francis Barker, Peter Hulme, and Margaret Iversen, eds., *Colonial Discourse / Postcolonial Theory*, Manchester: Manchester UP, 72–88; also in *Jean Rhys Review*, 6/1 (1993): 20–35.

——(1994b), 'Tales of Distinction: European Ethnography and the Caribbean', in Stuart Schwartz, ed., *Implicit Understandings: Encounters between Europeans and Other Peoples in the Wake of Columbus*, New York: CUP, 157–97.

——(1997a), 'El encuentro con Anacaona: Frederick Albion Ober, y la historia del Caribe autóctono', in *El Caribe Entre Imperios (Coloquio de Princeton)*, ed. Arcadio Díaz Quiñones (*Op. Cit. Revista del Centro de Investigaciones Históricas, no. 9, edición extraordinaria*), Río Piedras: Universidad de Puerto Rico, 75–109.

——(1997b), 'Under the Cuban Flag: Notions of Indigeneity at the End of the Nineteenth Century', paper presented at the conference Indigenous Legacies of the Caribbean, Baracoa, Cuba, 16–23 Nov.

——(1997c), 'In the Wake of Columbus: Frederick Ober's Ambulant Gloss', *Literature & History*, 6/2: 18–36.

——(1999a), 'Meditation on Yellow: Trade and Indigeneity in the Caribbean', paper presented at the conference Trading Places: Colonialism and Commerce, University of Queensland, Brisbane, 11–15 July.

——(1999b), 'Black, Yellow, and Red in the Caribbean', paper presented at the conference 'Crossings: Racial and Sexual Intermixture in Africa and the New World', The Clark Library, Los Angeles, 15–16 Oct.

——(2000), 'Islands and Roads: Hesketh Bell, Jean Rhys, and Dominica's Imperial Road', *The Jean Rhys Review* 11/2.

——and Neil L. Whitehead, eds. (1992), *Wild Majesty: Encounters with Caribs from Columbus to the Present Day*, Oxford: Clarendon Press.

Huth, Hans (1972), *Nature and the American: Three Centuries of Changing Attitudes* [1957], Lincoln, Nebr.: University of Nebraska Press.

Im Thurn, Everard (1884), 'Notes on West Indian Stone Implements; and Other Indian Relics (Illustrated)', *Timehri*, 3: 103–37.

Irving, Washington (1981), *The Life and Voyages of Christopher Columbus* [1828], ed. John Harmon McElroy [*The Complete Works of Washington Irving*, vol. xi], Boston: Twayne.

Jaimes, M. Annette (1992), 'Federal Indian Identification Policy: A Usurpation of Indigenous Sovereignty in North America', in M. Annette Jaimes, ed., *The State of Native America: Genocide, Colonization, and Resistance*, Boston: South End Press, 123–38.

James, C. L. R. (1977), *The Future in the Present: Selected Writings*, Westport, Conn.: Lawrence Hill & Co.

Johnson, Amryl (1988), *Sequins for a Ragged Hem*, London: Virago.

Johnson, Rossiter, ed. (1897–8), *A History of the World's Columbian Exposition Held in Chicago in 1893*, 4 vols., New York: D. Appleton & Co.

Jones, Siân (1997), *The Archaeology of Ethnicity: Constructing Identities in the Past and Present*, London: Routledge.

Kass, Amalie M. and Edward H. Kass (1988), *Perfecting the World: The Life and Times of Dr. Thomas Hodgkin, 1798–1866*, Boston: Harcourt Brace Jovanovich.

Kastarlak, Bulent (1975), *Tourism and its Development Potential in Dominica*, St Lucia: United Nations Development Program.

Keegan, William F. (1994), 'West Indian Archaeology. 1. Overview and Foragers', *Journal of Archaeological Research*, 2: 255–84.

——(1996a), 'West Indian Archaeology. 2. After Columbus', *Journal of Archaeological Research*, 4: 265–94.

——(1996b), 'Columbus was a Cannibal: Myth and the First Encounters', in Robert L. Paquette and Stanley L. Engerman, eds., *The Lesser Antilles in the Age of European Expansion*, Gainesville, Fla.: UP of Florida, 17–32.

Keim, DeB. Randolph (1870), *San Domingo. Pen Pictures and Leaves of Travel, Romance and History, from the Portfolio of a Correspondent in the American Tropics*, Philadelphia: Claxton, Remsen & Haffelfinger.

Kennedy, James (1855), 'On the Probable Origin of the American Indians, with Particular Reference to the Caribs', in *Ethnological Essays*, London: Arthur Hall, Virtue & Co., 1–42.

Kennedy, Roger G. (1996), *Hidden Cities: The Discovery and Loss of Ancient North American Civilization*, New York: Penguin.

Kerns, Virginia (1983), *Women and the Ancestors: Black Carib Kinship and Ritual*, Urbana, Ill.: University of Illinois Press.

Kersey, Harry A., Jr. (1975), *Pelts, Plumes, and Hides: White Traders among the Seminole Indians, 1870–1930*, Gainesville, Fla.: UP of Florida.

Kidd, Benjamin (1896), *Social Evolution* [1894], London: Macmillan & Co.

——(1898), *The Control of the Tropics*, New York: Macmillan & Co.

Kloepfer, Deborah Kelly (1989), *The Unspeakable Mother: Forbidden Discourse in Jean Rhys and H.D.*, Ithaca, NY: Cornell UP.

Knight, Melvin M. (1928), *The Americans in Santo Domingo*, Vanguard Press: New York.

Kubicek, Robert V. (1969), *The Administration of Imperialism: Joseph Chamberlain at the Colonial Office*, Durham, NC: Duke University Press.

Kuklick, Henrika (1993), *The Savage Within: The Social History of British Anthropology, 1885–1945*, Cambridge: CUP.

Kuper, Adam (1988), *The Invention of Primitive Society: Transformations of an Illusion*, London: Routledge.

Labat, Jean Baptiste (1931), *The Memoirs of Père Labat 1693–1705*, trans. and abridged John Eaden, London: Constable & Co.

——(1722), *Nouveau Voyage aux Isles de L'Amérique*, 6 vols., Paris: P. F. Giffart.

LaFeber, Walter (1963), *The New Empire: An Interpretation of American Expansion, 1860–1898*, Ithaca, NY: Cornell UP.

Laguna, Frederica de, ed. (1960), *Selected Papers from the American Anthropologist, 1888–1920*, Evanston, Ill.: Row, Peterson.

Lanfant, Marie-Françoise and Nelson H. H. Graburn (1992), 'International Tourism Reconsidered: The Principle of the Alternative', in Valene L. Smith and William R. Eadington, eds., *Tourism Alternatives: Potentials and Problems in the Development of Tourism*, Philadelphia: University of Pennsylvania Press, 88–112.

Langley, Lester D. (1976), *Struggle for the American Mediterranean. United States—European Rivalry in the Gulf-Caribbean, 1776–1904*, Athens, Ga.: University of Georgia Press.

Larcom, Lucy (1884), *The Poetical Works of Lucy Larcom*, Boston: Houghton, Mifflin and Company.

——(1961), *A New England Girlhood* [1889], introduction by Charles T. Davis, New York: Corinth Books.

Lasserre, Guy (1961), *La Guadeloupe: Etude géographie*, 2 vols., Bordeaux: Union Française d'Impression.

Layng, Anthony (1976), 'The Carib Population of Dominica', Ph.D. diss. Department of Anthropology: Case Western Reserve University.

——(1979–80), 'Ethnic Identity, Population Growth, and Economic Security on a West Indian Reservation', *Revista/Review Interamericana*, 9/4: 577–84.

——(1983), *The Carib Reserve: Identity and Security in the West Indies*, Washington: University Press of America.

Layng, Anthony (1985), 'The Caribs of Dominica: Prospects for Structural Assimilation of a Territorial Minority', *Ethnic Groups*, 6/2–3: 209–21.

Lee, Simon (1996), 'In the Land of the Kalinago', *Caribbean Week*, 11–28 May: 24–5.

Lent, John A. (1977), *Third World Mass Media and their Search for Modernity: The Case of the Commonwealth Caribbean 1717–1976*, Lewisburg: Bucknell UP.

Le Toumelin, Jacques-Yves (1963), *Kurun in the Caribbean*, trans. and adapted by Lawrence Wilson, London: Rupert Hart-Davis.

Levin, Harry (1972), *The Myth of the Golden Age in the Renaissance*, New York: OUP.

Lewis, Gordon K. (1969), *The Growth of the Modern West Indies*, New York: Monthly Review Press.

Linnekin, Jocelyn (1983), 'Defining Tradition: Variations on the Hawaiian Identity', *American Ethnologist*, 10: 241–52.

Longfellow, Henry Wadsworth (1855), *The Song of Haiwatha*, London: David Boyne.

Longmore, Zenga (1990), *Tap-Taps to Trinidad: A Caribbean Journey*, London: Arrow Books.

Loring, Katharine P. and May Toomey (1941), *Genealogy of the Ober Family*, privately printed: copy in Beverly Room, Beverly Public Library, Mass..

Loti, Pierre (1976), *The Marriage of Loti*, trans. Wright and Eleanor Frierson, Honolulu: UP of Hawaii.

Lowenthal, David (1972), *West Indian Societies*, London: OUP.

Lucas, Charles Prestwood (1890), *A Historical Geography of the British Colonies*, vol. ii: *The West Indies*, Oxford: Clarendon Press.

Luke, Sir Harry (1950), *Caribbean Circuit*, London: Nicholson & Watson.

Lynch, Mrs Henry (1856), *The Wonders of the West Indies*, London: Seeley, Jackson and Halliday.

MacCannell, Dean (1976), *The Tourist: A New Theory of the Leisure Class*, New York: Schocken Books.

——(1992), *Empty Meeting Grounds: The Tourist Papers*, London: Routledge.

McGregor, Russell (1997), *Imagined Destinies: Aboriginal Australians and the Doomed Race Theory, 1880–1939*, Melbourne: Melbourne UP.

Mackenzie, Chief Tom, and Bill Logan (1985), *Caribbean Report. Recommendations for Training and Education for Indigenous Communities and Organizations in the Countries of Dominica, St. Vincent and Belize*, Regina: Saskatchewan Indian Federated College.

McKinnen, Daniel (1804), *A Tour of the British West Indies, in the Years 1802 and 1803*, London: J. White.

Macmillan, W. M. (1936), *Warning from the West Indies: A Tract for Africa and Empire*, London: Faber & Faber.

Madden, A. F. (1959), 'Changing Attitudes and Widening Responsibilities, 1895–1914', in *The Cambridge History of the British Empire*, vol. iii: *The Empire-Commonwealth 1870–1919*, ed. E. A. Benians, James Butler, C. E. Carrington, Cambridge: CUP, 338–99.

Mahan, Capt. A. T. (1918), *The Interest of America in Sea Power, Present and Future*, Boston: Little, Brown & Co.

Mahon, John K. (1967), *History of the Second Seminole War, 1835–1842*, Gainesville, Fla.: University of Florida Press.

Marchalonis, Shirley (1989), *The Worlds of Lucy Larcom, 1824–1893*, Athens, Ga.: University of Georgia Press.

Marshall, Bernard (1976), 'Maronage in Slave Plantation Societies: A Case Study of Dominica, 1785–1815', *Caribbean Quarterly*, 22/2–3: 26–32.

Martin, R. Montgomery (1852–7), *The British Colonies; Their History, Extent, Condition, and Resources*, 6 vols., London: London Printing and Publishing Co.

Mason, Otis T. (1877), 'The Latimer Collection of Antiquities from Porto Rico in the National Museum, at Washington, D.C.', *Smithsonian Institution Annual Report for 1876*, Washington, Government Printing Office, 372–93.

——(1885), *The Guesde Collection of Antiquities in Pointe-à-Pitre, Guadeloupe, West-Indies*, Washington: Government Printing Office.

Matthiessen, Peter (1992), *In the Spirit of Crazy Horse*, London: Harvill.

Maxwell, Anne (1999), *Colonial Photography & Exhibitions: Representations of the 'Native' People and the Making of European Identities*, Leicester: Leicester University Press.

Mead, Margaret (1981), *Coming of Age in Samoa: A Study of Adolescence and Sex in Primitive Societies* [1928], Harmondsworth: Penguin.

Merk, Frederick (1963), *Manifest Destiny and Mission in American History*, New York: Alfred A. Knopf.

Mitchell, Carleton (1955), *Islands to Windward: Cruising the Caribbees* [1948], New York: D. Van Nostrand Company.

——(1971), *Isles of the Caribbees*, Washington: National Geographic Society.

Mitchell, Lee Clark (1981), *Witnesses to a Vanishing America: The Nineteenth-Century Response*, Princeton: Princeton UP.

Montlezun, Baron de (1818), *Souvenirs des Antilles: voyage en 1815 et 1816, aux États-Unis, et dans l'archipel Caraïbe*, 2 vols., Paris: Librairie de Gide Fils.

Moore, John H. (1994), 'Putting Anthropology Back Together Again: The Ethnogenetic Critique of Cladistic Theory', *American Anthropologist*, 96: 925–48.

Moore, Thomas (1929), *The Poetical Works of Thomas Moore*, ed. A. D. Godley, London: OUP.

Murra, John V., ed. (1976), *American Anthropology: The Early Years*, St. Paul: West Publishing Co.

Murray, William H. H. (1869), *Adventures in the Wilderness; or, Camp-life in the Adirondacks*, Boston: Fields, Osgood, & Co.

Naftel, C. O. (1898), *Report on the Agricultural Capabilities of Dominica*. Presented to the House of Commons, March 1898. P.P. 59, Accounts and Papers (PRO, ZHC1/6084).

[Napier, Elma] (1933), 'The Native Remnant in Dominica' (from a correspondent), *Manchester Guardian Weekly* (8 Sept. 1933).

Napier, Elma (MS), 'Black and White Sands', unpublished manuscript in possession of Patricia Honychurch, Dominica.

Nash, Roderick (1973), *Wilderness and the American Mind*, rev. edn., New Haven: Yale UP.

Nassief, Yvor (1994a), 'The True Lesson of Geneva', *New Chronicle*, 16 Sept.

——(1994b), 'In Response to Dr. Henderson', *New Chronicle*, 25 Nov.

Neveu-Lemaire, M. (1921), 'Les Caraïbes des Antilles', *Géographie*, 35/2: 127–46.

New York: Museum of the American Indian (1913–15), *Contributions from the Heye Museum*, vol. 1, New York: Heye Museum.

Nicholls, David (1995), *The Lost Prime Minister: A Life of Sir Charles Dilke*, London: Hambledon Press.

Nott, Josiah C. and George R. Gliddon (1857), *Indigenous Races of the Earth; or, New Chapters of Ethnological Enquiry*, Philadelphia: J. B. Lippincott & Co.

Ober, Frederick A. (1873a), 'Wild Life in Florida: Camping among the Seminoles', *Forest and Stream*, 1/13 (6 Nov.): 193–4.

——(1873b), 'Wild Life in Florida: Camping among the Seminoles', *Forest and Stream*, 1/14 (13 Nov.): 209–10.

——(1875), 'Ten Days with the Seminoles', *Appleton's Journal*, 14 (31 July): 142–4; (7 Aug.): 171–3.

——(1879), 'Ornithological Exploration of the Caribbee Islands', *Annual Report of the Smithsonian Institution for 1878*, Washington: Government Printing Office, 446–51.

——(1880), *Camps in the Caribbees: The Adventures of a Naturalist in the Lesser Antilles* [1879], Edinburgh: David Douglas.

——(1884), *Travels in Mexico and Life among the Mexicans*, Boston: Estes & Lauriat.

——(1891), *The Knockabout Club on the Spanish Main*, Boston: Estes & Lauriat.

——(1893), *In the Wake of Columbus. Adventures of a Special Commissioner Sent by World's Columbian Exposition to the West Indies*, Boston: D. Lothrop Company.

——(1894), 'Aborigines of the West Indies', *Proceedings of the American Antiquarian Society*, NS 9: 270–313.

——(1897), *Under the Cuban Flag, or the Cacique's Treasure*, Boston: Estes and Lauriat.

——(1898), *Crusoe's Island: A Bird-Hunter's Story*, New York: D. Appleton and Co.

——(1901), *The Last of the Arawaks: A Story of Adventure on the Island of San Domingo*, Boston and Chicago: W. A. Wilde and Co.

——(1908), *With Osceola in Florida: Being the Adventures of Two Boys in the Seminole War in 1835*, New York: A. L. Burt Company.

Ober, Sara Endicott (n.d.), 'Looking Back from "Borrowed Time": Kim's Store', ed. Augustus Peabody Loring, Jr., MS in Beverly Historic Society, Mass..

O'Connor, Teresa F. (1986), *Jean Rhys: The West Indian Novels*, New York: New York UP.

——(1992), 'Jean Rhys, Paul Theroux, and the Imperial Road', *Twentieth Century Literature*, 38: 404–14.

Oliver, Vere Langford (1927), *The Monumental Inscriptions of the British West Indies*, Dorchester: F. G. Longman.

Ortiz, Fernando (1922), *Historia de arqueología indocubana*, Havana: Imprenta 'Siglo XX'.

Owen, Nancy H. (1974), 'Land and Politics in a Carib Indian Community: A Study of Ethnicity', Ph.D. diss. Department of Anthropology, University of Massachusetts.

——(1975), 'Land, Politics, and Ethnicity in a Carib Indian Community', *Ethnology*, 14: 385–93.

——(1980), 'Conflict and Ethnic Boundaries: A Study of Carib/black Relations', *Social and Economic Studies*, 29/2–3: 264–74.

——(1981), 'Witchcraft in the West Indies: The Anthropologist as Victim', *Anthropology and Humanism Quarterly*, 6/2–3: 15–22.

Palacio, Joseph (1992), 'The Sojourn Toward Self Discovery Among Caribbean Indigenous People', *Caribbean Quarterly*, 38/2 and 3: 55–72.

Pané, Ramón (1978), *Relación acerca de las antigüedades de los indios: el primer tratado escrito en América*, ed. José Juan Arrom, Mexico: Siglo Veintiuno.

Paravisini-Gebert, Lizabeth (1996), *Phyllis Shand Allfrey: A Caribbean Life*, New Brunswick, NJ: Rutgers UP.

Paravisini-Gebert, Lizabeth (1999), ' "A Forgotten Outpost of Empire": Social Life in Dominica and the Creative Imagination', *Jean Rhys Review*, 10/1–2: 13–26.

Parmer, Charles B. (1937), *West Indian Odyssey: The Complete Guide to the Islands of the Caribbean*, New York: Dodge Publishing Co.

Parry, J. H., and P. M. Sherlock (1956), *A Short History of the West Indies*, London: Macmillan.

Paton, William A. (1888), *Down the Islands: A Voyage to the Caribbees*, London: Kegan Paul & Co.

Patterson, Thomas C. (1986), 'The Last Sixty Years: Toward a Social History of Americanist Archeology in the United States', *American Anthropologist*, 88: 8–26.

Pattullo, Polly (1992), 'The Egg Man', MS.

——(1996), *Last Resorts: The Cost of Tourism in the Caribbean*, London: Cassell.

Pézéron, Simone Magay (1993), *The Carib Indians of Dominica Island in the West Indies Five Hundred Years After Columbus*, New York: Vantage Press.

Plante, David (1979), 'Jean Rhys: A Remembrance', *Paris Review*, 21/76: 238–84.

——(1983), *Difficult Women: A Memoir of Three*, London: Victor Gollancz.

Poey, Andrés (1851), 'Cuban Antiquities. A Brief Description of Some Relics Found in the Island of Cuba', *Transactions of the American Ethnological Society*, 3 (pt. 1): 185–202.

Pound, Francis (1983), 'Lowville Alumnus Leads Tribal Struggle', *Watertown Times*, 7 May.

Powell, John Wesley (1875), *Exploration of the Colorado River of the West and Its Tributaries*, Washington, Government Printing Office.

——(1895), *The Exploration of the Colorado River and Its Canyons*, Meadville, PA: Flood & Vincent.

——(1901), 'Report on Bureau of American Ethnology', in *Annual Report of the Smithsonian Institution for the year 1900*, Washington: Government Printing Office, Appendix II.

Pratt, Mary Louise (1992), *Imperial Eyes: Travel Writing and Transculturation*, London: Routledge.

Purchas, Samuel (1905–7), *Purchas His Pilgrimes* [1625], 20 vols., Glasgow: James MacLehose.

Pybus, Cassandra (1991), *Community of Thieves*, Melbourne: Minerva.

Quick, Richard (1902), 'Carib Stone Implements in the

Horniman Museum', *Reliquary and Illustrated Archaeologist*, NS 8: 169–81.

Rafinesque, Cornelius Samuel (1836), *The American Nations; or, Outlines of their General History, Ancient and Modern*, 2 vols., Philadelphia: privately published.

Rainger, Ronald (1978–9), 'Race, Politics, and Science: The Anthropological Society of London in the 1860s', *Victorian Studies*, 22: 51–70.

Raiskin, Judith (1996), ' "Great Mistake to Go by Looks": Jean Rhys, the Caribbean Creole, and Cultural Colonialism', in her *Snow on the Cane Fields: Women's Writing and Creole Subjectivity*, Minneapolis: University of Minnesota Press, 97–143.

Raspail, Jean (1973), *Secouns le Cocotier*. Édition revue et augmentée, Paris: Éditions Robert Laffont.

——(1980), *Bleu Caraïbe et Citrons Verts: Mes Derniers Voyages aux Antilles*, Paris: Éditions Robert Laffont.

——(1988), *Who Will Remember the People?* [1986], trans. Jeremy Leggatt, San Francisco: Mercury House.

——(1995), *The Camp of the Saints* [1973], trans. Norman Shapiro, Petoskey: Social Contract Press.

Rat, Joseph Numa (1897), 'The Carib Language as now Spoken in Dominica, West Indies', *Journal of the Anthropological Institute of Great Britain and Ireland*, 27 (Feb.), 293–315.

Rennie, Neil (1996), *Far-Fetched Facts: The Literature of Travel and the Idea of the South Seas*, Oxford: Clarendon Press.

Reynolds, Henry (1995), *Fate of a Free People*, Ringwood, Victoria: Penguin.

Rhys, Jean (1981), *Smile Please. An Unfinished Autobiography*, Harmondsworth: Penguin.

——(1982), *Voyage in the Dark* [1934], Harmondsworth: Penguin.

——(1985), *Letters 1931–66*, ed. Francis Wyndham and Diana Melly, Harmondsworth: Penguin.

——(1987), *The Collected Short Stories*, New York: W. W. Norton & Company.

——(1997), *Wide Sargasso Sea* [1966], Harmondsworth: Penguin.

——(2000), 'The Imperial Road', *The Jean Rhys Review* 11/2.

Rich, Paul (1986), *Race and Empire in British Politics*, Cambridge: CUP.

Richardson, Bonham C. (1992), 'Depression Riots and the Calling of the 1897 West India Royal Commission', *New West Indian Guide*, 66: 169–92.

Rivero de la Calle, Manuel, comp. (1966), *Actas: Sociedad antropológica de la isla de Cuba*, Havana: Comisión Nacional de la UNESCO.

Rivinus, E. F. and E. M. Youssef (1992), *Spencer Baird of the Smithsonian*, Washington: Smithsonian Institution Press.

Roberts, Leslie (1992), 'Anthropologists Climb (Gingerly) on Board', *Science*, 258: 1300–1.

Roberts, Peter (1997), 'The (Re)construction of the Concept of *indio* in the National Identities of Cuba, Puerto Rico and the Dominican Republic', in Lowell Fiet and Janette Becerra, eds., *Caribe 2000: Definiciones, Identidades y Culturas Regionales y/o Nacionales*, Río Piedras: Facultad de Humanidades, UPR, 99–120.

Rochefort, Charles de (1665), *Histoire naturelle et morale des Îles Antilles de l'Amérique* [1658], 2nd. edn., Rotterdam: Arnour Leers.

Rogin, Michael Paul (1991), *Fathers and Children: Andrew Jackson and the Subjugation of the American Indian* [1975], New Brunswick, NJ: Transaction Publishers.

Romero, Lora (1991), 'Vanishing Americans: Gender, Empire, and the Now Historicism', *American Literature*, 63/3: 385–404.

Roosevelt, Theodore (1901), *The Strenuous Life* (from *The Works of Theodore Roosevelt in Fourteen Volumes*), New York: P. F. Collier & Son.

Roth, Henry Ling (1887), 'The Aborigines of Hispaniola', in *Journal of the Royal Anthropological Institute of Britain and Ireland*, 16: 247–86.

——(1899), *The Aborigines of Tasmania*, Halifax: F. King & Sons.

Rountree, Helen C. (1990), *Pocahontas's People: The Powhatan Indians of Virginia Through Four Centuries*, Norman, Okla.: University of Oklahoma Press.

Rouse, Irving (1992), *The Tainos: The Rise and Decline of the People Who Greeted Columbus*, New Haven: Yale UP.

Ryan, Lyndall (1981), *The Aboriginal Tasmanians*, St Lucia: University of Queensland Press.

Rydell, Robert W. (1987), *All the World's a Fair: Visions of Empire at American International Expositions, 1876–1916*, Chicago: University of Chicago Press.

St-Johnston, Reginald (1936), *From a Colonial Governor's Note-book*, London: Hutchinson & Co.

Salmon, C. S. (1888), *The Caribbean Confederation*, London: Cassell & Co.

Savarin, Charles A. (1994), 'Spearheading the Development Process in Industry, Tourism & Small Business', *New Chronicle*, 2 Nov., National Development Corporation Supplement, i–xii.

Savory, Elaine (1998), *Jean Rhys*, Cambridge: CUP.

Schlereth, Thomas J. (1992), 'Columbia, Columbus, and Columbianism', *Journal of American History*, 79/2: 937–68.

Sclater, P. L. (1889), 'List of Birds Collected by Mr. Ramage in

Dominica, West Indies', *Proceedings of the Zoological Society of London*, part 57: 326–7.

Seeley, John R. (1914), *The Expansion of England: Two Courses of Lectures* [1883], 2nd edn., London: Macmillan.

Sell, Henry B. and Victor Weibright (1955), *Buffalo Bill and the Wild West*, New York.

Shukman, Henry (1993), *Travels with My Trombone: A Caribbean Journey*, London: Flamingo.

Sider, Gerald M. (1993), *Lumbee Indian Histories: Race, Ethnicity, and Indian Identity in the Southern United States*, Cambridge: CUP.

Sketches and Recollections of the West Indies. By a Resident (1828), London: Smith, Elder & Co.

Slocum, Joshua (1962), *Sailing Alone Around the World, and Voyage of the Liberdade*, ed. Walter Magnes Teller, New York: Collier Books.

Smith, Bradley (1961), *Escape to the West Indies: A Guidebook to the Islands of the Caribbean with Photographs by the Author* [1956], New York: Alfred A. Knopf.

Smith, Raymond T. (1962), 'Report on the Caribs of Dominica,' Institute of Social and Economic Research, University of the West Indies, Jamaica. Mimeo.

Smith, Valene L. and William R. Eadington (1992), *Tourism Alternatives: Potentials and Problems in the Development of Tourism*, Philadelphia: University of Pennsylvania Press.

Snipp, C. Matthew (1986), 'Who Are the American Indians? Some Observations about the Perils and Pitfalls of Data for Race and Ethnicity', *Population Research and Policy Review*, 5: 237–52.

Sollors, Werner (1997), *Neither Black Nor White Yet Both: Thematic Explorations of Interracial Literature*, New York: OUP.

Some Observations; which may contribute to afford a just idea of the nature, importance, and settlement, of our new West-India colonies (1764), London: no publisher.

Stafford, Fiona J. (1994), *The Last of the Race: The Growth of a Myth from Milton to Darwin*, Oxford: Clarendon Press.

Stegner, Wallace (1954), *Beyond the Hundredth Meridian: John Wesley Powell and the Second Opening of the West*, Boston: Houghton Mifflin.

Stepan, Nancy (1985), 'Biological Degeneration: Races and Proper Places', in *Degeneration: The Dark Side of Progress*, ed. J. Edward Chamberlin and Sander L. Gilman, New York: Columbia UP, 97–120.

Stocking, George W. (1971), 'What's in a Name? The Origins of the Royal Anthropological Institute, 1837–1871', *Man*, 6: 369–90.

——(1973), 'From Chronology to Ethnology: James Cowles Prichard and British Anthropology', in J. C. Prichard, *Researches into the*

Physical History of Man [1913], Chicago: University of Chicago Press, pp. ix–cx.

——(1982), *Race, Culture, Evolution. Essays in the History of Anthropology*, Chicago: University of Chicago Press.

——(1987), *Victorian Anthropology*, New York: The Free Press.

Stoddard, Lothrop (1971), *The Rising Tide of Color Against White World-Supremacy* [1921], Westport, Conn.: Negro Universities Press.

Sturtevant, William C. (1971), 'Creek into Seminole', in Eleanor Burke Leacock and Nancy Oestreich Lurie, eds., *North American Indians in Historical Perspective*, New York: Random House, 92–128.

Suaudeau, Père René (1927), *Au Pays des Caraïbes. Lettres d'un missionnaire pendant son séjour dans l'ile de la Dominique (Antilles Anglaises)*, Fontenay-le-Comte: Des Presses de l'Imprimerie Fontenaisienne.

Sued Badillo, Jalil (1978), *Los Caribes: realidad o fábula?*, Río Piedras: Editorial Antillana.

——(1985), 'Las Cacicas Indoantillanas', *Revista del Instituto de Cultura Puertorriqueña*, 87: 17–26.

——(1992), 'Facing up to Caribbean History', *American Antiquity*, 57: 599–607.

Sütterlin, Georg (1991), 'The Caribs of Dominica', *Swiss Review of World Affairs*, 41 (July): 27–8.

Tagg, John (1988), *The Burden of Representation: Essays on Photographies and Histories*, Basingstoke: Macmillan.

Tansill, Charles C. (1938), *The United States and Santo Domingo, 1798–1873: A Chapter in Caribbean Diplomacy*, Baltimore: Johns Hopkins Press.

Tauli-Corpuz, Victoria (1993), 'First Step Towards Patenting Indigenous Peoples?', *New Chronicle*, 85/30 (23 July): 10.

Taylor, Douglas (1935), 'The Island Caribs of Dominica, B.W.I.', *American Anthropologist*, NS 37: 265–72.

——(1936), 'Additional Notes on the Island Carib of Dominica, B.W.I.', *American Anthropologist*, NS 38: 462–8.

——(1938), 'The Caribs of Dominica', *Bureau of American Ethnology*, Bulletin 119, Anthropological Papers no. 3, Washington: Smithsonian Institution.

——(1941), 'Columbus Saw Them First', *Natural History*, 48 (June): 40–9.

——(1945), 'Carib Folk-Beliefs and Customs from Dominica, B.W.I.', *Southwestern Journal of Anthropology*, 1: 507–30.

——(1946a), 'Notes on the Star Lore of the Caribbees', *American Anthropologist*, NS 48: 215–22.

——(1946*b*), 'Kinship and Social Structure of the Island Carib', *Southwestern Journal of Anthropology*, 2: 180–212.

——(1949), 'The Interpretation of Some Documentary Evidence on Carib Culture', *Southwestern Journal of Anthropology*, 5: 379–91.

——(1951), *The Black Carib of British Honduras*, Viking Fund Publications in Anthropology, 17, New York, Wenner-Gren Foundation.

——(1952), 'Tales and Legends of the Dominica Caribs', *Journal of American Folklore*, 65: 267–79.

——(1956), 'Languages and Ghost-Languages of the West Indies', *International Journal of Linguistics*, 22: 180–2.

——(1958), 'Use and Disuse of Languages in the West Indies', *Caribbean Quarterly*, 5/2: 67–77.

——(1961), 'New Languages for Old in the West Indies', *Comparative Studies in Society and History*, 3: 277–88.

——(1963), 'The Origin of West Indian Creole Languages: Evidence from Grammatical Categories', *American Anthropologist*, 65: 800–14.

——(1977), *Languages of the West Indies*, Baltimore: Johns Hopkins UP.

——and Berend J. Hoff (1980), 'The Linguistic Reportory of the Island-Carib in the Seventeenth Century: The Men's Language—A Carib Pidgin?', *International Journal of American Linguistics*, 46: 301–12.

——and Harvey C. Moore (1948), 'A Note on Dominican Basketry and Its Analogues', *Southwestern Journal of Anthropology*, 4: 328–43.

——and Irving Rouse, (1956), 'Linguistic and Archeological Time Depth in the West Indies', *International Journal of American Linguistics*, 21: 105–15.

Taylor, Frank Fonda (1993), *To Hell with Paradise: A History of the Jamaican Tourist Industry*, Pittsburgh: University of Pittsburgh Press.

Teller, Walter Magnes (1971), *Joshua Slocum*, New Brunswick, NJ: Rutgers UP.

Tennyson, Alfred (1987), *The Poems of Tennyson*, ed. Christopher Ricks, 3 vols., Harlow: Longman.

Teuscher, Philip Thorneycroft, dir. (1983), *Last of the Karaphuna*, 16mm film/video, produced by Teuscher/Pettys Productions.

Thomas, J. J. (1969), *Froudacity: West Indian Fables by James Anthony Froude* [1889], London: New Beacon Books.

Thomas, Léon (1953), 'La Dominique et les derniers Caraïbes insulaires', *Cahiers d'outremer*, 6: 37–60.

Thomas, Nicholas (1989), 'The Force of Ethnology: Origins and Significance of the Melanesia/Polynesia Division', *Current Anthropology*, 30: 27–41.

Thomas, Sue (1996*a*), 'William Rees Williams in Dominica', *Jean Rhys Review*, 7/1–2: 3–14.

——(1996*b*), 'Conflicted Textual Affiliations: Jean Rhys's "The Insect World" and "Heat" ', in Hena Maes-Jelinek *et al.*, eds., *A Talent(ed) Digger: Creations, Cameos, and Essays in Honour of Anna Rutherford*, Amsterdam: Rodopi, 287–94.

——(1999), *The Worlding of Jean Rhys*, Westport, Conn.: Greenwood Press.

Tobin, Jeffrey (1994), 'Cultural Construction and Native Nationalism: Report from the Hawaiian Front', *boundary 2*, 21/1: 111–33.

Trask, Haunani-Kay (1991), 'Natives and Anthropologists: The Colonial Struggle', *Contemporary Pacific*, 2: 159–67.

——(1992), *'Kupa'a 'Aina*: Native Hawai'an Nationalism in Hawai'i', in Zachary A. Smith and Richard C. Pratt, eds., *Politics and Public Policy in Hawai'i*, Albany, NY: State University Press of New York, 243–60.

Tree, Isabella (1998), 'Dominica', *Islands Magazine* (Sept./Oct.): 103–10.

Trennert, Robert A., Jr. (1974), 'A Grand Failure: The Centennial Indian Exhibit of 1876', *Prologue*, 6: 118–29.

Treves, Sir Frederick (1908), *The Cradle of the Deep: An Account of a Voyage to the West Indies*, London: Smith, Elder, & Co.

Trollope, Anthony (1968), *The West Indies and the Spanish Main* [1859], London: Frank Cass.

Trouillot, Michel-Rolph (1988), *Peasants and Capital: Dominica in the World Economy*, Baltimore: Johns Hopkins UP.

——(1989), 'Discourses of Rule and the Acknowledgment of the Peasantry in Dominica, W.I., 1838–1928', *American Ethnologist*, 16: 704–18.

——(1992), 'The Inconvenience of Freedom: Free People of Color and the Political Aftermath of Slavery in Dominica and Saint-Domingue/Haiti', in *The Meaning of Freedom: Economics, Politics, and Culture after Slavery*, ed. Frank McGlynn and Seymour Drescher, Pittsburgh: University of Pittsburgh Press: 147–82.

Turnbull, Paul (1999), 'Enlightenment Anthropology and the Ancestral Remains of Australian Aboriginal people', in Alex Calder, Jonathan Lamb, and Bridget Orr, eds., *Voyages and Beaches: Pacific Encounters, 1769–1840*, Honolulu: University of Hawai'i Press, 202–25.

Tylor, Edward B. (1892), *Anthropology: An Introduction to the Study of Man and Civilization*, London: Macmillan and Co.

Urry, John (1990), *The Tourist Gaze: Leisure and Travel in Contemporary Societies*, London: Sage.

Van Dyke, John C. (1932), *In the West Indies: Sketches and Studies in Tropic Seas and Islands*, New York: Charles Scribner's Sons.

'Vaquero' (1914), *Life and Adventure in the West Indies*, London: John Bale, Sons & Danielsson.

Verrill, Alpheus Hyatt (1929), *Thirty Years in the Jungle*, London: John Lane.

——(MS), 'Never a Dull Moment', unpublished manuscript in the Archives of the Museum of the American Indian, Smithsonian Institution, New York: Box Oc 32 No. 5.

Vitier, Cintio (1970), *Lo cubano en la poesía*, La Habana: Instituto del Libro.

Warner, Marina (1997), 'Siren, Hyphen; or, The Maid Beguiled', *New Left Review*, 223: 101–13.

Watters, David Robert (1976), 'Caribbean Prehistory: A Century of Researchers, Models, and Trends', unpublished MA thesis, University of Nevada, Reno.

Waugh, Alec (1952), *Where the Clocks Chime Twice*, London: Cassell & Co.

——(1958), 'Typical Dominica' [1952], in his *The Sugar Islands: A Collection of Pieces Written About the West Indies Between 1928 and 1953*, London: Cassell, 281–315.

Wearne, Phillip (1996), *Return of the Indian: Conquest and Revival in the Americas*, London: Cassell.

Weaver, David B. (1991), 'Alternative to Mass Tourism in Dominica', *Annals of Tourism Research*, 18: 414–32.

Weller, Anthony (1983), 'Conquerors of the Caribbean', *Geo*, 5 (Apr.), 68–76, 102, 105–6.

Wertheimer, Eric (1999), *Imagined Empires: Incas, Aztecs, and the New World of American Literature, 1771–1876*, Cambridge: CUP.

White, Hayden (1980), 'The Value of Narrativity in the Representation of Reality', *Critical Inquiry*, 7/1: 5–28.

White, M. G., *et al.* (1976), *Rural Sector Case Study Report, with Proposals for Development of Geneva Estate, Grandbay, Dominica*, Case study presented at Eleventh West Indies Agricultural Economics Conference, Roseau, Dominica, 20–24 Apr. 1976.

Whitehead, Neil L. (1988), *Lords of the Tiger Spirit: A History of the Caribs in Colonial Venezuela and Guyana 1498–1820*, Dordrecht: Foris.

——ed. (1995), *Wolves from the Sea: Readings in the Anthropology of the Native Caribbean*, Leiden: KITLV.

Wickman, Patricia R. (1991), *Osceola's Legacy*, Tuscaloosa, Ala.: University of Alabama Press.

Wilkie, Tom (1993), *Perilous Knowledge: The Human Genome Project and its Implications*, London: Faber & Faber.

Wilkins, Thurman (1958), *Clarence King: A Biography*, New York: Macmillan.

Will, H. A. (1970), *Constitutional Change in the British West Indies, 1880–1903*, Oxford: Clarendon Press.

Willey, Gordon R. and Jeremy A. Sabloff (1980), *A History of American Archaeology*, 2nd. edn., San Francisco: W. H. Freeman and Company.

Williamson, J. A. (1926), *The Caribbee Islands under the Proprietary Patents*, London: Humphrey Milford.

Wolfe, Linda (1970), *The Cooking of the Caribbean Islands*, New York: Time-Life Books.

Wormell, Deborah (1980), *Sir John Seeley and the Uses of History*, Cambridge: CUP.

Wright, J. Leitch, Jr. (1986), *Creeks & Seminoles: The Destruction and Regeneration of the Muscogulge People*, Lincoln, Nebr.: University of Nebraska Press.

Young, Elspeth (1995), 'The Role of Parks and Tourism in Aboriginal Development', in her *Third World in the First: Development and Indigenous Peoples*, London: Routledge, 189–222.

Index

Bold numbers denote reference to illustrations